60 HIKES
WITHIN 60 MILES

3RD Edition

DALLAS–FORT WORTH

Including Tarrant, Collin, and Denton Counties

Joanie Sánchez

MENASHA RIDGE PRESS
Your Guide to the Outdoors Since 1982

60 HIKES WITHIN 60 MILES: DALLAS–FORT WORTH

Published by Menasha Ridge Press

Third edition, first printing

Library of Congress Cataloging-in-Publication Data

Names: Sánchez, Joanie, author.
Title: 60 hikes within 60 miles : Dallas/Fort Worth, including Tarrant, Collin, and Denton counties /
   Joanie Sánchez.
Other titles: Sixty hikes within sixty miles
Description: Third Edition. | Birmingham, Alabama : Menasha Ridge Press, an imprint of AdventureKEEN,
   [2018] | Includes index.
Identifiers: LCCN 2018021525| ISBN 9781634042574 | ISBN 9781634040952 (ebook)
Subjects: LCSH: Hiking—Texas—Dallas Region—Guidebooks. | Hiking—Texas—Fort Worth Region—Guidebooks.
   | Walking—Texas—Dallas Region—Guidebooks. | Walking—Texas—Fort Worth Region—Guidebooks. |
   Mountaineering—Texas—Dallas Region—Guidebooks. | Mountaineering—Texas—Fort Worth Region—
   Guidebooks. | Rock climbing—Texas—Dallas Region—Guidebooks. | Rock climbing—Texas—Fort Worth
   Region—Guidebooks. | Backpacking—Texas—Dallas Region—Guidebooks. | Backpacking—Texas—Fort Worth
   Region—Guidebooks. | Trails—Texas—Dallas Region—Guidebooks. | Trails—Texas—Fort Worth Region—
   Guidebooks. | Outdoor recreation—Texas—Dallas Region—Guidebooks. | Outdoor recreation—Texas—Fort
   Worth Region—Guidebooks. | Dallas Region (Tex.)—Guidebooks. | Fort Worth Region (Tex.)—Guidebooks. |
   Texas—Guidebooks.
Classification: LCC GV199.42.T492 D35 2018 | DDC 796.51097642812—dc23
LC record available at https://lccn.loc.gov/2018021525

Project editor: Kate Johnson
Cover and text design: Scott McGrew
Cartography and elevation profiles: Scott McGrew and Joanie Sánchez
Photos: Joanie Sánchez, except where noted on page and the following: page 30: f11photo/Shutterstock and page 62:
   Earth Trotter Photos/Shutterstock
Copy editor: Susan Roberts McWilliams
Proofreader: Rebecca Henderson
Indexer: Rich Carlson

Front cover photo: Lake Mineral Wells State Park (Hike 55, page 252) by Mike Oropeza-Fossati

MENASHA RIDGE PRESS
An imprint of AdventureKEEN
2204 First Ave. S, Ste. 102
Birmingham, Alabama 35233

Visit menasharidge.com for a complete listing of our books and for ordering information. Contact us at our website, at facebook.com/menasharidge, or at twitter.com/menasharidge with questions or comments. To find out more about who we are and what we're doing, visit our blog, blog.menasharidge.com.

DISCLAIMER This book is meant only as a guide to select trails in the Dallas–Fort Worth area and does not guarantee hiker safety in any way—you hike at your own risk. Neither Menasha Ridge Press nor Joanie Sánchez is liable in any way for property loss or damage, personal injury, or death that may result from accessing or hiking the trails described in the following pages. Please be aware that hikers have been injured in the Dallas–Fort Worth area. Be especially cautious when walking on or near boulders, steep inclines, and drop-offs, and do not attempt to explore terrain that may be beyond your abilities. To help ensure an uneventful hike, please read carefully the introduction to this book, and perhaps get further safety information and guidance from other sources. Familiarize yourself thoroughly with the areas you intend to visit before venturing out. Ask questions, and prepare for the unforeseen. Familiarize yourself with current weather reports, maps of the area you intend to visit, and any relevant park regulations.

Dedication

To my mother and father, for teaching me my first few steps and guiding me on each one thereafter.

60 Hikes Within 60 Miles: Dallas–Fort Worth

TABLE OF CONTENTS

MAP LEGEND

←→ → Directional arrows	Featured trail	Alternate trail
Freeway	Highway with bridge	Minor road
Boardwalk	Unpaved road	Railroad
Park/forest	Water body	River/creek/intermittent stream

♨ Amphitheater	⚓ Footbridge	P Parking
☂ Beach access	●━ Gate	⚘ Picnic area
⌐ Bench	● General point of interest	⚒ Playground
▲ Campground	🏌 Golf course	⚡ Radio tower
✝ Cemetery	⑦ Information/kiosk	⚹ Restroom
⛪ Church	▯ Lookout tower	⚐ Scenic view
⊘ Closed trail	▮ Monument	⚶ Trailhead
⬟ Dam	◄ One-way (road)	⊓ Trash receptacle
⊔ Drinking water	▲ Overlook	⌂ Viewing platform
⯛ Electrical tower		

ACKNOWLEDGMENTS

Without question, it would have been impossible for me to write this book without the enthusiasm of the park rangers, office staff, and volunteers who promote and stand guard over the trails in their domain. On my first visits, they had me eagerly lacing up my boots and seeking out their trailheads. Since then, their passion has kept me eager to revisit and explore more. I cannot thank these watchful custodians enough for their tips, insights, recommendations, and knowledge that help and inspire all who pass through their doors.

I would also like to thank others without whose help the first edition of this book truly would never have been written, much less updated: my father, Orlando Sánchez, whose enthusiasm and excitement motivate me; Bob Shauchunas, who always seems to have the right tip at the right time; my mother, Joan Shauchunas, who inspires me with her company and impresses me with her own adventures; and my brother, Andrew Sánchez, who has never—regardless of weather, insects, or logistics—turned me down for an adventure. These hikes would not have been nearly as easy or as fun to execute without his assistance, advice, and companionship.

—Joanie Sánchez

FOREWORD

Welcome to Menasha Ridge Press's *60 Hikes Within 60 Miles,* a series designed to provide hikers with the information they need to find and hike the very best trails surrounding metropolitan areas.

Our strategy is simple: First, find a hiker who knows the area and loves to hike. Second, ask that person to spend a year researching the most popular and very best trails around. And third, have that person describe each trail in terms of difficulty, scenery, condition, elevation change, and other categories of information that are important to hikers. "Pretend you've just completed a hike and met up with other hikers at the trailhead," we told each author. "Imagine their questions; be clear in your answers."

An experienced hiker and writer, author Joanie Sánchez has selected 60 of the best hikes in and around the Dallas–Fort Worth metropolitan area. This third edition includes new hikes, as well as additional sections and new routes for some of the existing hikes. Joanie provides hikers (and walkers) with a great variety of hikes—all within roughly 60 miles of Dallas–Fort Worth—from urban strolls on city sidewalks to flora- and fauna-rich treks along the cliffs and hills in the hinterlands.

You'll get more out of this book if you take a moment to read the Introduction, which explains how to read the trail listings. The "Topographic Maps" section will help you understand how useful topos are on a hike and will also tell you where to get them. And though this is a where-to, not a how-to, guide, readers who have not hiked extensively will find the Introduction of particular value.

As much for the opportunity to free the spirit as to free the body, let these hikes elevate you above the urban hurry.

All the best,
The Editors at Menasha Ridge Press

PREFACE

If this is your first time picking up this book, welcome! Within these pages 60 adventures await. From native prairies to bottomland forests and to canyon rims, your hikes and treks will take you on a tour of North Texas you'll never forget—and likely never even knew existed within the metroplex.

On the other hand, for those of you who already have a copy of this book, welcome back! This new edition has been revised with updates to existing hikes as well as many miles of new hikes—many of which are likely to become fast favorites.

In the last edition of this book, I commented on the population boom that the Dallas–Fort Worth area has seen over the past few years. Since then, DFW has continued to see record growth. In fact, recent Census Bureau estimates show that Dallas–Fort Worth had the second largest population gain of any other metropolitan area in the entire country! With more than 7.2 million people, DFW now ranks as the fourth largest metropolitan area in the nation. However, this comes as no surprise to those of us who live here. Signs of growth are everywhere—new housing construction and highway expansions are visible wherever you live. Once-empty tracts of land seem to give way overnight to new development.

When I set out to update *60 Hikes Within 60 Miles: Dallas–Fort Worth,* the questions that plagued me on the last edition were once again foremost in my mind. What does this population growth mean for the outdoors enthusiast, adventure seeker, and hiker? Will the trails that we love be reclaimed for necessities like housing, roads, and new developments? The answer is simple and clear.

Despite record growth—or perhaps because of it—the cities and towns that make up the general area are even *more* committed to making accessible and preserving tracts of wilderness within their domains. One of the most outstanding examples of this is the Great Trinity Forest in Dallas—what is believed to be the largest urban bottomland hardwood forest in the country. For many years it was accessible only to the most stout-hearted of adventurers. In recent years, however, the city of Dallas has made considerable strides in improving upon and expanding trail access to its 6,000-plus acres. This is a direct result of the city's desire to introduce new and old residents alike to the wealth of outdoor opportunities the area has to offer.

In the last edition of this book, I tried to select trails from all corners of the metroplex so that no matter where you lived, you could find something close to home. For this edition I've taken out a few trails and replaced them with new ones that impressed me in different ways. Happily, though, I've kept most of your favorites, and many of these are now better than ever in terms of length and amenities.

As I mentioned in the last edition, I've done my best to describe the trails in this book, but don't be surprised if, on your own explorations, you discover things that differ slightly from what I've found. A trail you've been on before (or heard about) can be an entirely new experience in another season. Don't like a trail in the winter? Go back in the spring, when the flowers are in bloom and the trees are budding. Conversely, a hot prairie path can be a delight on a sunny winter day, but it's probably not as pleasant at the peak of summer.

Regardless of when you go or where you go, just make sure that you *go*. If you know of a hike I haven't included here, that doesn't mean it's not worthy—some hikes didn't make my list because of weather or logistics; nevertheless, don't be afraid to check them out. If you've thumbed through this book and found a hike that interests you but that seems too short or too long, try it anyway: any hike can be shortened, and many of these can be lengthened.

And when you're done trying the hikes in this book . . . keep going! So many more trails out there await your discovery. I hope you enjoy them as much as I have.

—Joanie Sánchez

The remains of an old chimney spark the imagination along the Lost Pines Trail at Ray Roberts Lake State Park (Hike 36, page 169).

60 HIKES BY CATEGORY

REGION Hike Number/Hike Name	page #	Less than 3 Miles	3-5 miles	More than 5 Miles	Children	Best Maintained	Busiest	Easiest	Flat
DALLAS AREA (Including Grand Prairie, Garland, and Irving)									
1 Boulder Park Trail	22	✓							
2 Campion Trail	26		✓				✓		✓
3 Downtown Dallas Urban Trail	30	✓							
4 Fair Park Loop	34	✓							
5 Joppa Preserve Trail	38			✓					✓
6 Katy Trail	42			✓			✓		✓
7 L. B. Houston Nature Trail	46	✓				✓			
8 Oak Cliff Nature Preserve Trail	50	✓				✓			
9 Rowlett Creek Nature Trail	54		✓			✓			
10 Trinity River Audubon Trail	58	✓			✓				
11 Trinity Skyline Trail	62	✓			✓			✓	✓
12 White Rock Lake Trail	66		✓			✓			
FORT WORTH AREA (Including Grapevine Lake, Colleyville, and Euless)									
13 Benbrook Dam Trail	72		✓					✓	✓
14 Benbrook Lake Trail	76		✓						
15 Eagle Mountain Park Trail	80		✓				✓	✓	
16 Fort Worth Nature Center: Canyon Ridge Trail	85		✓						
17 Fort Worth Nature Center: Prairie Trail	89	✓			✓			✓	✓
18 Horseshoe Trail	93		✓				✓		
19 Knob Hills Trail	97			✓					
20 Northshore Trail	101			✓			✓		
21 River Legacy Trail	105			✓				✓	✓
22 Rocky Point Trail	109		✓						
23 Sansom Park Trail	113	✓							
24 Tandy Hills Trail	117	✓							
25 Trinity River Trail (McMillan Plaza)	121		✓						
26 Trinity River Trail (Oakmont Park)	125		✓						
NORTH OF DALLAS–FORT WORTH (Including Plano, McKinney, Lake Ray Roberts, and Lake Lewisville)									
27 Arbor Hills Loop	132	✓			✓		✓		
28 Black Creek–Cottonwood Hiking Trail	136			✓					
29 Cicada–Cottonwood Loop	141	✓			✓	✓		✓	✓
30 Elm Fork Trail	145		✓						
31 Erwin Park Loop	149	✓							

xiii

More Hikes by Category

REGION Hike Number/Hike Name		Best for Dogs	Bodies of Water	Flora or Fauna	Historical Interest	Most Scenic	Runners	Steepest	Urban	Wheelchair Friendly
DALLAS AREA (Including Grand Prairie, Garland, and Irving)										
1	Boulder Park Trail									
2	Campion Trail	✓	✓				✓		✓	
3	Downtown Dallas Urban Trail				✓				✓	
4	Fair Park Loop				✓				✓	
5	Joppa Preserve Trail	✓					✓		✓	✓
6	Katy Trail	✓					✓		✓	
7	L. B. Houston Nature Trail									
8	Oak Cliff Nature Preserve Trail								✓	
9	Rowlett Creek Nature Trail									
10	Trinity River Audubon Trail			✓		✓				
11	Trinity Skyline Trail	✓	✓				✓		✓	✓
12	White Rock Lake Trail		✓			✓	✓		✓	✓
FORT WORTH AREA (Including Grapevine Lake, Colleyville, and Euless)										
13	Benbrook Dam Trail		✓				✓			
14	Benbrook Lake Trail		✓	✓						
15	Eagle Mountain Park Trail		✓			✓		✓		
16	Fort Worth Nature Center: Canyon Ridge Trail			✓				✓		
17	Fort Worth Nature Center: Prairie Trail			✓						
18	Horseshoe Trail	✓	✓			✓	✓		✓	✓
19	Knob Hills Trail			✓						
20	Northshore Trail		✓			✓	✓	✓		
21	River Legacy Trail	✓	✓				✓		✓	✓
22	Rocky Point Trail		✓							
23	Sansom Park Trail		✓					✓		
24	Tandy Hills Trail			✓		✓	✓			
25	Trinity River Trail (McMillan Plaza)		✓						✓	✓
26	Trinity River Trail (Oakmont Park)		✓							
NORTH OF DALLAS–FORT WORTH (Including Plano, McKinney, Lake Ray Roberts, and Lake Lewisville)										
27	Arbor Hills Loop	✓		✓						✓
28	Black Creek–Cottonwood Hiking Trail		✓	✓						
29	Cicada–Cottonwood Loop			✓	✓					
30	Elm Fork Trail		✓		✓					
31	Erwin Park Loop			✓						

More Hikes by Category (Continued)

REGION Hike Number/Hike Name	Best for Dogs	Bodies of Water	Flora or Fauna	Historical Interest	Most Scenic	Runners	Steepest	Urban	Wheelchair Friendly
NORTH OF DALLAS–FORT WORTH *(Continued)* (Including Plano, McKinney, Lake Ray Roberts, and Lake Lewisville)									
32 Lavon Lake: Trinity Trail		✓							
33 Parkhill Prairie Trail			✓		✓				
34 Pilot Knoll Trail		✓	✓						
35 Ray Roberts Greenbelt	✓		✓			✓			
36 Ray Roberts Lake State Park, Isle du Bois Unit: Lost Pines Trail	✓			✓					
37 Ray Roberts Lake State Park, Johnson Branch Unit: Johnson Branch Trail						✓			
38 Sister Grove Loop			✓						
39 Tribute Shoreline Trail	✓	✓	✓		✓	✓			✓
40 Walnut Grove Trail		✓	✓						
SOUTH OF DALLAS–FORT WORTH (Including Cedar Hill, Glen Rose, and Cleburne)									
41 Bardwell Lake Multiuse Trail	✓		✓						
42 Cedar Hill State Park: Talala–Duck Pond Loop			✓						
43 Cedar Mountain Preserve Trail									
44 Cedar Ridge Preserve Trail			✓		✓		✓		
45 Cleburne State Park Loop Trail							✓		
46 Cottonwood Creek Trail					✓				
47 Dinosaur Valley Trail			✓	✓	✓		✓		
48 Dogwood Canyon Audubon Trail			✓		✓		✓		✓
49 Goat Island Preserve Trail		✓							
50 Purtis Creek Trail		✓							
51 Visitor's Overlook: Joe Pool Lake Dam Trail		✓							
52 Walnut Creek Trail		✓							
53 Waxahachie Creek Hike & Bike Trail	✓	✓	✓			✓		✓	
54 Windmill Hill Preserve Trail	✓								
WEST OF FORT WORTH									
55 Lake Mineral Wells State Park: Cross Timbers Trail									
56 Lake Mineral Wells State Trailway			✓			✓			
57 Lost Creek Reservoir State Trailway		✓	✓			✓			
EAST OF DALLAS									
58 Lake Tawakoni Nature Trail			✓						
59 Post Oak Trail					✓				
60 Samuell Farm Trail			✓	✓					

About This Book

Many people who arrive in Dallas–Fort Worth form a first impression of the area that can persist: hot summers; a dry, flat landscape; and a lack of wildlife. And while the first is certainly true (North Texas summers have an average high of near 100 degrees in July and August, and have been known to get over 110 degrees in the summer), the latter two descriptors are anything but accurate. The Dallas–Fort Worth region has a fascinating and varied terrain teeming with a surprising diversity of wildlife.

The metroplex sits in what the Texas Parks and Wildlife Department describes as the "Prairies and Lakes" region—a geographic area of the state defined by woodlands, grasslands, lakes, and hills. Distinctive features divide the area into specific ecoregions, identified as cross timbers, blackland prairie, and post oak savannah.

The cross timbers ecoregion encompasses a wide section of North Texas, covering areas to the west of Dallas, including Fort Worth. It is characterized by a mix of woodland trees and prairie grasses. Just to the east of the cross timbers, the blackland prairie covers a section of North Texas from just north of Dallas south to San Antonio; it is associated with tallgrass prairies and heavy clay soil. Finally, just to the east of the blackland prairie ecoregion is the post oak savannah, a grassy savannah with oak trees. In selecting the 60 trails for this book, I've tried to include hikes throughout the metroplex to ensure a mix of representatives of each of these ecoregions. Hikes are listed alphabetically and are 60 miles from either Dallas or Fort Worth, whichever city is closer.

How to Use This Guidebook

The following information walks you through this guidebook's organization to make it easy and convenient for planning great hikes.

OVERVIEW MAP AND MAP LEGEND

Use the overview map on page iv to assess the general location of each hike's primary trailhead. Each hike's number appears on the overview map and in the table of contents. As you flip through the book, a hike's full profile is easy to locate by watching for the hike number at the top of each page. The book is organized by region, as indicated in the table of contents. A map legend that details the symbols found on trail maps appears on page xiii.

REGIONAL MAPS

The book is divided into regions, and prefacing each regional section is an overview map. The regional maps provide more detail than the overview map, bringing you closer to the hikes.

TRAIL MAPS

A detailed map of each hike's route appears with its profile. On each of these maps, symbols indicate the trailhead, the complete route, significant features, facilities, and topographic landmarks such as creeks, overlooks, and peaks.

To produce the highly accurate maps in this book, the author used a handheld GPS unit to gather data while hiking each route, and then sent that data to the publisher's expert cartographers. However, your GPS is not really a substitute for sound, sensible navigation that takes into account the conditions you observe while hiking.

Further, despite the high quality of the maps in this guidebook, the publisher and author strongly recommend that you always carry an additional map, such as the ones noted in each entry's listing for "Maps."

ELEVATION PROFILES (DIAGRAM)

For trails with any significant elevation changes, the hike description *will* include this profile graph. Entries for fairly flat routes, such as a lake loop, will *not* display an elevation profile.

For hike descriptions where the elevation profile is included, this diagram represents the rises and falls of the trail as viewed from the side, over the complete distance (in miles) of that trail. On the diagram's vertical axis, or height scale, the number of feet indicated between each tick mark lets you visualize the climb. To avoid making flat hikes look steep and steep hikes appear flat, varying height scales provide an accurate image of each hike's climbing challenge. For example, one hike's scale might rise to 1,200 feet, while another goes to 900 feet.

THE HIKE PROFILE

Each hike contains a brief overview of the trail, a description of the route from start to finish, key at-a-glance information—from the trail's distance and configuration to contacts for local information—GPS trailhead coordinates, and directions for driving to the trailhead area. Each profile also includes a map (see "Trail Maps," above) and elevation profile (if the elevation gain is 100 feet or more). Many hike profiles also include notes on nearby activities.

KEY INFORMATION

The information in this box gives you a quick idea of the statistics and specifics of each hike.

DISTANCE & CONFIGURATION Distance notes the length of the hike round-trip, from start to finish. If the hike description includes options to shorten or extend the hike, those round-trip distances will also be factored here. Configuration defines the trail as a loop, an out-and-back (taking you in and out via the same route), a figure eight, or a balloon.

DIFFICULTY   The degree of effort that a typical hiker should expect on a given route. For simplicity, the trails are rated as easy, moderate, or strenuous.

SCENERY   A short summary of the attractions offered by the hike and what to expect in terms of plant life, wildlife, natural wonders, and historic features.

EXPOSURE   A quick check of how much sun you can expect on your shoulders during the hike.

TRAFFIC   Indicates how busy the trail might be on an average day. Trail traffic, of course, varies from day to day and from season to season. Weekend days typically see the most visitors. Other trail users who may be encountered on the trail are also noted here.

TRAIL SURFACE   Indicates whether the trail surface is paved, rocky, gravel, dirt, boardwalk, or a mixture of elements.

HIKING TIME   How long it takes to hike the trail. A slow but steady hiker will average 2–3 miles an hour, depending on the terrain.

DRIVING DISTANCE   Listed in miles from a major intersection or landmark.

ACCESS   Fees or permits required to hike the trail are detailed here—and noted if there are none. Trail-access hours are also shown here.

If you plan to do a lot of hiking, consider buying a Texas State Parks Pass, which waives the daily entrance fee to the state parks and historic sites within the state, allowing pass holders unlimited free access. The annual pass costs $60 for a one-card membership or $75 for a two-card membership (with the stipulation that both pass holders live at the same residence) and allows everyone in the vehicle admittance. If you don't have a State Parks Pass, you'll need to pay the daily entrance fee, which varies from park to park (most within 60 miles of Dallas–Fort Worth cost $5). Passes can be purchased at the visitor centers at most state parks. Seniors and veterans may be eligible for reduced or free admission. For more information, visit tpwd.state.tx.us/spdest/parkinfo/passes.

Most of the parks I've listed that are operated by the U.S. Army Corps of Engineers require no admission or parking fees, but most city parks offering recreation areas, such as camping, boating, and picnicking, typically charge a small entrance fee.

MAPS   Resources for maps, in addition to those in this guidebook, are listed here. (As previously noted, the publisher and author recommend that you carry more than one map—and that you consult those maps before heading out on the trail in order to resolve any confusion or discrepancy.)

WHEELCHAIR TRAVERSABLE At a glance, you'll see if there are paved sections or other areas for safely using a wheelchair.

FACILITIES This item alerts you to restrooms, water, picnic tables, and other basics at or near the trailhead.

CONTACT Listed here are phone numbers and website addresses for checking trail conditions and gleaning other day-to-day information.

LOCATION The address of the trail.

COMMENTS Here you will find assorted nuggets of information, such as whether or not dogs are allowed on the trails.

IN BRIEF

Think of this section as a taste of the trail, a snapshot focused on the historical landmarks, beautiful vistas, and other sights you may encounter on the hike.

DESCRIPTION

The heart of each hike. Here, the author provides a summary of the trail's essence and highlights any special traits the hike has to offer. The route is clearly outlined, including landmarks, side trips, and possible alternate routes along the way. Ultimately, the hike description will help you choose which hikes are best for you.

NEARBY ACTIVITIES

Look here for information on things to do or points of interest: nearby parks, museums, restaurants, and the like.

DIRECTIONS

Used in conjunction with the GPS coordinates, the driving directions will help you locate each trailhead. Once at the trailhead, park only in designated areas.

GPS TRAILHEAD COORDINATES

As noted in "Trail Maps," page 2, the author used a handheld GPS device to obtain geographic data and sent the information to the publisher's cartographers. The coordinates listed with each profile—the intersection of the latitude (north) and longitude (west)—will orient you to the trailhead. In some cases, you can drive within viewing distance of it. Other hiking routes require you to walk a short distance from a parking area.

You will also note that this guidebook uses the degree–decimal minute format for presenting the latitude and longitude GPS coordinates:

N32° 51.733' W96° 55.517'

The latitude and longitude grid system is likely quite familiar to you, but here is a refresher, pertinent to visualizing the GPS coordinates:

Imaginary lines of latitude—called parallels and approximately 69 miles apart from each other—run horizontally around the globe. The equator is established to be 0°, and each parallel is indicated by degrees from the equator: up to 90°N at the North Pole, and down to 90°S at the South Pole.

Imaginary lines of longitude—called meridians—run perpendicular to latitude lines. Longitude lines are likewise indicated by degrees. Starting from 0° at the Prime Meridian in Greenwich, England, they continue to the east and west until they meet 180° later at the International Date Line in the Pacific Ocean. At the equator, longitude lines are also approximately 69 miles apart, but that distance narrows as the meridians converge toward the North and South Poles.

To convert GPS coordinates given in degrees, minutes, and seconds to the format shown above, the seconds are divided by 60. For more on GPS technology, visit usgs.gov.

Topographic Maps

The maps in this book have been produced with great care and, used with the hike text, will direct you to the trail and help you stay on course. However, you'll find superior detail and valuable information in the U.S. Geological Survey's 7.5-minute-series topographic maps. At mytopo.com, for example, you can view and print free USGS topos of the entire United States. Online services such as Trails.com charge annual fees for additional features such as shaded relief, which makes the topography stand out more. If you expect to print out many topo maps each year, it might be worth paying for such extras. The downside to USGS maps is that most are outdated, having been created 20–30 years ago; nevertheless, they provide excellent topographic detail. Of course, Google Earth (earth.google.com) does away with topo maps and their inaccuracies . . . replacing them with satellite imagery and its inaccuracies. Regardless, what one lacks, the other augments. Google Earth is an excellent tool whether you have difficulty with topos or not.

If you're new to hiking, you might be wondering, "What's a topo map?" In short, it indicates not only linear distance but elevation as well, using contour lines. These lines spread across the map like dozens of intricate spiderwebs. Each line represents a particular elevation, and at the base of each topo a contour's interval designation is given. If, for example, the contour interval is 20 feet, then the distance between each contour line is 20 feet. Follow five contour lines up on the same map, and the elevation has increased by 100 feet. In addition to the sources listed previously and in Appendix B, you'll find topos at major universities, outdoors shops, and some public libraries, as well as online at nationalmap.gov and store.usgs.gov.

Weather

There's an old saying—"If you don't like the weather, wait 5 minutes"—and nowhere is that more true than in North Texas. You can find yourself wearing a winter jacket one day and shorts the next, or be dismayed by severe thunderstorms wreaking havoc on your day, only to find the sun shining an hour later.

Winters are usually mild, with average daily temperatures in the 50s during December and January, with occasional days of below-freezing temperatures. Though winter storms rarely bring snow, a few times each year storms combine with overnight freezing temperatures to cause "black ice" to form on roads and bridges, temporarily immobilizing the city. The coldest month is January, with temperatures rising around 7–8 degrees each subsequent month before finally peaking in July.

Spring peaks in mid-April, when Texas's favorite wildflower, the bluebonnet, blankets medians, parks, and undeveloped fields. Daytime temperatures are typically in the high 70s, and it's not uncommon for showers and thunderstorms to threaten at least a couple of days a week. In conjunction with the storms, the threat of tornadoes also increases. Summers are typically hot, with temperatures in the 90s, and include an average of two weeks when readings are above 100—these are typically during the months of July and August. The following chart lists average temperatures and precipitation by month for the Dallas–Fort Worth region.

AVERAGE DAILY TEMPERATURES						
	JAN	FEB	MARCH	APRIL	MAY	JUNE
High	56°F	60°F	68°F	76°F	84°F	91°F
Low	36°F	39°F	47°F	55°F	64°F	71°F
	JULY	AUG	SEPT	OCT	NOV	DEC
High	96°F	96°F	88°F	78°F	67°F	57°F
Low	75°F	75°F	68°F	57°F	46°F	37°F

AVERAGE PRECIPITATION					
JAN	FEB	MARCH	APRIL	MAY	JUNE
2.1"	2.7"	3.5"	3.0"	4.9"	3.8"
JULY	AUG	SEPT	OCT	NOV	DEC
2.2"	1.9"	2.6"	4.2"	2.7"	2.6"

Water

How much is enough? Well, one simple physiological fact should convince you to err on the side of excess when deciding how much water to pack: a hiker walking steadily in 90° heat needs approximately 10 quarts of fluid per day. That's 2.5 gallons. A good rule of thumb is to hydrate prior to your hike, carry (and drink) 6 ounces of water for every mile you plan to hike, and hydrate again after the hike. For most people, the pleasures of hiking make carrying water a relatively minor price to pay to remain safe and healthy. So pack more water than you anticipate needing even for short hikes.

If you are tempted to drink "found" water, do so with extreme caution. Many ponds and lakes encountered by hikers are fairly stagnant, and the water tastes terrible. Drinking such water presents inherent risks for thirsty trekkers. Giardia parasites contaminate many water sources and cause the dreaded intestinal giardiasis, which can last for weeks after ingestion. For information, visit the Centers for Disease Control website at cdc.gov/parasites/giardia.

In any case, effective treatment is essential before using any water source found along the trail. Boiling water for 2–3 minutes is always a safe measure for camping, but day hikers can consider iodine tablets, approved chemical mixes, filtration units rated for giardia, and UV filtration. Some of these methods (for example, filtration with an added carbon filter) remove bad tastes typical in stagnant water, while others add their own taste. As a precaution, carry a means of water purification to help in a pinch and if you realize you have underestimated your consumption needs.

Clothing

Weather, unexpected trail conditions, fatigue, extended hiking duration, and wrong turns can individually or collectively turn a great outing into a very uncomfortable one at best—and a life-threatening one at worst.

You want to be comfortable on the trail, and that means keeping yourself cool in summer and warm in winter—especially in Texas, where temperatures can be extreme. In warm weather, a cotton T-shirt and shorts are great for urban hikes; cargo shorts are popular for their loose, comfortable fit. If you'll be in the grasslands or woodlands, a pair of hiking pants will protect your legs from ticks and snakes commonly found in these areas. You can find lightweight, quick-drying, UV-protective pants at many outdoors shops; these will keep you suitably cool. Consider a pair that converts into shorts so that you can unzip them when you're finished walking through the risky areas.

Hiking in cooler weather brings its own set of problems. Even though it might be cold out, you'll find yourself sweating after a little exertion. Layering is a good solution and an important part of keeping you comfortable. Wear a T-shirt or, better yet, a moisture-wicking shirt under your clothes, and top it with a lightweight fleece or sweater. In winter, wear an outer jacket. You'll more than likely find yourself taking off and putting on layers throughout the hike.

Year-round you need a good pair of hiking shoes. Day hikers are a great choice for most North Texas trails: they come in both low-top and high-top versions, are lightweight, and have good tread and support. Running/exercise shoes are suitable for paved trails but aren't ideal for dirt paths. Essential at any time of year, a hat not only keeps the hot Texas sun from burning your face but also doubles as protection against insects and low-hanging limbs. Another useful item is a rain jacket that can be compressed small enough to be stuffed in your pack; if you're caught out in the rain, you'll be thankful for it.

Proper attire plays a key role in staying comfortable and, sometimes, in staying alive. Here are some additional helpful guidelines to keep in mind:

➤ **Choose silk, wool, or synthetics for maximum comfort in all of your hiking attire**—from hats to socks and in between. Cotton is fine if the weather remains dry and stable, but you won't be happy if that material gets wet.

➤ **Always wear a hat, or at least tuck one into your day pack or hitch it to your belt.** Hats offer all-weather sun and wind protection as well as warmth if it turns cold.

➤ **Be ready to layer up or down as the day progresses and the mercury rises or falls.** Today's outdoor wear makes layering easy, with designs such as jackets that convert to vests and zip-off or button-up legs.

➤ **Wear hiking boots or sturdy hiking sandals with toe protection.** Flip-flopping along a paved urban greenway is one thing, but never hike a trail in open sandals or casual sneakers. Your bones and arches need support, and your skin needs protection.

➤ **Pair that footwear with good socks!** If you prefer not to sheathe your feet when wearing hiking sandals, tuck the socks into your day pack; you may need them if the weather plummets or if you hit rocky turf and pebbles begin to irritate your feet. And, in an emergency, if you have lost your gloves, you can adapt the socks into mittens.

➤ **Don't leave rainwear behind, even if the day dawns clear and sunny.** Tuck into your day pack, or tie around your waist, a jacket that is breathable and either water-resistant or waterproof. Investigate different choices at your local outdoors retailer. If you are a frequent hiker, ideally you'll have more than one rainwear weight, material, and style in your closet to protect you in all seasons in your regional climate and hiking microclimates.

Essential Gear

Today you can buy outdoor-recreation vests that have up to 20 pockets shaped and sized to carry everything from toothpicks to binoculars. Or, if you don't aspire to feel like a burro, you can neatly stow all of these items in your day pack or backpack. The following list showcases never-hike-without-them items, in alphabetical order, as all are important:

➤ **Extra clothes** Raingear, warm hat, gloves, and change of socks and shirt

➤ **Extra food** Trail mix, granola bars, or other high-energy foods

➤ **Flashlight or headlamp with extra bulb and batteries**

➤ **Insect repellent** For some areas and seasons, this is extremely vital.

➤ **Maps and a high-quality compass** Even if you know the terrain from previous hikes, don't leave home without these tools. And, as previously noted, bring maps in addition to those in this guidebook, and consult your maps prior to the hike. If you are versed in GPS usage, bring that device too, but don't rely on it as your sole navigational tool, as battery life can dwindle or die, and be sure to compare its guidance with that of your maps.

➤ **Pocketknife and/or multitool**

➤ **Sunscreen** Note the expiration date on the tube or bottle; it's usually embossed on the top.

➤ **Water** As emphasized more than once in this book, bring more than you think you will drink. Depending on your destination, you may want to bring a container and iodine or a filter for purifying water in case you run out.

➤ **Whistle** This little gadget will be your best friend in an emergency.

➤ **Windproof matches and/or a lighter, as well as a fire starter**

FIRST AID KIT

In addition to the aforementioned items, those below may appear overwhelming for a day hike. But any paramedic will tell you that the products listed here—in alphabetical order, because all are important—are just the basics. The reality of hiking is that you can be out for a week of backpacking and acquire only a mosquito bite. Or you can hike for an hour, slip, and suffer a bleeding abrasion or broken bone. Fortunately, these listed items will collapse into a very small space. You also may purchase convenient, prepackaged kits at your pharmacy or on the Internet.

➤ **Adhesive bandages**

➤ **Antibiotic ointment** Neosporin or the generic equivalent

➤ **Athletic tape**

➤ **Benadryl** or the generic equivalent, diphenhydramine In case of allergic reactions

➤ **Blister kit,** such as Moleskin/Spenco 2nd Skin

➤ **Butterfly-closure bandages**

➤ **Elastic bandages or joint wraps**

➤ **Epinephrine in a prefilled syringe** Typically by prescription only, and for people known to have severe allergic reactions to hiking occurrences such as bee stings

➤ **Gauze** One roll and a half dozen 4-by-4-inch pads

➤ **Hydrogen peroxide or iodine**

➤ **Ibuprofen or acetaminophen**

Note: Consider your intended terrain and the number of hikers in your party before you exclude any article cited above. A botanical garden stroll may not inspire you to carry a complete kit, but anything beyond that warrants precaution. When hiking alone, you should always be prepared for a medical need. And if you are a twosome or with a group, one or more people in your party should be equipped with first aid material.

General Safety

The following tips may have the familiar ring of your mother's voice as you take note of them.

➤ **Always let someone know where you will be hiking and how long you expect to be gone.** It's a good idea to give that person a copy of your route, particularly if you are headed into any isolated area. Let that person know when you return.

➤ **Always sign in and out of any trail registers provided.** Don't hesitate to comment on the trail condition if space is provided; that's your opportunity to alert others to any problems you encounter.

➤ **Do not count on a cell phone for your safety.** Reception may be spotty or nonexistent on the trail, even on an urban walk—especially if it is embraced by towering trees.

➤ **Always carry food and water, even for a short hike.** And bring more water than you think you will need. (That cannot be said often enough!)

➤ **Ask questions.** State forest and park employees are there to help. It's a lot easier to solicit advice before a problem occurs, and it will help you avoid a mishap away from civilization when it's too late to amend an error.

➤ **Stay on designated trails.** Even on the most clearly marked trails, there is usually a point where you have to stop and consider which direction to head. If you become disoriented, don't panic. As soon as you think you may be off track, stop, assess your current direction, and then retrace your steps to the point where you went astray. Using a map, a compass, and this book, and keeping in mind what you have passed thus far, reorient yourself, and trust your judgment on which way to continue. If you become absolutely unsure of how to continue, return to your vehicle the way you came in. Should you become completely lost and have no idea how to find the trailhead, remaining in place along the trail and waiting for help is most often the best option for adults and always the best option for children.

➤ **Always carry a whistle, another precaution that cannot be overemphasized.** It may be a lifesaver if you do become lost or sustain an injury.

➤ **Be especially careful when crossing streams.** Whether you are fording the stream or crossing on a log, make every step count. If you have any doubt about maintaining your balance on a log, ford the stream instead: use a trekking pole or stout stick for balance *and face upstream as you cross*. If a stream seems too deep to ford, turn back. Whatever is on the other side is not worth risking your life.

➤ **Be careful at overlooks.** While these areas may provide spectacular views, they are potentially hazardous. Stay back from the edge of outcrops, and make absolutely sure of your footing; a misstep can mean a nasty and possibly fatal fall.

➤ **Standing dead trees and storm-damaged living trees pose a significant hazard to hikers.** These trees may have loose or broken limbs that could fall at any time. While walking beneath trees, and when choosing a spot to rest or enjoy your snack, look up!

➤ **Know the symptoms of subnormal body temperature, known as hypothermia.** Shivering and forgetfulness are the two most common indicators of this stealthy killer. Hypothermia can occur at any elevation, even in the summer, especially when the hiker is wearing lightweight cotton clothing. If symptoms present themselves, get to shelter, hot liquids, and dry clothes as soon as possible.

➤ **Know the symptoms of heat exhaustion (hyperthermia).** Light-headedness and loss of energy are the first two indicators. If you feel these symptoms, find some shade, drink your water, remove as many layers of clothing as practical, and stay put until you cool down. Marching through heat exhaustion leads to heatstroke—which can be fatal. If you should be sweating and you're not, that's the signature warning sign. Your hike is over at that point—heatstroke is a life-threatening condition that can cause seizures, convulsions, and eventually death. If you or a companion reaches that point, do whatever can be done to cool the victim down and seek medical attention immediately.

➤ **Most important of all, take along your brain.** A cool, calculating mind is the single-most important asset on the trail. It allows you to think before you act.

➤ **In summary:** Plan ahead. Watch your step. Avoid accidents before they happen. Enjoy a rewarding and relaxing hike.

Watchwords for Flora and Fauna

Hikers should remain aware of the following concerns regarding plant- and wildlife, described in alphabetical order.

BLACK BEARS

Black bears can be found in West Texas, and very occasionally in Hill Country but are not to be found in North Texas. If your hiking adventures take you beyond these 60 hikes and out into far West Texas, keep in mind that though attacks by black bears are uncommon, the sight or approach of a bear can give anyone a start. If you encounter a bear while hiking, remain calm and avoid running in any direction. Make loud noises to scare off the bear and back away slowly. In primitive and remote areas, assume bears are present; in more-developed sites, check on the current bear situation prior to hiking. Most encounters are food related, as bears have an exceptional sense of smell and not particularly discriminating tastes. While this is of greater concern to backpackers and campers, on a day hike, you may plan a lunchtime picnic or munch on an energy bar or other snack from time to time. So remain aware and alert.

CHIGGERS

If you've ever been attacked by chiggers, you won't soon forget it. I personally have never encountered these annoying insects on the trail, but those who have will tell you their chigger stories over and over for years to come.

Chiggers are tiny red mites so small that you are unlikely to spot them until evidence of their bites signals that you have traipsed through an infested area. An unsuspecting hiker who wanders into their midst could easily go home with hundreds of bites on bare, exposed legs.

Though certainly a pest and maddening annoyance, the worst a chigger will cause is an itchy welt. They are most active from spring until late summer, and love damp areas as well as tall grasses. The best deterrent is keeping them away from your skin by wearing long pants, socks, and enclosed shoes. Insect repellents, especially those containing DEET, are effective as well.

MOSQUITOES

Ward off these pests with insect repellent and/or repellent-impregnated clothing. Although it's not a common occurrence, individuals can become infected with the West Nile virus if they're bitten by an infected mosquito. *Culex* mosquitoes, the primary varieties that can transmit West Nile virus to humans, thrive in urban rather than natural areas. They lay their eggs in stagnant water and can breed in standing water that remains for more than five days. Most people infected with West Nile virus have no symptoms of illness, but some may become ill, usually 3–15 days after being bitten.

In the Dallas–Fort Worth metroplex, the summer months—especially August and September—bring mosquitoes, and with them the highest risk for West Nile. Mosquitoes are especially prolific on trails with tall grasses, in marshy/swampy areas, and around dusk and dawn. Anytime you expect mosquitoes to be buzzing around, wear protective clothing, such as long sleeves, long pants, and socks. Loose-fitting, light-colored clothing is best. Spray clothing with insect repellent. The Centers for Disease Control and Prevention notes that repellents containing the active ingredients DEET or picaridin supply the best protection; the agency also suggests oil of lemon eucalyptus (a citrus-scented variety of the eucalyptus tree) as an effective plant-based repellent. Follow the instructions on the repellent, and take extra care with children. Insect-repellent clothing, available at outdoor retailers, is another source of protection against mosquitoes and other bothersome bugs.

POISON IVY, OAK, AND SUMAC

On any given North Texas trail, you'll want to keep a mindful eye as to where you step. Poison ivy grows commonly in the region, though staying on established trails will by and large help you avoid unknowingly traipsing through the leaves. Poison oak and sumac are similar plants to beware of.

Recognizing and avoiding poison ivy, oak, and sumac (pictured, top to bottom, at left) are the most effective ways to prevent the painful, itchy rashes associated with these plants. Poison ivy occurs as a vine or ground cover, three leaflets to a leaf; poison oak occurs as either a vine or shrub, also with three leaflets; and poison sumac flourishes in swampland, each leaf having 7–13 leaflets.

Urushiol, the oil in the sap of these plants, is responsible for the rash. Within 14 hours of exposure, raised lines and/or blisters will appear on the affected area, accompanied by a terrible itch. Refrain from scratching because bacteria under your fingernails can cause an infection. Wash and dry the affected area thoroughly, applying a calamine lotion to help dry out the rash. If itching or blistering is severe, seek medical attention.

Look up a few pictures of the plants in order to gain some familiarity with what to avoid, and

Photo: Tom Watson

Photo: Jane Huber

Photo: Kevin Hansen/Freekee/Wikimedia Commons/CCO (creativecommons.org /license/CCO)

remember the adage to identify poison ivy—"Leaves of three, let them be." Another helpful tip, especially if you're heading onto a less used trail that may be slightly overgrown, is to wear protective clothing including long pants, socks, and enclosed shoes.

If you do come into contact with one of these plants, remember that oil-contaminated clothes, hiking gear, and pets can easily cause an irritating rash on you or someone else, so wash not only any exposed parts of your body but also anything the oil might have touched.

SNAKES

In the region described in this book, you will possibly encounter snakes on the trail. Most of the snakes you might encounter on your hikes will be nonvenomous and pose no threat to humans. Many folks even consider the most common snake in the area—the Texas rat snake—a welcome visitor. This snake, as its name implies, feasts on rodents, and though it may rear and act defensive if you antagonize it, its bite is harmless. Of the more than three dozen types of snakes in the area, only a handful are venomous, the most common ones being the rattlesnake (pictured at right), the cottonmouth, and the copperhead. On many trails, you'll spot signs warning that you're in a snake habitat. As long as you stay on the trail and out of tall grasses, however, you're unlikely to have a problem. In fact, in all my times hiking the trails in this book, I've met only the occasional snake, and those encounters were uneventful and brief.

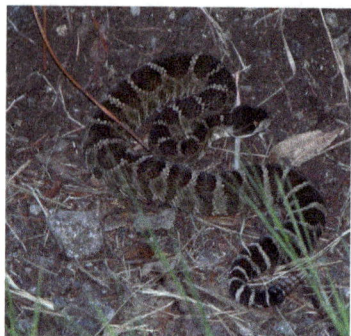

The best rule is to leave all snakes alone, give them a wide berth as you hike past, and make sure any hiking companions (including dogs) do the same.

When hiking, stick to well-used trails, and wear over-the-ankle boots and loose-fitting long pants. Do not step or put your hands beyond your range of detailed visibility, and avoid wandering around in the dark. Step *onto* logs and rocks, never *over* them, and be especially careful when climbing rocks. Always avoid walking through dense brush or willow thickets.

TICKS

Ticks are often found on brush and tall grass, where they seem to be waiting to hitch a ride on a warm-blooded passerby. Adult ticks are most active April–May and again October–November. Among the varieties of ticks, the black-legged tick, commonly called the deer tick, is the primary carrier of Lyme disease. Wear light-colored clothing to make it easier for you to spot ticks before they migrate to your skin. At the end

14

of the hike, visually check your hair, back of neck, armpits, and socks. During your posthike shower, take a moment to do a more complete body check. For ticks that are already embedded, removal with tweezers is best. Grasp the tick close to your skin, and remove it by pulling straight out firmly. Do your best to remove the head, but do not twist. Use disinfectant solution on the wound.

OTHER WILDLIFE

Some of the other common wildlife you can spot on trails in the region include:

- Beaver
- Black-tailed jackrabbit
- Bobcat
- Brown bat
- Coyote
- Goose
- Gray fox
- Mexican free-tailed bat
- Mountain lion
- Nine-banded armadillo
- Porcupine
- Rabbit
- Raccoon
- Red fox
- Striped skunk
- Texas horned lizard
- Turkey
- Virginia opossum
- White-tailed deer

Hunting

Separate rules, regulations, and licenses govern the various hunting types and related seasons. Although there are generally no problems, hikers may wish to forgo their trips during the big-game seasons, when the woods suddenly seem filled with orange and camouflage. For further information on hunting season by animal and by county, visit tpwd.texas.gov/huntwild/hunt/season.

Regulations

Fishing in any of the public waters of Texas requires a fishing license, with one exception: if you are fishing from the bank of a state park, no license is required. For further information on regulations and fees, tpwd.texas.gov/business/licenses.

Burn bans can sometimes be implemented within different counties or areas, especially during periods of severe drought. During a burn ban, things like campfires, sparklers, and fireworks are prohibited. The Texas Forest Service can provide a current list of burn bans implemented in the state: txforestservice.tamu.edu/texasburnbans.

Backcountry/Primitive Camping Advice

Backcountry/primitive camping is available in the LBJ National Grasslands and in many state parks and wildlife-management areas. Practice low-impact camping and adhere to the adages "Pack it in, pack it out" and "Take only pictures, leave only footprints." Practice "leave no trace" camping ethics while in the backcountry. Some backcountry areas are also public hunting areas, so research your destination before your visit.

Solid human waste should be buried in a hole at least 3 inches deep and at least 200 feet away from trails and water sources; a trowel is basic backpacking equipment.

Rules on open fires vary depending on where you go, so check before your visit; when collecting firewood, many places ask you to collect downed wood instead of chopping branches. In addition, Texas State Parks allow fires only in fire rings, fireplaces, and campsite grills. Burn bans, especially during drought periods, can restrict fires—including those at campsite grills. Double-check before your trip, because state parks may or may not be affected by a countywide burn ban.

A fishing license is required if you plan to fish. You can get one from many outdoor retailers, sports stores, and bait and tackle shops, online, or over the phone. Visit tpwd.state.tx.us for information on regulations, fees, permits, and how to purchase.

Following the previous guidelines will increase your chances of having a pleasant, safe, and low-impact interaction with nature. The suggestions are intended to enhance your experience. Regulations can change over time; contact the appropriate park office to confirm the status of any regulations before you enter the backcountry.

Trail Etiquette

Always treat the trail, wildlife, and fellow hikers with respect. Here are some guidelines to keep in mind.

➤ **Plan ahead in order to be self-sufficient at all times.** For example, carry necessary supplies for changes in weather or other conditions. A well-planned trip brings satisfaction to you and to others.

➤ **Hike on open trails only.** In seasons or construction areas where road or trail closures may be a possibility, use the website addresses or phone numbers shown in the "Contacts" line for each of this guidebook's hikes to check conditions prior to heading out for your hike. And do not attempt to circumvent such closures.

➤ **Avoid trespassing on private land, and be sure to obtain all permits and authorization as required.** Also, leave gates as you found them or as directed by signage.

Scenic views abound on the Canyon Ridge Trail at the Fort Worth Nature Center and Refuge (Hike 16, page 85).

➤ **Be courteous to other hikers,** bikers, equestrians, and others you encounter on the trails.

➤ **Never spook wild animals or pets.** An unannounced approach, a sudden movement, or a loud noise startles most critters, and a surprised animal can be dangerous to you, to others, and to itself. Give any animals you encounter plenty of space.

➤ **Observe the yield signs around the region's trailheads and backcountry.** Typically they advise hikers to yield to horses, and bikers to yield to both horses and hikers. By common courtesy on hills, hikers and bikers yield to any uphill traffic. When encountering mounted riders or horsepackers, hikers can courteously step off the trail, on the downhill side if possible. So the horse can see and hear you, calmly greet the riders before they reach you, and do not dart behind trees. Also resist the urge to pet horses unless you are invited to do so.

➤ **Stay on the existing trail and do not blaze any new trails.**

➤ **Be sure to pack out what you pack in, leaving only your footprints.** No one likes to see the trash someone else has left behind.

Tips on Enjoying Dallas and Fort Worth

If you plan on hiking in one of the state parks, Army Corps of Engineers sites, or national grasslands, visit a corresponding website for information to help you get oriented to the roads, features, and attractions of where you're going. General and detailed maps of the specific wilderness areas are often available online or, if you're visiting a state park, at the park office. In addition, the following tips will make your visit enjoyable and more rewarding.

➤ **Get out of your car and onto a trail.** Auto touring allows a cursory overview of the area, but only visually. On the trail, you can use your ears and nose as well. Even if you don't use the trails recommended in this guide, any trail is better than no trail at all.

➤ **North Texas summers can be unbearably hot, making a day hike in late July or August seemingly impossible.** If it's a nice day and you don't want to miss out on hiking because of the heat, go early in the morning. If you're on the trail at dawn, you can find temperatures 10–20 degrees lower than they'll be later in the day, and there's no better way to start your day than listening to the cheerful singing of birds along the trail.

➤ **Take your time along the trails.** Pace yourself. North Texas is filled with wonders both big and small. Don't rush past a tiny lizard to get to that over-look. Stop and smell the wildflowers. Peer into a clear creek for minnows.

North Texas trails are at their most beautiful in the spring when the wildflowers are in full bloom.

Don't miss the trees for the forest. Shorter hikes allow you to stop and linger more than long hikes do. Something about staring at the front end of a 10-mile trek naturally pushes you to speed up. That said, take close notice of the elevation maps that accompany each hike. If you see many ups and downs over large altitude changes, you'll obviously need more time. Inevitably, you'll finish some of the hikes more or less quickly than the estimated time. Nevertheless, leave yourself plenty of time for those moments when you simply feel like stopping and taking it all in.

➤ **Try to hike during the week and avoid the traditional holidays, if possible.** Trails that are packed in the spring and fall are often clear during the hotter or colder months. If you're hiking on a busy day, go early in the morning; it'll enhance your chances of seeing wildlife. The trails really clear out during rainy times; however, don't hike during a thunderstorm.

➤ **Investigate different areas around the metroplex.** The scenery you'll find hiking through meadows and grasslands is pleasantly different from the riparian forest alongside a fork of the Trinity River or lakeside water views. Sample a few of each to see what the area has to offer and what most appeals to you.

➤ **Hike during different seasons.** Trails change dramatically from spring to winter and can transform themselves into something you might not even recognize.

Hiking with Children

No one is too young for a hike in the outdoors. Be mindful, though. Flat, short, and shaded trails are best for infants. Toddlers who haven't quite mastered walking can ride on an adult's back in a child carrier. Use common sense to judge a child's capacity to hike a particular trail, and always expect that the child will tire quickly and need to be carried. A list of hikes suitable for kids is provided on pages xiii–xiv.

When packing for the hike, remember children's needs in addition to your own. Make sure they are adequately clothed for the weather, have proper shoes, and are protected from the sun with sunscreen. Kids dehydrate quickly, so make sure you have plenty of fluid for everyone.

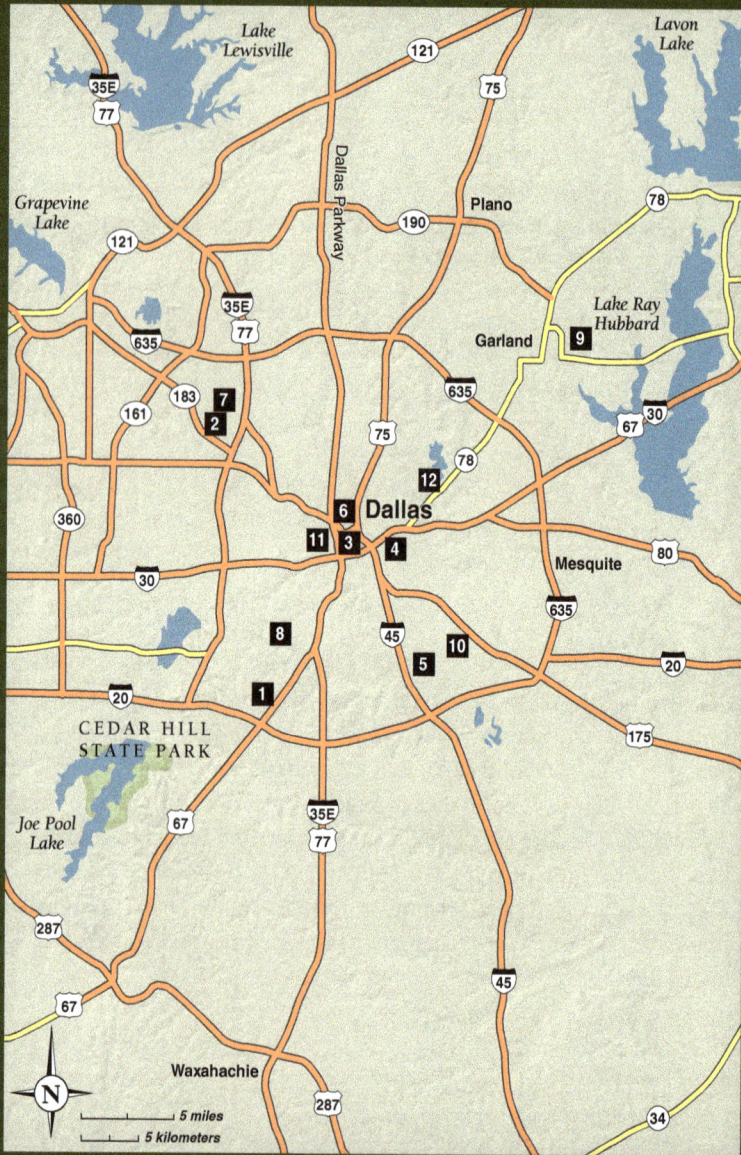

DALLAS AREA
(Including Grand Prairie, Garland, and Irving)

1 BOULDER PARK TRAIL

The trail alternates between open, sunny sections and densely shaded portions.

THIS FUN HIKE twists and turns haphazardly through dense, shaded woodland. Many junctions provide ample opportunities for exploring, and color-coded trails prevent you from getting too lost.

DESCRIPTION

Boulder Park was purchased in 1967 by the city of Dallas and is near Red Bird Airport, north of Duncanville. It's maintained by DORBA—the Dallas Off-Road Bicycle Association—which has built 12 miles of trails through its woodlands. The trails are quite pretty, offering a few deeply wooded sections that are especially lovely in the springtime, when everything is green.

On any given weekend, the gravel parking lot fills up with cars as hikers and bikers flock from nearby in search of outdoor fun. DORBA cautions that visitors are not to park in the nearby church parking lot. If the trail parking lot is full, alternate parking is available on the side streets of Hallet and Calhoun.

Although this is a favorite DORBA spot and you're likely to meet some bikers on the trail, don't let this discourage you from visiting; the trail is long enough to accommodate both hikers and bikers without too much inconvenience for either. Most bikers are hiker-savvy and will voice their approach when they see you, allowing you ample time to step onto the side of the trail.

DISTANCE & CONFIGURATION: 2.4-mile loop

DIFFICULTY: Easy

SCENERY: Woodlands

EXPOSURE: Partial shade

TRAFFIC: Moderate

TRAIL SURFACE: Dirt

HIKING TIME: 50 minutes

DRIVING DISTANCE: 2 miles from US 67 and I-20

ACCESS: Daily, 6 a.m.–11 p.m.; free

MAP: dorba.org/trail.php?t=4

WHEELCHAIR TRAVERSABLE: No

FACILITIES: Portable toilets, picnic tables

CONTACT: dorba.org

LOCATION: 6600 Bailey Dr., Dallas

COMMENTS: Don't park in the church parking lot. Check the trail website for temporary trail closures after rains.

The trailhead has picnic tables along with a kiosk featuring a map of the park's trails. There are five loops, labeled A–E and color-coded as blue for easy and red for more difficult. Although you're unlikely to get too lost, as the land the trail sits on is not too vast, it's a good idea to bring a GPS or compass with you to help you get oriented. Trail signage along the way will help keep you on track; however, not all junctures are clearly marked, and with 12 miles of trail and multiple loops, it's easy to get confused.

From the trailhead, you'll see a break in the trees just to the south. Heading down the path, immediately enter the woods. Above you, the trees have intertwined their limbs, welcoming you into a tunnel-like entrance.

The hike is fairly straightforward at this point, heading south and then east through the woods with no turnoffs. This quickly changes, however, and soon you'll reach the first of many trail splits. For this hike, you'll want to follow the A Loop. At the first trail split, you'll therefore stay to the left.

Stay left at the next two junctures you reach, always following the A Loop trail sign when there is one. A couple of small clearings are interspersed throughout the trail, and you'll soon leave the woods and enter the first of these, where cacti and wildflowers dot the open ground. As you head back into a grove of hardwood trees, the trail twists and turns a few times. The ground is relatively flat in this section, but as you continue, the terrain changes and you'll encounter a couple of small ups and downs—nothing extensive, just enough to give the trail some interest.

At the next trail split, take the left fork. The trail follows a deep ravine with a river flowing quietly at its bottom. Trees clinging to the walls of the ravine are convenient perches for birds attracted to the area by the river waters. Here the trail continues its gentle winding through a pocket of woods where the trees tower high above, sheltering an understory of shrubs and saplings. The ground, rich with the remains of bark and leaves, becomes soft and cushy, making for a comfortable path.

Another trail soon meets up with the trail you're hiking on; continue to the right at this split. At the next three splits, you'll also want to turn right; follow these turns with a left then another right at the next two junctures. As you hike, the trees

Boulder Park Trail

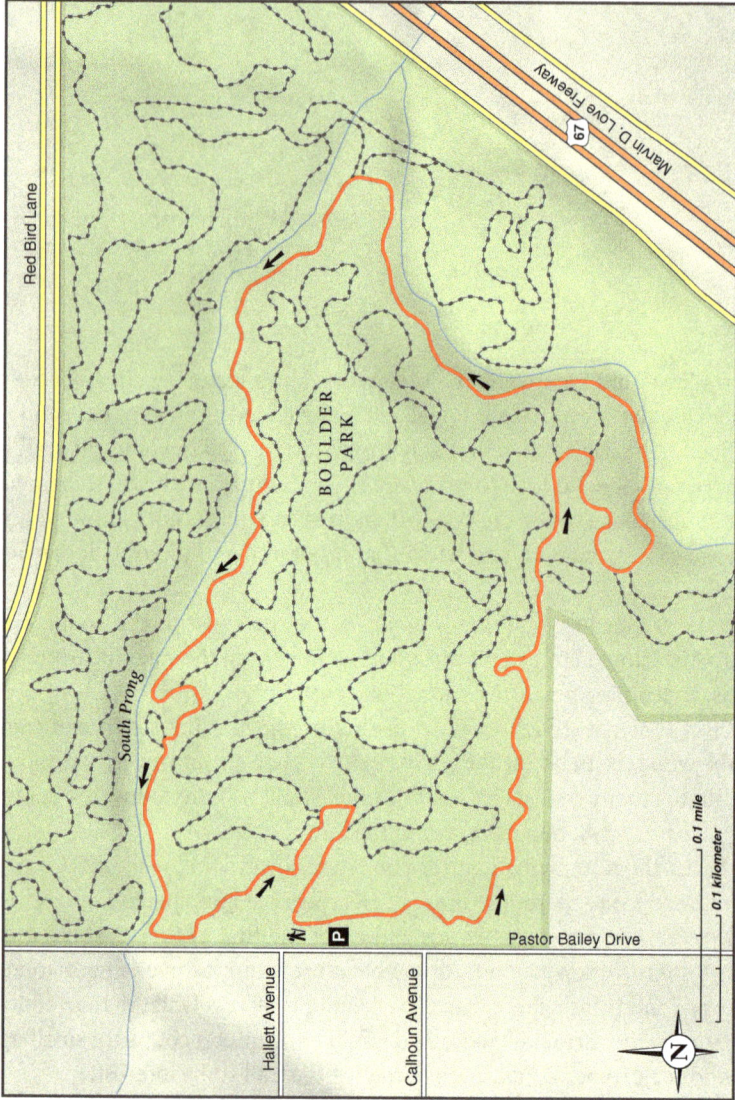

become shorter and thinner, until they finally break and you find yourself once again in a cactus- and tree-dotted grassy clearing. No longer soft and welcoming, the ground has changed with the scenery, hardening into a chalky-white mixture that reflects the sunlight.

Wind back into the woods, and soon the sounds of the roadway will become audible. At the next trail splits, turn left, followed by two more rights. You'll soon see a wide, grassy strip cutting through the park. Turn right, following the grassy path.

Well-maintained trails twist and turn through the wilderness.

A few hundred feet farther, turn left at the last trail split and you'll suddenly find yourself emerging from the woods back at the trailhead.

NEARBY ACTIVITIES

Just down the street on Camp Wisdom Road, you can do some retail shopping in the Southwest Center Mall (aka Red Bird Mall) and the nearby Uptown Village at Cedar Hill. To get to Southwest Center Mall, head south on US 67, then turn right onto Camp Wisdom Road. Cedar Hill is another 7 miles south on US 67.

• •

GPS TRAILHEAD COORDINATES N32° 40.130' W96° 52.450'

DIRECTIONS Boulder Park is adjacent to Dallas's Executive Airport, just north of Duncanville. To get there, take US 67 and exit west onto Red Bird Lane; then turn south onto Pastor Bailey Drive.

Enjoy scenic views of the Trinity River at various stops along the trail.

IN NORTH IRVING, this pleasant trail affords easy access to river views as it follows lazily alongside the Trinity River. A packed-dirt trail and wide, paved path attract hikers, dog walkers, joggers, bikers, and skaters. Keep an eye out for a state-record elm tree on the return leg.

DESCRIPTION

When completed, Irving's Campion Trail is expected to comprise a 22-mile network of trails throughout the city. Currently about 8 miles long, the trail will eventually link to north-central Texas's much more expansive Trinity Trails System—a multicity effort to create 250 miles of accessible greenbelt along the Trinity River corridor.

Throughout the year you can choose from a variety of events along the trail: workshops, organized walks, and guided night hikes highlighting the native nocturnal critters that call the area home. On any given weekend, the trail hums with the activity of outdoors enthusiasts eager to take advantage of this little stretch of green in a city of more than 200,000 residents.

A number of parks along the trail help chronicle the pioneer settlement of the area. Kiosks along the length of the greenbelt link the past with the present. This hike starts at California Crossing Park, where in the mid- to late 1800s settlers crossed the Trinity River on wagon trains.

DISTANCE & CONFIGURATION: 3-mile loop

DIFFICULTY: Easy

SCENERY: Woods, river

EXPOSURE: Partially shady–sunny

TRAFFIC: Moderate

TRAIL SURFACE: Pavement, packed dirt

HIKING TIME: 50 minutes

DRIVING DISTANCE: 2 miles from Loop 12 and TX 114

ACCESS: Daily, 5 a.m.–midnight; free

MAP: irvingtexas.com/listings/campion-trails/491

WHEELCHAIR TRAVERSABLE: Yes

FACILITIES: Portable toilet, benches

CONTACT: 972-721-2501, cityofirving.org

LOCATION: 5198 Riverside Dr., Irving

COMMENTS: Bring insect repellent if hiking during warmer months.

The parking lot at the trailhead is fairly small, but there is usually an available spot, as many folks tend to pick up the trail farther down at the larger Bird's Fork Trail Park. You'll want to start your hike here, however, as this section offers the opportunity to hike a natural path alongside the river before joining with the paved portion of the greenbelt.

Pick up the trail adjacent to the parking lot and follow it north a couple hundred feet until you reach a sign advertising a river view to your right. Turn right onto this path to reach a viewpoint overlooking the sparkling waters of the Elm Fork of the Trinity River. From here, a natural trail starts just where the pavement ends on your left. Pick it up and follow it as it hugs the river and meanders through the shade. Hikers who require wheelchair access can opt to follow the paved portion of the greenbelt, which parallels and ultimately joins the natural trail.

As you hike, a smattering of small signs posted off the trail help you identify the different types of trees—green ash, American elm, and hackberry—that shelter you from the sun. To your right, the river flows quietly, disturbed only by the occasional bird flying through. You are likely to spot the tracks of native wildlife in the dirt below your feet.

Continue along the trail as it parallels the river until you emerge from the trees at 0.4 mile and join the main paved portion of the greenbelt. You'll be unprotected from the sun for a bit as the trail crosses a road at 0.55 mile, then veers back toward the woods and the river.

At 0.73 mile, turn onto the natural-trail entrance and reenter the woods, with the river once again accompanying you on your right. There is no shortage of benches, and at 0.93 mile you'll reach one that's ideally positioned for those who want to absorb a scenic view of the river. At 1.25 miles, cross under an overpass, then over a wooden bridge before you bear right toward more benches and then pick up the trail alongside the river.

At 1.63 miles, reach the end of the natural trail, where you're faced with a choice. If you're not quite ready to return, you can turn right, where the Campion Trail continues for several miles, offering more greenbelt to explore. If you want to go back,

Campion Trail

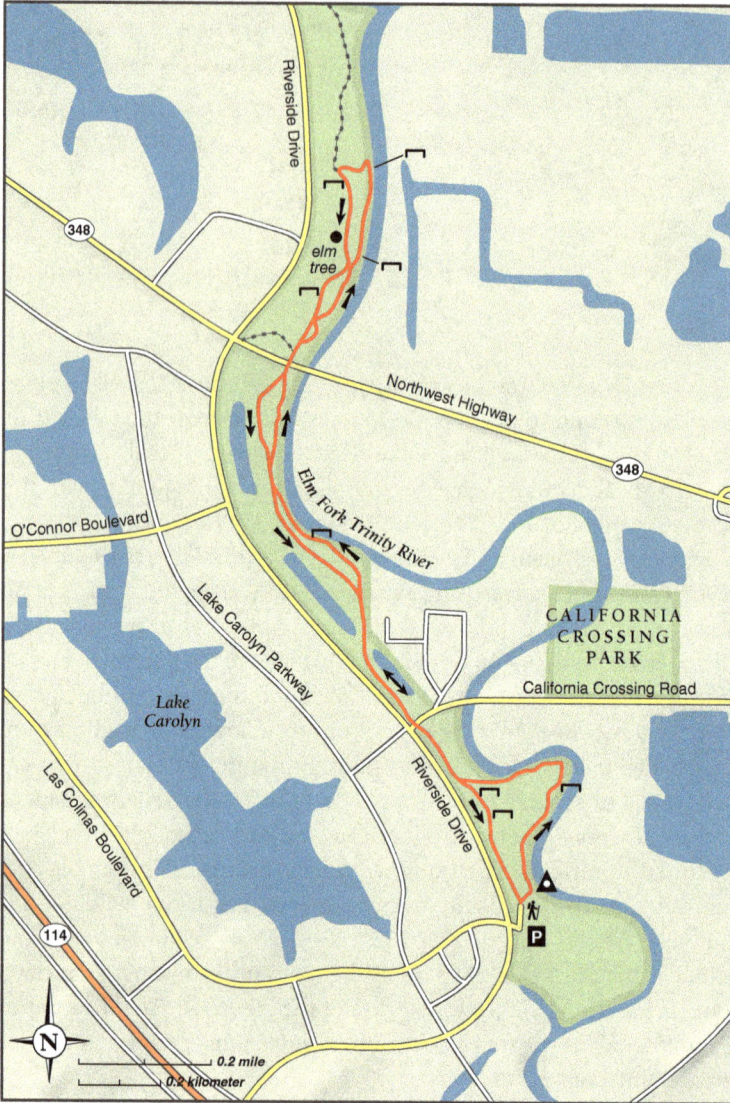

the trail will take you south back down the paved trail. At 1.73 miles, come to a sign-post for a state-record elm tree just off the trail. As you continue back toward the trailhead, a few intersections allow you to rejoin the natural trail by the river, if you desire. If you prefer not to retrace the path you've already taken, simply keep right at the intersections, following the paved portion of the trail, and you'll soon find yourself back at the trailhead.

NEARBY ACTIVITIES

Just down the road, in Las Colinas' Williams Square, is the largest equestrian sculpture in the world: *The Mustangs at Las Colinas,* a collection of huge, lifelike bronze mustangs racing through a fountain in the middle of a plaza. A few restaurants in the area serve lunch. To reach Williams Square, head north on Riverside Drive about 0.8 mile. Turn left onto North O'Connor Boulevard; you'll see the mustangs in about 0.3 mile.

• •

GPS TRAILHEAD COORDINATES N32° 51.733' W96° 55.517'

DIRECTIONS Take TX 114 E toward Irving and exit at Riverside Drive/Rochelle Boulevard. Turn left onto Rochelle Boulevard, which becomes Riverside Drive. The trailhead is about 0.5 mile down on the right.

Don't miss the state-champion cedar elm adjacent to the trail.

View of Dealey Plaza (in the foreground) and the Old Red Courthouse (center)

THIS URBAN HIKE beneath glistening skyscrapers combines the walking routes suggested by the city's visitor center into a loop of some of the best points in the downtown jungle.

DESCRIPTION

Start in front of the Old Red Courthouse. One of the most recognizable buildings downtown, the beautiful red-sandstone building, built in the late 19th century, also houses the Visitor Information Center, where you can pick up brochures and maps of the area. From here, head east on Main Street. At about 150 feet, pass the Kennedy Memorial Plaza, an open, grassy space in the center of which sits a huge square monument designed by architect Philip Johnson and erected in honor of John F. Kennedy. Across the street to the left sits a treasured reminder of Dallas's history: the John Neely Bryan Cabin. The one-room log cabin is a replica of what Dallas's founder, Bryan, would have lived in around the time the city was founded.

Cross Market Street, trek a few blocks, then reach Griffin Street and turn right, following the road 0.25 mile to the Convention Center District. At 0.53 mile, come to Young Street; turn left and head toward the 4-acre grassy hill where the heads of dozens of longhorn cattle are just visible.

Follow the gravel trail toward the steers, which are part of the Pioneer Plaza Cattle Drive, an amazing congregation of 70 bronze longhorn cattle driven by three mounted cowboys. Shawnee Trail, an old route along which cowboys herded cattle in the 1800s, ran near Pioneer Plaza, which commemorates this heritage. Continue

DISTANCE & CONFIGURATION: 3.08-mile loop

DIFFICULTY: Easy

SCENERY: Historic landmarks, cityscape, bronze statues, fountains

EXPOSURE: Sunny

TRAFFIC: Light

TRAIL SURFACE: Paved

HIKING TIME: 2 hours

DRIVING DISTANCE: 0.5 mile from I-35E and Commerce St.

ACCESS: Free

MAP: visitdallas.com/meeting-planners/promote/maps.html

WHEELCHAIR TRAVERSABLE: No

FACILITIES: None

CONTACT: 214-571-1000, visitdallas.com

LOCATION: 100 S. Houston St., Dallas

COMMENTS: You won't need to feed the meters on Sundays.

along the trail, cross the stream, and turn left, heading uphill alongside the cattle. The sculptures are impressive; you can see the veins bulging in their necks and the muscles rippling beneath their skin. Take a moment to examine the intricately detailed cowboys before returning to the path and toward Pioneer Cemetery.

Turn left onto the short dirt path through the cemetery, which honors Dallas's founders. Many of the names, such as Harwood, Stemmons, and Flynn, have been bestowed on Dallas streets. At about 0.7 mile, the dirt path ends; turn left and cross Marilla Street. Join the sidewalk heading diagonally through a 2-acre grassy park that is home to the Dallas Police Memorial. This stainless-steel sculpture casts shadows on the ground, revealing the badge numbers of fallen officers.

At 0.75 mile, turn left onto Akard Street. To the right, you'll see the US, Texas, and Dallas flags flying in front of City Hall. To the left is an excellent view of a famous Dallas landmark, Reunion Tower—a 55-story tower topped with a dome housing a revolving restaurant and an observation deck. Cross Young Street and follow tree-lined Akard Street. Pass the historic old Federal Reserve Bank on the right. Straight ahead, if you look up you'll see a huge statue of Pegasus resting atop another famous Dallas building, the Magnolia Hotel. The building—and its logo, the winged horse—originally belonged to the Magnolia Petroleum Company and is now listed on the National Register of Historic Places. Across the street, you'll see the Adolphus Hotel, another ornate and historic building dating from 1912.

At about 0.9 mile, Akard ends. Cross the street and head through the brick plaza toward and past the Magnolia. Just beyond some patio tables where folks are enjoying the outdoors, cross Commerce Street and rejoin Akard Street on its northern section. Now turn right onto Main Street, passing Pegasus Plaza on the right, Neiman Marcus at 1.1 miles, and then a skyscraper—the Mercantile Bank building—at 1.18 miles.

Turn left onto St. Paul Street and pass the building that once housed the Titche-Goettinger department store. When you reach Elm, look to the right to see the vertical sign of the historic Majestic Theatre, here since the 1920s. Continue one block and head west (left) down Pacific Avenue; at 1.43 miles, make a right onto Ervay Street.

Downtown Dallas Urban Trail

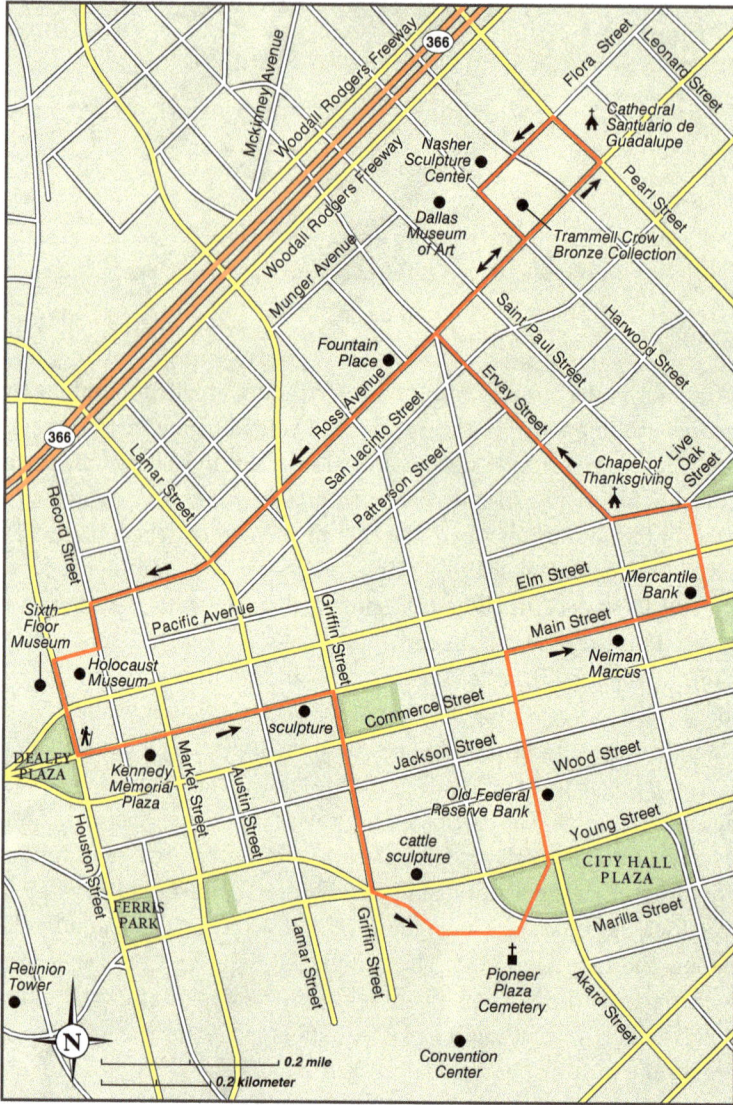

Thanks-Giving Square, which celebrates the world's thanksgivings, is on the left and is a nice spot for a break. Enjoy the courtyard, the outdoor fountains, and the prominent white spiral tower, called the Chapel of Thanksgiving. Inside the chapel you can view a beautiful stained-glass design called the "Glory Window."

Continue over the trolley tracks and past the post office until you reach Ross Avenue, at 1.7 miles. Turn right. On the left is the Dallas Museum of Art, fronted by a huge orange-red steel sculpture. Finally, reach the Cathedral Santuario de

Guadalupe, a cathedral dating to the 19th century, featuring stained glass windows and a bell tower housing 49 bells. Turn left just in front of the cathedral onto North Pearl Street, and at 2 miles make another left onto Flora Street.

Continuing, you'll see the Nasher Sculpture Center on your right and the Crow Collection of Asian Art on your left, with its magnificent sculptural waterfall entrance. The road dead-ends in front of the Dallas Museum of Art; turn left onto Harwood Street. At the next intersection, turn right to get back onto Ross Avenue.

At 2.4 miles, pass Fountain Place on the right. At the base of this prism-shaped skyscraper is a waterfall with ledges and pools. This is a nice place to explore, with a few acres of fountains and waterfalls. Cross Lamar Street and then see redbrick buildings, indicating you've reached the West End Historic District, an attractive area of old warehouses that have been converted into stores and restaurants. At 2.83 miles, turn left onto Record Street. Walk to Pacific Avenue, where you'll see the Dallas Holocaust Museum across the street. Turn right, following the trolley tracks.

A block down, turn left onto Houston Street. On the right is the former Texas School Book Depository, where on November 22, 1963, Lee Harvey Oswald shot and killed President John F. Kennedy from its sixth floor. Today, the building houses the Sixth Floor Museum, which harbors exhibits on JFK's life and death. A few steps farther, and you're at the entrance to Stemmons Freeway and in the middle of Dealey Plaza, a National Historic Landmark. Here lies the infamous grassy knoll—the controversial hill where some theorize another shooter in the Kennedy assassination was hidden. Crowds always gather in this spot, reading brochures and pamphlets about the incident. An *X* in the street marks where the motorcade was at the time of the shooting.

Cross the street and find a reflecting pool and a statue honoring George Bannerman Dealey, the Dallas businessman and civic planner after whom the plaza is named. From here, turn left back onto Main Street to reach the trailhead.

NEARBY ACTIVITIES

A few blocks east of downtown, visit Deep Ellum, Dallas's arts and entertainment district, where retail shops sell unusual items and an array of restaurants beckons you to grab a bite to eat. In the evenings, the area is a popular nightlife hub. To get to Deep Ellum, head east down Elm Street—it's just past the Central Expressway.

• •

GPS TRAILHEAD COORDINATES N32° 46.750' W96° 48.450'

DIRECTIONS Follow I-30 E toward Dallas and take Exit 44 (Industrial Boulevard). Turn left onto Industrial Boulevard and right onto Commerce Street, then continue straight onto Main Street. The Old Red Courthouse is on the right, just in front of Dealey Plaza. Park at any metered spot along the street.

Swan boats offer visitors a chance to spend some time on the lagoon.

THIS TRAIL LOOPS through the fairgrounds, passing historic Art Deco buildings, the Cotton Bowl football stadium, the Texas Vietnam Memorial, various statues and museums, and a small lagoon.

DESCRIPTION

Listed as a National Historic Landmark, the Fair Park Buildings in Dallas are a group of Art Deco structures built in the 1930s for the Texas Centennial Exposition. According to the National Historic Landmark Registry, they form one of the largest such collections in the country. Today the area is the site of the State Fair of Texas. Its mascot—Big Tex, a statue more than 50 feet tall depicting a Texan complete with a cowboy hat and a Lone Star shirt—sits at the entrance while the fair is in attendance, greeting millions of visitors each year during its annual three-week run. When the fair is not on the grounds, Big Tex is taken down and the visitors dwindle. The buildings, gigantic Ferris wheel, and permanent exhibits and displays, however, remain; entrance to the area is free, and visitors are welcome to roam around. A lagoon with swan boats and fountain, the Texas Vietnam Memorial, and an esplanade decorated with huge sculptures—not to mention the Cotton Bowl and various museums— make for an enjoyable hike.

DISTANCE & CONFIGURATION: 2.95-mile loop

DIFFICULTY: Easy

SCENERY: Lagoon, Art Deco buildings, fairgrounds

EXPOSURE: Sunny

TRAFFIC: Moderate

TRAIL SURFACE: Paved

HIKING TIME: 1 hour

DRIVING DISTANCE: 1.3 miles from I-30 and US 75

ACCESS: Daily when fair is not in town; free

MAP: fairpark.org/images/pdfs/fair-park-map.pdf

WHEELCHAIR TRAVERSABLE: Yes

FACILITIES: Restrooms, water fountains

CONTACT: 214-426-3400, fairpark.org

LOCATION: 1121 First Ave., Dallas

COMMENTS: There is an admission charge for the grounds when the State Fair of Texas is in town; in the off-season, there is no charge. Museums are open year-round (with admission), so plan for a whole day if you intend to visit some after the hike.

From the parking lot, head to the pedestrian gate at the Grand Avenue entrance. Start the hike by heading northeast on Grand and down a wide promenade, keeping the Dallas Museum of Natural History to your right. At 0.1 mile, reach a kiosk with a map of the grounds. Continue straight, then turn left onto First Avenue at the roundabout, keeping the Old Mill Inn on your right. Established in 1936, the building was originally a flour-mill exhibit, built to resemble an 1836 mill. Today the structure, complete with waterwheel, houses a restaurant.

Continue along the redbrick path, with the Dallas skyline rising in the distance. At 0.42 mile, reach a metal sculpture called *The Gulf Cloud,* erected in 1916 in memory of the first secretary of the State Fair of Texas, Captain Sydney Smith. The sculpture depicts a woman and her daughters, each representing an aspect of Texas's geography: the prairies, the mountains, and the Gulf Coast. Beyond the sculpture is a short field of grass and, beyond that, the Texas Vietnam Memorial. To get there, turn right, heading down the half-circular driveway, and turn left onto the memorial's walkway. The walls list the names of more than 3,000 casualties of the war.

Continue by turning right to follow the walkway out. Ahead is the Women's Museum. Walk a few hundred feet, then turn right at the statue and head down the walkway. To your left is the Continental DAR (Daughters of the American Revolution) House, a small, white Colonial-style house with green trim. During the fair, the house is open to the public, displaying exhibits on American history.

Continue straight, and at 0.75 mile reach the esplanade, a long corridor lined with buildings and six huge sculptures surrounding a reflecting pool. At the far end of the esplanade rises the Hall of State. As you walk through the esplanade, you'll see some magnificent murals by the artist Pierre Bourdelle on the buildings. During the winter holidays, the esplanade is lined with lights and Christmas trees.

At 1 mile, reach the Hall of State, a magnificent Art Deco building in front of which stands a gold archer. Along the frieze, the names of dozens of important Texas figures—among them Travis, Hogg, Ellis, Lamar, and Milam—adorn the building. A column of statues at the front steps—representing Spain, France,

Fair Park Loop

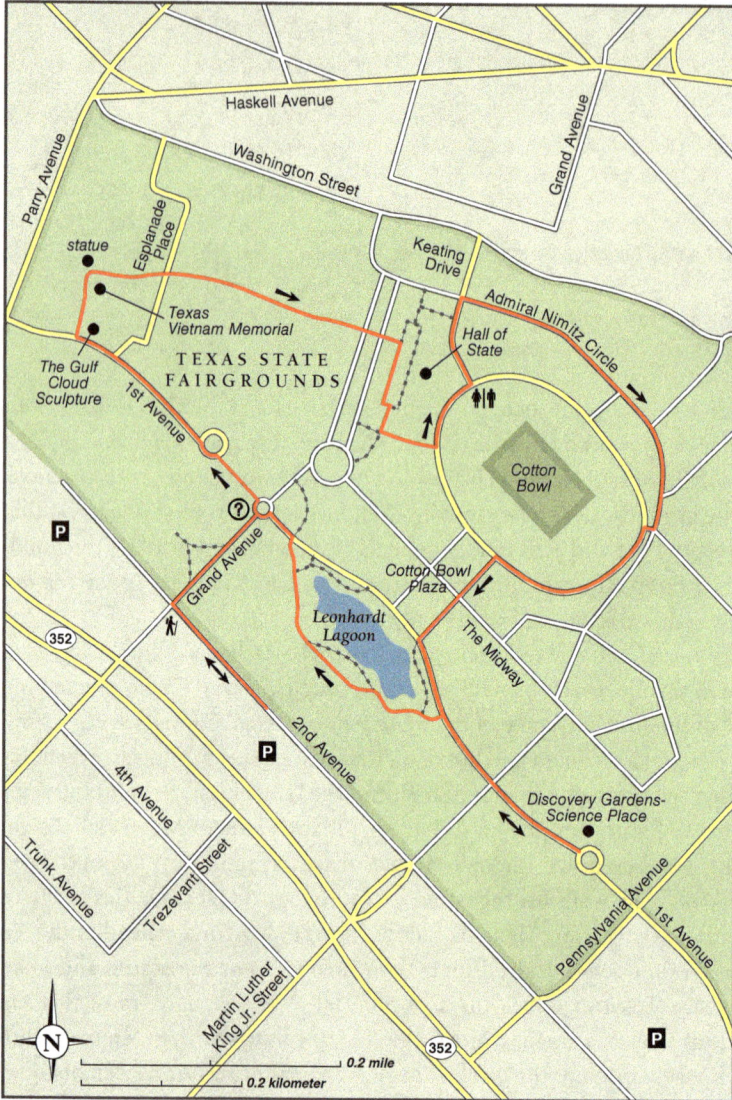

Haskell Avenue

Washington Street

Parry Avenue

Grand Avenue

Esplanade Place

Keating Drive

Admiral Nimitz Circle

statue

Texas Vietnam Memorial

Hall of State

The Gulf Cloud Sculpture

TEXAS STATE FAIRGROUNDS

1st Avenue

Cotton Bowl

Grand Avenue

Cotton Bowl Plaza

Leonhardt Lagoon

The Midway

352

2nd Avenue

Discovery Gardens-Science Place

4th Avenue

Trunk Avenue

Trezevant Street

Pennsylvania Avenue

1st Avenue

Martin Luther King, Jr. Street

352

N

0.2 mile

0.2 kilometer

Mexico, the Republic of Texas, the Confederate States, and the United States—compose the Six Flags of Texas.

From the state hall, turn right, heading south. At the end of the building, head left onto the walkway, keeping the Tower Building on your right. Ahead, seemingly out of place, looms the historic Cotton Bowl, a huge football stadium dating back to 1932. The stadium has a long and rich history, having hosted not only popular football teams such as the Dallas Cowboys and the SMU Mustangs but also having been the site of events such as the 1994 Fifa World Cup and concerts by performers such as Elvis Presley and Aerosmith. At 1.4 miles, turn left onto the drive encircling the Cotton Bowl. After a couple hundred feet, take a left onto Keating Drive and then the first right onto Admiral Nimitz Circle.

Follow Nimitz past some exhibition halls and the Creative Arts Show Place Theatre to head toward the Children's Petting Zoo, which is open during the fair. On your right, you'll see the back side of the Cotton Bowl. Continue walking down the road toward the Ferris wheel. You'll soon see a MIDWAY sign atop a closed-off entrance to a section holding the fair's amusement rides and games. The road curves to the right and comes out onto a plaza in front of the Cotton Bowl.

Head southwest through the plaza, away from the Cotton Bowl and toward the Leonhardt Lagoon. Take a left at the benches in front of the water. Along the water's edge, you'll see oddly shaped red walkways, which actually make up a sculpture designed to resemble a fern. Kids can often be seen leaning from its edges looking into the waters for the many turtles that inhabit the lagoon. Among the fish are yellow bluehead and longear sunfish; the plants include lizard tail, water hyacinth, and cattails. Swan boats regularly circle the lagoon, completing the tranquil scene.

Continue following the walkway southeast alongside and past the lagoon. As you walk, you'll get closer to the gigantic Texas Star Ferris Wheel to the left, allowing you to appreciate its beauty and size. The pathway continues past the Science Place and the Discovery Gardens before ending at a parking lot. From here, turn back, retracing your steps to the lagoon, this time turning left to follow the walkway along the opposite side of the lagoon, past the IMAX, and back toward the trailhead.

NEARBY ACTIVITIES

You could spend the entire day here after the hike enjoying the sights, including the Dallas Aquarium at Fair Park, the Women's Museum, the African American Museum, and the Texas Discovery Gardens. If you intend to visit multiple museums, ask about purchasing a ticket that allows entrance to all of them. For a bite to eat, stop by the Old Mill Inn, open year-round, 11 a.m.–2:30 p.m.

• •

GPS TRAILHEAD COORDINATES N32° 46.700' W96° 45.850'

DIRECTIONS Take I-30 E to Exit 47 (Second Avenue/Fair Park). Continue straight to reach Fair Park. Park at the Grand Avenue entrance in front of the Perot Museum.

Tranquil views from the trail transport you miles from the hustle and bustle of Dallas–Fort Worth.

PROVIDING ACCESS TO the Great Trinity Forest, this trail offers a pleasant hike through one of the largest urban hardwood forests in the country.

DESCRIPTION

Most local residents are probably not aware that Dallas has what is considered to be the largest urban bottomland hardwood forest in the country. Known as the Great Trinity Forest, the 6,000-acre parcel of land is located along a section of the Trinity River in South Dallas.

Dallas County is working hard to make the Great Trinity Forest a destination for outdoors enthusiasts and explorers, and in recent years has worked hard to construct, expand, and maintain a trail system providing access to this hidden gem. The trails, known as the Trinity Forest Trails, include more than 8 miles of paved-surface paths targeted toward bikers, joggers, walkers, and hikers. There are various access points to the Trinity River Trails and Great Trinity Forest, including Eco Park, the Trinity River Audubon Center, and Joppa Preserve.

Though the 307-acre Joppa Preserve has been there for decades, you've probably never heard of it. Located in South Dallas, it has been around since 1986, though originally it was known as Lemmon Lake, named after the small drought-prone lake within its boundaries. In the 1990s, the preserve was renamed Joppa (pronounced

DISTANCE & CONFIGURATION:
7-mile out-and-back

DIFFICULTY: Easy

SCENERY: Forest

EXPOSURE: Shady–sunny

TRAFFIC: Light

TRAIL SURFACE: Paved

HIKING TIME: 3.5 hours

DRIVING DISTANCE: 3.5 miles from the intersection of I-20 and I-45

ACCESS: Daily; free

MAP: trinityrivercorridor.com/recreation/trinity-trails-phase-1-and-2

WHEELCHAIR TRAVERSABLE: Yes

FACILITIES: Water fountain, picnic tables

CONTACT: trinityrivercorridor.com

LOCATION: 4911 River Oaks Rd., Dallas

COMMENTS: To shorten this hike, turn around just after you exit the preserve, making the outing a pleasant 3-mile round-trip trek.

Joppee) in honor of a freedman's community that existed nearby. The community was established in the 1860s–'70s by former slaves emancipated during the Civil War, some of whom came from the nearby Miller Plantation. Interestingly, plantation owner William Brown Miller's log cabin, which was at one point located in this area, has been moved and is now preserved in Dallas Heritage Village next to the historic Millermore Mansion. Today, the Joppa community still exists and, according to Preservation Dallas, is considered one of the last remaining freedman communities.

From the trailhead, you'll start your hike by heading east down the paved path toward an opening in the forest. Lemmon Lake lies hidden behind the trees and brush just to the east. Though the trail has no overlooks onto the main body of the lake, as you hike, glimpses of water will occasionally pop into view. During hot summers, it's not unusual to find the lake all but dried out, as it is fairly small. Beyond the lake, farther east, the Trinity River winds along, hidden in the forest just out of sight.

The wide paved path that started the hike continues the entire length of the trail and leaves plenty of room for outdoor enthusiasts of all kinds; however, because the preserve is still relatively unknown, you're unlikely to pass too many people aside from the occasional biker.

As you head down the trail, the Great Trinity Forest will quickly close in around you. Tall trees loom on either side of the path, forming a peaceful green canopy and casting much of the trail in shade. As you hike it's easy to understand why there is so much interest by activists in preserving and providing access to this old-growth woodland. Accessible yet remote. Peaceful yet wild. The forest feels undiscovered and untouched, though you know that civilization is just a stone's throw away.

Wildlife is abundant deeper in the forest and includes deer, raccoons, and coyotes. On the trail, however, you aren't likely to see these larger animals, but don't be surprised if you spot smaller creatures like frogs, turtles, and snakes. An amazing variety of birds is also readily visible, making the preserve a popular spot with birders. The Trinity River Audubon Center lies just to the east and offers activities such as early morning birding hikes and nighttime owl-prowl hikes

Joppa Preserve Trail

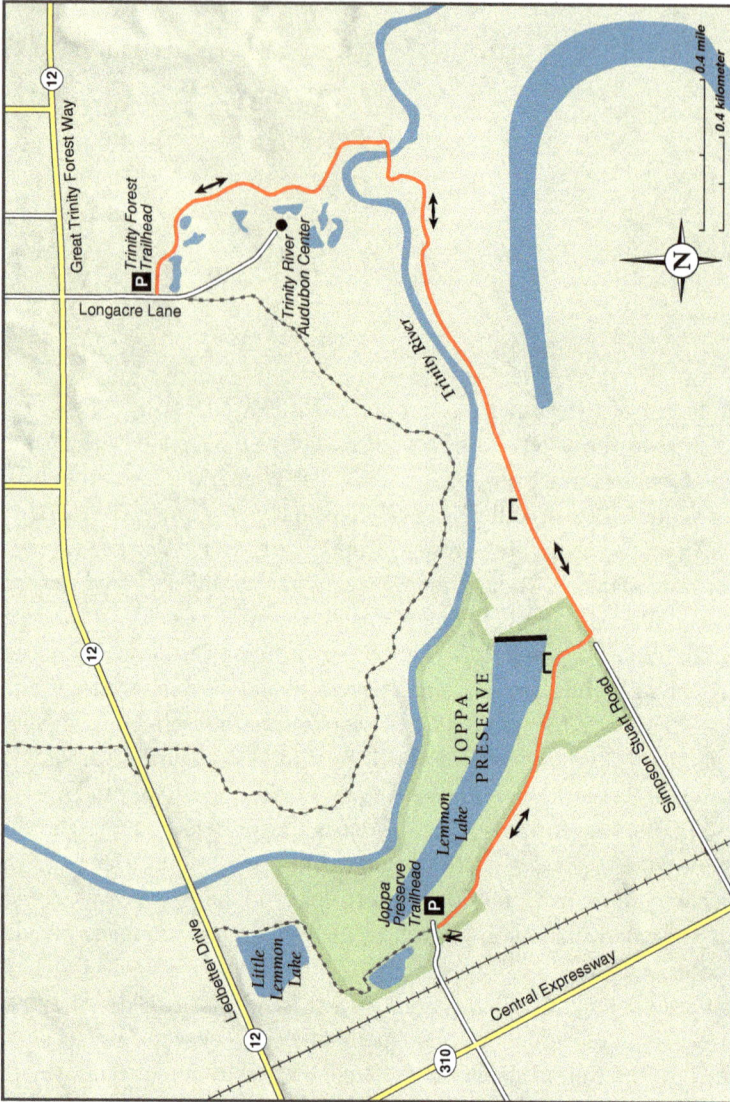

through the forest. The Audubon Center has its own hiking trails, which are featured on page 58.

The entire length of the trail is straight and flat, with benches interspersed throughout. It will continue heading southeast through thick forest before emerging from the trees at 0.9 mile. At this point, the trail splits. To the right, the trail ends at the Eco Park Trailhead on Simpson Stuart Road. To the left, the trail continues heading east. Turn left.

At this point, the scenery surrounding the trail changes dramatically as you head out of Joppa Preserve and skirt the edge of the forest. The trail, which before had been mainly shady, now becomes almost entirely exposed. To the right, glimpses of old pastures can be seen peeking from behind closed gates. Beyond, in the distance, you'll see tractors and machinery, evidence of the nearby McCommas Bluff Landfill. This pesky reminder of civilization will soon disappear as the trail continues to make its way east. Just past a stone bench at 1.5 miles at a creek crossing, you can turn around, making the entire hike a pleasant 3-mile outing. Or you can continue following the trail. If you do, the trail will cross the Trinity River before curving north, where it passes right by the Trinity River Audubon Center. From here, the trail winds back to the west, where it meets up with another trailhead just behind the Trinity River Audubon Center. At this point, you can follow the driveway up to the Audubon Center to explore the center's offerings or retrace your steps back to the Joppa Preserve Trailhead.

NEARBY ACTIVITIES

Just 6 miles away, Dallas Heritage Village (1515 South Harwood in Dallas, dallas heritagevillage.org) is a living village of historic buildings from the late 1800s. It showcases 21 structures, including a saloon, a general store, a church, a school, a hotel, and even the Old Miller Cabin, which was originally located near the Joppa Preserve. The Millermore House, a plantation house the Miller family subsequently moved into, is also on display. Admission is $9 for adults and $5 for children. To get there, take I-45 N to the I-30 W exit. Keep right on the service road, following the signs for Ervay Street. From here, turn left on St. Paul Street, left onto Ervay Street, then left again onto Gano Street. At the end of Gano Street, turn right onto St. Paul Street. The Heritage Village parking lot will be on your left.

• •

GPS TRAILHEAD COORDINATES N32° 41.844' W96° 44.236'

DIRECTIONS Take I-45 S and exit Loop 12 E. Turn right, heading south onto TX 310/ South Central Expressway. After 0.7 mile turn left onto River Oaks Drive.

6 KATY TRAIL

Don't anticipate being alone on the Katy Trail—it's always bustling with activity.

POPULAR WITH A YOUNG, URBAN CROWD, this linear trail creates a pedestrian-friendly corridor between downtown Dallas and the Mockingbird DART station and has become a place to see and be seen.

DESCRIPTION

No trail is more well known in Dallas than the Katy Trail. Without question, it is one of the most popular trails in the metroplex. Crowds of people overtake it on weekends and holidays, offering the adventurous visitor an always lively experience. And if you think you can avoid the crowds by visiting during the scorching summer months, well, think again. This trail is always hopping, thanks in part to its easy accessibility in highly populated areas of the city. In fact, according to the Friends of the Katy Trail, a nonprofit organization dedicated to the trail's expansion and development, more than 300,000 people live within 1 mile of the trail.

To accommodate the many folks who live in the area, the trail has a number of access points. In addition, it passes several city parks and intersects a couple of major streets, affording further access. Because of its popularity, you'll encounter a wide assortment of outdoor types, including walkers, joggers, bikers, dog walkers, skateboarders, and in-line skaters. The trail is about 3.5 miles in total length, stretching from the American Airlines Center to Mockingbird Station near the Southern Methodist University campus.

DISTANCE & CONFIGURATION: 5.64-mile out-and-back

DIFFICULTY: Easy

SCENERY: Trees, city views

EXPOSURE: Mostly sunny, some shade

TRAFFIC: Heavy

TRAIL SURFACE: Concrete

HIKING TIME: 1.75 hours

DRIVING DISTANCE: 1.4 miles from Woodall Rodgers Freeway and I-35E

ACCESS: Daily, 5 a.m.–midnight; free

MAP: katytraildallas.org/map

WHEELCHAIR TRAVERSABLE: Yes

FACILITIES: None

CONTACT: 214-303-1180, katytraildallas.org

LOCATION: 2500 Victory Ave., Dallas

COMMENTS: If you can't find a spot near the trailhead, try parking at one of the parks adjacent to the trail.

In recent years, a massive publicity campaign to promote safety along the trail has been implemented with the help of names such as former Dallas Cowboys quarterback Troy Aikman (a high-profile user of the trail). In particular, the campaign focuses on trail etiquette and safety awareness so that visitors know how to share the trail when there is both biker and pedestrian traffic.

The trail's history dates back to the late 1800s, when the Missouri–Kansas–Texas (MKT) Railroad began operating a passenger and freight line into Texas, connecting it with states to the north. The MKT, nicknamed the "Katy," eventually connected St. Louis with Dallas and Fort Worth and extended as far south as Galveston. In the late 1980s, to avoid financial losses, the MKT merged with the Missouri Pacific Railroad Company, part of the Union Pacific Railway. Dallas's Katy Trail owes its existence in part to Union Pacific, which donated the abandoned tracks to the city. In Missouri, another old abandoned section of the Katy Trail has been similarly donated and forms a 225-mile trail known as Katy Trail State Park.

The trailhead for this hike is in Victory Park behind the American Airlines Center, across the street from the facility's parking lot. A plaque identifying this entrance point as Victory Promenade marks the trailhead. If you prefer not to drive into downtown Dallas and the West End, other entrance points for the trail include Reverchon Park and the David's Way plaza.

From the Victory Park trailhead, the path ascends a small incline to reach the elevated trailbed, from the top of which you have a decent, though slightly obstructed, view of the Dallas skyline if you turn around. Because of its old railway status, the trail from here to the end is relatively level, with only a few gentle turns. The scenery is mostly a thick curtain of trees obscuring the highways, streets, and autos only a short distance below. If you're interested in orienting yourself, the trail runs roughly between Oaklawn Avenue and Stemmons Freeway to the left, and the busy Central Expressway to the right. Surprisingly, the sounds of urban life do not overwhelm, and at many points you'll even be unaware that you're hiking through the busiest part of Dallas.

The trail is about 12 feet wide and divided into two lanes—one for bikers, the other for pedestrians. You'll find the division of lanes a welcome feature, as the trail is

Katy Trail

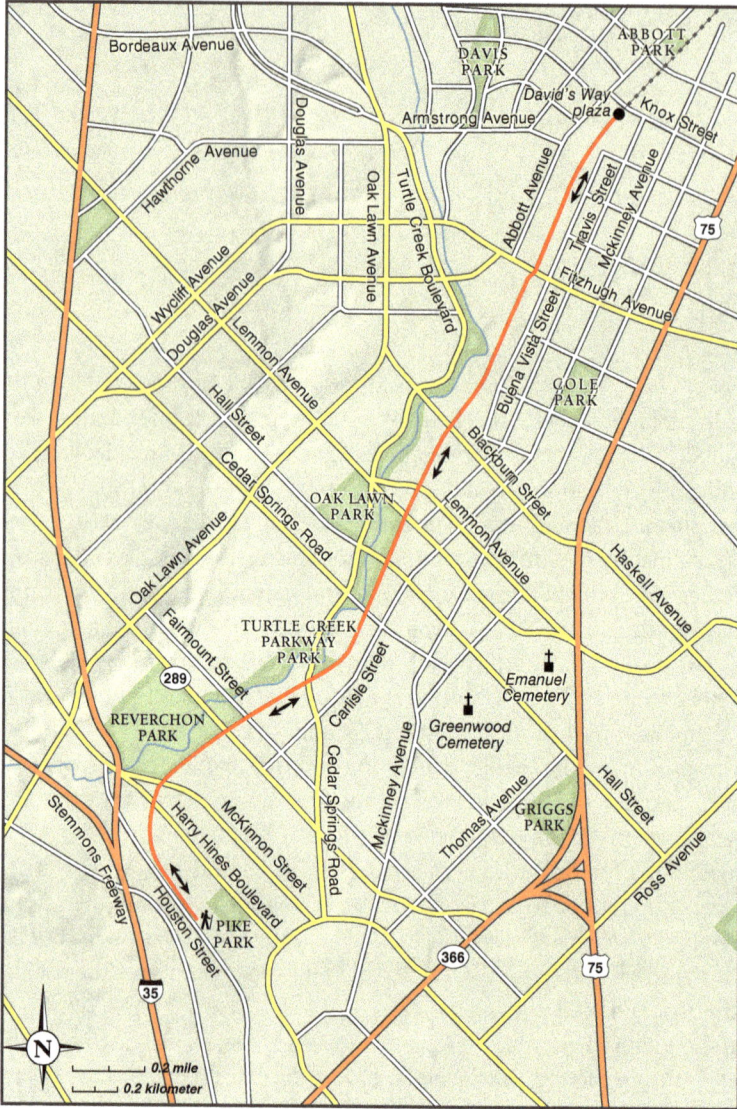

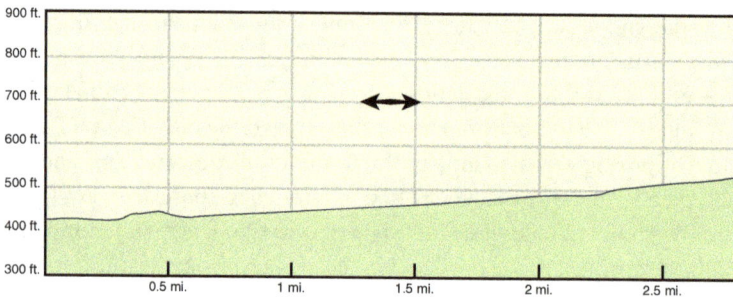

always heavily trafficked. The path is very nicely maintained; you'd be hard-pressed to find any litter, or even a spot where the grass comes close to encroaching on the path. The trail developers have also done an excellent job marking the trail: when you cross a highway or pass a park, you'll see signs telling you exactly where you are.

You won't find much wildlife along the path, though you may spot a few squirrels scurrying in front of you or a stray cat walking along the path's edge. The backyards of condos and homes abut the trail at various spots along the way, serving as a reminder of the trail's urban location.

At 0.6 mile, just after you pass over Harry Hines Boulevard and McKinnon Street, look left for Reverchon Park (conceived as Dallas's version of Central Park), named for James Reverchon, a late-19th-century botanist who lived nearby.

From here, the trail passes over Maple and Cedar Springs Roads. At about 1.6 miles, just after you cross Lemmon Avenue, pass Turtle Creek Park on the left. As you continue northeast, you'll reach the Highland Park area. The intersection of David's Way and Travis Street, at 2.8 miles, is a good turnaround spot. If you need to cool off or grab a drink before the hike back, a couple of restaurants and a convenience store are just within reach. To extend the hike, you can continue straight another mile, where the trail ends at some bike lockers not far from SMU and Mockingbird Station.

NEARBY ACTIVITIES

The West End is a pedestrian-friendly district with several restaurants. Once the hub of Dallas's commercial activities, the renovated warehouses now make up one of the city's main entertainment areas. Listed on the National Register of Historic Places, the West End is also the home of Dealey Plaza, where John F. Kennedy was shot.

• •

GPS TRAILHEAD COORDINATES N32° 47.550' W96° 48.650'

DIRECTIONS The trail is behind the American Airlines Center, at Victory Park. When there are no events at the center, you can park in its north parking lot; at other times, you can park in a metered space in nearby West End. If you're traveling south from I-35E toward downtown, you can get directly to the center by taking the Oaklawn/Victory Avenue/Hi Line Drive exit. Stay on the service road, then turn left onto Victory Avenue.

To get to the parking in West End from I-35E S, take the Continental Avenue exit and turn left onto Continental, which turns into Lamar. At the intersection of Lamar and McKinney Avenue, West End is on the right. Continue one block to Munger Avenue and turn right. Park in any lot or metered space, and walk north down North Houston Street (which parallels Lamar) toward the American Airlines Center. The trailhead is across the street from the parking lot of the American Airlines Center on North Houston.

A small pond beckons curious adventurers.

THIS FLAT TRAIL through the woods offers glimpses of the Elm Fork of the Trinity River and is a cool, shady hike for a hot summer's day.

DESCRIPTION

Tucked away in a corner of North Irving, this fun little trail offers locals easy access to a little bit of wilderness close to home. To me, this trail is a perfect example of how city dwellers craving the outdoors can turn an otherwise unremarkable location into a happening weekend spot. If it's nice out, you're likely to find the trailhead hopping with all kinds of activities: kayakers prepping their gear for an outing along the nearby river, anglers meandering down to the water with poles and tackle box in hand, joggers stretching in preparation for a run, or bikers readying their bikes for a spin along the trail.

Maintained by DORBA, the Dallas Off-Road Bicycle Association, the several miles of trails here are open to both bikers and hikers. An impressive amount of energy has been put into the trail's maintenance, and though in years past the vicinity had a reputation for attracting vagrants and partiers, the care and maintenance of volunteers have completely turned the area around. You'll find the trail clean, well maintained, and well used.

DISTANCE & CONFIGURATION: 1.61-mile loop

DIFFICULTY: Easy

SCENERY: Cedar, elm, and oak woodlands; river views

EXPOSURE: Shady

TRAFFIC: Heavy on weekends

TRAIL SURFACE: Packed dirt

HIKING TIME: 40 minutes

DRIVING DISTANCE: 2.7 miles from TX 114 and Loop 12

ACCESS: Daily; free

MAP: dorba.org/trail.php?t=17

WHEELCHAIR TRAVERSABLE: No

FACILITIES: None

CONTACT: dorba.org

LOCATION: 1366 California Crossing Road, Dallas

COMMENTS: Rains cause the trail to become muddy and impassable. If it rained the day before you plan to hike, choose a different trail.

As you approach from the parking lot, to your left you'll see a pond whose still waters attract birds, such as herons and egrets, searching for a meal. When the water is low, a sandbar attracts local kids looking to hone their fishing skills. Straight ahead, you'll see a tree-lined, wide, grassy lane down which trickles a steady stream of folks exiting the trail from both sides of the wood.

To the right, you'll see the trailhead. A small kiosk in front of it bears a trail map. The trail is intended to be one long loop, encouraging traffic to flow in one direction. The first part, however—which is ideal for hikers because of its smooth, level terrain—comes back out onto the grassy median before continuing. This allows for a pleasant walk while avoiding the more technical sections of the latter half of the trail. If you were to venture on, the trail crosses the central grass strip into the southeast section. The dips in these sections appeal to mountain bikers.

Begin the hike by entering the trail as it heads right and disappears into the woods. Keep right to follow the main trail. The trail immediately starts to twist and turn gently as it haphazardly makes its way through the trees. Off to the right, catch glimpses of California Crossing Road. At first you'll hear the background hum of the occasional car, but that quickly gives way to the chirping of birds and the rustling of trees. The trees are closely packed all along the trail, bathing most of the path in shade. At some points the branches converge tightly just overhead, enveloping the walkway in lovely tunnels of foliage. In other parts, the trees are a little more spaced apart, allowing wild grass to grow tall and thick at their bases.

The trail itself is narrow, allowing for only single-file walking. It approaches trees only to curve away at the last minute, keeping the hike interesting as your attention is naturally drawn outward to the cedar, elm, oak, and other trees and plants you pass. Stay right, following the outer trail as it makes a rough loop along the banks of Elm Fork of the Trinity River. At a couple of spots, you can glimpse the river through the trees to the right. Birds are often seen flying over the water before disappearing into the trees on the far side of the river.

The day of our hike, DORBA volunteers were on the trail cutting back limbs, clipping bushes, and cleaning debris. Judging from the excellent condition of parts

L. B. Houston Nature Trail

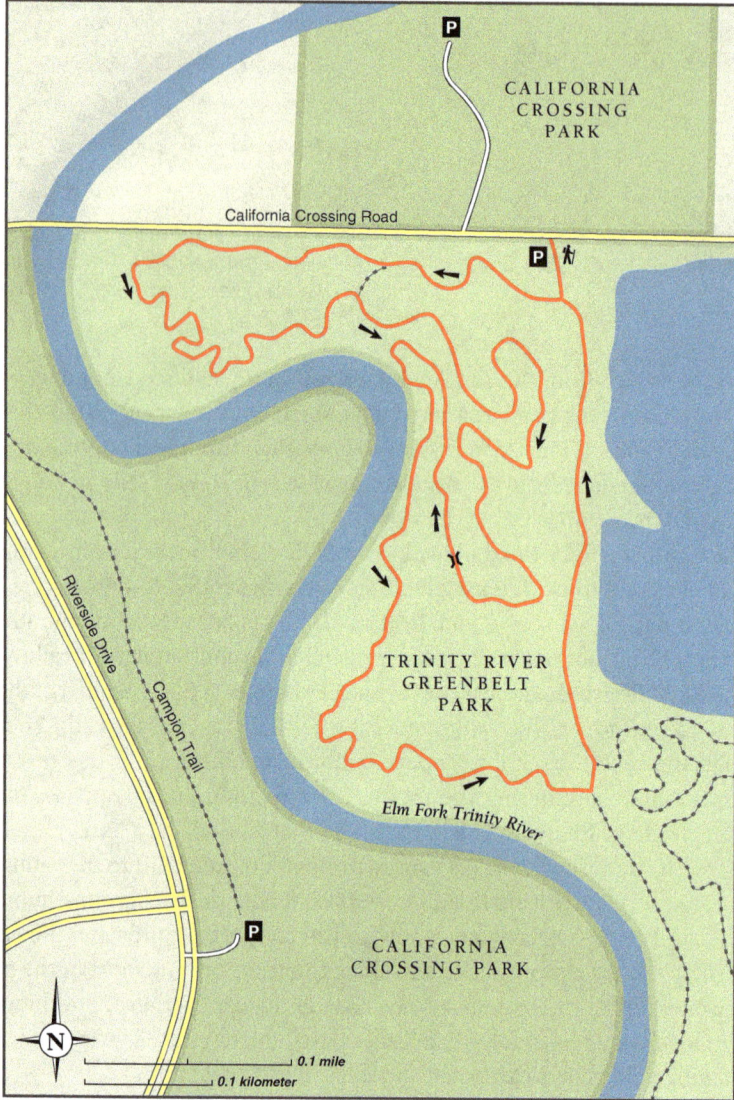

of the trail they had not yet reached, this is not a one-time undertaking, but rather a continuous effort.

At about 0.95 mile, reach a nice vantage point for viewing the wide expanse of river, whose waters are a muddy greenish-gray. In the spring and summer, colorful butterflies flutter through the foliage at the river's edge.

The trail crosses a short wooden footbridge, heads slightly uphill, and, at 1.3 miles, leaves the woods, whereupon you'll find yourself again on the wide, grassy lane just south of the trailhead. Turn left and follow the trail 0.25 mile back to the trailhead. Pass the pond on the right before arriving back at the parking lot.

NEARBY ACTIVITIES

In nearby Williams Square in Las Colinas, a section of North Irving, is the largest equestrian sculpture in the world: *The Mustangs at Las Colinas,* a collection of huge, lifelike bronze mustangs racing through a fountain in the middle of a plaza. A few restaurants in the area serve lunch. To get to Williams Square, head west on California Crossing and turn right onto Riverside Drive. Turn left onto North O'Connor Boulevard; you'll see the horses about 0.5 mile ahead on the right.

• •

GPS TRAILHEAD COORDINATES N32° 51.983' W96° 55.367'

DIRECTIONS From TX 183, take the TX 114 exit toward Grapevine and then the Tom Braniff Drive/Loop 12 exit. Turn north onto Tom Braniff Drive, which becomes Wildwood Drive. The trailhead is about 1 mile ahead on the right, at the intersection of Wildwood Drive and California Crossing Road, across the street from the National Guard Armory.

The narrow dirt path winds through dense foliage.

8 OAK CLIFF NATURE PRESERVE TRAIL

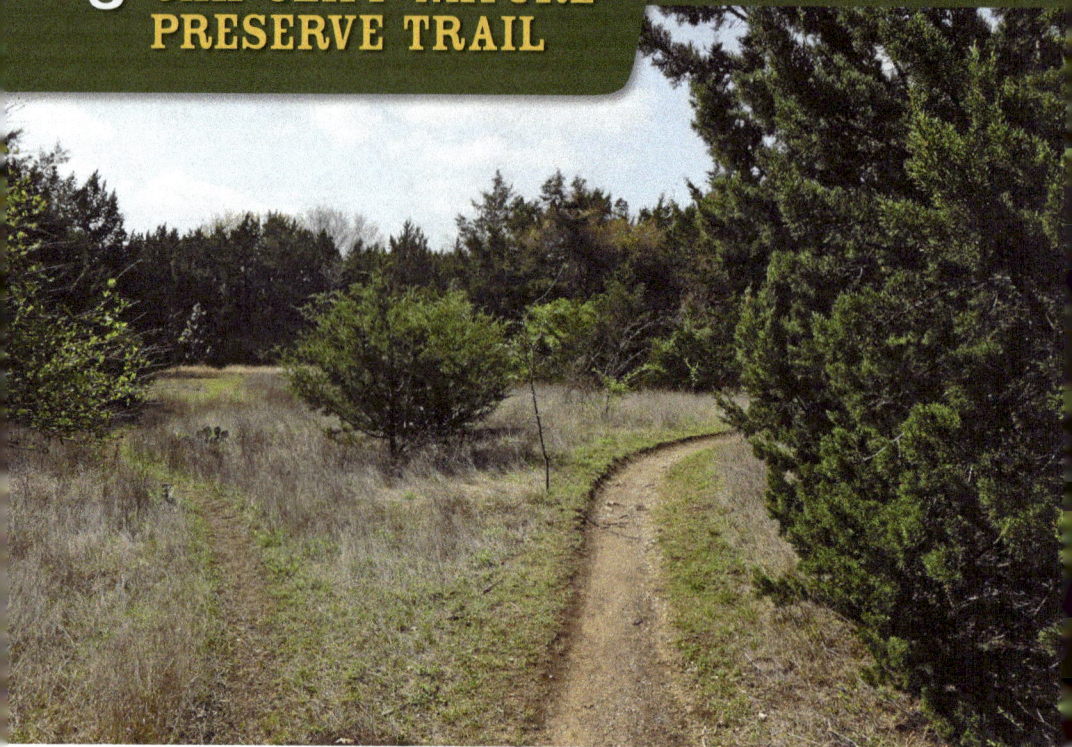

Well-maintained trails and surprises around every curve make this a fun hike for all ages.

WITH 8 MILES OF TRAILS and an impromptu collection of urban art that includes bicycles hanging from treetops, a metal spider sculpture, and a pink Christmas tree, the Oak Cliff Nature Preserve Trail is full of interest.

DESCRIPTION

Nestled deep within the city in the southwest Dallas community of Oak Cliff, the 121-acre Oak Cliff Nature Preserve continuously shows up on Dallasites' lists of favorite urban hikes. Oak Cliff might seem like an odd location for a popular hike, but once you've been there, you'll understand. Convenient, surprisingly picturesque, and with an extensive trail network, this preserve will quickly earn a spot on your list of favorite urban hikes as well.

Originally a Boy Scout camp known as Camp Brooklawn, the land was acquired in 1999 by the Texas Land Conservancy (TLC) after the scouts relocated to Camp Wisdom. In 2006 the Dallas Off-Road Bicycle Association (DORBA) partnered with TLC to develop and maintain trails on the preserve. The result is a wonderfully wild tract of land in the middle of the city with more than 8 miles of trails open to hikers and bikers. Arrive early on pleasant weekends, as the parking lot quickly fills with mountain bikers, families, and locals eager to explore a favorite haunt.

DISTANCE & CONFIGURATION: 2.5-mile double loop

DIFFICULTY: Easy

SCENERY: Woods

EXPOSURE: Partially sunny

TRAFFIC: Moderate

TRAIL SURFACE: Packed dirt

HIKING TIME: 1.25 hours

DRIVING DISTANCE: 9 miles from Loop 12 and I-30

ACCESS: Daily; free

MAP: dorba.org/trail.php?t=20

WHEELCHAIR TRAVERSABLE: No

FACILITIES: Picnic tables

CONTACT: dorba.org

LOCATION: 2875 Pierce St., Dallas

COMMENTS: A network of intersecting trails makes it easy to get disoriented in the preserve; bring a GPS or compass with you. The preserve is being upgraded with an interactive map for mobile use to be rolled out soon.

Adjacent to the trailhead you'll find a trail map detailing the trails. The first thing you'll notice is that they seem to network throughout the whole preserve in a haphazard fashion. In truth, there are six main color-coded loops. Loop 1, the white trail, is the longest loop at approximately 2.25 miles and is considered a "beginner/intermediate" trail for mountain bikers and an easy trail for hikers. The other trails, which range from 0.5 mile to 1 mile, are loops that spur off the main white trail.

It's important to note that although the trail system seems fairly organized and clear on the map, signage is poor and confusing on the trail itself. With this in mind, I suggest that if you own a GPS or compass, bring it! Another tip is to take a picture of the trail map prior to your hike so you have a reference if needed.

I set out on this hike with the intention of traversing the white trail to the yellow trail and returning. On my hike, however, poorly labeled trail intersections made it very difficult to tell if I stayed exclusively on these two trails. I've done my best to describe the route I took, but if you find yourself on a different route, don't panic. Enjoy the hike—discovery and exploration are part of the adventure.

From the trailhead, pass the picnic tables and then turn left (north) onto the white trail. The trail winds roughly east, following the perimeter of the preserve, winding through trees interspersed with grass and cactus. You'll see a number of side trails branching off; bypass them all and continue east. Occasionally, white arrows reaffirm that you are on the right track. The trail meanders pleasantly and soon starts to loop south, then west, then back north before reaching a main trail juncture. Follow the wider of the two trails southwest. About 70 feet later, at the next juncture, you'll again continue southwest. The trail takes you in and out through groves of trees. Birds, attracted by the overhead canopy, provide a relaxing auditory backdrop.

The trail heads south about 0.1 mile before you reach another trail split. At the split, head east. As you continue down the trail you'll have the distinct feeling you've left the city far, far behind. So it will come as a complete surprise when, through the trees, you catch glimpses of the preserve's perimeter. The brief glimpse of

Oak Cliff Nature Preserve Trail

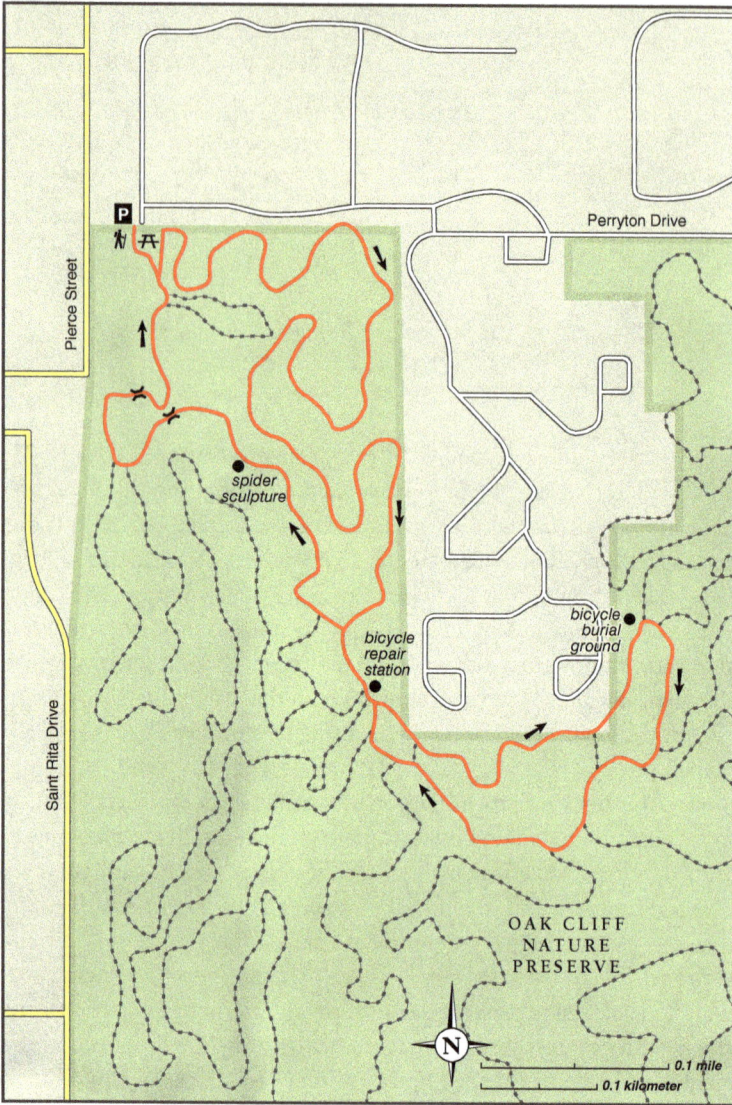

Pierce Street

Saint Rita Drive

P

Perryton Drive

spider
sculpture

bicycle
repair
station

bicycle
burial
ground

OAK CLIFF
NATURE
PRESERVE

N

0.1 mile

0.1 kilometer

civilization is fleeting, however, as the trail again veers south and you reach the next trail juncture. At this point, follow the southeast split.

After about 200 feet, you'll reach a bicycle tire pump. Beyond it, a small clearing with a tree in the middle marks the preserve's main hub, where trails branch off in multiple directions. Head southeast through the clearing toward the tree in the center. Behind the tree, you'll find a comprehensive trail map, showing the different loops. Head down the trail directly behind you, following the path as it loops southwest then southeast. At the first main trail juncture, continue southeast, bypassing any turnoffs. Sixty feet farther, at the next trail juncture, continue by taking the southeast branch.

The trail then loops back west. At the next two junctures, continue by heading northeast. After 250 feet, follow the trail sign that directs you toward the white, blue, and purple trails. More hiking through the trees will bring you to yet another sign that points you down the white loop trail to the northwest.

The wooded forest here is charming and relaxing, a natural place of solitude and beauty. As you round a bend in the trail, you'll suddenly find yourself in an artsy wonderland. An impromptu gallery of urban art decorates a small clearing, resulting in a charming point of interest. Attached to trunks of trees in every direction are dozens of street signs of all shapes and sizes. Plastic flowers artfully arranged draw the eye to different spots. Bicycles defy gravity, dangling from tree branches. And in the center of it all, an artificial pink Christmas tree perfectly captures the whimsical feeling of the spot. After you've explored, continue down the trail, and you'll find yourself back at the main hub in the middle of the preserve.

From the main hub, head north. At the next two trail junctures, continue north. A little farther, you'll come across a giant metal sculpture of a spider, positioned just off the trail, looking unexpectedly lifelike.

Just beyond the spider, the trail starts downhill then emerges onto an incredibly picturesque ravine where trees form a canopy overhead and footbridges cross a quiet creek. The beauty and peace of the spot leave no doubt as to why the preserve is a favorite of many. Cross the bridges and continue north. Turn east at the next two junctures and you'll find yourself back at the trailhead.

NEARBY ACTIVITIES

Just 5 miles north, the Bishop Arts District is a great place to grab a bite to eat. Trendy shops and unique boutiques mixed with local restaurants and coffee shops make this neighborhood a favorite. To get there, head north on South Hampton Road, then turn right, heading east on West 12th Street. At South Llewellyn Avenue turn left (north), then right onto West Davis Street until you get to North Bishop Avenue.

• •

GPS TRAILHEAD COORDINATES N32° 42.842' W96° 51.918'

DIRECTIONS From Dallas, take I-35E south to West Illinois Avenue. Turn right onto West Illinois, then left onto Pierce Street. The preserve will be on the left up a short driveway just before the entrance to an apartment complex.

From Fort Worth, take I-30 E to Exit 41, Westmoreland Road. Turn right onto North Westmoreland Road, left onto West Illinois Avenue, then right onto Pierce Street.

9 ROWLETT CREEK NATURE TRAIL

Take a break from your hike with a picnic lunch in the cool shade of a towering tree.

THIS HEAVILY TRAVELED TRAIL is an excellent choice for a hot, sunny day because most of it is shaded by woods. Because of the dense woodland along the entire length of the trail, this hike will appeal more to those looking for exercise than to those looking for scenic views.

DESCRIPTION

You'll be lucky if you can find a parking space in the Rowlett Creek Preserve in Garland. If you look closely, however, you're likely to see bike racks, helmets, and aerodynamic clothing—indicators of the activity that's most popular on this trail: mountain biking. The trails are, however, open to hikers, and because there are more than 16 miles of trails, it does not feel overwhelmingly crowded (though you certainly won't feel lonely). The trails are arranged in numbered loops; the higher the number, the more difficult the trail for a biker. What makes this trail particularly appealing is that almost all of it is shaded, making for an ideal summer hike.

This hike starts with the Loop 1 Trail. Find the trailhead on the north side of the parking lot, to the left of a gazebo and just behind a kiosk displaying a map of the preserve. The narrow dirt path disappears north into the woods and curls lazily in a half-loop through the trees until you reach a turnoff at 0.57 mile for the Loop 7 Trail. Turn left onto the trail; at about 0.63 mile, the path crosses beneath

DISTANCE & CONFIGURATION:
4-mile double loop

DIFFICULTY: Moderate

SCENERY: Woodland, creek

EXPOSURE: Shady with a section of sun

TRAFFIC: Heavy

TRAIL SURFACE: Packed dirt

HIKING TIME: 1.5 hours

DRIVING DISTANCE: 8.3 miles from I-30 and I-635

ACCESS: Daily, 6 a.m.–midnight; free

MAP: dorba.org/trail.php?t=22

WHEELCHAIR TRAVERSABLE: No

FACILITIES: Portable toilets, water fountain, picnic tables

CONTACT: dorba.org

LOCATION: 2525 Castle Rd., Garland

COMMENTS: Watch for snakes sunning on the trail.

the bridge for Centerville Road and then heads into more woods. The trail then follows a narrow creek north toward the northern edge of the preserve. Dense woods in this section cast a deep shade over the trail, providing welcome relief during a sunny day. To the right, the woods end at the backyards of private homes that abut the opposite side of the creek.

Continue on the trail, reaching a fence and a small sign at the edge of the preserve; the trail winds along this fence before coming to a junction at 1 mile. Take the trail to the left, heading downhill. The trails that cut through this section are close enough together that you're likely to glimpse bikers or hikers winding through the woods on trails completely obscured by the dense trees. This gives the confusing illusion that people might be heading toward you or coming up from behind you, when in fact they are on a completely different part of the trail. Keep alert, because when a rider is on the same trail, the path's twists and turns prevent you from knowing it until he or she is right in front of you, leaving you little time to step aside.

Reach the next junction at 1.1 miles, where trails head to the left and right while one continues straight ahead; choose this middle path to avoid the steep hills intended for mountain bikers. At 1.23 miles, go right and follow a long wooden boardwalk overlaying the trail. You'll dodge a couple of low-hanging limbs, then reach the end of the boardwalk's wooden planks. At 1.4 miles there is yet another junction—head right. At this point, the trail climbs out of the woods and onto a small, sun-drenched ridge, where Centerville Road stretches in front of you. Bear right, heading downhill; the path curls in a short loop through another section of woods, then, at 1.8 miles, comes back up onto the sunny, treeless ridge. Follow the trail back into the woods; the trees lean together, forming a cavelike entry into the inviting relief of deep shade.

A couple hundred feet farther and you'll be back at the bridge. Just after the overhang, stay to the right to pick up a trail that brings you back to the Loop 7 turn-off. At about 1.9 miles, approach the split and bear left. At about 2 miles, bear left again, following the sign for Loop 1a. Cross a small brook; follow it for 2.25 miles and then bear right, continuing on Loop 1a. The trail is level for the rest of the hike, making for easy walking. Keep your eyes peeled for snakes—it isn't unusual to spot

Rowlett Creek Nature Trail

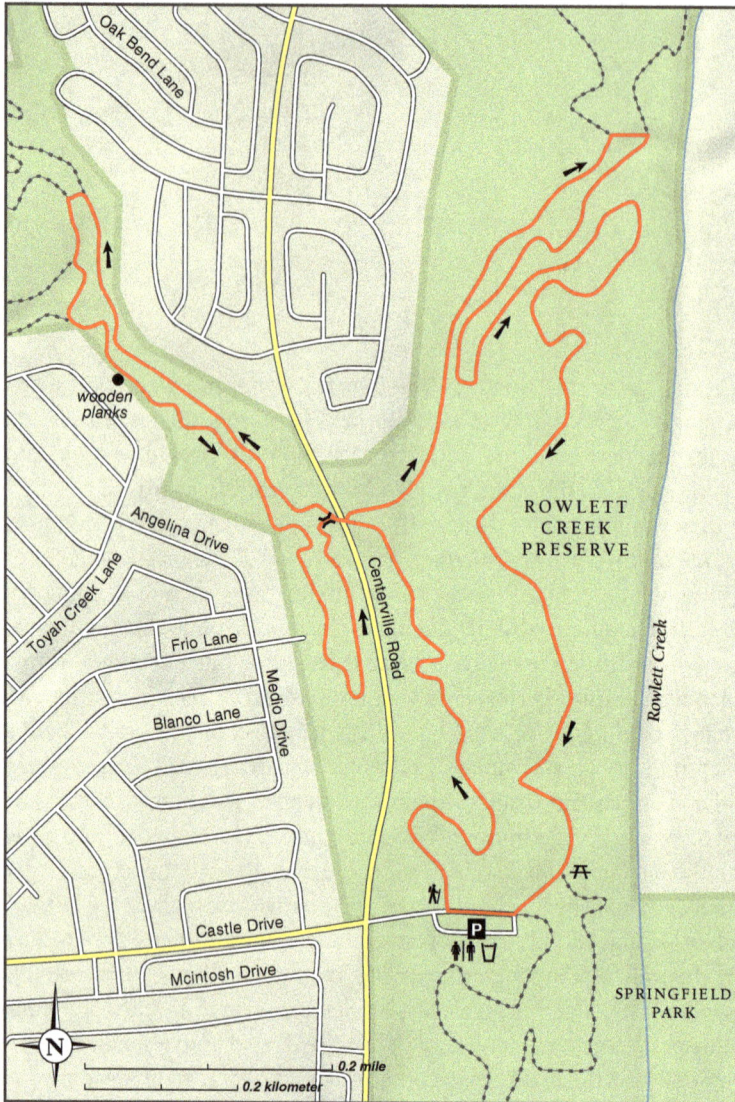

them curled in the middle of the trail, and I once spied a 3-foot one just barely slithering out of the way as bikers whizzed past.

At 2.9 miles, join Loop 1. The trail passes straight through a wide field, the only sunny portion of the trail. At 3.88 miles, come to a picnic table set conveniently in the shade of a huge lone tree—a nice spot at which to stop and eat lunch before heading home. From the picnic table, the trail merges onto a paved pathway that ends at the parking lot.

NEARBY ACTIVITIES

Just a few miles away, the Firewheel Town Center—an open-air complex of department stores, retail shops, and restaurants—is a good place to grab a bite to eat and do some shopping. It's about 2 miles northwest, at the intersection of TX 78 N and the President George Bush Turnpike (TX 190).

• •

GPS TRAILHEAD COORDINATES N32° 55.200' W96° 35.733'

DIRECTIONS Take the President George Bush Turnpike (TX 190) to its end, at TX 78 N (Lavon Drive). Turn right onto TX 78 N, toward Garland. Go about 2 miles and turn left onto Castle Drive to Rowlett Creek Preserve. The parking lot is about 1.7 miles ahead, at the intersection of Castle Drive and East Centerville Road.

This shady trail passes through dense woodland.

The Trinity River Audubon Center guards the entrance to the Wetland, Prairie, and Forest Trails.

THE AUDUBON CENTER does its best to keep you entertained with hands-on indoor exhibits and displays. When you finally venture outside, you'll find well-maintained trails that explore the diversity of the Great Trinity Forest. Bird-watching areas, picnic tables, and signage combine to give you a fun, family-friendly afternoon on the trail.

DESCRIPTION

Opened in October 2008, the Trinity River Audubon Center is an exciting collaboration between the City of Dallas and the National Audubon Society to make the surrounding area—the Great Trinity Forest—accessible to hikers, birders, and other outdoors enthusiasts. The forest is one of Dallas's special natural features: a forested urban park, one of the largest such parks in the country. Situated primarily south of Dallas, the preserve consists of 6,000 acres of bottomland forest and is part of the Trinity River Project, an effort to develop transportation and flood protection, foster nature preservation, and provide recreation for area residents.

The Trinity River Audubon Center was constructed to showcase the Great Trinity Forest and its resources, and it does so spectacularly. Designed with the nature lover in mind, the center contains displays and interactive exhibits, as well as a network of well-laid-out trails that entice you to explore the forest beyond.

As you walk into the beautifully designed building, you'll be hard-pressed to imagine that not so long ago the area was uninviting. Today, the landscape of rolling

DISTANCE & CONFIGURATION: 2.5-miles, 3 loops

DIFFICULTY: Easy

SCENERY: Forest, wetlands, river

EXPOSURE: Sunny

TRAFFIC: Moderate

TRAIL SURFACE: Packed dirt

HIKING TIME: 45 minutes

DRIVING DISTANCE: 3 miles from I-45 S and Loop 12

ACCESS: Tuesday–Friday, 9 a.m.–4 p.m.; Saturday, 7 a.m.–3 p.m.; Sunday, 11 a.m.–5 p.m.; closed on Mondays and holidays; $6 adults, $3 children, $4 seniors age 60 and over

MAP: tinyurl.com/trinityriverauduboncenter

WHEELCHAIR TRAVERSABLE: No

FACILITIES: Restrooms, water fountain, picnic tables, benches

CONTACT: 214-398-8722, trinityriver.audubon.org

LOCATION: 6500 Great Trinity Forest Way, Dallas

COMMENTS: Admission is free on the third Thursday of the month.

hills and dense green forest betrays no hint of its rocky past, but rather welcomes you to hike through native wetlands, grasslands, and bottomland hardwoods.

The starting point for the trails is the center itself: a beautiful LEED-certified facility uniquely designed to resemble a bird in flight. A small admission fee entitles you to explore the center and access the trails. If you're with a group, consider going on the third Thursday of the month, when admission is free. Set aside time before or after your hike to peruse the exhibits and displays. The largest is an interactive flood simulator, demonstrating the flooding that occurs along the Trinity River. With the press of a button, water seeps onto the large display, showing what happens during a 100-year flood, a 500-year flood, and a catastrophic flood. Nearby, an equally compelling exhibit targeted to kids shows how to shape and route a river.

Plenty of other diversions will catch your interest. Informational plaques on the birds and animals of the forest, wetlands, tallgrass and blackland prairies, and floodplains abound. Kids and parents alike will be enthralled by displays of skulls, spiders, and snakeskins. Small aquariums built into the walls housing catfish and turtles will keep you mesmerized; exhibits emitting the sounds of river animals such as frogs, crickets, and birds will keep you entertained.

When you pay your admission fee, the attendant will provide you with a map that directs you to pick up the trails behind the main building. For this hike, I've combined several trails into one trek that takes you through different landscapes.

From the back of the center, head down the raised walkway to the first junction. Signs point out the Wetland Trail to your left and the Forest Trail to your right. Turn right, following the Forest Trail until you reach the intersection marked TRINITY RIVER VISTA. Turn left, winding past wildflowers, over a small bridge, into the shelter of the forest, and out toward picnic tables and a view of the Trinity River as it bends around a curve. I've yet to see a prettier river vista in the metroplex.

When you're done admiring the view, retrace your steps to the Trinity River Vista junction and bear left back onto the Forest Trail. Pass two small junctions; continue straight on the main trail until you reach an intersection at 0.85 mile into the

Trinity River Audubon Trail

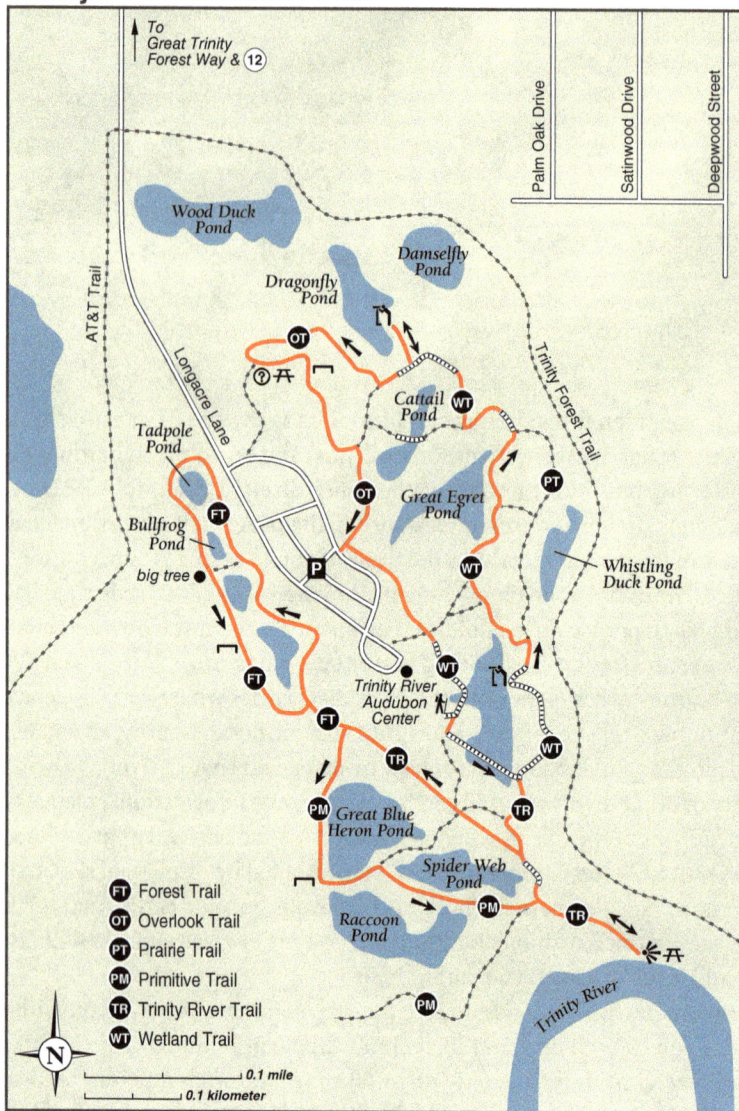

Map labels:

To Great Trinity Forest Way & 12

Palm Oak Drive
Satinwood Drive
Deepwood Street

AT&T Trail

Wood Duck Pond

Damselfly Pond

Dragonfly Pond

Longacre Lane

Cattail Pond

Trinity Forest Trail

Tadpole Pond

Great Egret Pond

Bullfrog Pond

big tree

Whistling Duck Pond

Trinity River Audubon Center

Great Blue Heron Pond

Spider Web Pond

Raccoon Pond

Trinity River

Legend:

- FT Forest Trail
- OT Overlook Trail
- PT Prairie Trail
- PM Primitive Trail
- TR Trinity River Trail
- WT Wetland Trail

N

0.1 mile
0.1 kilometer

hike. From here, make a right up the steps built into the trail and enter the cool shade of the woods. Tall trees surround you, and a pleasant feeling of solitude envelops you as you hike through the quiet forest. The trail makes a short loop before reaching a huge tree surrounded by benches where programs and presentations are held. Continue past the tree and bear right when you rejoin the main trail.

Quickly loop out of the shade and back into the sun, bearing right at the next junction to head down around a pond and over to a well-positioned bench at about 1.4 miles.

When you're ready to continue, turn right onto the trail heading between the ponds. Butterflies will flutter out of your way and birds will chirp from above as this trail merges onto the Trinity River Trail. The path here should look familiar—just follow it until you've returned to the Wetland–Forest Trail junction, where your hike began.

From here, explore the northern trails by following the WETLAND TRAIL sign. This section of trail is a boardwalk constructed above the swampy wetlands. A few hundred feet from the junction, arrive at a lookout platform where you can survey the wetland habitat of creatures you may have seen in the visitor center, such as frogs, turtles, and fish. From the lookout, continue following the Wetland Trail past a pond and to a junction about 1.9 miles into the hike. Bear left, following signs pointing the way to the Overlook Trail.

It's hard to imagine now, but the land you're trekking on was formerly known as the Deepwood Landfill—an illegal dumping ground for more than 1.5 million tons of construction debris. The land was reclaimed and the debris molded and shaped to provide an area upon which native flora and fauna could grow and thrive.

About 500 feet farther, come to another junction; turn right, following the WETLAND TRAIL sign. A couple hundred feet ahead, reach a well-designed bird blind where you can survey the native birds that populate the surrounding ponds.

From the bird blind, continue to the next trail junction and turn right, following the OVERLOOK TRAIL signs. The trail climbs slightly, looping around until you reach the top of a small hill where, in addition to a cool breeze and commanding view, you'll find picnic tables, benches, and a kiosk. This is an excellent spot to break for lunch.

Return to the trailhead by bearing right at the junction, past the kiosk, and retracing your steps until you reach the center.

NEARBY ACTIVITIES

Fair Park is only 8 miles away. When you're done with your hike, visit one of its museums or gardens, including the African American Museum, the Museum of the American Railroad, the Texas Discovery Gardens, and the Women's Museum. For more information, call 214-426-3400 or visit fairpark.org. To get to Fair Park from the Trinity River Audubon Center, head northeast on Loop 12 E/East Ledbetter Drive. Take I-45 N to Dallas/Sherman. Take Exit 284A to merge onto I-30 E, then take Exit 47 (Second Avenue/Fair Park) and follow the signs.

• •

GPS TRAILHEAD COORDINATES N32° 42.217' W96° 42.300'

DIRECTIONS From downtown Dallas, take I-45 S and exit at Loop 12 E/East Ledbetter Drive. Go about 2 miles to reach the entrance, on the right.

11 TRINITY SKYLINE TRAIL

There is no better view of the Dallas skyline than from this trail.

PACK YOUR CAMERA and play the *Dallas* theme song when you head to this greenbelt, which offers striking views of the Dallas skyline as it meanders alongside the Trinity River.

DESCRIPTION

Unapologetically urban, the Trinity Skyline Trail offers something few other Dallas trails have: unobstructed and absolutely stunning views of the Dallas skyline. Loved by joggers, walkers, and bikers, this trail has the same urban appeal as the extremely popular Katy Trail. It's a scenic, flat grade, easily accessible greenbelt in the heart of one of the most populous cities in the state. If you love the Katy Trail, you will without a doubt love this trail as well. If you've never been to the Katy Trail, start with this one; it's lesser known and so has only a fraction of the crowds, and the views just can't compare to what you'll find anyplace else. This trail also makes for an excellent spot to bring out-of-town guests—being a greenbelt, it does not require special footwear, and postcard-worthy photographs are almost guaranteed on any visit.

The Trinity Skyline Trail is part of a wider effort to revitalize the Trinity River Corridor, a project covering 10,000 acres of land along the Trinity River. Eventually, it is anticipated that the Skyline Trail will connect with the Santa Fe Trestle Trail to the east and the Trinity Strand Trail to the northwest.

DISTANCE & CONFIGURATION: 2.6-mile loop

DIFFICULTY: Easy

SCENERY: Dallas skyline, Trinity River

EXPOSURE: Sunny

TRAFFIC: Moderate

TRAIL SURFACE: Paved, packed dirt

HIKING TIME: 1.25 hours

DRIVING DISTANCE: 3 miles from intersection of I-30 and I-35E

ACCESS: Daily; free

MAP: dallasparks.org/documentcenter/view/2868

WHEELCHAIR TRAVERSABLE: Yes

FACILITIES: Portable toilets

CONTACT: 214-670-4100, dallasparks.org

LOCATION: Gulden Lane at Canada Dr., Dallas

COMMENTS: Leave time after your hike to explore the pedestrian bridge.

Ample parking and a trailhead are located on the west end of the Ronald Kirk Bridge, a pedestrian bridge that spans the Trinity River. Listed on the National Register of Historic Places, the bridge was originally named the Lamar-McKinney Bridge and was later renamed the Continental Avenue Bridge.

The bridge was designed and opened as a vehicular bridge in 1932 in order to ease travel across the chronically flooding waters of the Trinity River, and it remained in use for more than 80 years. In 2013 the bridge was closed, and vehicles were redirected to the nearby newly opened Margaret Hunt Hill Bridge. The following year, the Continental Avenue Bridge reopened as a pedestrian-friendly park for foot traffic only. The pedestrian bridge is now quite popular, offering benches and shade, a children's play area, and a giant chess set as well as various events and activities throughout the year.

Although most people still know it as the Continental Avenue Bridge, in 2016, Dallas City Council voted to rename the bridge in honor of Dallas's first African American mayor, Ronald Kirk. Keep in mind that because of the relative newness of the bridge's renaming, maps and literature could refer to the bridge by either moniker.

At the trailhead, you'll find portable toilets, benches, a map, and a spectacular view of the Dallas skyline. Follow the paved path down and under the Ronald Kirk Pedestrian Bridge to begin your hike. A sunny day will see the trail busy with a variety of outdoor enthusiasts, including dog walkers, families, joggers, skaters, hikers, and bikers.

After you pass under the Ronald Kirk Bridge, the trail splits. To the south, the paved section ends and becomes soft surface. To the east, the paved portion continues. Head south (right) onto the soft surface track. You'll pass under the Margaret Hunt Hill Bridge and continue your hike.

The Margaret Hunt Hill Bridge, easily identifiable by its distinctive 400-foot white arch, is a vehicular bridge that opened in 2012. It is a cable-stayed bridge designed by Santiago Calatrava and has become a distinguishing feature of the Dallas skyline. The bridge was named after local philanthropist and civic leader Margaret

Trinity Skyline Trail

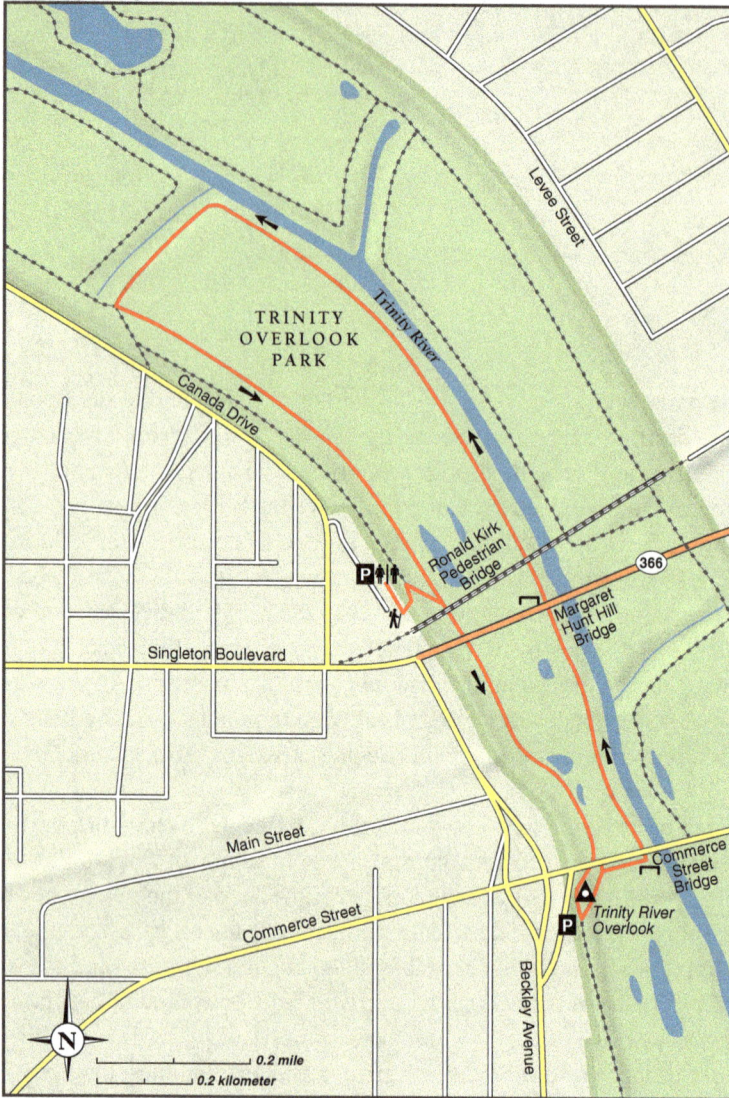

TRINITY OVERLOOK PARK

Levee Street

Trinity River

Canada Drive

Ronald Kirk Pedestrian Bridge

366

Margaret Hunt Hill Bridge

Singleton Boulevard

Main Street

Commerce Street

Commerce Street Bridge

Trinity River Overlook

Beckley Avenue

N

0.2 mile
0.2 kilometer

Hunt Hill, who was the daughter of Texas oil tycoon H. L. Hunt Jr. (the man who served as inspiration for the character of J. R. Ewing on the TV show *Dallas*).

After a short trek, the soft surface trail once again becomes paved and you'll reach another trail split. Turn right heading southwest and follow the paved path up the levee slopes to the Trinity River Overlook. At the overlook you'll find a shaded rest spot, replete with interpretive signage and uninterrupted views of the Dallas skyline. You'll also notice that there is street parking adjacent to the overlook, making it an alternative entry point onto the Skyline Trail.

Once you've taken in the views and read about the history of the trail, return to the trailhead by heading back down the levee slope onto the trail to the last trail split. This time, take the right fork onto the paved path heading west under the Commerce Street Bridge toward a bench placed conveniently in its shadow. From here, the trail turns left heading north.

As you hike, you'll enjoy views typical of the Trinity River floodplain—a green swath of low grass running adjacent to the winding river, occasionally disturbed by wading birds. Trees do not grow here, so most of the trail (other than portions under bridges) is entirely exposed. On any given summer day, you'll want to come prepared with sunscreen and a hat.

The trail continues north back under the Margaret Hunt Hill Bridge, under the Ronald Kirk Pedestrian Bridge, continuing alongside the Trinity River. A sharp left (southwest) turn in the trail followed by another sharp left (southeast) turn signals that the path is winding back to the trailhead.

NEARBY ACTIVITIES

Just across the bridge, downtown Dallas is only minutes away and has an endless array of museums, restaurants, and historic landmarks to explore. Some highlights include the Sixth Floor Museum at Dealey Plaza, which has exhibits covering the assassination of President John F. Kennedy. Reunion Tower, an iconic feature of the Dallas Skyline, has an observation deck and cafe on its upper floor. The Dallas World Aquarium and the Perot Museum of Nature and Science are other enjoyable ways to spend the afternoon. To get downtown, just cross the Margaret Hunt Hill Bridge heading east and exit onto Continental Avenue.

• •

GPS TRAILHEAD COORDINATES N32° 46.787' W96° 49.550'

DIRECTIONS The trailhead is located adjacent to the Continental Avenue Bridge West Dallas Gateway at the intersection of Canada Drive and Gulden Lane. To get there, cross the Trinity River using the Margaret Hunt Hill Bridge heading west on TX 366. After you cross the bridge you'll be on Singleton Boulevard. Take the first right onto Gulden Lane; you'll see the parking lot on your right. From Fort Worth, take I-30 E to Exit 44A toward Beckley Avenue/I-35E S/Riverfront Boulevard. Turn left onto North Beckley Avenue. North Beckley Avenue will turn left and become Singleton Boulevard. Take the first right onto Gulden Lane; you'll see the parking lot on your right.

A pier provides a fantastic spot to take in the views.

POPULAR WITH JOGGERS, bikers, walkers, and hikers, this lengthy trail runs along White Rock Lake. The hike starts just past the waterfall-like spillway and hugs the shoreline, offering constant views of the water as it winds past the Dallas Arboretum and Botanical Garden.

DESCRIPTION

White Rock Lake is one of the most well-known outdoor spots among Dallasites. Its 9-mile trail circumnavigates the lake and attracts joggers, walkers, hikers, bikers, and skaters. One of the lake's draws is that it's only 6 miles northeast of Dallas, in a populated area just 4 miles east of Highland Park.

Completed in 1911, the lake was originally intended as a primary reservoir for the city of Dallas. The city quickly outgrew the lake, though, and eventually the larger Lake Dallas was created to supply water. In its early days, White Rock Lake was also a popular local swimming hole; I even ran into an older gentleman by the trailhead who reminisced about the days he spent as a child with his father playing in the waters. Swimming there was banned in the early 1950s and hasn't been permitted since. The lake is also widely known for the annual White Rock Marathon, which started in 1971. The route runs a loop from downtown to the lake and back.

DISTANCE & CONFIGURATION: 4.66-mile out-and-back

DIFFICULTY: Easy

SCENERY: Lake, spillway

EXPOSURE: Sunny

TRAFFIC: Heavy

TRAIL SURFACE: Paved

HIKING TIME: 1.75 hours

DRIVING DISTANCE: 4.5 miles from I-30 and US 75

ACCESS: Daily; free

MAP: dallasparks.org/documentcenter/view/1009

WHEELCHAIR TRAVERSABLE: Yes

FACILITIES: Water fountains, benches

CONTACT: 214-670-4100, dallasparks.org

LOCATION: Winsted Dr. and Garland Rd., Dallas

COMMENTS: Bring a windbreaker—the wind can really pick up over the water.

In years past, the lake's urban location gave it a reputation for being unsafe. Its image has been rehabilitated, however, thanks in large part to a volunteer group known as For the Love of the Lake (FTLOTL), which has worked hard to clean and renovate the lake. Because of FTLOTL's efforts, it is very well kept, feels safe, and is surprisingly scenic. Also contributing to the feeling of safety is the fact that this section of the trail is not isolated and well exposed. During the day, you'll find it very busy— there are folks with baby strollers, dogs, and kids. Remember, though, that this is an urban trail, and heed the signs by the parking lot advising you to keep your valuables in your trunk. It's also a good idea for women and kids to bring a buddy along.

The land surrounding the lake is part of White Rock Park, which has several entrances. This hike starts from the southern end of the lake, at an entrance near the spillway. The small parking lot stays fairly full on weekends, although you can almost always manage to find at least one spot to squeeze your car into. The path comes into view to the left, running just in front of the spillway. Get on the trail and turn right, heading away from the parking lot toward Garland Road. The trail immediately curves left, crosses a concrete bridge that bounces as folks jog by, and takes you directly alongside the massive, tiered spillway. Water cascades down its huge steps, creating a thunderous noise. Ducks can often be spotted paddling on the top level, ignoring the nearby waterfall.

Just across the bridge, the trail, which once wound very close to the edge of the lake, has been rerouted along Garland Road. This is the loudest and least pleasant section of the trail because for a few hundred feet you'll find yourself essentially on the sidewalk of a busy road. The trail soon curves downhill, away from the road and back toward and alongside the shoreline to your left. You'll have a good view of the path curving out before you, following the shoreline until it disappears around a bend in the shore. Expect the path to be busy. Bikers and joggers are constantly coming and going, and if you stop for a minute or two, expect to be overtaken by other hikers or dog walkers.

At 0.4 mile, pass a pier; walk out to the water and you might see ducks just around the shore. Thanks in part to the Adopt-a-Shoreline program, you'll find the

White Rock Lake Trail

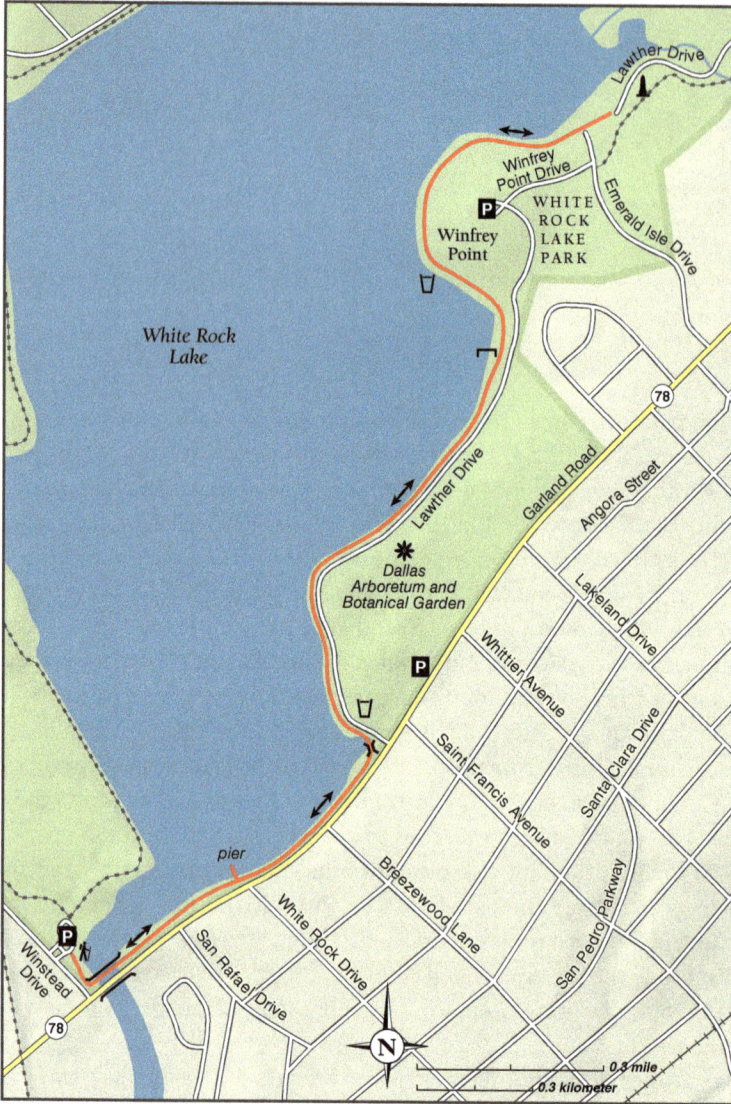

shore well kept. Through this program, various groups agree to be caretakers of certain sections of the trail. You'll see wooden signs along the shore as you hike, identifying the group—such as Boy Scout troops and REI—whose section you're in. Trash receptacles along the trail also help keep the area clean.

As you continue, you'll catch sight of a few nice residences bordering Garland Road on your right before the trail curves northwest away from the street and over a bridge at 0.78 mile. Take a moment to glance over your shoulder for a nice view of the Dallas skyline. A couple hundred feet farther, reach a water fountain where you can refresh yourself and read a nearby historical marker.

Continue down the trail, following the shoreline. To your right, a fence runs behind the Dallas Arboretum; to your left, you'll have a complete view of the lake's grassy, tree-dotted shoreline. The trail is mostly sunny and exposed, allowing great visibility wherever you are on the trail; at 1.55 miles, however, you'll reach one of the few sections with a small grouping of trees, providing some much-needed shade.

At 1.63 miles, note a parking lot to your right and kids playing on the shoreline to your left. This lake entrance is known as Winfrey Point. Joggers joining the trail here are likely to merge and pass you on their quest for fitness. The trail then turns into a wide path painted with double lanes on each side. Continuing north, you'll soon round another curve and see a densely wooded section ahead. A playground on your right marks yet another entrance. To your left, a shallow inlet attracts wading and shorebirds. A short dock extends into the waters, offering a good spot from which to view the birdlife. Here you'll also find a statue honoring the Civilian Conservation Corps, which worked at White Rock Lake from 1935 to 1942. Take a few minutes to rest before turning and retracing your steps to the trailhead. If you want to extend the hike, the trail continues another 6.5 miles, looping the rest of the way around the lake before returning you to the trailhead.

NEARBY ACTIVITIES

Head downtown and explore the Arts District. The Dallas Museum of Art is known for its collection of European paintings. Visit dallasmuseumofart.org for lists of the current exhibitions. Other nearby museums include the Nasher Sculpture Center, which houses pieces by Matisse, de Kooning, Picasso, and Rodin, and the Crow Collection of Asian Art. From White Rock, take I-30 W about 2 miles, then exit onto I-45 S/US 75 N to reach Elm Street. Turn right on North Central Expressway, then left onto North Pearl Street. Drive about 0.5 mile. Turn left onto Flora Street, then left again onto North Harwood Street; the Dallas Museum of Art is at 1717 N. Harwood.

• •

GPS TRAILHEAD COORDINATES N32° 48.850' W96° 43.633'

DIRECTIONS Follow I-30 E toward I-45 S, and take Exit 488 (Barry Avenue) onto East R. L. Thornton Freeway toward East Grand Avenue. Turn left onto East Grand and drive 2 miles. East Grand will become Garland Road. Turn left onto Winsted Drive and you'll see a sign for White Rock Park. Park in the lot on the right.

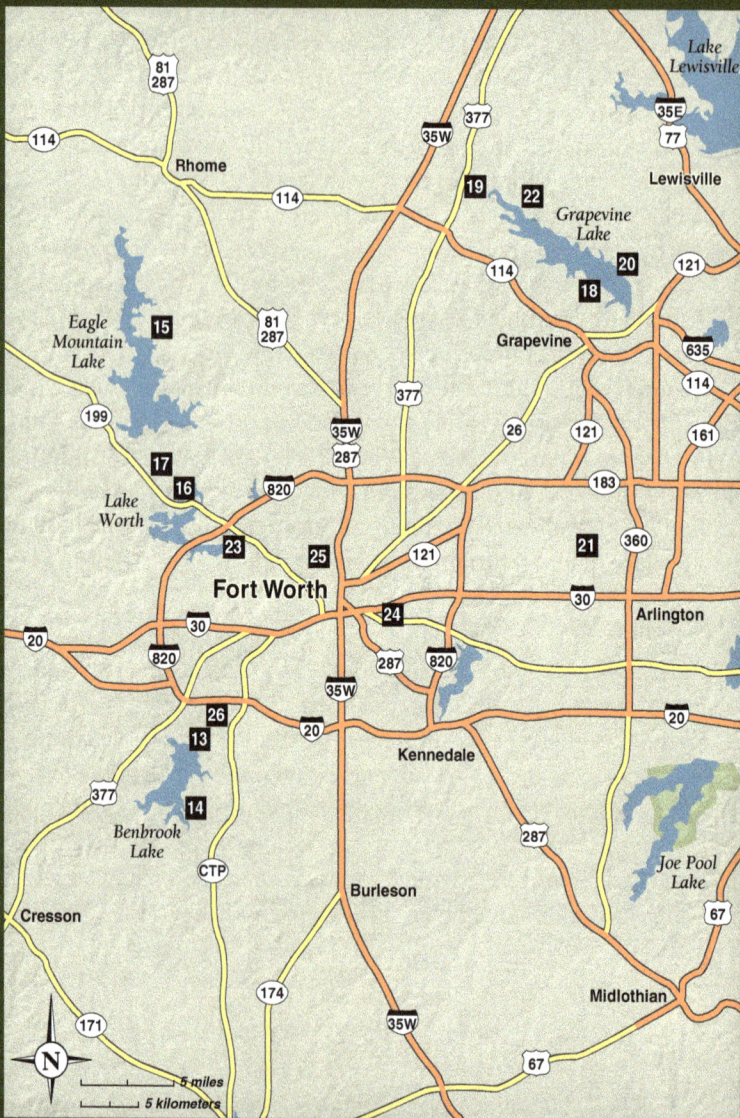

FORT WORTH AREA
(Including Grapevine Lake, Colleyville, and Euless)

A windless day creates a mirrorlike surface on Benbrook Lake.

THIS TRAIL RUNS along a grassy strip atop the Benbrook Dam and ends at the dam's spillway. Appealing for its unobstructed views of the lake and surrounding area, the flat, straight path is ideal for walkers and joggers.

DESCRIPTION

On the Clear Fork of the Trinity River just southwest of Fort Worth, Benbrook Lake offers impressive stretches of trail that extend for miles, affording hikers plenty of room to stretch their legs and roam around.

The lake, impounded in 1952, serves as a flood-control reservoir for the surrounding area. According to the Army Corps of Engineers, which operates the lake, it has served its purpose quite well, preventing flooding and destruction of populated areas during periods of severe rainfall, most notably in the early 1990s. The lake is also a popular spot for summer recreational activities and is lined with parks offering picnicking, swimming, fishing, camping, and hiking opportunities.

The trailhead is a short walk east of the roundabout, at the gated road. As you drive in, pass the gated road just to the right before you reach the parking lot. A tall locked metal gate blocks the road to car traffic; however, foot traffic is permitted. Although the latter was light on my visit due to overcast weather, the path is said to

DISTANCE & CONFIGURATION: 3.1-mile out-and-back

DIFFICULTY: Easy

SCENERY: Lake

EXPOSURE: Sunny

TRAFFIC: Light

TRAIL SURFACE: Paved, grassy

HIKING TIME: 1.5 hours

DRIVING DISTANCE: 5.4 miles from I-820 and I-20

ACCESS: Daily; free

MAP: None

WHEELCHAIR TRAVERSABLE: No

FACILITIES: Restrooms, picnic tables

CONTACT: 817-292-2400, www.swf-wc.usace .army.mil

LOCATION: Longhorn Park, located in the 7000 block of Lakeside Dr., Fort Worth

COMMENTS: After the hike, walk or drive south down the park road to the boat ramp for an up-close view of the water.

be especially popular with joggers. To access the area, you'll need to step over the low barrier adjacent to the gate. Then head down the road toward the lake.

Yucca sprouts alongside the road, drinking in the sun on this exposed section of path. Continue west, following the road until you reach the lake. The trail surface changes from paved to partial grass as it keeps going west atop the crest of the dam, an earth-fill embankment that stretches 1.5 miles across the north end of the lake to a spillway at the western end. Steep, grassy slopes lead down to the lake level; you'll hike along the flat top. Be aware, however, that even though there is no fence restricting access to the dam's steep slopes, walking down or on them is strictly prohibited.

Because it was overcast the day I hiked this trail, I was concerned that the hike might not be enjoyable. To my surprise, the weather proved ideal. The cloud cover kept the temperature cool, allowing me to maintain a fast clip on the ridge's flat, even, exposed surface without even breaking a sweat. Lack of wind left the lake ripple-free and eerily still. The water reflected the gray sky perfectly, making it impossible to discern where sky ended and lake began. Overall, the weather was perfect. If you come on a sunny day, though, bring a hat and sunscreen, because there's no shade on this trail.

Regardless of the weather, your hike across the dam will afford fantastic views of the lake spreading below and to the left. To the right you'll enjoy a bird's-eye view of encroaching development to the north. You'll also be able to spot golf carts roaming the nearby Pecan Valley Golf Course, and you'll hear the rumble of cars as they barrel down Lakeside Drive.

As you hike, keep an eye out for birds flying low over the lake or standing along the shoreline. You're most likely to see waders and shorebirds such as herons, grebes, cormorants, ducks, and egrets. Bird-watchers have spotted more than 269 species in the area, so bring some binoculars.

As you approach the western side of the dam, you'll see a narrow road running down along the shoreline to your left and curling out to a small inlet. Unfortunately,

Benbrook Dam Trail

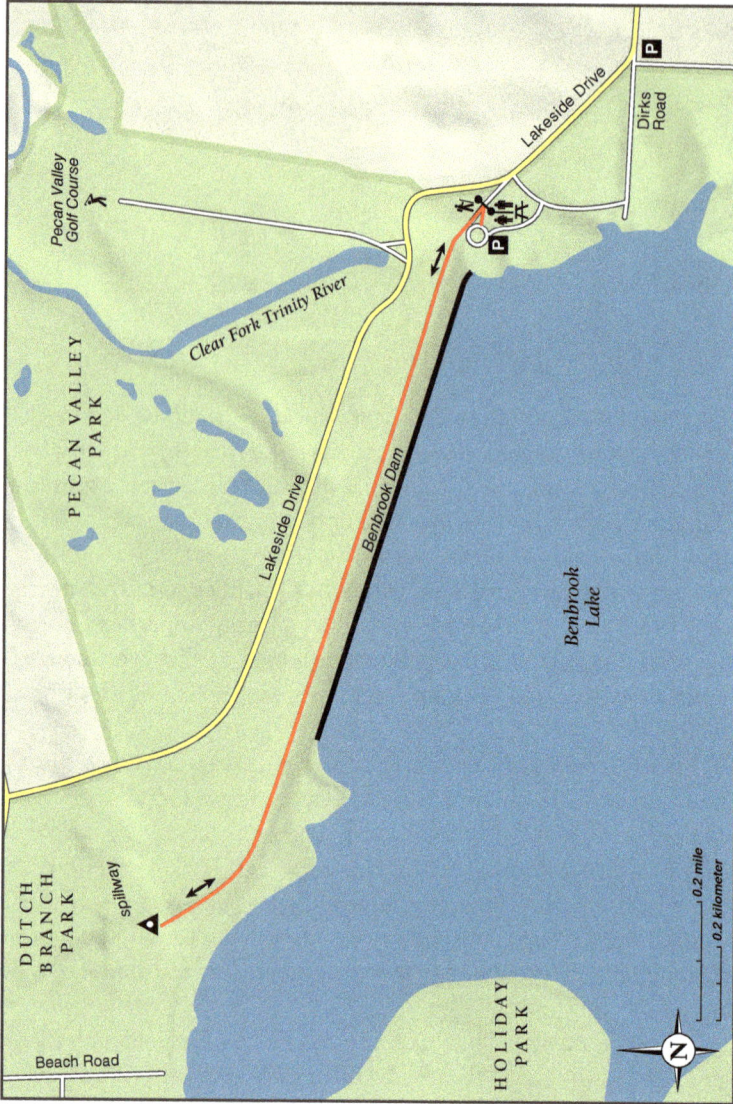

the road starts on the opposite side of the lake and is inaccessible from this side of the dam.

A short walk farther and you'll have reached the spillway, where the path ends at a locked gate. Although the gate prohibits you from crossing to the other side of the lake, you'll find a nice overlook with views of the spillway. From here, just retrace your steps across the dam to the trailhead.

Spectacular lake views are the highlight of this trail.

NEARBY ACTIVITIES

The Fort Worth Botanic Garden (3220 Botanic Garden Blvd.) comprises 109 acres with more than 2,500 species of plant life, including a Japanese garden, rose garden, and fragrance garden. The grounds are open 8 a.m.–sunset; visit fwbg.org for specifics on fees and the hours of the on-site restaurant.

Near the garden, Forest Park offers a few acres and the Log Cabin Village, a living-history museum featuring interpreters and demonstrators. For more information, visit logcabinvillage.org. To get to Forest Park from the trail, drive down Dirks Road and turn left onto Bryant Irvin Boulevard. After 6 miles, turn right onto Camp Bowie Boulevard. After 0.5 mile, bear right onto I-30 E; go 2 miles, then take Exit 12A onto West Rosedale Street toward University Drive. Bear right, heading south onto South University Drive; the Log Cabin Village is about 1 mile ahead on the right. To get to the garden from the intersection of I-30 and University Drive, go north on University Drive. The entrance is on the left.

• •

GPS TRAILHEAD COORDINATES N32° 39.017' W97° 26.750'

DIRECTIONS Follow I-20 W toward Abilene and take Exit 434A toward Granbury Road/South Drive. Turn left onto Granbury Road and go about 3 miles, then turn right onto Dirks Road and travel 2 miles. Bear right onto Lakeside Drive and go 0.5 mile. The parking lot will be on the left, just past the lake office. Park near the roundabout, to the right.

14 BENBROOK LAKE TRAIL

The trail runs alongside the lake through tall grasses and shaded woods.

THIS HIKE ALONG the lakeshore yields scenic views and sections of wooded trail with plenty of opportunities to spot local wildlife. Bring your lunch to a tucked-away cove at the water's edge.

DESCRIPTION

On the Clear Fork of the Trinity River just southwest of Fort Worth, Benbrook Lake offers impressive stretches of trail that extend for miles, affording hikers plenty of room to stretch their legs and roam around.

The lake, impounded in 1952, serves as a flood-control reservoir for the surrounding area. According to the Army Corps of Engineers, which operates the lake, it has served its purpose quite well, preventing flooding and destruction of populated areas during periods of severe rainfall, most notably in the early 1990s. The lake is also a popular spot for summer recreational activities and is lined with parks offering picnicking, swimming, fishing, camping, and hiking opportunities.

Rocky Creek Park, on the eastern side of the lake, serves as the starting point for this hike. Find the trailhead just before you reach the gatehouse at the park entrance, off a small gravel parking lot to the right. You'll often spot a horse trailer or two parked here, as the trails are open not only to hikers but also to equestrians.

DISTANCE & CONFIGURATION: 6-mile out-and-back

DIFFICULTY: Easy

SCENERY: Lake views, woodlands

EXPOSURE: Partially shady–sunny

TRAFFIC: Moderate

TRAIL SURFACE: Packed dirt

HIKING TIME: 1 hour

DRIVING DISTANCE: 12 miles from I-20 and I-35W

ACCESS: Daily, sunrise–sunset; free

MAP: www.swf-wc.usace.army.mil/benbrook /Information/Maps.asp

WHEELCHAIR TRAVERSABLE: No

FACILITIES: None

CONTACT: 817-292-2400, www.swf-wc.usace .army.mil

LOCATION: Rocky Creek Park Rd. at Benbrook Lake in Crowley

COMMENTS: This hike can easily be extended for many miles. Bring binoculars, sunscreen, and plenty of water, and spend the whole day exploring.

Before you start your hike, decide how long you want to be out, and plan your water and food needs accordingly. This hike covers only 3 miles of the Benbrook Lake Trail, but if you're interested in something a little lengthier, you can simply continue on at the turnaround point. The total trail length is about 10 miles.

Pick up the trail on the far side of the parking lot. At the first junction bear right, following the trail past the edge of fenced property lines, through tall grasses, and toward the lake.

At about 0.6 mile into the hike, the trail joins a slightly overgrown road—an indication that you've entered the outskirts of the park. To the left, the waters of Benbrook Lake welcome you. But don't stop to enjoy the view just yet: at 0.9 mile you'll reach a bench positioned by the Boy Scouts as a place to rest. Take in the views; search for gulls, pelicans, or cormorants; and enjoy the cooling breeze.

When you're ready, continue down the road and pick up the trail a couple hundred feet down, where it parallels the road along a grassy bank that yields pleasant lake views along the way. You're likely to pass not only the occasional hiker but also the occasional equestrian—horseback riders favor the trail because of its length and location.

At 1 mile and 1.13 miles, you'll cross roads before leaving civilization and heading back into the brush, where the flatness of the trail starts to give way to a few small hills. Pass plenty of cactus (particularly beautiful in the spring), a creek crossing, and a few trail markers before you reach a horse watering hole at 1.6 miles. Views of the lake persist until the trail curves out of the sun and into a thick grove of trees. When you reach an old sign labeled PIER ONE, you're about 2.1 miles into the hike. In this area you'll stand a good chance of spotting wildlife: on a recent hike, I heard a rustling in the trees and sudden movement in the woods, which manifested as a couple of huge white-tailed deer. Upon realizing they'd been spotted, they bolted quickly out of view, only to reappear farther down the trail. Birders may be rewarded with sightings of painted buntings or, for the especially lucky, the Rio Grande turkey,

Benbrook Lake Trail

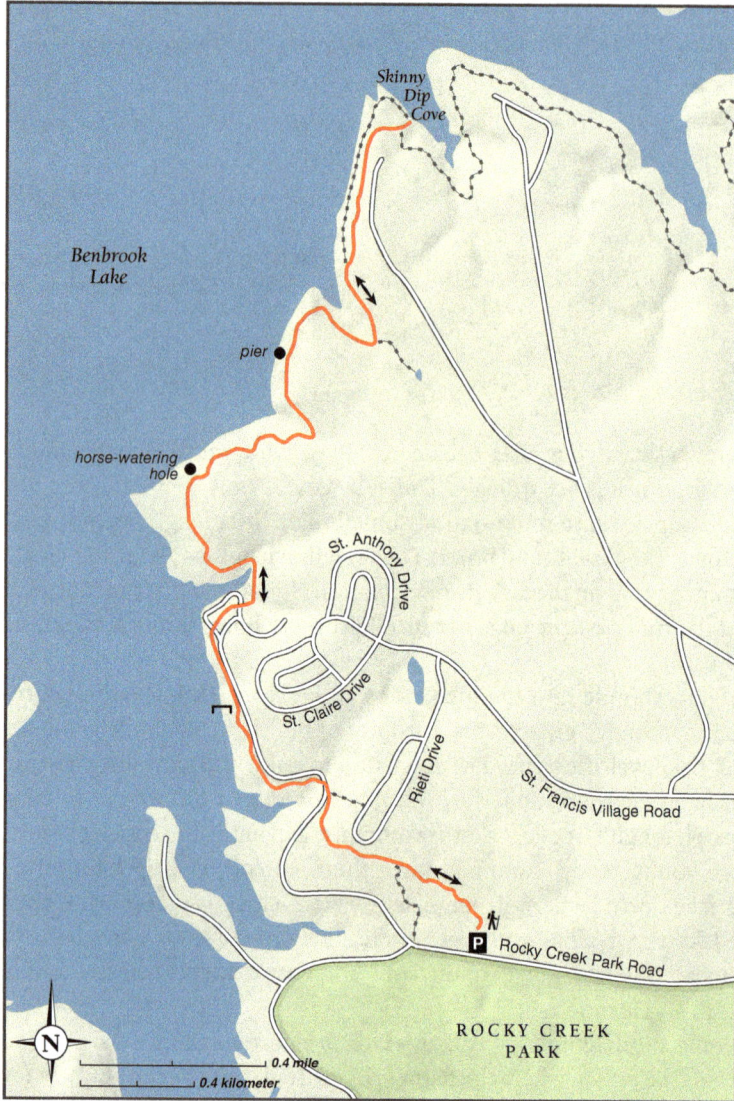

which, according to the Texas Parks and Wildlife Department, can sometimes be spotted in this area very early in the morning.

At 2.5 miles, go left over a small brook, then left again at the next trail intersection. The trail winds back toward the lake and Skinny Dip Cove, an intriguing name for a spot known as a horse-watering hole. Follow the trail another 150 feet toward the small cove, where the lake waters lap onto an intimate, rocky beach area. This is an ideal place to stop and enjoy lunch, after which you can examine the fossils embedded in the rocky bank or simply spend some time watching fishing boats float quietly past you. When you're ready, retrace your steps to the trailhead or return to the Skinny Dip Cove junction and hike on. The trail continues about 7 more miles.

NEARBY ACTIVITIES

Adjacent to the trailhead, Rocky Creek Park (817-346-2199, www.swf-wc.usace .army.mil/benbrook/Recreation/Parks/Corpsparks.asp) provides primitive camping as well as opportunities for picnicking, fishing, and swimming. The admission fee is $3 per car for day-use activities and $10 per night for tent camping.

• •

GPS TRAILHEAD COORDINATES N32° 36.400' W97° 27.033'

DIRECTIONS The trailhead is just outside Rocky Creek Park on Benbrook Lake. From I-35W south of Fort Worth, take I-20 W to Exit 434A onto Granbury Road; turn left (southwest) on Granbury. Turn right onto Sycamore School Road, which becomes Columbus Trail then Old Granbury Road. Continue on Rocky Creek Park Road to the park entrance.

Hikers share the trail with equestrians.

15 EAGLE MOUNTAIN PARK TRAIL

After a rigorous hike, you're rewarded with spectacular views of Eagle Mountain Lake.

A SUNNY DAY draws adventure seekers to Eagle Mountain Park like moths to a flame—and for good reason! Miles of trails suitable for everyone, lake views, and varied terrain make this park a hiking must.

DESCRIPTION

Sitting on the eastern shores of Eagle Mountain Lake, Eagle Mountain Park encompasses 400 acres of ruggedly beautiful North Texas habitat. Although the land was originally acquired in the 1980s and conceptualized as a possible location for a state park, decades passed with no further action. Eventually, the land caught the attention of conservationists, who worked to preserve the area as a local park; it opened to the public in April 2008. The lake, an impoundment of the West Fork of the Trinity River, is popular as a boating and fishing destination. A number of marinas sit on its banks.

On any given weekend, the generously sized parking lot is likely to be nearly full—this is a popular park with lots of natural beauty, and locals throughout the metroplex tend to return once they find out about it. Don't let the crowds scare you, though. You can expect to see hikers all along the route, but the bottleneck you might encounter in the parking lot quickly thins. Trails are plentiful and varied enough that visitors are spread reasonably throughout the park. Arriving early or on a weekend can help you avoid the crowds that build up later in the day.

DISTANCE & CONFIGURATION:
4.8-mile balloon

DIFFICULTY: Moderate, with some strenuous sections

SCENERY: Panoramic lake views

EXPOSURE: Sunny–shady

TRAFFIC: Heavy on weekends

TRAIL SURFACE: Packed dirt

HIKING TIME: 3 hours

DRIVING DISTANCE: 12 miles from Business US 287 and I-820

ACCESS: Daily; gates close 30 minutes after sunset; free

MAP: trwd.com/wp-content/uploads/eagle-mountain-park.pdf

WHEELCHAIR TRAVERSABLE: No, but the park has a separate 0.24-mile wheelchair-accessible trail.

FACILITIES: Portable toilets, covered picnic tables, water fountains

CONTACT: trwd.com/contact-trwd

LOCATION: 11601 Morris Dido Newark Rd., Fort Worth

COMMENTS: A hiking stick is useful on the rockier uphill sections of the trail.

The trailhead is a welcoming feature of the park, replete with interpretative signage, a covered patio dedicated to picnic tables, and a detailed trail map. In addition, adjacent to the trailhead you'll find what remains of an old farm that used to operate on the land that the park is on. You'll want to start or end your hike by exploring the preserved farm buildings, which include a windmill, a water tank, an old barn, and an outhouse. Interpretive signage explains that the windmill and barn date back to 1938. At that time, wealthy Fort Worth businessman Kay Kimbell owned the land. Interestingly, Kimbell was also an art patron who established the Kimbell Art Foundation, which runs the internationally renowned Kimbell Art Museum in nearby Fort Worth.

Orient yourself at the trail map adjacent to the picnic area. The hike I've outlined here will take you down the Main Park Trail then connect to the South Overlook Trail. From there, you will connect to the Shoreline Trail before rejoining the Main Park Trail on your return to the trailhead. This route will ensure you get the best out of the park's trails and has something to delight every hiker.

From the map kiosk, you'll start by heading south down the wide gravel path that marks the entrance to the Main Park Trail. Stay left (south) at the first two junctures, following the trail as it winds past cacti and scrub brush. Through the trees to the east, you'll hear the faint sounds of Farm to Market Road 1220/Morris Dido Newark Road.

Approximately 0.25 mile into the hike, you'll reach a juncture where you'll head west (the other path dead-ends at a maintenance road). The sounds of civilization soon disappear, to be replaced by the chirping of birds and a soft breeze in your ears.

The trail will become somewhat rugged as you make your way down a rocky hillside. At 0.4 mile you'll reach an outcrop that serves as a makeshift overlook where you can catch your breath. From here, the trail continues its rough and rugged route with a few steeper sections.

Eagle Mountain Park Trail

Morris Dido Newark Road

old farm buildings

Eagle Mountain Lake

EAGLE MOUNTAIN PARK

MP	Main Park Trail
NT	Northwest Trail
OT	Overlook Trail
RL	Ridge Loop Trail
ST	Shoreline Trail
SO	South Overlook Trail

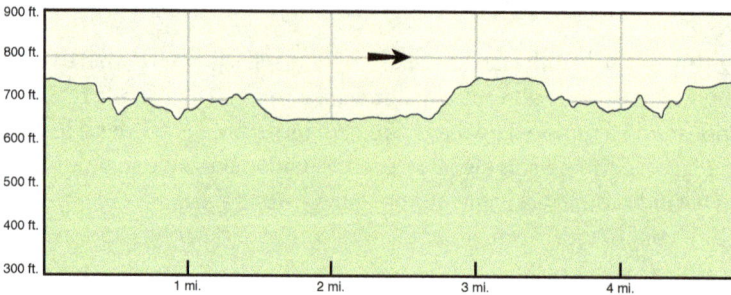

N

0.3 mile
0.3 kilometer

900 ft.
800 ft.
700 ft.
600 ft.
500 ft.
400 ft.
300 ft.

1 mi.   2 mi.   3 mi.   4 mi.

Persevere, and at 0.85 mile you'll find a trail map with a nearby bench where you can reorient and refresh yourself. The trail splits at this point. Turning right (west) will take you to the lakeshore, where you will catch your first glimpse of the lake. To continue, you'll want to head south (left), past the bench and back onto the sun-drenched trail. An additional 0.42 mile will take you past another bench and to the next trail map, where the trail splits. This is where the Shoreline Trail and the Main Park Trail meet. Head southwest (left) to continue on the Main Park Trail. After hiking 0.12 mile more, you'll reach another map and trail juncture. This is the spot where the South Overlook Trail and the Main Park Trail join. You'll continue by heading onto the South Overlook Trail to the southeast (left).

At this point, you may be starting to tire from the uphill trek. Continue another 0.5 mile to reap your reward: a spectacular overlook onto the lake down below. A bench and perfectly positioned picnic tables provide a shaded spot to have lunch and take in the cool breeze and inspiring views.

When you're ready, continue onto the trail. A hundred feet from the overlook, a map signals that the trail heads downhill and becomes the Shoreline Trail. The short trek will bring you parallel with the lake's shoreline. Dense tree coverage in this section canopies the trail and obscures the water. You'll pass a picnic table nestled in the trees, offering another opportunity to break for a snack.

Eventually, 0.75 mile from the last trail map, you'll reach another juncture and map noting that this is where the Main Park Trail and the Shoreline Trail meet. Head north (left) on the Shoreline Trail. You'll pass a couple of scenic spots overlooking the lake. The trail traverses the shoreline then rejoins the Main Park Trail, completing the Overlook/Shoreline Loop. Head east, retracing your steps to the trailhead.

NEARBY ACTIVITIES

Also on Eagle Mountain Lake, just 11 miles south, Twin Points Park is open from Memorial Day Weekend through Labor Day and offers a sandy swimming beach along with a swim platform, picnic pavilions, and barbecue pits. Admission is $20 per carload Friday–Sunday and holidays, and $10 on all other days. To get there, take Morris Dido Newark Road south until it becomes Boat Club Road. Turn right, heading west onto Robertson Road, and then take another right onto Ten Mile Bridge Road. The park is located at 10200 Ten Mile Bridge Road.

If you're up for more hiking, you can also check out the Fort Worth Nature Center and Refuge, just 15 miles to the south at 9601 Fossil Ridge Road. The nature center has more than 20 miles of hiking trails, a Bison Range, and water access for your canoe or kayak. It also offers monthly canoe tours down the West Fork of the Trinity River, along with a monthly canoe fest—for a small fee, you're provided with canoes, paddles, and life jackets and can float around Greer Island. Check fwnaturecenter.org for a calendar of events and fees.

· ·

GPS TRAILHEAD COORDINATES N32° 56.115' W97° 28.827'

DIRECTIONS From Dallas, take I-30 W to I-820 N to I-35W heading north. Take Exit 60 to US 287/US 81 N. Exit onto West Bonds Ranch Road. After 3 miles, turn right (north) on Business US 287. In 1 mile, turn left on East Peden Road. In 3.6 miles you'll reach Morris Dido Newark Road, where you'll turn right (north). The park is immediately on your left.

From Fort Worth, head north on Business US 287/South Saginaw Boulevard. Turn left (west) onto East Peden Road. In 3.6 miles you'll reach Morris Dido Newark Road, where you'll turn right (north). The park is immediately on your left.

The park is easily identifiable by a towering windmill visible on approach.

16 FORT WORTH NATURE CENTER:
Canyon Ridge Trail

Early-morning hikers are rewarded with a sunrise that's not to be missed.

THIS RIGOROUS TRAIL climbs into the hills, winds through massive patches of yuccas, and provides scenic views of Lake Worth before descending back to lake level. Deer are abundant on this trail.

DESCRIPTION

One of the best places in the metroplex to spot wildlife while hiking is on a trail at the Fort Worth Nature Center and Refuge. The center's sprawling 3,600 acres make up one of the largest city-owned nature centers in the country and include miles of hiking trails covering a range of habitats, including woodlands, grasslands, and wetlands.

With such a wide range of habitats, it should come as no surprise that the area is abundantly full of wildlife, and visitors are almost guaranteed an animal sighting. If you don't spot something on the trail, you're almost certain to catch sight of something in the enclosed bison range, in the field housing the well-established prairie dog population, or on the boardwalk.

Although wildlife can be spotted at any time, you'll have a particularly good chance if you arrive early in the morning. Hikers have encountered everything from white-tailed deer, wild turkeys, rabbits, opossums, raccoons, and bobcats to alligators.

DISTANCE & CONFIGURATION: 4.71-mile loop

DIFFICULTY: Strenuous

SCENERY: Woodlands, canyon views, yucca

EXPOSURE: Partially shady–sunny

TRAFFIC: Light

TRAIL SURFACE: Dirt

HIKING TIME: 2.5 hours

DRIVING DISTANCE: 3.5 miles from Jacksboro Hwy. and I-820

ACCESS: May–September, Monday–Friday, 7 a.m.–5 p.m., and Saturday–Sunday, 7 a.m.–7 p.m.; October–April, daily, 8 a.m.–5 p.m.; $5 adults, $2 children ages 3–12, free for kids under age 3, $3 seniors 65 and older. Hardwicke Interpretive

Center: Daily, 9 a.m.–4:30 p.m.; $1 discount for active/retired military (show military ID)

MAP: fwnaturecenter.org/trails

WHEELCHAIR TRAVERSABLE: No

FACILITIES: Restrooms, water fountains, picnic tables

CONTACT: 817-392-7410, fwnaturecenter.org

LOCATION: 7551 North Shore Dr., Fort Worth

COMMENTS: Bring repellent for spiders, gnats, and other flying insects. Pets are welcome but must be leashed. Because bicycles are prohibited on the trails, many cyclists take advantage of the slow and sparse traffic on the nature center's roads to ride around.

More-obscure sightings include the Lake Worth Monster—a tall, hairy, half-man, half-goat creature last seen on the lake in 1969 but still celebrated by the nature center.

There's enough variety in the center's trails to appeal to anyone. Hikes climb the hillsides, which offer pretty views, or meander along the river bottom. Of the many hikes worth trying, I've selected two that will give you a good introduction to the nature center. (To explore the entire center, though, you'll need more than one visit.)

The center charges a small entrance fee, which goes toward improvements. In exchange for your fee, you'll receive a map of the park, which is worth a review, especially if you plan on visiting the Hardwicke Interpretive Center (in the middle of the nature center) or driving by the bison range. Water fountains, picnic areas, and restrooms can be found at the interpretive center.

To get to the trailhead from the entrance booth, take a right at the first intersection and another right at the next intersection. The road ends 1 mile down, at a small parking area—the trailhead is on the southwest side of the lot. The trail heads steeply uphill and is marked with the Canyon Ridge Trail insignia: a picture of a flowering yucca. Your map has a key to help you identify the other trail signs.

The first part of this hike takes you gradually uphill. Stairs worked into the hillside at the steep points make this a fairly easy climb. The trail continues up wooded hillsides and over some wooden bridges. As you gain altitude, look to your right for views of Lake Worth, which the nature center abuts. The trail runs fairly parallel to the road in this section, and you'll catch glimpses of it to your right before the path veers away from the road and enters a section of towering trees. At 0.73 mile, reach a long staircase built into a towering hill. From here, the trail winds through the hilltops after circumventing a couple of fields overtaken by hundreds of yucca. Overlooks at 0.83 mile and 0.98 mile offer vistas of Lake Worth and Greer Island below.

Fort Worth Nature Center: Canyon Ridge Trail

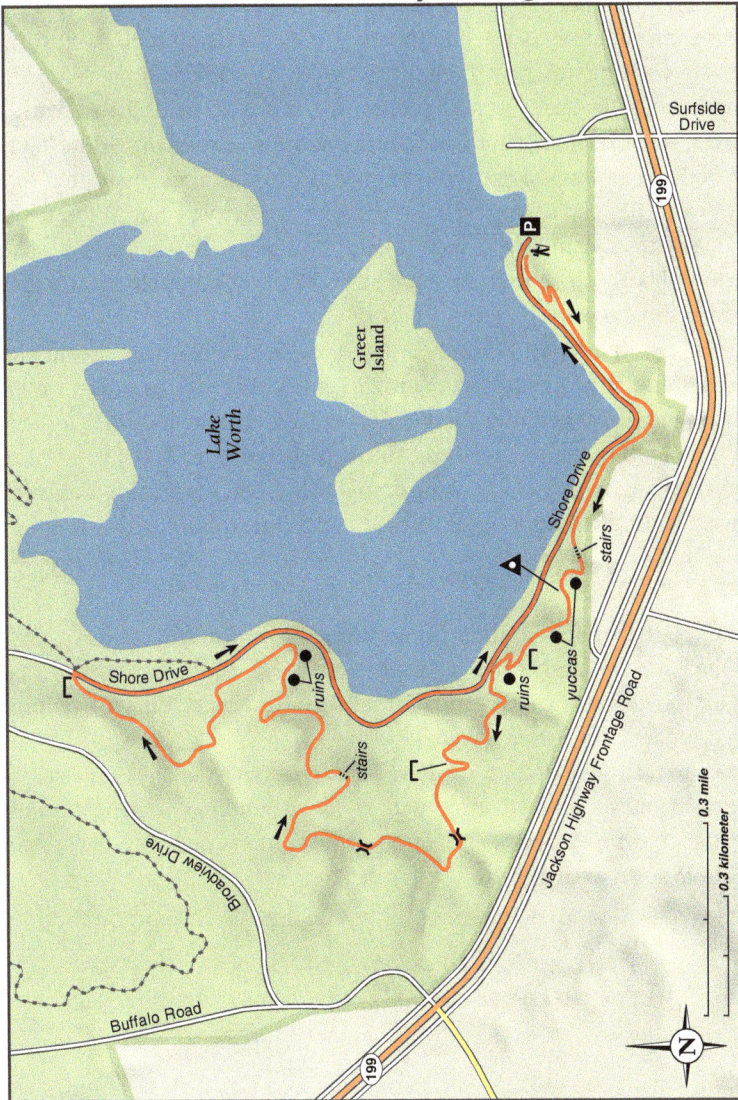

At 1.08 miles, the trail splits. To your left, note the dilapidated remnants of an old bathroom. If you decide to explore, look out for spiders hanging from its entryway and corners. Ruins such as these, left over from work done in the area by the Civilian Conservation Corps, can be found all along the trail.

The rocky trail climbs a little more through the wooded hillside and, at 1.4 miles, reaches a bench positioned to overlook the canyon—a nice spot to take a break. If you like to hike early in the day, be aware that the webs of orb-weaving spiders sometimes span the trail in this section. The large spiders sitting in the center of the webs can be intimidating to arachnophobes. Carry a walking stick to clear the path. Alternatively, consider hiking later in the day after other hikers have cleared the trail.

Continuing, the trail passes through a couple of fields filled with purple wildflowers—an excellent spot for sighting some of the many white-tailed deer that live here. I came upon a couple of groups of them that I was able to admire before they saw me and scampered out of sight. On my way out of the nature center, I spoke with a visitor who was equally impressed by the deer he had seen, having spotted both a ten-point stag and an eight-point stag bolting into the woods elsewhere in the park.

The trail continues past a couple bridges and starts a gradual descent past more old building remnants, including one at 2.61 miles that affords a beautiful view of Lake Worth. Just after the ruins, there are stairs built into the hillside. Descend these and you'll quickly spot the park road through the woods. At 3.11 miles, the trail intersects the road, then picks back up across the street, continuing as Riverbottom Trail. For this hike, turn right onto the road and follow it back to the trailhead.

NEARBY ACTIVITIES

The nature center offers monthly canoe tours down the West Fork of the Trinity River, along with a monthly canoe fest—for a small fee, you're provided with canoes, paddles, and life jackets and can float around Greer Island. Check fwnaturecenter .org for a calendar of events and fees.

Year-round, stop by downtown Fort Worth to visit Sundance Square, the city's entertainment and shopping district, with restored buildings housing museums, galleries, gift shops, and a diverse selection of restaurants covering everything from sandwiches to sushi to steaks.

• •

GPS TRAILHEAD COORDINATES N32° 49.467' W97° 27.583'

DIRECTIONS Take Loop I-820 to Jacksboro Highway (TX 199). Go 4 miles west and exit at Confederate Park Road. Go about 0.5 mile and turn right onto Buffalo Road to reach the entrance to the Fort Worth Nature Center and Refuge. From the entrance, take a right at the first two forks to get to the trailhead. The road ends at the trailhead parking lot.

Bring a sense of adventure and binoculars, for hidden among the grasses and trees, wildlife abounds.

CHILDREN WILL LOVE this flat trail that winds alongside a bison range and prairie dog town, then through a wide prairie with excellent wildlife viewing.

DESCRIPTION

From the entrance, get to the trailhead by turning left at the first fork in the road. About 1 mile down, you'll see a small parking lot on the right with a BISON RANGE sign; a smaller sign next to it announces PRAIRIE DOG TOWN. The trailhead is to the right of the signs. A fenced-in prairie adjacent to the trailhead keeps the bison and prairie dogs separated from hikers so they can be viewed from a safe distance.

If you look closely at the prairie, you'll spot dozens of dirt mounds, marking prairie dog burrows. These rodents can be difficult to spot at first because their fur is close to the color of the dirt. Look for them by their burrows—you'll see them bobbing up and down—and listen for their barks, which alert the colony to predators.

You may or may not see the other prairie resident—the bison—in this area; the bison range is actually quite large, and the animals have a lot of space in which to

DISTANCE & CONFIGURATION: 1-mile loop

DIFFICULTY: Easy

SCENERY: Prairies

EXPOSURE: Sunny

TRAFFIC: Moderate

TRAIL SURFACE: Packed dirt

HIKING TIME: 25 minutes

DRIVING DISTANCE: 3.5 miles from Jacksboro Hwy. and I-820

ACCESS: May–September, Monday–Friday, 7 a.m.–5 p.m.; Saturday–Sunday, 7 a.m.–7 p.m.; October–April, daily, 8 a.m.–5 p.m. $5 adults, $2 children ages 3–12, free for kids under age 3, $3 seniors age 65 and older; Hardwicke Interpretive Center: Daily, 9 a.m.–4:30 p.m.;

$1 discount for active/retired military (show military ID)

MAP: fwnaturecenter.org/trails

WHEELCHAIR TRAVERSABLE: No

FACILITIES: Restrooms, water fountains, picnic tables

CONTACT: 817-392-7410, fwnaturecenter.org

LOCATION: 9601 Fossil Ridge Rd., Fort Worth

COMMENTS: This is a sun-drenched trail, so be sure to bring sunscreen and water. Binoculars are also useful because the prairie dogs are small and stay a few hundred feet behind a fence. Pets are allowed but must be leashed. Because bicycles are prohibited on the trails, many cyclists take advantage of the slow and sparse traffic on the nature center's roads.

roam. Benches along the trail face the fence, offering a nice spot to linger while looking for wildlife. I stopped at various points along the fence, waiting with high hopes for even a single sighting, but the prairie dogs seemed to have taken over the entire prairie and there was not a single bison to be seen. I did not, however, leave the park disappointed—as we drove away from the trailhead, I spotted a whole herd roaming another section of their range, within a dozen feet of a fenced enclosure alongside the park road. Park staff at the interpretive center or the gate entrance can often tell you where the herd is.

The trail follows the fence east. At about 400 feet, bear left (north), away from the bison range and through some brush. Keep an eye out for the variety of birds that migrate through the refuge. The Fort Worth Audubon Society lists the refuge as good for bird-watching and notes that in the summer you'll find a variety of hummingbirds, whereas in winter sightings include the yellow-bellied sapsucker, purple finch, and blue warbler.

At 0.25 mile, the trail crosses a grassy maintenance road and continues northeast into a huge, sunny prairie filled with tall grasses and small red and purple flowers. This is a good spot for sighting some of the many white-tailed deer that live here. The prairie buzzes with the pleasant hum of grasshoppers, crickets, and the occasional flying insect, so it's a good idea to apply insect repellent before your hike.

Reach a split at 0.45 mile. Bear right to loop back south through the prairie. Heading left would take you to the Hardwicke Interpretive Center, which has refuge information and exhibits, including a reclusive bobcat that can sometimes be seen in his outdoor enclosure. The center is also adjacent to an interesting short trail along a fossil-shell outcrop.

Fort Worth Nature Trail: Prairie Trail

CT Caprock Trail
DM Deer Mouse Trail
LL Limestone Ledge Trail
OM Oak Motte Trail
PT Prairie Trail
RT Riverbottom Trail
WP Wild Plum Trail

Lake Worth

Shoreline Drive

Hardwicke Interpretive Center

FORT WORTH NATURE CENTER AND REFUGE

Shoreline Drive

Buffalo Road

Fossil Ridge Road

prairie dog town

Buffalo Road

To 199

bison range

N

0.1 mile
0.1 kilometer

Continue straight, following the trail until you reach the bison range again at 0.7 mile; turn left. The trail splits again at 0.9 mile. Following the left trail takes you alongside the bison range another 500 feet until you're back at the trailhead. On my visit, I noticed that at least one trail in this area had been blocked off and marked with an EARTH HEALING sign—encourage children to stay on the trails to minimize visitor impact to the refuge.

NEARBY ACTIVITIES

The nature center offers monthly canoe tours down the West Fork of the Trinity River, along with a monthly canoe fest—for a small fee, you're provided with canoes, paddles, and life jackets and can float around Greer Island. Check fwnaturecenter .org for a calendar of events and fees.

Year-round, stop by downtown Fort Worth to visit Sundance Square, the city's entertainment and shopping district, with restored buildings housing museums, galleries, gift shops, and a diverse selection of restaurants covering everything from sandwiches to sushi to steaks.

• •

GPS TRAILHEAD COORDINATES N32° 50.500' W97° 28.700'

DIRECTIONS Take Loop I-820 to Jacksboro Highway (TX 199). Go 4 miles west and exit at Confederate Park Road. Go about 0.5 mile and turn right onto Buffalo Road to the entrance of the Fort Worth Nature Center and Refuge. From the entrance, bear left at the fork in the road to get to the trailhead; you'll see a parking area about 1 mile ahead on the right.

A local resident takes a break in the shade.

18 HORSESHOE TRAIL

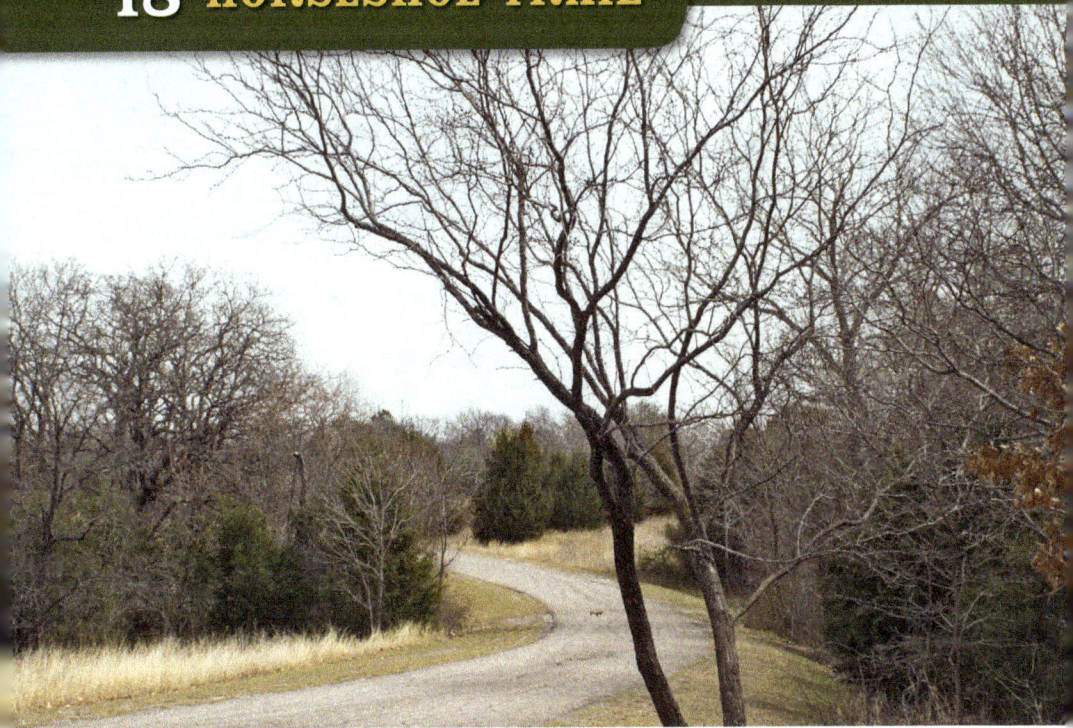

Don't let this photo fool you—the trail is hardly ever empty unless it's cold and overcast. The sunnier the day, the more people you'll find enjoying the trail with you.

POPULAR WITH LOCALS, Horseshoe Trail offers a lively hike along a paved path circling a small section of Lake Grapevine's southern edge. It is enjoyed by dog walkers, hikers, joggers, and bikers. You also have the opportunity to hike some dirt paths, if you're so inclined.

DESCRIPTION

Horseshoe Trail is inside Oak Grove Park, which sits on the southern shoreline of Grapevine Lake, very close to downtown Grapevine. When you enter the park, turn left at the park sign and park by the restrooms, a short drive down on the right.

The trailhead is on the pathway across the road from the restrooms. To your left, the paved pathway has a yellow stripe down its center; to your right, you'll see an old park road just beyond a gate blocking auto traffic. A marker adjacent to the gate identifies the road as Horseshoe Trail. Take a right here. Small brush and trees adjacent to the trail conceal the lake (which is off to the right) as you make your way southwest. Train your eyes upward for brilliant red cardinals.

This is not a trail for those looking to be alone with their thoughts—to the contrary, it's almost always bubbling with the infectious cheer of fellow outdoors sorts. Folks wave or smile as they pass by, giving you a few minutes alone before another

DISTANCE & CONFIGURATION:
4.08-mile out-and-back

DIFFICULTY: Easy

SCENERY: Lake, woods

EXPOSURE: Sunny

TRAFFIC: Heavy

TRAIL SURFACE: Paved

HIKING TIME: 1.5 hours

DRIVING DISTANCE: 6 miles from TX 121 S and TX 114 W

ACCESS: Daily; free

MAP: gograpevine.com/grapevine-trails

WHEELCHAIR TRAVERSABLE: Yes

FACILITIES: Restrooms, picnic tables, benches

CONTACT: 817-410-3450

LOCATION: Catfish Lane, Grapevine

COMMENTS: Dogs are welcome on this lively trail.

group passes by. Trail users include everyone from in-line skaters and bikers to dog walkers and joggers to those just looking to get outside. Unlike other trails, which can become popular with a certain niche, folks on this trail seem to include every age group. I've spotted every demographic, from young families out for the day to older couples out for a stroll to teenagers and 20-somethings out for some sun. Once I spotted a group of Boy Scouts marching happily along an adjacent path, following their Scoutmaster.

At regular intervals along the path, singletrack dirt trails veer off the road and disappear beneath the trees to the right. These trails loop out to the lake, providing a nice detour for those looking to explore the woods. If you miss a path, just keep walking and another one will appear soon enough. Many of the dirt trails you'll see to the left lead only to the back porches of local residents' houses.

The road curls southwest past more thickets and scrubby trees. At 0.55 mile, reach a junction with another park road, which is gated and inaccessible; keep straight. You'll come upon the intersection of Horseshoe Trail and Colt Drive 0.1 mile later. Near the intersection is a solitary bench. It may have served a purpose at some time, but it now sits almost inaccessible amid a small patch of grassland at the junction of two roads open only to foot traffic. Continue straight on Horseshoe Trail. A short trek later, come to a junction with Bronco Drive. Again, continue straight along the trail.

On the left, the backyards and back porches of houses abutting the trail spring into view. A short distance farther, reach another junction. At this point, the trail changes from old paved road to a narrower paved path with a yellow dividing line down its center. To the left, you'll see an alternate trailhead and parking lot with a plastic-bag dispenser for cleaning up after your dog. This is a busy access point, and the parking lot is often quite full. To the right, the trail continues northwest. Bear right and follow the trail downhill past much of the same scenery: trees and underbrush. The trail follows the shoreline, making its way around the end of the lake.

As you round a bend of the lake the foliage clears, and you find yourself sandwiched between a road to the left and the lake to your right. Thankfully, the roadway is slightly raised above the trail and mostly blocked from view, so you won't find the

Horseshoe Trail

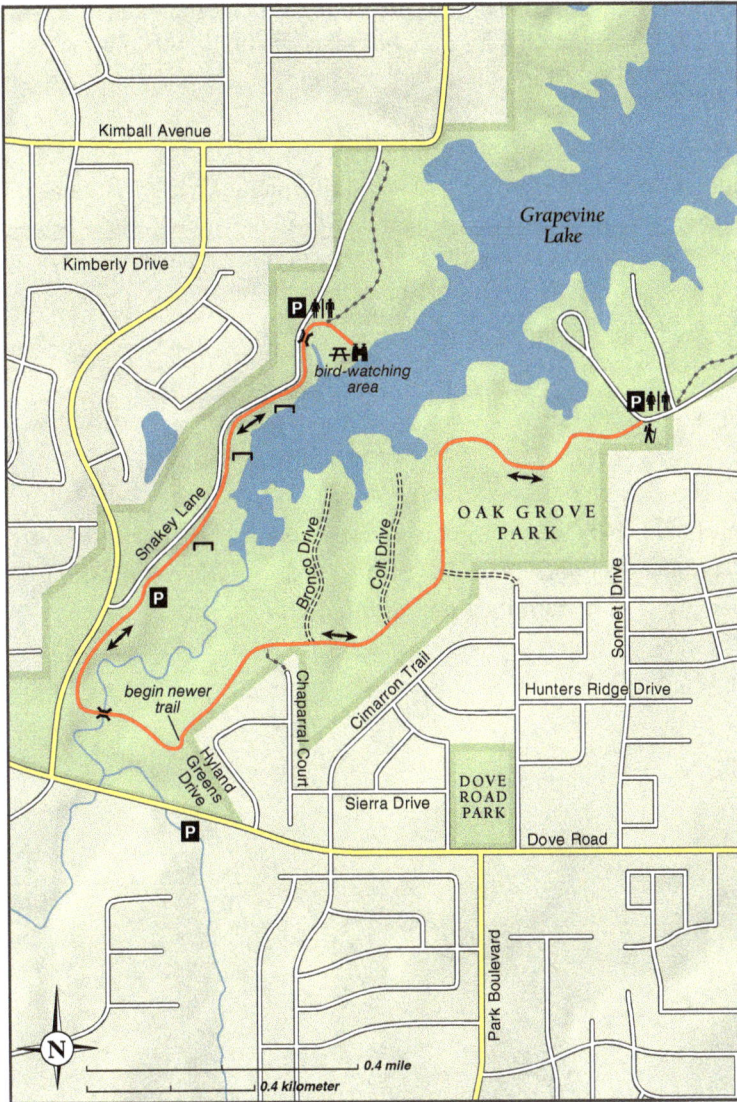

Kimball Avenue

Kimberly Drive

Grapevine Lake

bird-watching area

Snakey Lane

Bronco Drive

Colt Drive

OAK GROVE PARK

Sonnet Drive

begin newer trail

Chaparral Court

Cimarron Trail

Hunters Ridge Drive

Hyland Greens Drive

Sierra Drive

DOVE ROAD PARK

Dove Road

Park Boulevard

N

0.4 mile

0.4 kilometer

car traffic distracting. At 1.23 miles, cross a bridge. Just 0.25 mile farther, a parking lot on the left marks another trail entrance. To the right, you have a clear view of the end of the lake—a barren expanse of marshland. A sign adjacent to the trail indicates that this section is part of a Blue Bonnet Naturalization Eagle Scout Project.

At 1.93 miles, cross another bridge before reaching yet another parking area at 2 miles. Just beyond the lot and to the right, find a bird-watching area dotted with a few picnic tables. My favorite spot is at the back of the picnic area, where one table has been placed on the edge of the outcrop to overlook the lake. This is the perfect spot to have lunch and scan for herons and egrets in the shallow waters and along the sandy shore below. From here, turn back and retrace your steps to the trailhead.

NEARBY ACTIVITIES

Head into downtown Grapevine and take a ride on the Grapevine Vintage Railroad. The steam locomotive and open-air coaches head down the Cotton Belt Route into Stockyards Station in Fort Worth. The train runs only on the weekends; for schedules and fees, visit grapevinesteamrailroad.com. The depot is at 707 S. Main St. in Grapevine, just off Northwest Highway.

• •

GPS TRAILHEAD COORDINATES N32° 57.817' W97° 05.650'

DIRECTIONS From Dallas, take TX 114 W toward Grapevine and exit at TX 26/Business TX 114, turning right onto Texan Trail. From here, turn left onto Northwest Highway, pass Main Street, and turn right onto North Dove Road (which becomes Dove Loop Road), heading north into Oak Grove Park. Turn left onto Horseshoe Trail. Parking will be ahead on the right.

Miles of trail make this the perfect spot for a weekend hike.

19 KNOB HILLS TRAIL

In the spring, cacti and wildflowers bloom in force alongside the trail.

WEST OF GRAPEVINE LAKE, this pleasant trail roughly traces Denton Creek on a trek through impressive displays of local flora. A bench atop a wildflower-covered hill awaits you at its end.

DESCRIPTION

This unexpectedly scenic trail lies just west of Grapevine Lake. From the trailhead, the path makes a roundabout loop toward the lake. In the spring, when the cactus flowers are blooming and the hills are green and dotted with wildflowers, the trail inspires a sense of renewal.

Maintained by the Dallas Off-Road Bicycle Association (DORBA), this trail sees its fair share of mountain bikers, who love it for its initial steep, winding sections. Though bike traffic can be moderate on the weekends, bikers pass by quickly, intent on doing the full 13-mile-plus round-trip in an hour, which makes traffic feel much lighter. Because the trail is winding and some parts are also narrow, allowing for only single-file walking, you'll need to let others know bikers are approaching, especially if you're bringing kids. Yelling "Bike!" as a signal for everyone to step to the same side of the trail works best. The trail is closed when muddy, so if it has just rained, you'll have to pick another hike.

DISTANCE & CONFIGURATION: 6.96-mile out-and-back

DIFFICULTY: Moderate with some strenuous sections

SCENERY: Cactus, wildflowers, woods, hilly meadow

EXPOSURE: Mix of sun and shade

TRAFFIC: Moderate

TRAIL SURFACE: Packed dirt

HIKING TIME: 3 hours

DRIVING DISTANCE: 13 miles from I-35E/I-35W split

ACCESS: Daily, 6 a.m.–9 p.m. (closed when muddy); free

MAP: None

WHEELCHAIR TRAVERSABLE: No

FACILITIES: No restrooms or water

CONTACT: dorba.org

LOCATION: US 377 near Flower Mound

COMMENTS: The trail can take some time to dry out after a rainstorm, so check dorba.org /trail.php?t=16 before you visit to see if it is open.

The trailhead is almost adjacent to the highway, but within a couple hundred feet the sounds of cars are replaced by the chirping of birds as the trail curls away from the road and around some small hills. The hillsides on the first half of this trail are blanketed with hundreds of prickly pear cacti. In the spring, they bloom with large, beautiful yellow flowers, creating an impressive display. Even the remnants of an old abandoned road have been taken over by the wild-cactus garden.

The trail winds gently downhill into a small section of woods, where the path has a few short, steep drops—a favorite section of mountain bikers. On my hike, helmet fragments littered a portion of the trail, evidence that some unfortunate person had misjudged the roughness of this section. Although there are a couple of steep, slick spots, careful hikers will find these sections easily maneuverable. The most difficult spot—a neck-breaking, clifflike drop of about 12 feet—has a gently sloping footpath encircling it. The trail soon crosses a small creek littered with horse apples (also known as hedge apples) from a nearby Osage orange tree. The path soon reaches a small opening in the brush overlooking the muddy, slow-moving waters of Denton Creek. Although the trail loosely follows the creek, this is the only glimpse of it you'll find on the hike.

From here, the trail's terrain quickly changes as you leave the woods and head into a sunny, flat section that leads through a large field of tall reeds. A little farther down the trail and just past the billowing, fluffy seed-clouds of a cottonwood tree, look for a large log, which marks the outbound midpoint and serves as an excellent place to take a break.

From here, the surrounding terrain changes yet again as the trail turns north through dense green foliage, where hundreds of delicate purple wildflowers do their best to flourish in patches of sun. If you listen beyond the cicadas, crickets, and birds, you're likely to hear the moos of nearby cows. As you emerge into an area open to the sky, the path soon changes from hard-packed brown dirt to packed red clay. Ahead, the trail curls through a rolling meadow dotted with Indian paintbrush and

Knob Hills Trail

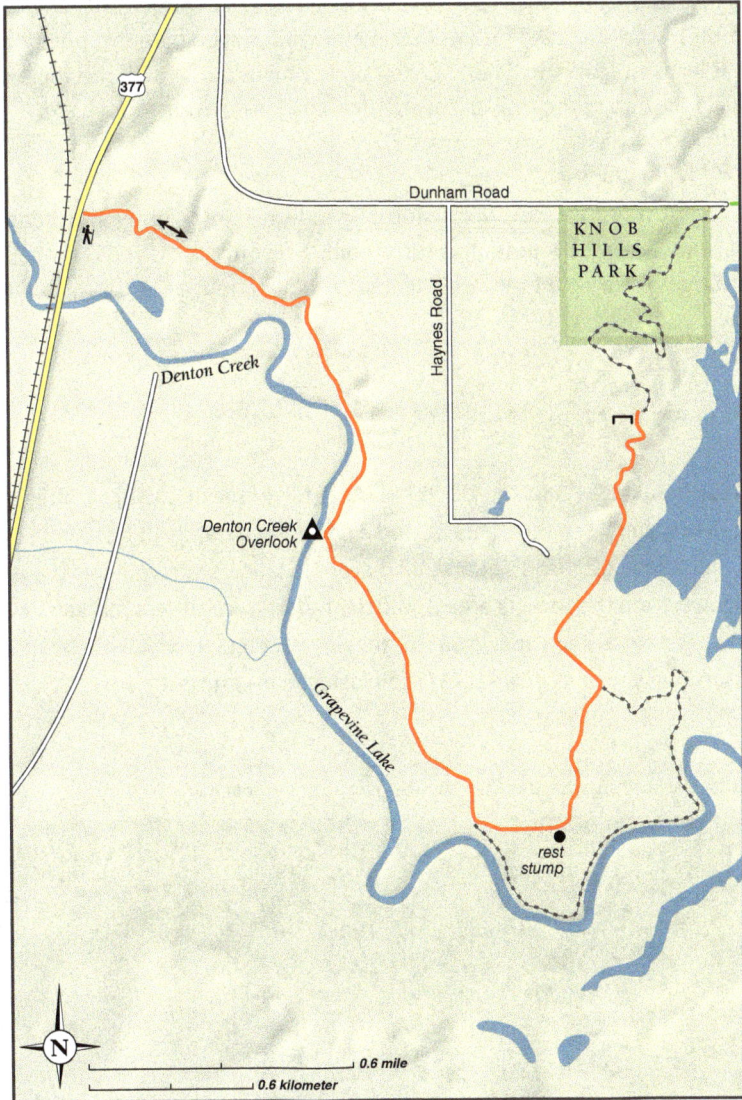

other wildflowers. The nearby mooing perfects the restful country feeling. Although I didn't see any cattle, I did see a couple of cow patties on the trail, so you may have company in the vicinity.

Where the path forks, choose the left branch for a longer walk; this spur winds around the hill before rejoining the main path. At the next fork, turn right to find a lonely bench surrounded by wildflowers atop a small hill. Take in the view before heading back.

To extend the hike, turn left at the previous fork. The trail winds downhill, continuing on toward the lake for another couple miles. The path eventually reaches a fork that leads to Dunham Trail. Staying on the main trail, you'll reach a bridge and eventually the end of the trail at Pocahontas Road, near Grapevine Lake.

NEARBY ACTIVITIES

If you're a NASCAR fan, the Texas Motor Speedway is just 6 miles away. For a schedule of events, visit texasmotorspeedway.com. Go south on US 377 about 1.2 miles and turn right onto TX 114 W. Go 3.8 miles and turn right on Allison Avenue.

• •

GPS TRAILHEAD COORDINATES N33° 02.683' W97° 12.433'

DIRECTIONS Take TX 114 W to US 377 N. About 1.3 miles down, just after you cross Denton Creek, you'll see the trailhead and a small dirt parking lot just off US 377 to the right. Don't let the trailhead's highway-adjacent location scare you: this is a secondary rural highway, and the parking area is sufficiently large and acceptably safe. When visiting for the first time, keep an eye out for the dirt parking lot, which often has at least a few cars in it—if you whiz down US 377 too fast, you may miss it.

Hikers enjoy the peaceful setting as they traverse the trail's narrow path.

Scenic lake views attract hikers to this popular trail.

NICE VIEWS FROM THE BLUFFS overlooking the lake dominate the first half of this hike. The second half is less busy because it twists and turns through the hardwood forest just out of view of the lake.

DESCRIPTION

Dammed in the 1950s, Grapevine Lake is a popular reservoir just north of Dallas–Fort Worth International Airport. The lake gets very busy on weekends with families who come to enjoy camping, boating, fishing, and picnicking, and miles of multiuse trails. Northshore Trail, certified as a National Recreation Trail in 1991, is one of the most popular trails on the lake and arguably the most popular in the area. A deserved favorite thanks to its accessibility, length, and scenic lake views, the trail sees a high volume of hikers, joggers, and bikers.

As its name indicates, the trail is on the north side of the lake in Rockledge Park. In years past, the trail was notorious for being incredibly crowded. More recently, the City of Grapevine began managing the park and started charging an admission fee. As a result, the massive number of visitors who once crowded the trailhead has decreased. On nice days, however, the small admission fee isn't much of a deterrent, so be prepared for plenty of company along the trail.

DISTANCE & CONFIGURATION: 8.96-mile out-and-back

DIFFICULTY: Easy–moderate

SCENERY: Lake views from bluffs, hardwood forest, birds

EXPOSURE: Mix of sun and shade

TRAFFIC: Heavy

TRAIL SURFACE: Packed dirt

HIKING TIME: 4.5 hours

DRIVING DISTANCE: 4.2 miles from I-635 and TX 121

ACCESS: (from Rockledge Park) Daily, 8 a.m.–sunset; $5 per vehicle, $1 per pedestrian or cyclist, $10 per vehicle on holiday weekends

MAP: tinyurl.com/northshoretrailmap

WHEELCHAIR TRAVERSABLE: No

FACILITIES: Restrooms, picnic area

CONTACT: dorba.org

LOCATION: 3600 Pilot Point, Grapevine

COMMENTS: Popular with mountain bikers and joggers in addition to hikers, this trail is especially busy on weekends and holidays.

The trailhead is tucked in the back corner of the parking lot. Immediately pass a small rock-strewn beach, which dog owners and amateur anglers scramble down to access the lake. Continue on the trail as it winds along the top of some small, rocky cliffs that hug the shoreline. On sunny days, watch for sailboats gliding past as they circle the lake.

The path then climbs uphill and meanders around some of the large rocks (which help give the park its name) before flattening and heading slightly away from the shoreline and among tall trees with an understory of dense brush. The path parallels the water slightly inland, offering occasional glimpses of the lake.

At the first two forks you encounter, go right. At the next fork, continue straight on the main trail. As you near the 1-mile mark, reach a long wooden bridge and then another junction, where you'll head right onto a wider trail. About 1.2 miles into the hike, gaze over the lake below at a scenic overlook at the top of a bluff. This spot is a good place to orient yourself. To the left, you'll see the 1,500-plus-room Gaylord Texan, a resort and convention center. The airport is also nearby, and though for the most part air traffic is not overly noticeable, you'll probably have already seen a plane or two approaching.

More interesting than airplanes, fossils have also been found nearby. Recent record heat has left the lake level substantially below normal, exposing million-year-old dinosaur tracks embedded in sandstone along the shoreline on this side of the lake. Unfortunately, visitors are prohibited from viewing the tracks because vandals destroyed a couple of them, prompting the lake's controlling authority, the Army Corps of Engineers, to block access and cover the tracks until the water levels rise enough to hide them again.

Continuing along the trail, head through grasslands and, at 1.6 miles, come to an old road. Cross the road and pick up the trail on the far side, continuing until you reach a clearing at about 1.8 miles. This area, which is virtually always empty, has a vacant parking lot and about a half-dozen old picnic tables tucked under the trees.

Northshore Trail

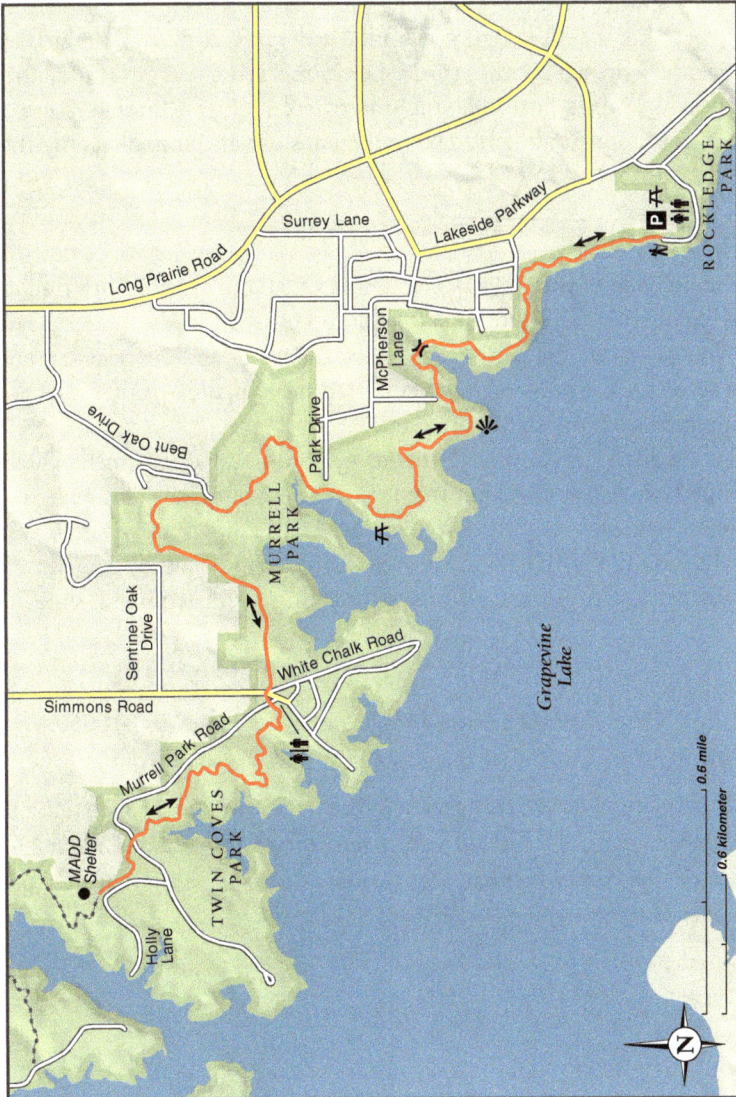

Probably attracted by the solitude, the birds here are loud and abundant. On my hike, I was able to spot only the most obvious—cardinals, whose telltale bright-red plumage makes them easy to pick out, and a vulture that slowly circled nearby. If you want to shorten this hike, this is a good spot to turn around.

Pick up the trail as it enters a patch of forest on the opposite side of the parking lot. At 2.2 miles, come to a small bridge and, shortly thereafter, cross an old gravel road. At 2.5 miles, reach another road where you'll hang a left, following the road until it deteriorates into a dirt path and then rejoins a paved road. When you reach a spot where the road forks, turn left and, at the next fork, at 3.1 miles, bear right. You'll eventually reach another road where you'll cross and pick up the trail on the opposite side. For the next mile, the trail twists and turns through the trees, more of a thrill for mountain bikers. The trail comes out at the trailhead by the MADD Shelter at Murrell Park.

NEARBY ACTIVITIES

After the first half of your hike, while you're still at the Murrell Park trailhead, walk over to the marina for a bite to eat at Little Pete's (littlepeteslakegrapevine.com), where you can sit on the patio overlooking the water and the boats and munch on comfort food such as burgers or chicken-fried steak. In the evenings, there's typically entertainment such as karaoke or poker.

The Gaylord Texan (marriott.com/gaylord-hotels/travel.mi), which sits on Grapevine Lake, is another fun place to stop after your hike. This huge resort has a 4.5-acre atrium, each section of which represents a different part of Texas. A short stroll takes you to the Hill Country, Palo Duro Canyon, and the San Antonio Riverwalk, where there are plenty of spots for grabbing a cold drink and some hot food.

• •

GPS TRAILHEAD COORDINATES N32° 58.967' W97° 04.060'

DIRECTIONS From I-635 W, take Exit 36B, Bass Pro Drive. Go 0.5 mile and turn left on Bass Pro, then go about 0.6 mile and turn left onto TX 26. Continue about 0.5 mile and turn right on Farm to Market Road 2499 (Fairway Drive). Cross the dam and turn left into Rockledge Park. Stay right; the road dead-ends at the parking lot.

21 RIVER LEGACY TRAIL

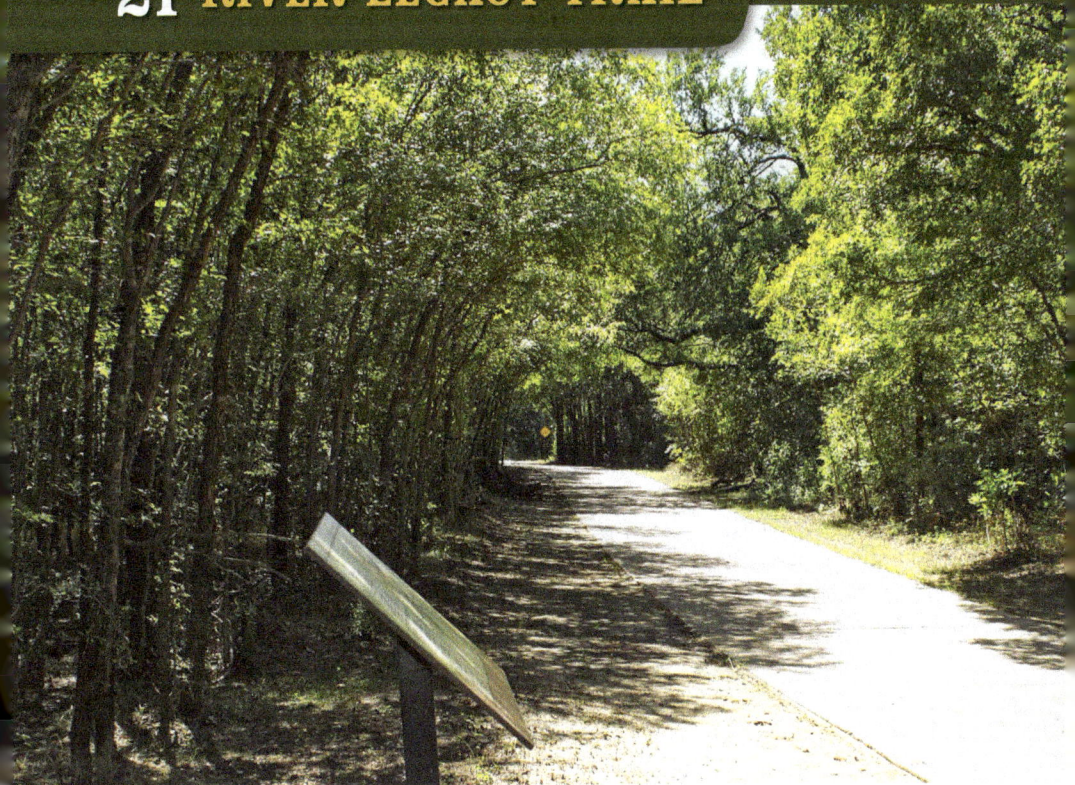

Early mornings are your best chance to have the trail to yourself, as it stays busy here.

THIS LENGTHY PAVED TRAIL stretches alongside the river, offering a few good overlooks for bird-watching.

DESCRIPTION

River Legacy Parks' 1,300 acres and 8 miles of trails are a popular attraction in Arlington, drawing hikers, bikers, joggers, and dog walkers. A few different access points to the parks' recreational trails help spread the visitors throughout. The parks' name originates from the River Legacy Foundation's vision of preserving a "living legacy for future generations."

Trail maps and park information are available a short drive from the trailhead at the River Legacy Living Science Center. The center's unique design was inspired by a children's fort built of sticks and leaves, a picture of which can be found at the center's website. According to the website, the center is not only designed to be part of its natural surroundings, but its construction included trees salvaged from a city project, and its maintenance relies on recycled gray water for landscaping. Another reason to stop by the center is its large exhibit hall and observation decks. A short trail winds through the grounds surrounding the center. To get to

DISTANCE & CONFIGURATION: 5.46-mile out-and-back

DIFFICULTY: Easy

SCENERY: Woods, river

EXPOSURE: Shady

TRAFFIC: Moderate–heavy

TRAIL SURFACE: Paved path

HIKING TIME: 1.5 hours

DRIVING DISTANCE: 4 miles from I-30 and TX 360

ACCESS: Daily, 5 a.m.–10 p.m.; free

MAP: tinyurl.com/riverlegacytrailmap

WHEELCHAIR TRAVERSABLE: Yes

FACILITIES: Water fountain, restrooms

CONTACT: 817-860-6752

LOCATION: 3020 N. Collins St., Arlington

COMMENTS: Presentations and festivals are among the events at the Living Science Center; check the calendar at riverlegacy.org.

the trailhead for this hike, however, you'll have to drive a few blocks to the lengthier paved sections of the parks.

The trailhead is adjacent to the parking lot. Head down the paved path toward the kiosk, which is adjacent to a water fountain and displays a huge aerial photo of the area. After getting oriented, head straight past the kiosk and turn right at the first junction onto the path with a dotted line down its center. Immediately come upon a wide bridge spanning the West Fork of the Trinity River. You're likely to find folks at its railings enjoying the relaxing views of its green, slow-moving waters.

The trail continues through the woods along the river. The route is mostly shaded, making it a good hike for a hot day. At 0.17 mile, bear right at the junction onto the path with a red-dotted stripe down its center.

A couple of interpretive signs along the trail provide information on local wildlife. You'll pass one of these signs on the left; it tells about raccoons: the small masked creatures, commonly associated with trash cans and late-night raids, are nocturnal animals that can often be found in hollowed-out tree trunks.

As you continue, you'll notice some smaller dirt trails heading toward the river. Some of these overlooks offer nice views of the river. Be careful not to step too close to the edge, which is slightly raised above the river. The banks easily erode and can cause you to slide right in. Farther down the trail, structured overlooks complete with benches offer safer viewing.

At 0.6 mile, reach another display on the left, describing a creature commonly found here: the wolf spider. These large brown spiders, which can grow to more than an inch long, are typically spotted scurrying along the ground as opposed to hanging in webs.

At 0.88 mile, reach a long wooden bridge across a narrow river. The path continues with woods on both sides until it forks at 0.92 mile; here, bear right onto a path with a blue line. In another couple hundred feet, come to another trail split. To the right, the trail terminates at a bench set alongside the river—a good spot for a quick break. The initials of two lovers are carved into a tall tree here.

River Legacy Trail

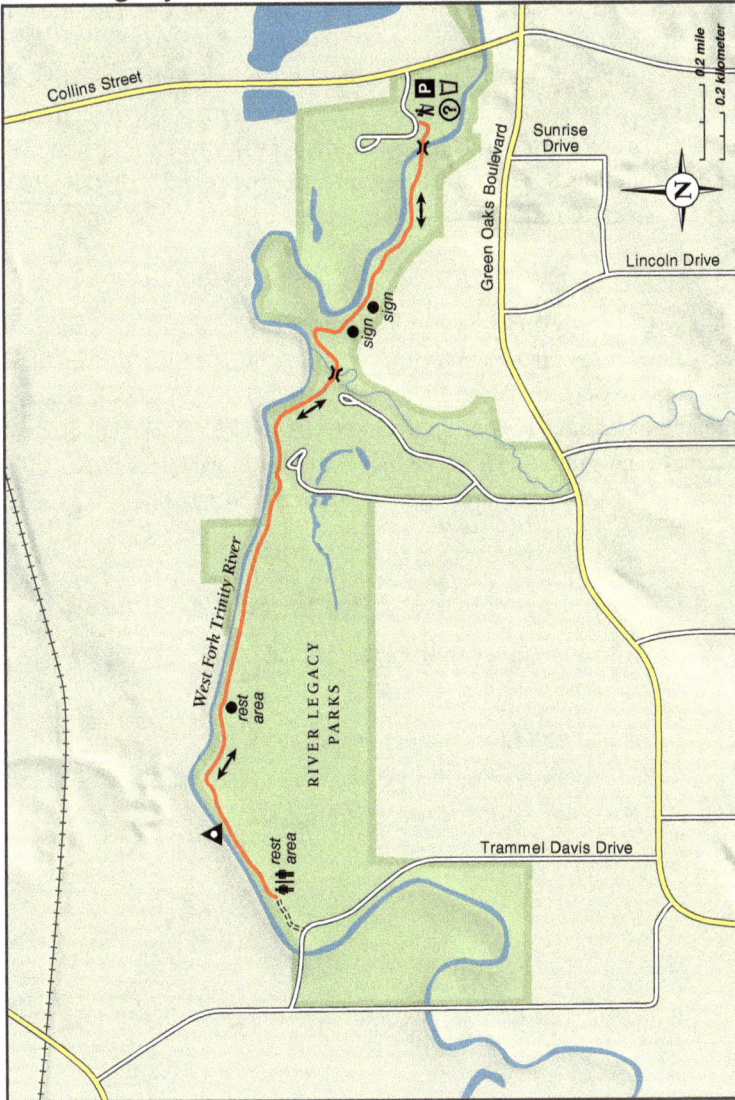

Collins Street

Green Oaks Boulevard

Sunrise Drive

Lincoln Drive

0.2 mile
0.2 kilometer

sign
sign

West Fork Trinity River

rest area

RIVER LEGACY PARKS

rest area

Trammel Davis Drive

When you've rested, continue on the path, staying to the right. The trail reaches a break in the trees, where, to the left, you'll see a large pavilion across a field. From here you'll pass a few more overlooks, which provide opportunities to scan for turtles and birds, before reaching 1.34 miles; at this point head right, following the yellow-striped path. The trail straightens here; among the few distractions are folks jogging with their dogs and others cruising on their bikes toward the end of the trail.

I was even passed by a fellow in his wheelchair, sailing along toward the turnaround just a little more than a mile down.

Pass a circular stone bench, to the right, at 1.82 miles, before reaching a wooden deck overlooking the river at 2.47 miles. The deck has high wooden railings, providing adequate cover for bird-watchers discreetly scoping the river. The trail continues another 0.26 mile to a dead end, where you'll find trees and a ring of seats. Retrace your steps to the trailhead.

NEARBY ACTIVITIES

Baseball fans will enjoy a visit to Ameriquest Field in Arlington, home of the Texas Rangers. Check texas.rangers.mlb.com for ticket information during baseball season. Year-round you can visit the Legends of the Game Museum, which is on the same site and has a huge collection from the National Baseball Hall of Fame. To get to the ballpark, go south on North Collins Street and turn left onto Northeast Green Oaks Boulevard. Continue 1.4 miles, then turn right onto Ballpark Way. The baseball stadium is 2 miles down.

• •

GPS TRAILHEAD COORDINATES N32° 47.333' W97° 05.933'

DIRECTIONS Follow I-30 toward Arlington, take Exit 28, and turn left onto Farm to Market Road 157. The entrance to River Legacy Parks is 0.6 mile down Collins Street on the left, at 3020 N. Collins. Park in the first parking area.

A peaceful view of Grapevine Lake beckons for a photograph.

THIS TREK DESCENDS a rocky hill and follows a wooded creek toward Grapevine Lake. When you near the lake, the path changes from dirt to soft sand as it leads onto the beach.

DESCRIPTION

This rocky trail is one of Grapevine Lake's less frequented paths, often overlooked in favor of other, more popular trails such as Northshore Trail (see page 101). Its small parking area—which holds maybe a half-dozen cars—is just off the shoulder of a secondary residential road and marked by nothing more than a small trail sign. If you're not paying attention, you're likely to drive past before you realize there's actually a trail here. You'll therefore be fairly surprised when you step onto the trail and discover a lovely tree-covered path following a creek. It's a great choice if you're looking for a winter hike; the cooler weather will allow you to spend as much time as you want beachcombing the long, sandy lakeshore at its end.

The trail heads east into a narrow, grassy, tree-covered strip of land sandwiched between private homes. The path parallels the boundary fence of a private driveway. After a few hundred feet, it starts to descend, becoming steep and rocky as it makes its way to a creek. If you have a hiking stick, bring it along—most of the trail is only slightly

DISTANCE & CONFIGURATION: 3.84-mile out-and-back

DIFFICULTY: A couple of rough patches in the beginning

SCENERY: Creek, woods, lake beach

EXPOSURE: Partially shady–sunny

TRAFFIC: Light

TRAIL SURFACE: Dirt, sand

HIKING TIME: 1.75 hours

DRIVING DISTANCE: 14 miles from I-35E and TX 121

ACCESS: Daily; free

MAP: tinyurl.com/rockypointtrailmap

WHEELCHAIR TRAVERSABLE: No

FACILITIES: None

CONTACT: 817-481-4541, www.swf-wc.usace .army.mil/grapevine/Recreation/Trails/Horse.asp

LOCATION: High Rd. and Sunnyview Lane, Flower Mound

COMMENTS: Bring a bag to carry the goodies you collect while beachcombing.

hilly, but you'll find the extra support useful for navigating the descent in this section, which, though short, is fairly steep, with rocks and roots making for uneven footing.

At 0.33 mile, come to the creek. Here the path splits, heading north toward Farm to Market Road 1171 and south toward the lake. Turn south (right). Lush green vegetation grows richly along the creek's banks, and unlike many streams, which stagnate in murky puddles, this one's waters flow briskly over the rocks, providing a pleasant gurgling backdrop for your hike. After a brief flat stretch, climb gently through wooded terrain, away from the creek. Bear right at the junction at 0.73 mile, and round a small pond decorated with bird boxes.

If you could see an aerial view of the trail, you'd realize that you're actually winding around the outskirts of a residential neighborhood on a small point that juts into the lake. Just after you pass the pond, you'll start to notice the backyards of some of these residences. They are, however, set amid wooded hilly lots and widely spaced; as a result, they don't feel overly obtrusive and are easily ignored. The trail curls back toward the creek—which by now has widened to the width of a river. It peeks in and out of view to your right and stays within sight the rest of the way to the lake.

You'll soon see Grapevine Lake ahead of you in the distance. The lake is popular, and if it's nice out you'll likely spot motorboats chugging to and from the more than half a dozen boat ramps along its shores. The trail progresses steadily toward the water, passing through a small stand of eastern red cedars, before emerging into the sun. To your left, huge houses sit atop a small hill, their backyards overlooking the lake.

With the lake only a short distance away, the trail becomes sandy and the trees fall back, leaving you in full sun. To your right, the river, which had been gradually widening, is now a couple hundred feet across. During droughts, the part nearest the lake dries out, forming a long, brown beach where the water should be. During my visit, the water was so low that an entire dock was stranded on the dry banks.

You'll soon reach a trail split; keep straight, heading up a short, rocky hill. A few hundred feet farther, reach a detour; going left will take you out to Rocky Point, whereas if you go right you'll reach the beach, where you can spend some time

Rocky Point Trail

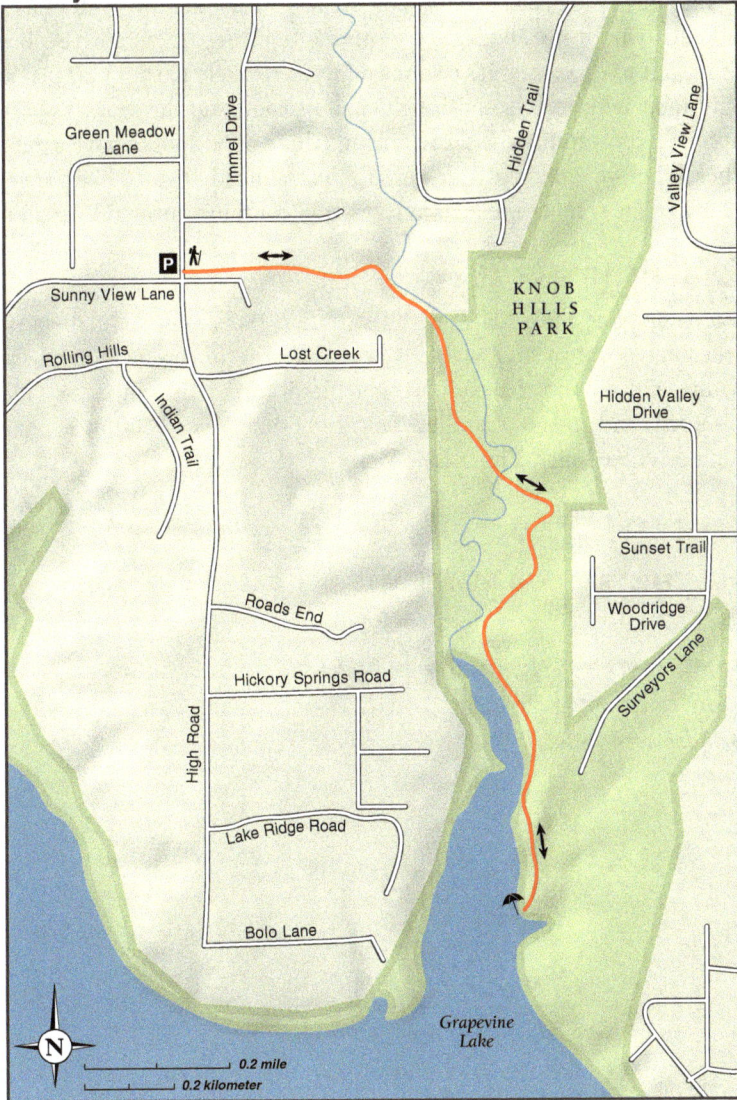

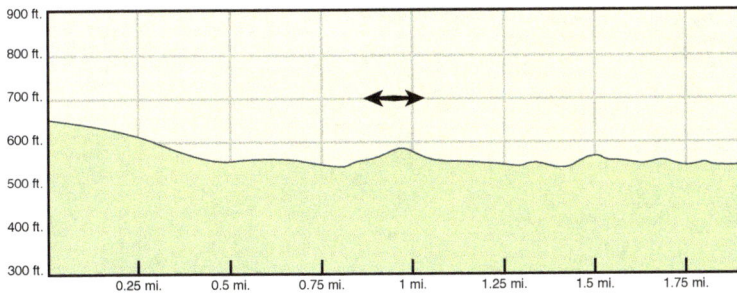

Green Meadow Lane

Immel Drive

Hidden Trail

Valley View Lane

KNOB
HILLS
PARK

Sunny View Lane

Lost Creek

Rolling Hills

Indian Trail

Hidden Valley Drive

Sunset Trail

Roads End

Woodridge Drive

Hickory Springs Road

Surveyors Lane

High Road

Lake Ridge Road

Bolo Lane

N

Grapevine Lake

0.2 mile

0.2 kilometer

900 ft.
800 ft.
700 ft.
600 ft.
500 ft.
400 ft.
300 ft.

0.25 mi.   0.5 mi.   0.75 mi.   1 mi.   1.25 mi.   1.5 mi.   1.75 mi.

walking the soft, sandy lakeshore. When the lake is low and the water has receded, shells, old driftwood, and all manner of other interesting artifacts are exposed, making it a fun spot to explore. If it's a sunny day, you're likely to spot kids playing in the water and folks with towels and beach chairs soaking up the rays. It's easy to lose track of time lazing around the shore, making this a good spot to have a picnic lunch on the beach before retracing your steps to the trailhead. If you'd like to keep going, just go back to the turnoff and bear left; the trail continues around Rocky Point.

NEARBY ACTIVITIES

The huge Grapevine Mills Mall—with more than 190 shops and a 30-screen AMC movie theater—is only a short drive away. You'll also find a selection of restaurants both within and around the mall. To get there, turn right onto FM 1171 (Cross Timbers Road) and go about 5 miles. Turn right onto FM 2499 south (Long Prairie Road) and drive 5.6 miles. The mall is on your left.

• •

GPS TRAILHEAD COORDINATES N33° 02.017' W97° 09.000'

DIRECTIONS Take FM 1171 (Road) west from I-35E in Lewisville or east from I-35W in Justin. Turn south onto High Road. There is a small parking area on the left, about 0.5 mile down, between Stallion Circle and Sunnyview Lane.

23 SANSOM PARK TRAIL

After a challenging hike on rough trail, you're rewarded with a beautiful vista.

ROCKY TRAIL DOMINATES this hike, which winds down a bluff and along the southeastern edge of Lake Worth to a scenic overlook. Fossils can easily be spotted in the path's rocky sediment.

DESCRIPTION

Thanks to the efforts of the Fort Worth Mountain Bikers' Association (FWMBA), Marion Sansom Park offers good hiking on hike-bike trails built along Lake Worth's shoreline. Although it looks fairly small from the park, which is on the lake's southeastern tip, the lake continues around to the north. An impoundment of the West Fork of the Trinity River, the lake was created in 1914. Parks, including the huge Fort Worth Nature Center and Refuge, abound along the lake's shoreline, offering plenty of recreation for locals. Fishing is a popular activity, and you're likely to see anglers searching for white crappie, largemouth bass, and catfish.

This city park has little by way of amenities, except for a couple of picnic tables and the trails; however, this doesn't deter visitors, and you'll often find at least a few cars in the large parking lot. Most of the visitors are bikers drawn in by FWMBA's efforts to build the trails, but the 11 miles of trails accommodate both hikers and

DISTANCE & CONFIGURATION: 1.6-mile balloon

DIFFICULTY: Strenuous

SCENERY: Lake

EXPOSURE: Partially shady–sunny

TRAFFIC: Heavy on weekends

TRAIL SURFACE: Dirt

HIKING TIME: 45 minutes

DRIVING DISTANCE: 1 mile from Jacksboro Hwy. and NW Loop 820

ACCESS: Daily; free

MAP: fwmba.org/sansom-park-trail

WHEELCHAIR TRAVERSABLE: No

FACILITIES: Picnic table

CONTACT: fwmba.org

LOCATION: 2501 Roberts Cut-Off Rd., Fort Worth

COMMENTS: A lot of winding and twisting back and forth, but it's rugged and fun.

bikers, so you won't feel overrun. Sections of the trail are fairly rugged, so come prepared with sturdy hiking shoes and a walking stick.

It's worth noting that there are many different loops of trails in the park, all seeming to intersect and cross each other, making it hard to keep track of where you are, and harder still to follow the exact path I took on this hike. The trail map shown in this book depicts only some of the trails to give you a general sense of where you are, so be aware that there are many more offshoots than shown on the map. Bring a GPS or compass with you to help navigate. The key feature in this hike is the overlook, which is located downhill to the southeast. Use your navigational skills to get you there. Once you reach the overlook, pick trails that lead you back uphill to the northwest. Don't worry if you get a little lost. Have fun and explore!

Start the hike just to the south of the parking lot, where you'll find a scenic overlook for viewing the southeastern end of the lake. A table here is an ideal spot to have lunch after the hike. Continue to the trailhead by walking down the wide, rutted dirt path to the right of the overlook. At 0.2 mile, bear left, continuing steeply downhill. Ignore any smaller side trails and stay on the wide dirt lane, following it downhill toward the lake. To the left, glimpse a rolled-earth dam abutting the southeastern edge of the lake. Cacti and small shrubs dot the trailside.

The trail winds parallel to the lake and west through steep, rocky terrain. Stay to the left at the first juncture, then follow the path as it swings left onto a narrow singletrack trail heading back northeast.

The trail winds uphill through scrubby trees and follows the shoreline, below and to your right. As you hike, keep an eye to the ground for fossils from millions of years ago, when this area was underwater. Without much effort, it's easy to find shells and imprints from ancient ammonites—extinct mollusks distinguishable by their spiral shape—in the trail's rocky sediment.

At the next two trail junctures, stay to your left. Yucca and juniper encroach upon the trail as you continue east. The lake stays almost constantly within view to your right. The gentle lapping of its waters on the shoreline below reminds you it's there even when it briefly disappears from sight. The trail starts a brief, rocky

Sansom Park Trail

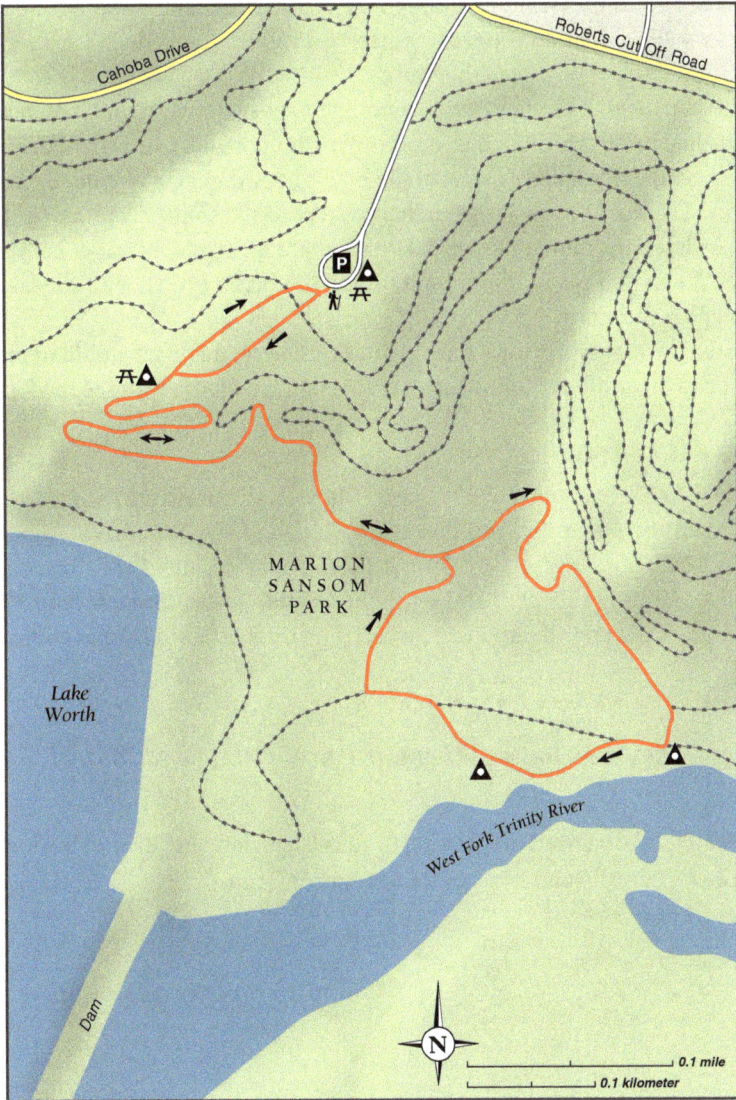

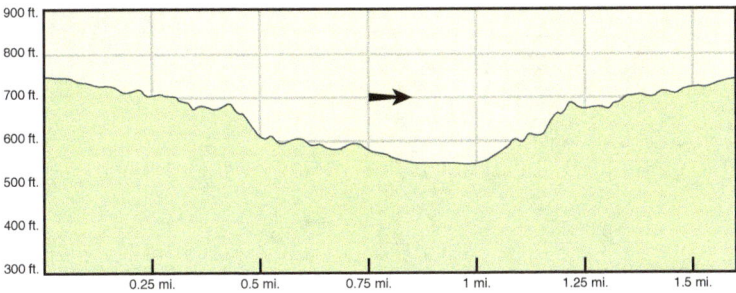

Cahoba Drive

Roberts Cut Off Road

P

MARION
SANSOM
PARK

Lake
Worth

West Fork Trinity River

Dam

N

0.1 mile

0.1 kilometer

900 ft.
800 ft.
700 ft.
600 ft.
500 ft.
400 ft.
300 ft.

0.25 mi.   0.5 mi.   0.75 mi.   1 mi.   1.25 mi.   1.5 mi.

descent as it continues winding through the brush, then climbs a small hill, exposing the rocky wall of the outcrop from which you've just descended. Turn right at the next trail split followed by another left.

The narrow dirt path continues winding its way downhill in an easterly direction, heading briefly through the woods before merging with an old road. Follow the road past an overlook with a view of the blue-green waters of an inlet of the lake on the right. The Fort Worth Fish Hatchery is just to the south. Continuing down the trail, bear left back onto a narrow dirt path that heads steeply up an uneven, rocky hillside. When you reach the summit, enjoy the bird's-eye view of the lake below, then bear left to return.

At the next two junctions, keep right. From here, trek back uphill to make your way back to the trailhead following the same path you initially descended from.

NEARBY ACTIVITIES

Head over to Exchange Avenue to see cowboys and cowgirls drive Texas longhorn steers down the street through Stockyard Station. The cattle drive happens twice daily, at 11:30 a.m. and 4 p.m. To get there from Sansom Park, turn right onto Jacksboro Highway (TX 199) and go about 1.5 miles, then turn left onto TX 183 N. Drive 2 miles, turn right onto Main Street, then turn left onto Exchange Avenue.

• •

GPS TRAILHEAD COORDINATES N32° 47.733' W97° 24.783'

DIRECTIONS Take Jacksboro Highway/TX 199 W. Turn left onto Biway Street, then right onto Roberts Cut-Off Road and into Marion Sansom Park.

24 TANDY HILLS TRAIL

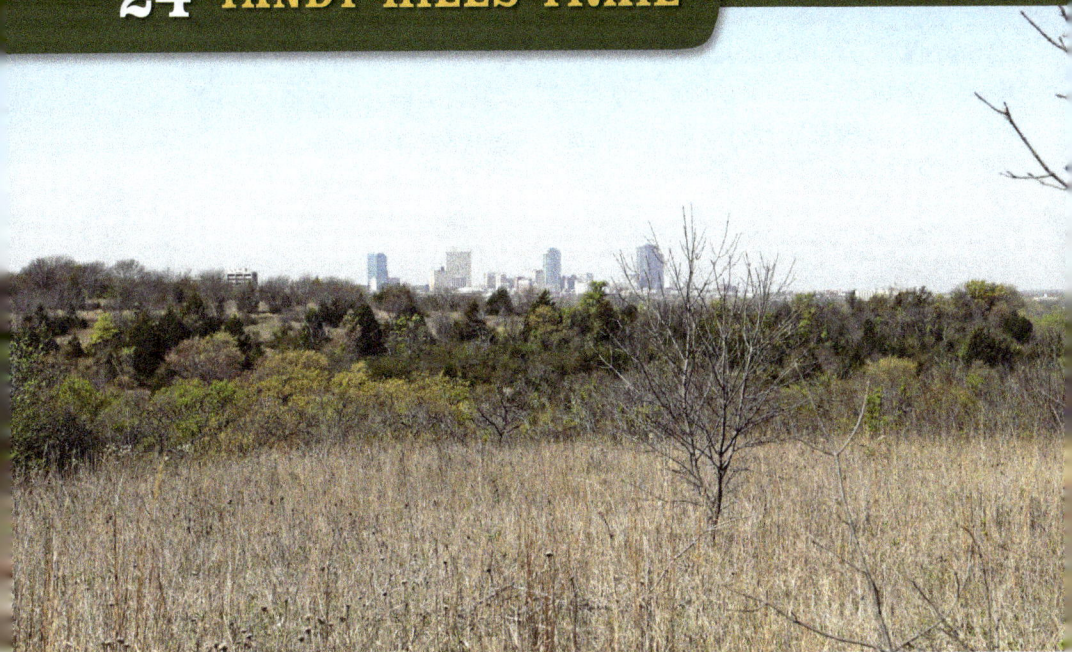

The Fort Worth skyline is easily visible from the trail's overlook.

WITH UNIMPEDED VIEWS of the skyline and spectacular wildflower displays, this hike through the rolling prairie hills of Fort Worth is a hidden gem.

DESCRIPTION

As you speed down I-30, you might be surprised that right in the shadow of the highway, a remarkable tract of land exists. Untouched from times before concrete, cars, and people moved in, a native patch of prairie has survived and thrived. Managed by the Fort Worth Nature Center and Refuge, the 160-acre Tandy Hills Natural Area is a step into the past and a lesson in native North Texas plants and geography.

Fort Worth acquired the land for Tandy Hills in 1960. When unsanctioned recreational use by four wheelers and mountain bikers increased in the 1980s, citizens stepped in, and in 1987 the land's designation changed to that of a Natural Area.

Research and studies have shown that Tandy Hills, with hundreds of species of native plants, is remarkable in terms of its diverse collection of flora, which includes prairie grasses and wildflowers such as trout lily, purple paintbrush, bluebell, and big bluestem. As a result, a hike at Tandy Hills in spring is a breathtaking experience and is oft touted as one of the best wildflower displays in the metroplex. At this time of year, lucky hikers are greeted with a rainbow-colored spread of flowers that brighten the prairie meadow in a display often only seen in photographs. As far as fauna goes, dozens of species of birds and butterflies have been identified, making it a favorite of birders and naturalists.

DISTANCE & CONFIGURATION: 1.9-mile balloon

DIFFICULTY: Moderate; some difficult sections

SCENERY: Native prairie, Fort Worth skyline

EXPOSURE: Sunny

TRAFFIC: Light

TRAIL SURFACE: Packed dirt

HIKING TIME: 1.5 hours

DRIVING DISTANCE: 2.2 miles from I-30 and TX 280

ACCESS: Daily, sunrise–sunset; free

MAP: tandyhills.org/maps

WHEELCHAIR TRAVERSABLE: No

FACILITIES: Picnic tables, portable toilets, water fountains, playground

CONTACT: tandyhills.org

LOCATION: 3400 View St., Fort Worth

COMMENTS: The prairie is at its most impressive in spring, when the wildflowers are blooming.

The preserve relies on street-side parking, and you'll often find at least a couple of cars parked alongside the preserve's entrance. To get to the trailhead, follow a short paved sidewalk north into the preserve. When the paved trail ends, continue northeast, following a faint path across a field toward a break in the trees. A map kiosk (empty on my visit) marks the trailhead and start of the hike.

Starting into the preserve, you'll be going northwest onto the Hawk Trail. A small side trail branches off to the east, toward the preserve's outdoor classroom, but you continue straight, past a signpost designating a monarch butterfly waystation.

Within a few more steps, the trail emerges onto the top of a small hillside. To the west spectacular views of downtown Fort Worth form the backdrop for this section of trail. To the east, across the rolling hills of the prairie, you'll see a broadcast tower. If you become disoriented, you can reorient yourself by locating the tower.

Continue on the trail and you'll soon reach an unmarked juncture that leads to a scenic overlook from which you can get excellent photographs of the city skyline. After a few photographs, follow the trail downhill into the tall grasses of the untouched prairie—a once common sight now just a rarity. As you admire the delicate grass strands waving in the breeze, take a moment to appreciate the complexity of what you don't see. Underneath the soil, the grass' roots can grow up to 14 feet long!

Continue down the trail, ignoring any small side trails you may encounter until you reach a trail marker with an image of a rabbit on one side and a hawk on the other. The images on the trail marker correspond with the names of the preserve's individual trails. Most of the junctures along the hike are well-marked like this one. For further reference on how the individual trails network together, you can visit the Tandy Hills website (tandyhills.org/maps), which has an overview map of the entire preserve.

For the purposes of this hike, head north, staying on the Hawk Trail. The hard-packed dirt trail narrows and leaves the prairie behind as it continues winding its way north in a rugged descent of the hill. When the trail levels out, you'll find yourself stepping across a small creek at the bottom of a ravine. The trail then winds southeast and you'll reach the next trail juncture. The trail marker is hidden in some vegetation along the side of the trail and indicates that you have reached the juncture

Tandy Hills Trail

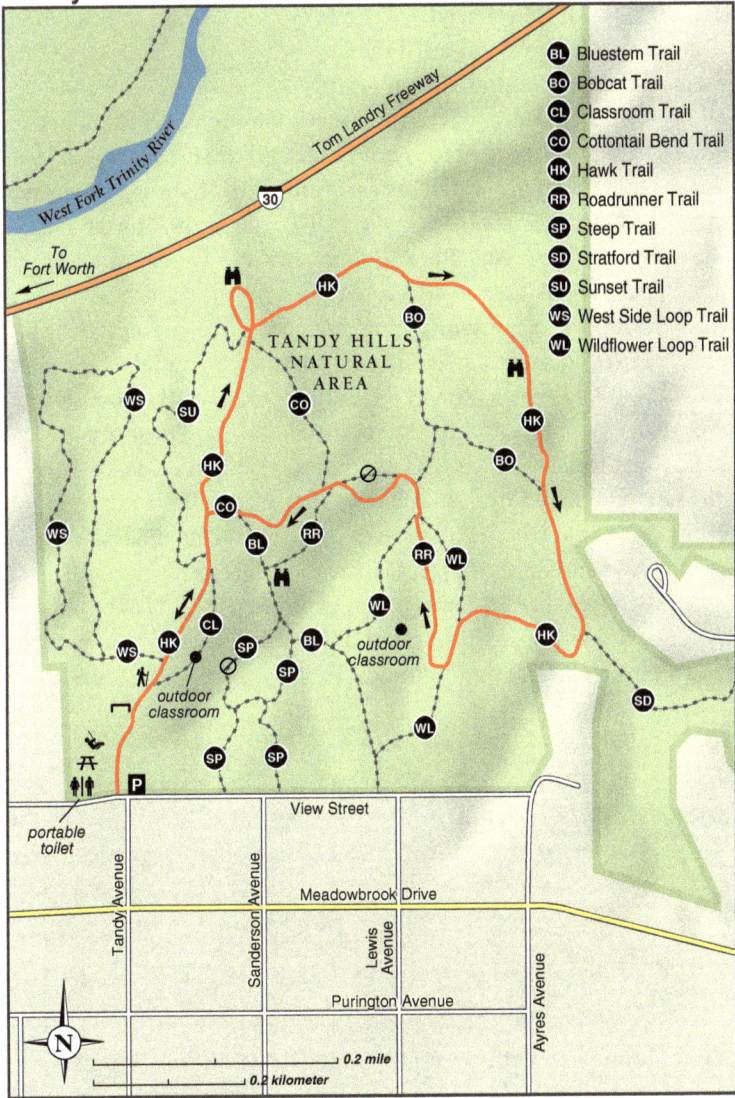

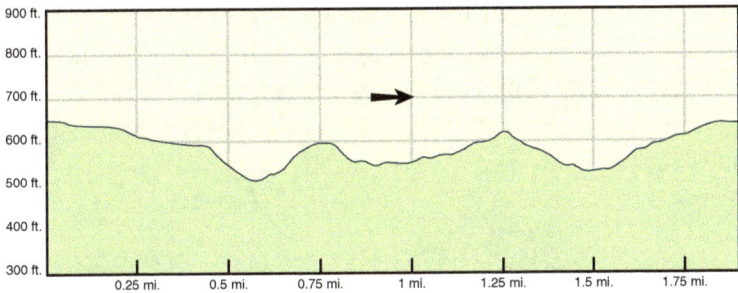

Tom Landry Freeway

West Fork Trinity River

30

To
Fort Worth

BL	Bluestem Trail
BO	Bobcat Trail
CL	Classroom Trail
CO	Cottontail Bend Trail
HK	Hawk Trail
RR	Roadrunner Trail
SP	Steep Trail
SD	Stratford Trail
SU	Sunset Trail
WS	West Side Loop Trail
WL	Wildflower Loop Trail

TANDY HILLS
NATURAL
AREA

WS   SU

HK   BO

CO

HK

BO

HK

CO

BL   RR

RR   WL

WS

WL

WS   HK   CL

BL

outdoor
classroom

HK

SP

SP

WL

SD

outdoor
classroom

SP   SP

portable
toilet

P

View Street

Tandy Avenue

Sanderson Avenue

Meadowbrook Drive

Lewis
Avenue

Purington Avenue

Ayres Avenue

N

0.2 mile

0.2 kilometer

900 ft.
800 ft.
700 ft.
600 ft.
500 ft.
400 ft.
300 ft.

0.25 mi.   0.5 mi.   0.75 mi.   1 mi.   1.25 mi.   1.5 mi.   1.75 mi.

of the Hawk Trail and Bobcat Trail. Continue east on the Hawk Trail, following the path as it heads steeply uphill toward the broadcast tower. When you finally make it to the top of the hill, the trail continues its lazy meander south through the sun-drenched prairie. At the next two junctures, stay on the Hawk Trail, heading south. You'll now be fairly close to the broadcast tower and can use it for orientation.

The trail winds downhill, widening as it reaches the bottom. The next trail junc-ture is marked as the intersection of the Hawk Trail and the Bobcat Trail. Continue south, following the Hawk Trail. Shortly after you cross a creek, you'll reach another trail juncture, partially hidden in the trees, where you'll head southwest. Keep an eye out for this turnoff, as it's easy to miss. A ribbon in the tree and a partially hidden trail marker will help you locate the split and confirm that you're still on the Hawk Trail.

The next trail juncture is unmarked; at this spot, take the north split. The trail crosses another creek, then winds up another hill. If you're starting to get disori-ented, locate the broadcast tower and use that as a general guide.

At the next unmarked trail split, continue west uphill. In 180 feet, you'll reach another unmarked split where you'll head south, following the trail up another hill. At yet another unmarked split 180 feet farther, head west downhill.

The next two junctures are unmarked; continue straight (north) through both. You'll soon reach another split; follow the trail northwest. At the next three junc-tures, head west to return to the Cottontail Trail. Retrace your steps to the trailhead.

NEARBY ACTIVITIES

Head 6 miles over to Sundance Square downtown, where you can grab a bite at one of its charming cafés or restaurants. Then explore the area's boutiques, shops, and galleries. Take I-30 W to US 287 N to TX 280 N. Exit onto East Fourth Street.

• •

GPS TRAILHEAD COORDINATES N32° 44.795' W97° 16.559'

DIRECTIONS From Fort Worth, take I-30 E to Exit 16C (Beach Street). Turn right on Beach and head south on the service road. At East Lancaster Avenue, turn left. After 0.9 mile, turn left on Tandy Avenue. Tandy will dead-end at View Street in front of Tandy Hills Natural Area. Parking is available on the street adjacent to the Natural Area.

From Dallas, take I-30 W to Exit 18 (Oakland Boulevard). Turn left (south) on Oak-land. In 0.9 mile turn right onto Meadowbrook Drive. At Tandy Avenue turn right. Tandy will dead-end at View Street in front of the Natural Area. Parking is available on the street.

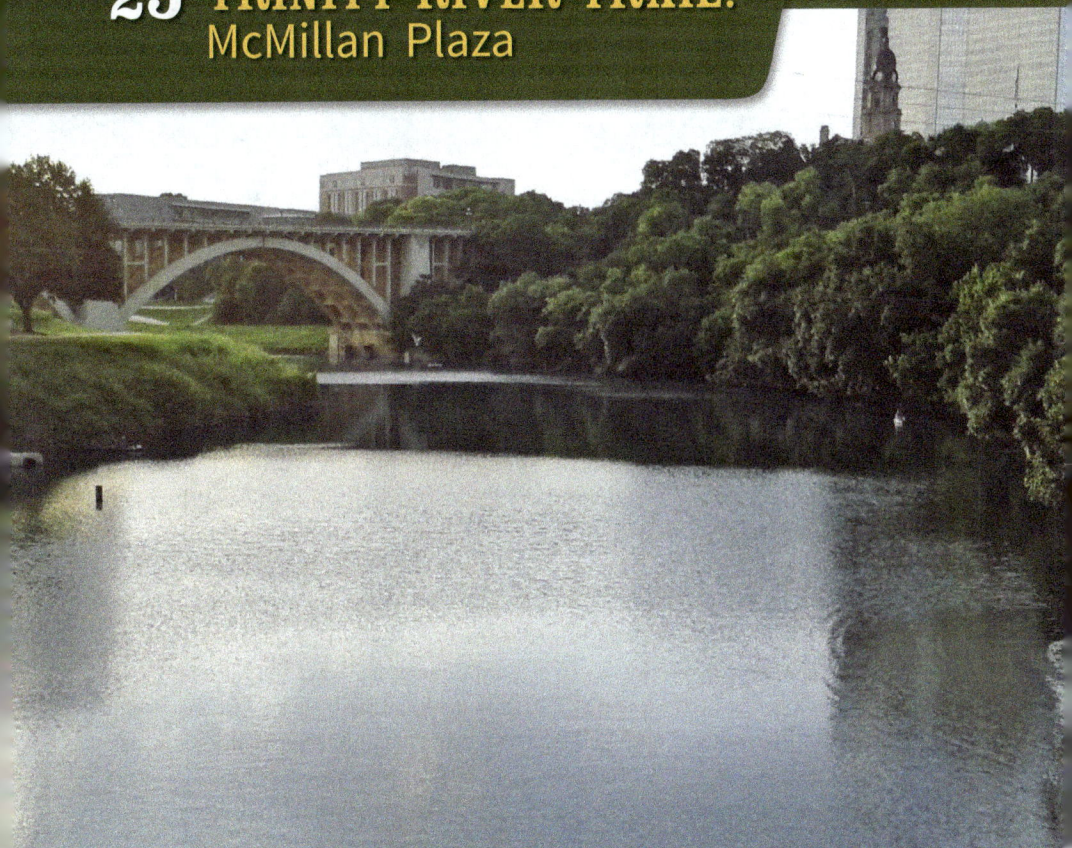

The trail parallels the Trinity River.

VIEWS OF SKYSCRAPERS in downtown Fort Worth dominate the skyline of this flat, sunny trail that winds alongside the West Fork of the Trinity River.

DESCRIPTION

Fort Worth's Trinity Trail system comprises about 40 miles of hike-bike trails along the Trinity River. It is readily accessible and is bordered by a number of city parks, including downtown Fort Worth's McMillan Plaza. The trail has a few different legs, all of which meet in or around the plaza, making it a popular starting point for new-comers to the trail system. Bikers, in-line skaters, joggers, and walkers all frequent the trail, attracted by the paved surface. Trinity Park, the Fort Worth Zoo, and the Fort Worth Botanic Garden also border sections of the trail. This hike covers a short section of one of the northern legs of the trail network.

McMillan Plaza is located at the end of a small cul-de-sac adjacent to Panther Island Pavilion. Named after John V. McMillan, a local businessman, it showcases a statue of Fort Worth's founder, Major Ripley Allen Arnold. Arnold was a U.S. Army

DISTANCE & CONFIGURATION: 3.9-mile out-and-back

DIFFICULTY: Easy

SCENERY: River

EXPOSURE: Sunny

TRAFFIC: Light

TRAIL SURFACE: Paved

HIKING TIME: 1.5 hours

DRIVING DISTANCE: 2 miles from I-30 W

ACCESS: Daily; free

MAP: trwd.com/wp-content/uploads/trinity-river-trail-map.pdf, trinitytrails.org

WHEELCHAIR TRAVERSABLE: Yes

FACILITIES: Benches

CONTACT: trwd.com

LOCATION: Ripley Arnold Plaza, Fort Worth

officer tasked with finding a military post on the Trinity River. In 1849 he established the post of Fort Worth, naming it after General William Jenkins Worth.

Plenty of parking lines the small cul-de-sac at the trailhead, offering joggers, hikers, and dog walkers a launch point for exploration. Self-service bike rentals are also available in the plaza. Bring your own water and wear plenty of sunscreen—this hike is completely exposed. To see a good map of the entire Trinity Trail network, visit trinitytrails.org before you leave home.

From the plaza, the trail branches in several directions. Start the hike by heading north across a bridge that spans the Trinity River. The trail curves east, then back north again, following the glistening river waters where ducks and geese can regularly be seen paddling in contentment or resting on the grassy banks. Kayakers can also often be seen lazing down the sunny river in search of their own adventures.

Houses and businesses sitting atop the embankment on the opposite side of the river signal that though you may feel removed from the hustle and bustle of the city, downtown is just an arm's reach away. Soon the shadows of the city's buildings will be replaced by open skies and grassy banks.

With little to block the scenery ahead, you'll have charming views of the upcoming sections of trail snaking off into the distance before they disappear around the bends of the river. At your back, the Fort Worth skyline becomes a small cluster of shiny skyscrapers, forming a picturesque juxtaposition to the calm, natural setting, making it a perfect spot to snap postcard-worthy pictures.

You'll soon reach a junction where the main path continues straight while a spur branches off, crossing the river and continuing along the opposite bank. Continue straight along the main trail, bypassing the river crossing. As you hike, you'll pass a few rocks with plaques describing the history and significance of portions of the trail.

The flat, smooth trail continues north and runs inside a greenbelt bordered by small earth embankments on the west and east. The embankments block the surrounding city and neighborhoods from view, isolating you from the stresses of urban life. Within the embankments is the Trinity River, just to your right. A neatly mowed strip of grass reaches toward the embankment to the left. Trees and benches, placed carefully at regular intervals along the trail, complete the parklike setting.

Trinity River Trail: McMillan Plaza

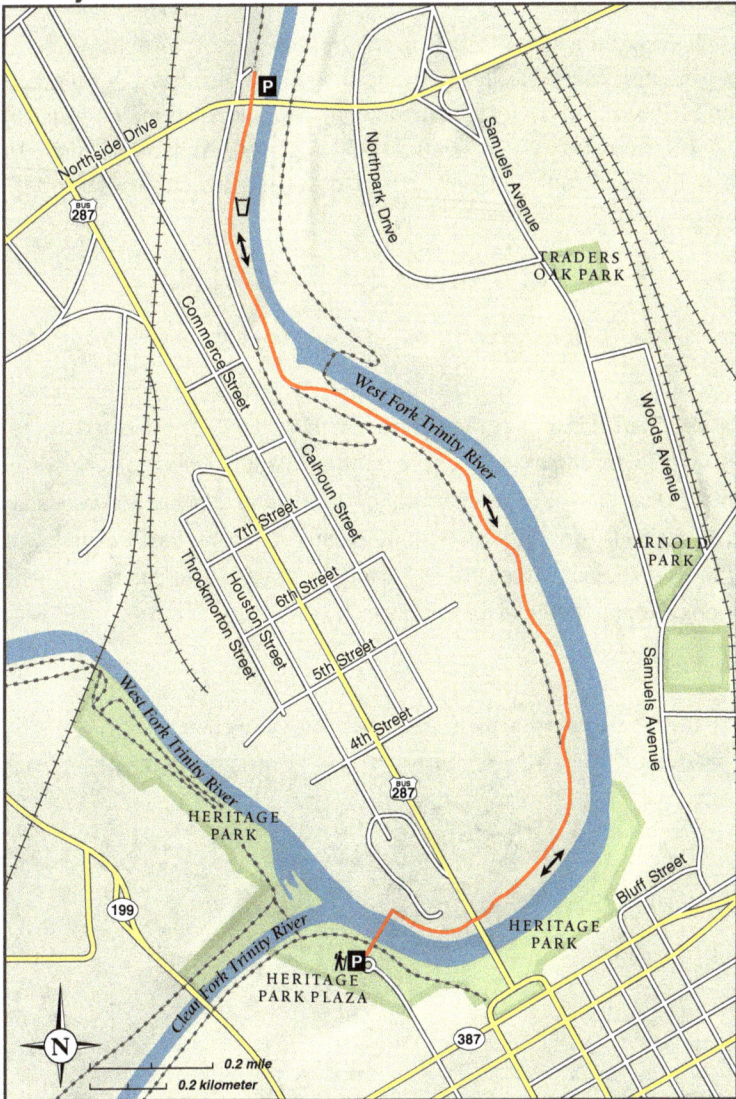

The trail continues north, until you reach the Northside trailhead. From here you can turn back or continue.

If you were to continue, you would soon reach a trail juncture where you can head either northwest, toward the Stockyards Historic District, or southeast toward Riverside Park, all while following the gentle curves of the Trinity River. When you're ready, retrace your steps back to the trailhead.

NEARBY ACTIVITIES

Only 8 miles away, the Fort Worth Zoo is a great spot to explore; its residents include raptors, primates, cheetahs, and Komodo dragons. It also has a petting corral and a rock-climbing wall. Visit fortworthzoo.com for information, entrance fees, and hours. To get there, take I-35W south to I-30 W toward Abilene. Take the University Drive exit and head south on University Drive 1 mile, then turn left onto Colonial Parkway.

• •

GPS TRAILHEAD COORDINATES N32° 45.532' W97° 20.255'

DIRECTIONS Start this trail at the trailhead in McMillan Plaza, located at the end of a cul-de-sac on Taylor Street, adjacent to Panther Island Pavilion, on the northeast side of downtown Fort Worth. To get there, follow I-30 W and take Exit 15A Lancaster Avenue toward downtown. Turn right on Commerce Street, left on East Belknap Street, then right onto North Taylor Street. North Taylor Street ends at a cul-de-sac, where you'll find parking and the trailhead for this hike.

Fort Worth looms in the distance as the trail meanders alongside the river.

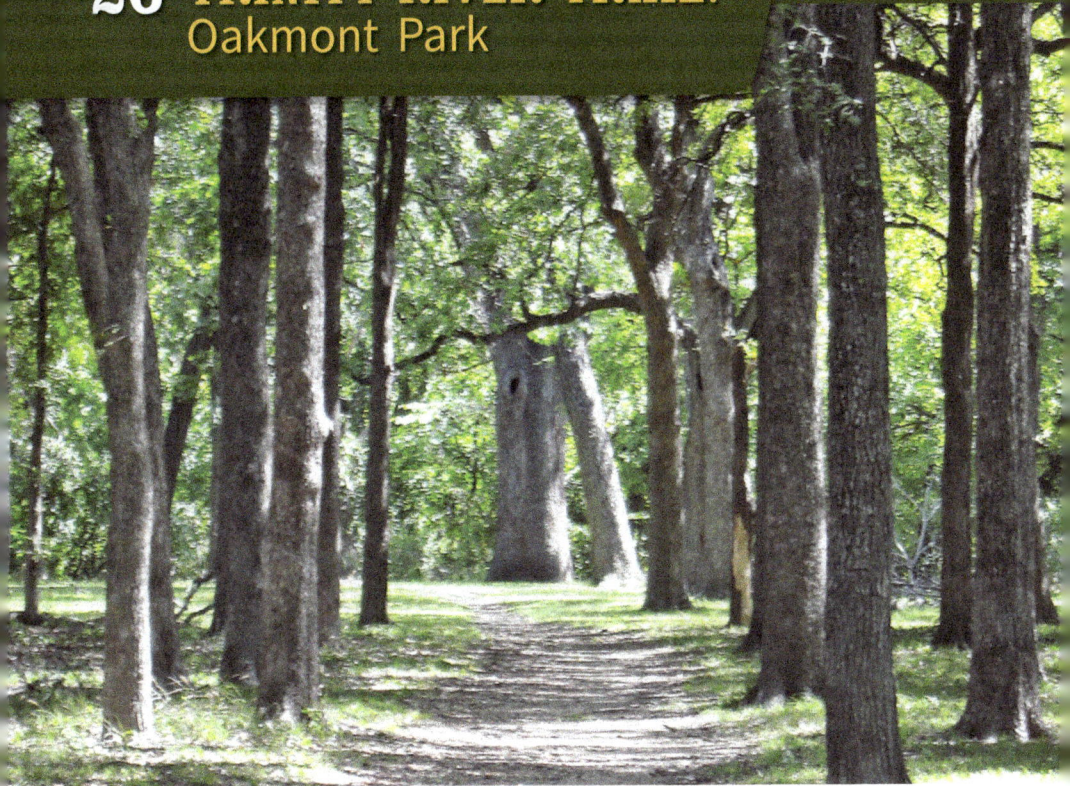

The path travels through a grove straight to the Memorial Oak.

A PAVED SECTION of the Trinity River Trail system, this pleasant trail is popular with bicyclists and dog walkers. The trail winds through the woods between two parks. A turnoff near the park at the other end takes you down a dirt trail to the huge state-champion bur oak tree.

DESCRIPTION

Part of the Trinity River Trail system—a network that spreads spiderlike for a total of 30 miles through Fort Worth—this paved trail follows the Clear Fork River (a branch of the Trinity River) southwest from Oakmont Park to Pecan Valley Park. The trail is popular with bikers, joggers, and walkers because it is level, with only gentle turns. Hikers will find the trail, which curls through the woods, a nice escape from the bustle of the nearby city. The Texas Parks and Wildlife Department recently listed Oakmont Park among its suggested routes for hikes in the Prairies and Pineywoods areas.

The small parking area at the trailhead fills up quickly on pretty days; arrive early to secure a spot. If the parking lot is full, you can do the hike in reverse, starting from Pecan Valley Park, which has much more parking.

DISTANCE & CONFIGURATION: 3.36-mile out-and-back

DIFFICULTY: Easy

SCENERY: Woods, champion oak tree

EXPOSURE: Partially shady

TRAFFIC: Light–moderate

TRAIL SURFACE: Paved path and short dirt trail

HIKING TIME: 1.25 hours

DRIVING DISTANCE: 6 miles from I-20/I-820 junction

ACCESS: Daily; free

MAP: trwd.com/wp-content/uploads/trinity-river-trail-map.pdf

WHEELCHAIR TRAVERSABLE: On paved portion

FACILITIES: Picnic tables

CONTACT: trwd.com

LOCATION: Oakmont Park (access off Bellaire Dr. S), Fort Worth

COMMENTS: The trail has only a few river overlooks, but they're great for birders nevertheless. Bring binoculars.

The trailhead is marked by a couple of picnic tables. Follow the trail over a bridge spanning a small creek. Pass the park's playground, then hike through a wide field dotted with trees. The trail then curls downhill, crosses a dried-up gully, and passes another field, this one dotted with purple wildflowers, bright-yellow sunflowers, and trees such as mesquite and oak.

Turn left at the junction, at 0.28 mile. Continue until you reach a bridge spanning a wide river at 0.63 mile. Enjoy the view, but don't lean too far into the railing—the posts often have large webs with huge spiders in them awaiting prey. Signs just across the bridge mark this spot as the entrance to Clear Fork Park. Continue southwest. Native trees line both sides of the trail, keeping the path in partial shade for most of the hike. Sunflowers bloom alongside the trail, and butterflies flutter across the path. Trail traffic is light, though cyclists occasionally pass. Many are kids accompanied by parents, and all respect the signs and cruise at low speeds. Once they've disappeared around the bend, you may find yourself completely alone again, with only the chirping of birds for company. Just when you've begun to wonder where the trail is going, pass a sign indicating that a rest area is 1 mile farther up the trail. The trail winds slowly here, passing more oak trees and wildflowers.

In another 0.6 mile, cross another bridge. Continuing straight, the trail passes a ranch on the right, where donkeys and horses sometimes linger by the fence. At 1.58 miles, you'll see a footbridge off to the left. Turn left and cross the bridge. (If you were to continue straight, you'd reach the Pecan Valley Park parking area, just 0.1 mile farther down the trail. In front of the parking lot there, you'll find a kiosk with a detailed map of the entire trail network.)

The small bridge spans a wide creek with pretty green water. As I crossed the bridge, I spotted a beautiful great blue heron perched on a log downstream stalking fish. Wishing I had brought my binoculars, I watched him for a few minutes, until the huge bird spread his wings and took off with a few elegant strokes. I later found out from the Texas Parks and Wildlife website that several herons nest in the area, and it is not unusual to see them.

Trinity River Trail: Oakmont Park

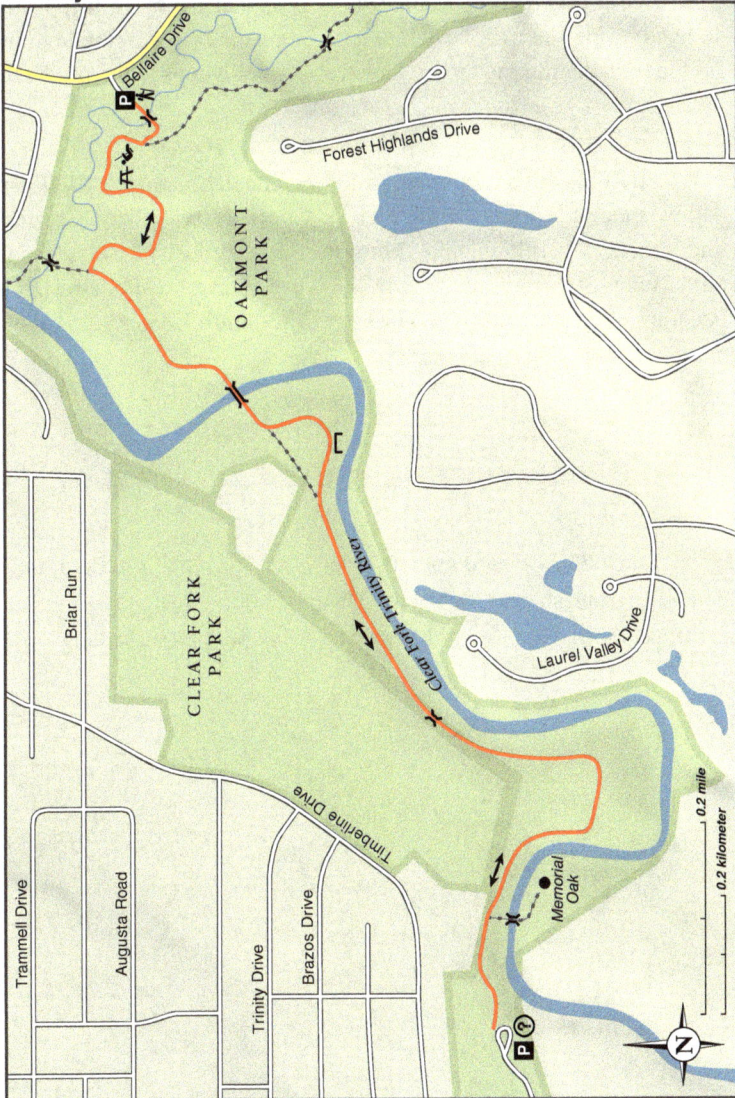

Across the bridge are a few narrow posts and a gate. Walk through the gate and onto the dirt trail. Within a few steps, reach a junction; take the trail to your left, which runs closest to the creek. Ahead, you'll see a lovely grove of tall trees, so unexpectedly picturesque that you'll feel as if you've just crossed a bridge into another world. After passing through the grove, you'll see a small fence to the right marking the boundary of a golf course. About 300 feet down the dirt trail, find the Memorial Oak, a huge bur oak tree. Listed on the Texas Big Tree Registry, sponsored by the Texas Forest

Service, this tree boasts recorded dimensions of 81 feet tall by 18 feet around. After you're done admiring the tree, have lunch at the picnic tables a couple hundred feet farther up the trail, behind the grove. Then retrace your steps to the trailhead.

NEARBY ACTIVITIES

The Fort Worth Zoo, which is home to primates, cheetahs, and the Komodo dragon, among other species, is only 8 miles away. Check fortworthzoo.com for special events and hours. To get there, take Oakmont Boulevard east 2 miles, then turn left onto South Hulen Street and drive 3 miles. Turn right onto Bellaire Drive South, which becomes West Berry Street. Turn left onto South University Drive and bear right onto Colonial Parkway.

• •

GPS TRAILHEAD COORDINATES N32° 40.217' W97° 25.867'

DIRECTIONS Take I-20 W toward Abilene to Exit 431. Turn left onto Bryant Irvin Boulevard, heading southwest. Turn right onto Oakmont Boulevard and go about 0.5 mile to Bellaire Drive South; then turn right again into Oakmont Park. Parking is on the left.

The Memorial Oak, a bur oak, is 81 feet tall and 18 feet around.

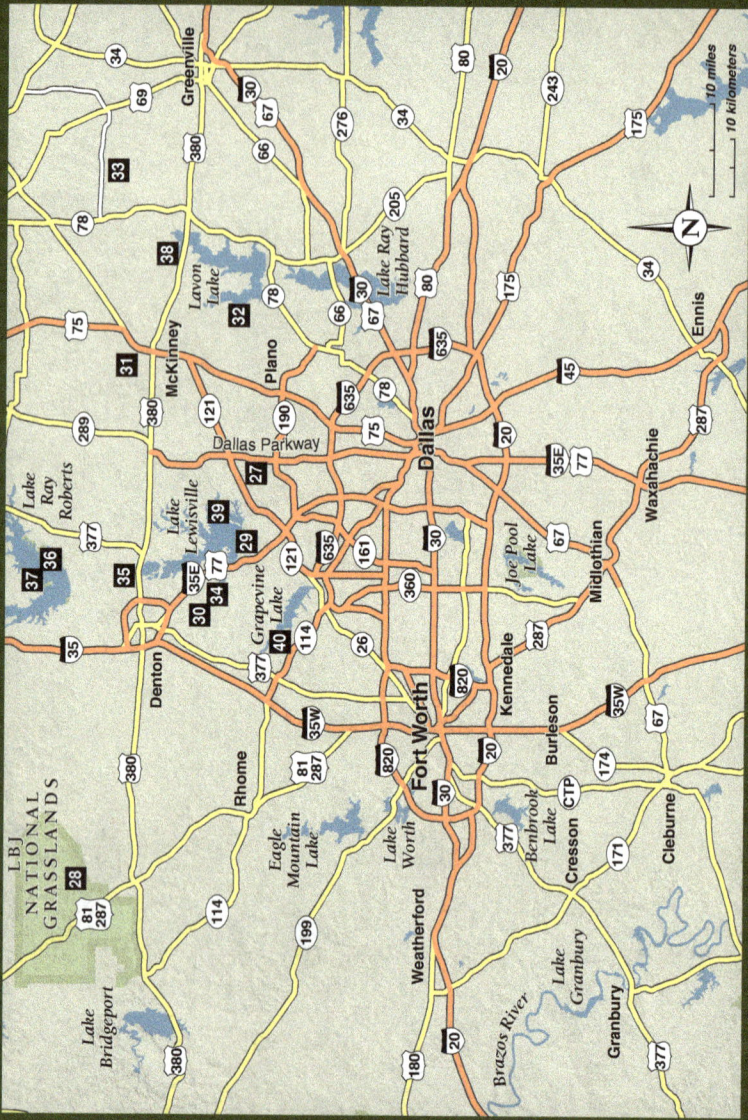

NORTH OF DALLAS–FORT WORTH

(Including Plano, McKinney, Lake Ray Roberts, and Lake Lewisville)

A wide, paved trail provides all ages an opportunity to explore the preserve's Blackland Prairie, Upland Forest, and Riparian Forest sections.

THIS TRAIL WINDS its way slowly uphill, moving from wetland to prairie to forest before looping back to the beginning. On any sunny weekend, you'll find the trails here bustling with families.

DESCRIPTION

In West Plano, the 200-acre Arbor Hills Nature Preserve is laid out in three sections: Blackland Prairie, Upland Forest, and Riparian Forest. On any given weekend you'll find the parking lot busy. Most visitors—young parents strapping their kids into strollers and young professionals leashing their dogs—are regulars who live in the area, already have their favorite routes in mind, and disappear down the trail within seconds. For newcomers, a map at the trailhead describes the three zones, offering a wealth of information for the nature maven, including the types of trees and animals you can find in each zone, and displays a map of the entire trail network. In addition to the paved trail, Arbor Hills boasts some primitive nature trails. These dirt trails are unstructured, and their access points unmarked, disappearing into the woods at various spots along the main paved trail.

The trailhead is inside the pavilion and picnic shelter adjacent to the parking lot. Follow the paved trail south through the pavilion and past the playground toward

DISTANCE & CONFIGURATION: 2.3-mile loop

DIFFICULTY: Easy–moderate

SCENERY: Blackland prairie, riparian forest, upland forest

EXPOSURE: Partially shady

TRAFFIC: Heavy

TRAIL SURFACE: Paved path

HIKING TIME: 55 minutes

DRIVING DISTANCE: 2 miles from Plano Pkwy. and Midway Rd.

ACCESS: Daily, 5 a.m.–11 p.m.; free

MAP: plano.gov/documentcenter/view/18597

WHEELCHAIR TRAVERSABLE: Yes

FACILITIES: Restrooms, water fountains, picnic tables, playground

CONTACT: plano.gov

LOCATION: 6701 Parker Rd., Plano

COMMENTS: Dogs are allowed but must be leashed.

West Parker Road. The trail quickly loops back north, heading into the Riparian Forest habitat. Mountain bikers are welcome here, but they do not pose a nuisance—most head straight for the DORBA (Dallas Off-Road Bicycle Association) trail. At about 0.2 mile, pass that trailhead, which diverges into the brush to the left.

Continue down the trail and reach a bridge crossing a creek at about 0.35 mile. The dense trees here, which make up the Upland Forest habitat, form a relaxing canopy of shade and make this a nice spot for lingering and trying to identify some of the area's avian inhabitants.

A little farther down the trail, just before the tree cover gives way to sky, you'll pass a huge bur oak tree nestled among other hardwoods. Keep an eye to the ground on the right side of the trail. You'll know you've reached it when you see its golf ball–sized acorns littering the ground; if you reach the stone bench, you've gone too far.

As you continue, the trees thin and the trail winds into the Blackland Prairie zone. This type of prairie, which is quickly disappearing because of urbanization, takes its name from its rich black clay soils. The prairie consists of tall grasses such as little bluestem, a bunchgrass that grows 2–4 feet tall. Wildflowers, such as Mexican hat, a red wildflower with a distinctive long, cone-shaped head; black-eyed Susan, a sunny yellow wildflower with a domelike head; and the bluebonnet, Texas's state flower, abound. In the fall, when the flowers aren't in bloom, the prairie is a dark mass of brittle yellow grasses that look black from a distance, thanks in part to the hundreds of spent flower heads. Visitors can often be seen here wandering the trails, entranced by the rippling of the tall grasses in the wind. The sun in this exposed area can be brutal in the summer, but you soon reenter forest just up the trail.

At 0.68 mile, you'll reach a junction where you should turn left, heading uphill alongside the prairie. Another junction, at 0.83 mile, leads to a tower overlooking the preserve; the trail you're on climbs to the tower the back way, so continue on this path, bypassing the turnoff. The trail continues, leaving the prairie behind as it heads slightly uphill, past wildflowers and into a forest of tall trees. To the right in the distance, you'll see apartment complexes abutting the edge of the preserve.

Arbor Hills Loop

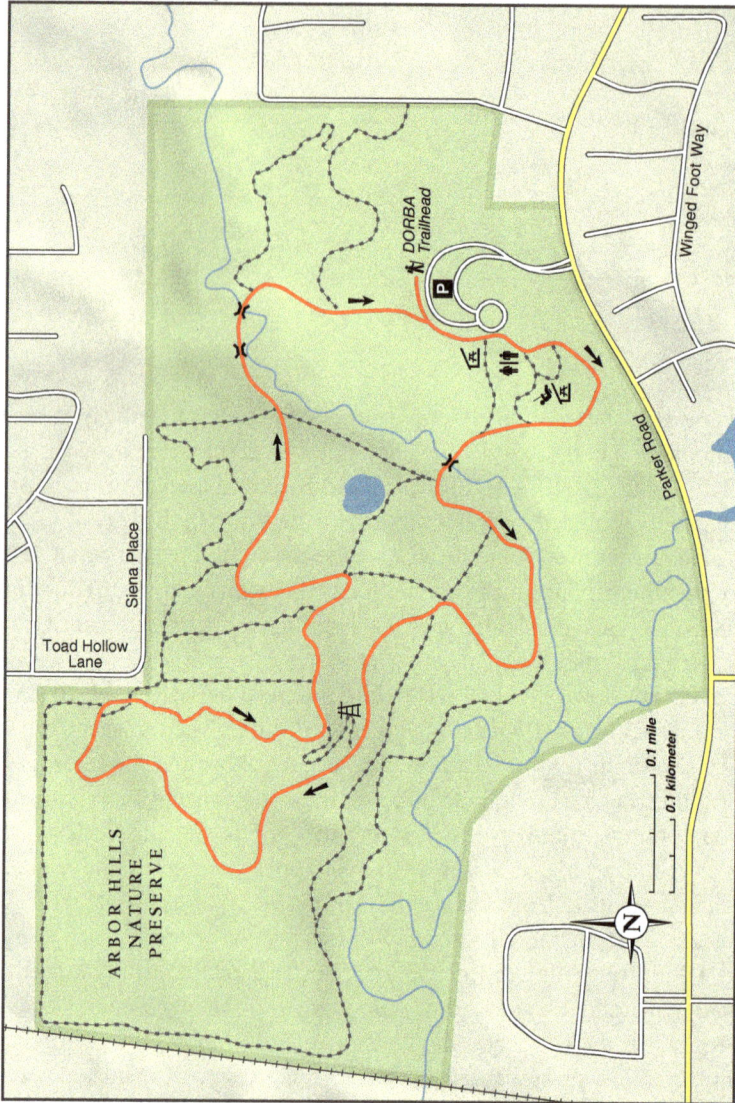

At 1.5 miles, reach the lookout tower. You'll usually find a few people at its railings enjoying the breeze and the views. You'll also have a bird's-eye view of the trail.

Back on the trail, you'll head through the forest, following the path as it winds slowly downhill. The trail easily accommodates wheelchairs, and alongside the hikers, dog walkers, and joggers, I encountered a couple of folks in wheelchairs, happily enjoying the outdoors. I also couldn't help but notice that the preserve's smooth, gentle slopes lured a surprising number of new and young parents, who

View of the lookout tower from the trail

were enjoying a nature walk and a workout as they pulled toddlers in little red wagons uphill or pushed strollers and baby carriages downhill.

At 1.63 miles, you'll find a wheelchair-access point. Head left, following the trail another 100 feet to a turnoff, on which you should again head left. Cross a couple of bridges, then, at 1.98 miles, come to a trail split where you'll bear right. Heading south now, reach the parking lot and trailhead from the other end.

NEARBY ACTIVITIES

Southfork Ranch (southfork.com), made famous on the TV show *Dallas,* lies just west of Plano. Its magnificent white mansion served as the home of the show's infamous J. R. Ewing from 1978 to 1991. The ranch was opened to the public in 1985 and continues to offer daily tours of the mansion and grounds. To get there from Arbor Hills, go east 15 miles down Parker Road toward Lavon Lake. Turn right onto Hogge Road.

• •

GPS TRAILHEAD COORDINATES N33° 02.850' W96° 50.917'

DIRECTIONS Take the Dallas Tollway north to the Parker Road exit. Turn left on West Parker Road. Arbor Hills Nature Preserve is a mile ahead on the right, past Midway Road.

28 BLACK CREEK-COTTONWOOD HIKING TRAIL

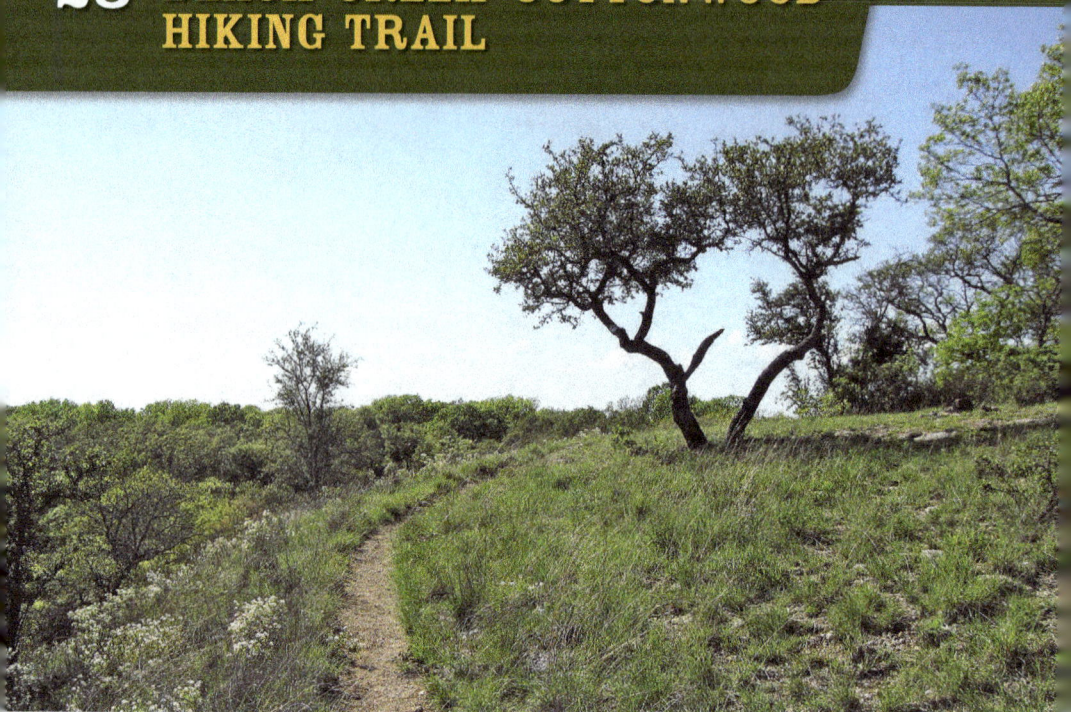

Enjoy stunning views of the surrounding countryside.

THIS LONG DAY HIKE explores the wild, grassy woodlands between the small Black Creek and Cottonwood Lakes of the LBJ National Grasslands. Although the bulk of the trail is open woodland, you will pass through many small pockets of sunny grassland as you make your way north.

DESCRIPTION

One of only 20 national grasslands in the country managed by the U.S. Forest Service, the Caddo–Lyndon B. Johnson (LBJ) National Grasslands consists of close to 40,000 acres of land. The grasslands are divided into two sections: the Caddo section, northeast of the metroplex, and the LBJ section, northwest of the metroplex.

The Caddo is slightly smaller than the LBJ and comprises a few recreational areas at Lake Coffee Mill and Lake Davy Crockett—small lakes built in the 1930s, when the land for the preserve was acquired. Its trails are popular with equestrians. The LBJ is a hiking hub. Not only does it have a 75-mile multiuse trail system accessible from its main campsite, TADRA Point, but it also has a 4-mile hiking trail connecting two of its small lakes—Black Creek and Cottonwood. This hike features the latter trail.

Be aware that there are designated hunting seasons in the grasslands. The trail, however, receives enough visitors that, as long as you stay on designated trails and

DISTANCE & CONFIGURATION: 9.58-mile out-and-back

DIFFICULTY: Moderate

SCENERY: Grasslands, woodlands, small lakes

EXPOSURE: Partially sunny

TRAFFIC: Light

TRAIL SURFACE: Dirt

HIKING TIME: 4.5 hours

DRIVING DISTANCE: 34 miles from I-35W/I-35E split

ACCESS: Daily; $2 day-use fee

MAP: tinyurl.com/blackcreekcottonwoodmap

WHEELCHAIR TRAVERSABLE: No

FACILITIES: Pit toilet, picnic tables

CONTACT: 940-627-5475, fs.usda.gov

LOCATION: Near Black Creek Reservoir, Decatur

COMMENTS: There is no water at either recreation area. Pack a lunch, plenty of water, and insect repellent.

aren't rooting through the underbrush, you're unlikely to encounter any problems. The U.S. Forest Service recommends that if you're hiking during hunting season, you should wear colorful clothing to be safe. Check the Texas Parks and Wildlife website (tpwd.state.tx.us) for specific information on hunting-season dates, which vary by animal.

It's a long drive down a remote, primarily gravel road to the trailhead, which is in the Black Creek Recreational Area. Although you'll feel like you're driving to a secluded, little-visited place, if you visit on a weekend you'll be surprised to find a fair number of folks at the rec area, which attracts a lively mixture of hikers, equestrians, hunters, and campers. I also noticed quite a few local teenagers who drove up for the day to splash around the 30-acre Black Creek Lake. There is a small day-use fee; drop your money in a box by the parking lot. There is no visitor center, office, or even park ranger on site, so make sure you've come with exact change.

Find the trailhead at the entrance to the recreational area, on the right side of the entrance road and just behind a large wooden sign with faded lettering that identifies this as Black Creek–Cottonwood Hiking Trail 901. The trail is hidden in the shrubbery behind the sign and is marked with a smaller 901 signpost. There are markers at regular intervals along the trail, so if you're ever in doubt at a junction, look for that number to get you back on the right track.

The trail heads northwest through thickets and shrubbery occasionally interspersed with small, sunny clearings filled with prairie grasses. On this hike, you won't find the expansive grasslands you might envision when you hear the term *national grassland*. Instead, this trail traverses a number of small clearings with tall grasses that harbor butterflies, crickets, and dragonflies, all of which emerge to greet you as you pass.

At 0.35 mile, reach a split where you'll bear right. The trail becomes rough, with a couple of short, steep, rocky grades before it reaches another junction. Bear right and cross the barbed-wire fence by going over the small step bridge intended to keep horseback riders out of the developed recreational area. At 0.75 mile, bear

Black Creek–Cottonwood Hiking Trail

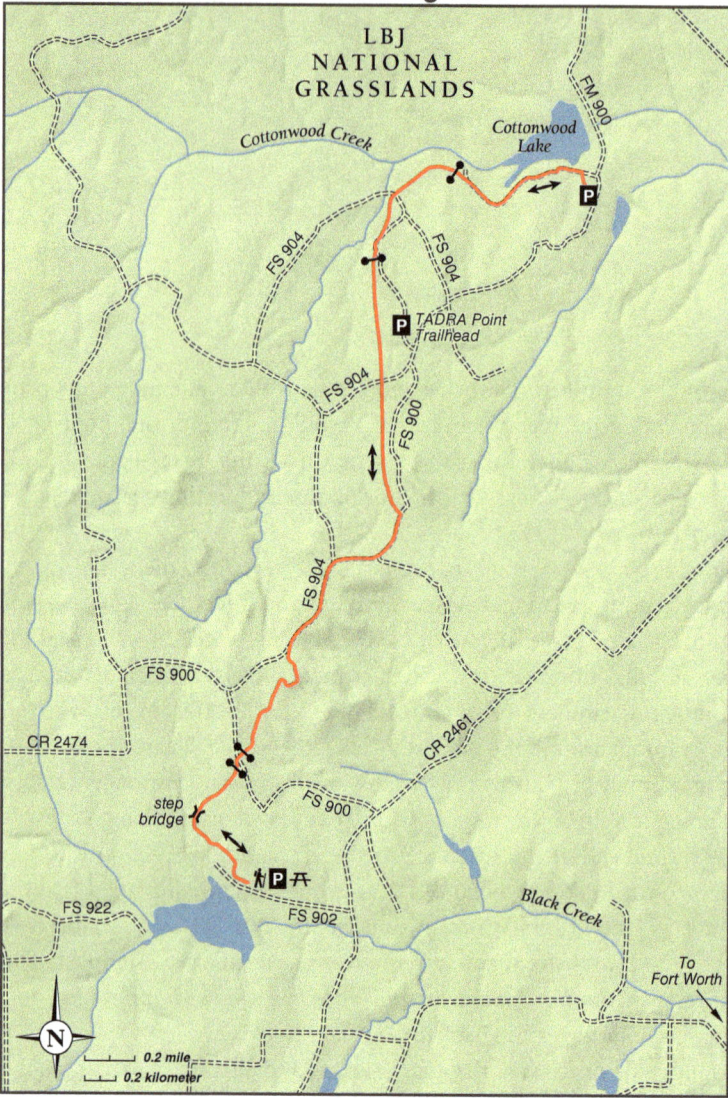

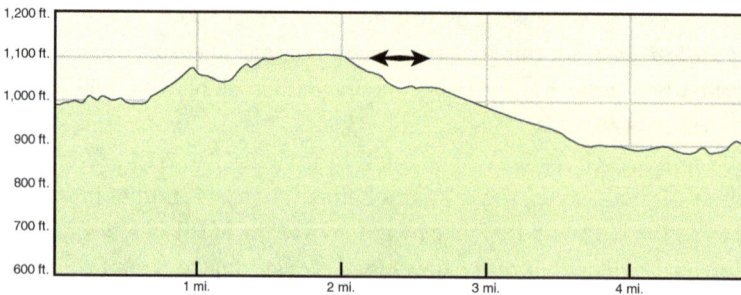

LBJ NATIONAL GRASSLANDS

Cottonwood Creek

Cottonwood Lake

FM 900

FS 904

FS 904

TADRA Point Trailhead

FS 904

FS 900

FS 904

FS 900

CR 2474

CR 2461

step bridge

FS 900

FS 922

FS 902

Black Creek

To Fort Worth

N

0.2 mile
0.2 kilometer

Visitors explore the banks of a small lake.

left. The trail becomes wider, following an old, partially overgrown park road enclosed by light woodlands. Pass through a few small patches of grassland that are quietly being overtaken by shrubs and small trees. White-tailed deer, cottontail rabbits, wild turkeys, and coyotes are all commonly found here. If you're not lucky enough to catch sight of these creatures, you're likely to spot their tracks in the loose dirt of the trail.

As you hike, you'll find a series of metal gates along the trail, separating tracts of land. Pass the first of these at 0.95 mile, where you bear right to head north just after you go through the gate. Bypass the next gate, keeping straight. At 1.35 miles, bear right and climb the steep grade to the top of the hill; the trail here has been severely eroded, so a hiking stick would be useful. This is one of the highest points on the trail, and at the top you'll find a pleasant breeze and a nice view. The path rounds the ridge, then emerges onto the hilltop—a grassy plain with a dirt park road passing through it. The road is used but not busy; this is the route you'd take if you were to drive to Cottonwood Lake. It's also the hiking route, and as you walk along you'll see the 901 trail markers.

Head straight (north) on the dirt road, then turn right onto the gravel road at 1.55 miles. It's sunny and hot in this section, but a cool breeze and the flat road make for fast, easy hiking. Bypass a small half-loop in the road where you may see campers or RVers; turn left at 2.3 miles. A few trails join in this section, and it can be hard to figure out which one you should take—just stay on the road until you see the dirt trail just off the road to the left at 2.45 miles; the 901 signpost marks it. Turn onto the dirt path and then bear right at the next junction.

At 3 miles, turn left onto a wide, flat trail. TADRA Point, which has a huge multiuse trail system popular with equestrians, is just to your right. (TADRA stands for the Texas Arabian Distance Riders Association, a horse club that worked closely with the Forest Service to develop the campsite and trail system.) The trails are color-coded, and as you hike you'll see signs pointing the way to the Blue, Yellow, and Red Trails. Bypass all turnoffs, cross the road, and pass through another metal gate at 3.45 miles. Bear right, descending through cacti and shrubs, then turn left through a wide grassland. At the next junction, bear right again.

Pass through another gate at 4.1 miles. Here the trail winds through a thicker mixture of trees and underbrush before finally emerging at Cottonwood Lake. Although the lake is only 40 acres, you'll still see a fair amount of activity, including ducks and egrets along its marshy edges, anglers settled onto its sandy banks, and possibly a boat or two sitting quietly on the lake's edge. Walk along the shoreline until you reach the shady parking area. If you're planning to eat lunch here, make sure you've brought along a picnic blanket to lay out on the grassy banks of the lake—besides the boat launch and parking area, you won't find any picnic tables or other facilities at this end of the trail. From here, retrace your steps to the trailhead.

NEARBY ACTIVITIES

Head 10 miles south to Decatur for a burger at the Whistle Stop Cafe, a lunchroom dating to 1929. It's part of the Texas Tourist Camp Complex, which was designated a Recorded Texas Historic Landmark in 1995. The complex also includes the Petrified Wood Gas Station and some cabins that, until the 1960s, were popular among travelers. There are even unsubstantiated rumors that Bonnie and Clyde may have stayed here. To reach the complex, take US 287/81 South back into Decatur and turn left on Business US 380. The cafe is about 0.5 mile ahead on the right.

• •

GPS TRAILHEAD COORDINATES N33° 20.700' W97° 35.700'

DIRECTIONS From Decatur, take US 287/TX 81 N and turn right at the rest area onto County Road 2175, heading east. Cross the railroad tracks and turn left, heading north on Old Decatur Road. After about 4 miles, turn right (east) onto CR 2372. Turn left (north) on CR 2461, then make another left onto FS 902, following it to the entrance of the Black Creek Recreational Area. Parking is on the left, adjacent to the lake.

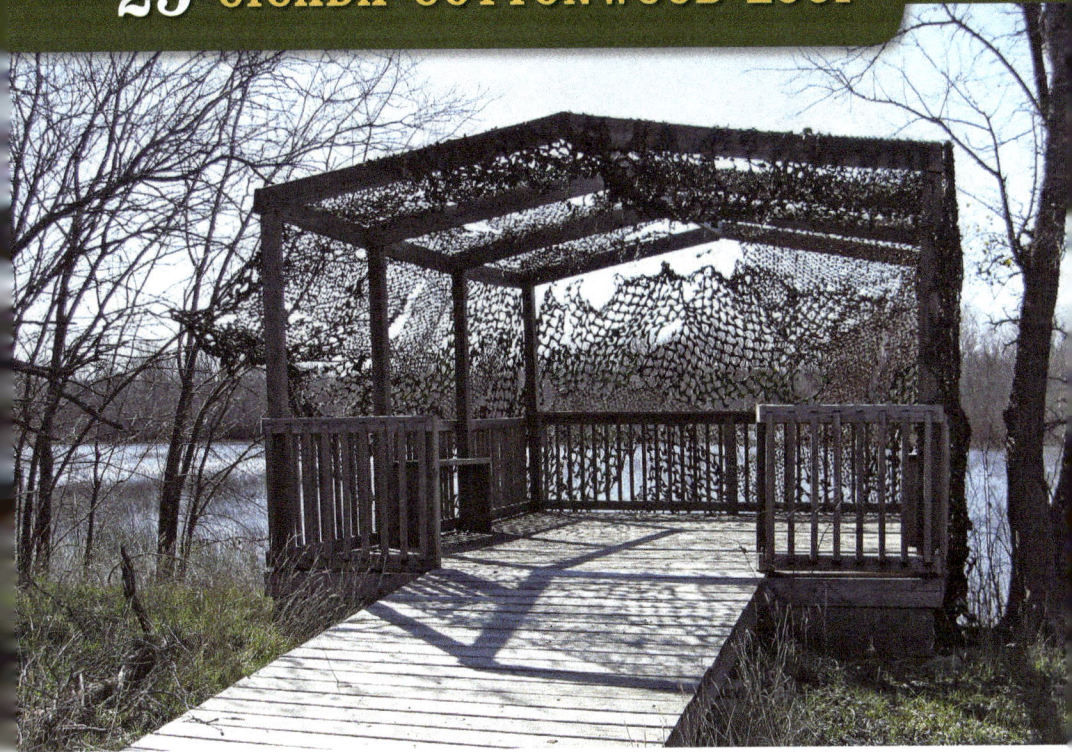

A camouflaged lookout offers views of the surrounding wetlands.

HIKE THROUGH THE WOODS to an overlook with a view of the wetlands, where a camouflaged blind allows for bird-watching. The trail's highlight is a restored pioneer cabin from the 1850s, complete with period furnishings.

DESCRIPTION

The 2,000-acre Lewisville Lake Environmental Learning Area (LLELA) is adjacent to the southern shore of Lake Lewisville, opposite the lake's dam. A Federal Wildlife Management Area, LLELA offers a variety of activities, including primitive camping, canoeing, kayaking, fishing, and hiking. The area also offers guided tours of its bison herd on the last Sunday of the month for an additional $2; if you're interested, call 972-219-3930 or 972-219-7980 to confirm tour times. The bison are in a separate enclosure, so there is no worry of being confronted by an errant bull while hiking.

Operated by a consortium of local universities, the city of Lewisville, and the Lewisville Independent School District, LLELA is involved in ongoing research and education programs, including prairie restoration, wetland research, and water retention. A number of graduate theses and dissertations have also focused on the habitat and ecology of LLELA and the surrounding lake area.

DISTANCE & CONFIGURATION: 1.7-mile loop

DIFFICULTY: Easy

SCENERY: Woods, wetlands, interpretive signs, pioneer log cabin

EXPOSURE: Shady–sunny

TRAFFIC: Light

TRAIL SURFACE: Packed dirt

HIKING TIME: 45 minutes

DRIVING DISTANCE: 8 miles from I-35E and TX 121

ACCESS: November 1–February 28, 7 a.m.–5 p.m.; March 1–October 31, 7 a.m.–7 p.m.; $5 per vehicle (cash or check only)

MAP: llela.org/explore/current-trail-and-camping-conditions

WHEELCHAIR TRAVERSABLE: No

FACILITIES: Toilet, picnic tables, benches

CONTACT: llela.org

LOCATION: 201 E. Jones St., Lewisville

COMMENTS: Bring binoculars and spend some time scoping the wetlands.

At the LLELA entrance, someone in the small booth will collect your admission fee and give you a pamphlet that includes a small map of the grounds. The hike starts on Cicada Trail, just south of the parking area and behind the Cicada Pavilion picnic tables. A small sign marks the trailhead.

Cicada Trail is a self-guided nature trail that meanders south through the woods and past signs describing the foliage, including cedar elm, coralberry, elderberry, and bois d'arc. The signs are actually quite descriptive, so plan on setting aside extra time along this section if you intend to read each marker.

Turn left at the trail junction at 0.33 mile. To the left, catch glimpses through the trees of a river that helps make the path a good place to spot birds. Year-round birds such as the redwing blackbird, the northern cardinal, and the Carolina chickadee are regularly spotted in the area.

At 0.4 mile, bear right at the split. Pass another interpretive sign; just beyond this, the trail splits. To the left, the trail ends at a lookout over a gully. Bear right and follow the trail downhill. It emerges from woods, then joins the wide Cottonwood Trail. Head right to take Cottonwood Trail, following the road as it heads west.

Pass a group of picnic tables abutting a narrow creek at 0.83 mile. Snakes such as the southern copperhead and the western cottonmouth are commonly spotted in the surrounding habitat. Although I haven't seen any, remind younger hikers to be cautious when traipsing off-trail through tall grass or dense underbrush.

Continuing down the road, reach a camouflaged lookout over the surrounding wetlands. The pavilion is nicely shielded, allowing you to view the wetland wildlife unnoticed. A peek through the netting on my hike revealed dozens of ducks resting peacefully on the calm waters. Keep an eye out for other common birds, including the great blue heron, great egret, and smaller snowy egret.

Heading back down the trail, the marsh stays within sight to the left, with small trees and shrubs to the right. You're likely to spot gulls, turkey vultures, and red-tailed hawks circling overhead. Power lines briefly cross the path, reminding you of civilization. Just a few feet past the towers, however, the present is forgotten and

Cicada–Cottonwood Loop

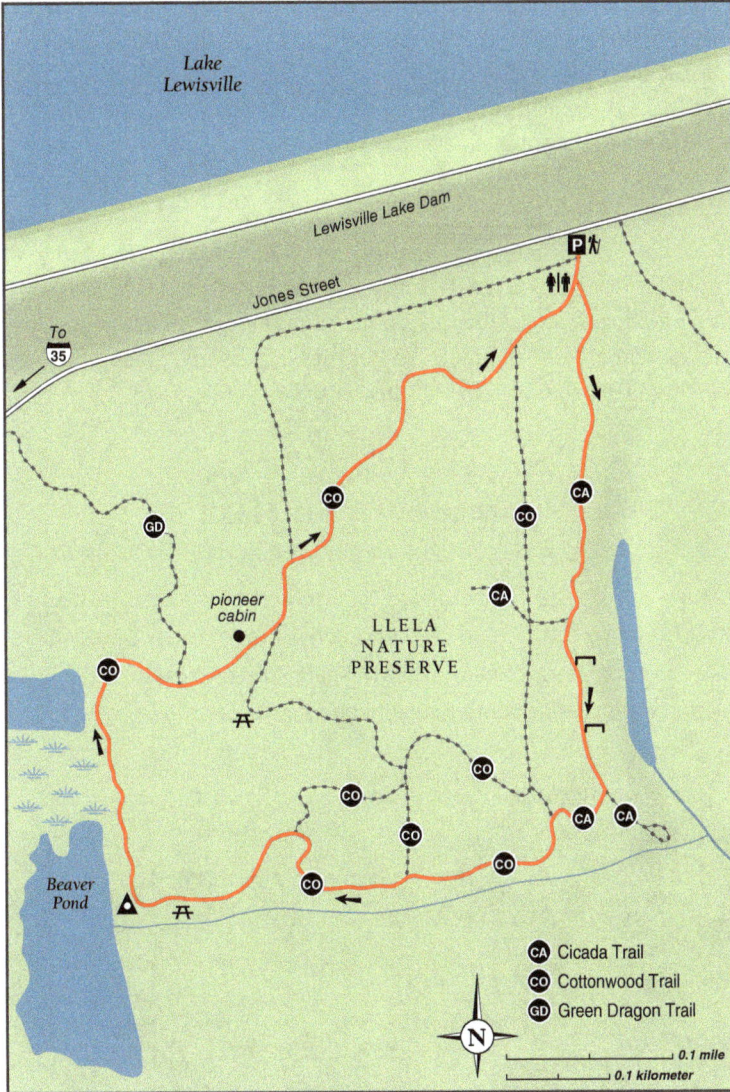

Lake Lewisville

Lewisville Lake Dam

Jones Street

To 35

LLELA NATURE PRESERVE

pioneer cabin

Beaver Pond

CA Cicada Trail
CO Cottonwood Trail
GD Green Dragon Trail

N

0.1 mile
0.1 kilometer

you're instantly transported into the past as an old log cabin comes into view amid woods on your right. The cabin is surrounded by a few other log buildings and suggests what life must have been like on the North Texas prairie in the pioneer days. A log fence encloses the complex.

The cabin, built in the 1850s, originally belonged to a local resident. It was donated and transported to LLELA, where it has since been carefully restored to create a pioneer setting. The house sports original period furnishings and has a separate garden and smokehouse out back. The buildings are all made of logs and insulated with packed mud. As you explore, don't be surprised if you see the remnants of ashes in the pit of the smokehouse—it has even been put to use to roast a pig at a recent LLELA event! From here, head 0.3 mile back down the road to finish the trail loop and reach the trailhead.

NEARBY ACTIVITIES

If you're looking for a change of pace after the hike, stop by Vista Ridge Mall, only 6 miles away. It has a few large department stores, such as Macy's, Sears, Dillard's, JCPenney, and dozens of smaller gift shops and boutiques. There are also a number of eateries in and around the mall. To get there, follow I-35E south 3.5 miles, and take Exit 448B. Turn left onto East Round Grove Road.

• •

GPS TRAILHEAD COORDINATES N33° 03.933' W96° 58.517'

DIRECTIONS Follow I-35E north toward Denton and take Exit 454A (Farm to Market Road 407/Justin Road). Turn right onto East Jones Street. The LLELA entrance is at the end of Jones, at the intersection with North Kealy Street. To get to the trailhead, follow the road from the entrance booth to the first parking area on your right.

A restored pioneer cabin from the 1850s abuts the trail.

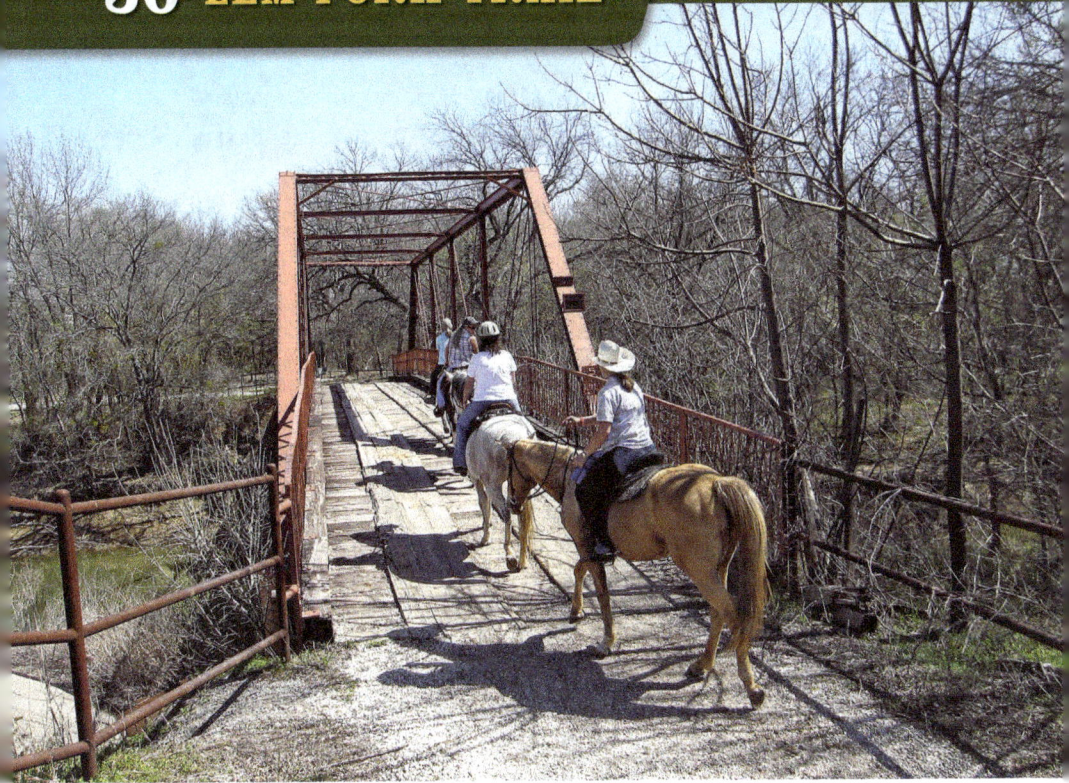

Equestrians enjoy a sunny day on the trail.

EXPLORE A HISTORIC BRIDGE associated with tales of spooky hauntings, and then enjoy a pleasant hike through the woods.

DESCRIPTION

The trailhead for this hike is in Old Alton Bridge Park, just outside Denton near the town of Copper Canyon. The park houses the historic Old Alton Bridge—not only well known for its historical importance but also notorious for its much-researched paranormal activity.

The bridge is just west of the parking lot. Built in 1884, it was added to the National Register of Historic Places in July 1988. More recently, Denton's population growth has prompted the creation of a new bridge for motor traffic; this new route bypasses the one-lane, iron-truss, wood-planked Old Alton Bridge, which is now open only to pedestrian and equestrian traffic.

From the parking lot, the trail splits, heading southeast (left) and southwest (right). If you go right, you'll cross the bridge and head south, eventually joining Pilot Knoll Trail, which descends toward Pilot Knoll Park. The hike described here does not cross the bridge in that direction, but rather follows the trail on the left. But

DISTANCE & CONFIGURATION: 3.8-mile out-and-back

DIFFICULTY: Moderate

SCENERY: Historic bridge, marshy banks of lake, woods

EXPOSURE: Partially shady–sunny

TRAFFIC: Moderate

TRAIL SURFACE: Dirt

HIKING TIME: 1.5 hours

DRIVING DISTANCE: 8 miles from I-35E/I-35W split

ACCESS: Daily; free

MAP: tinyurl.com/elmforktrailmap

WHEELCHAIR TRAVERSABLE: No

FACILITIES: Picnic tables

CONTACT: None

LOCATION: Old Alton Bridge Park, Argyle (Lake Lewisville, North Shore)

COMMENTS: Bring water; there are no drinking fountains. Avoid this trail after rainstorms, as the latter portion can stay muddy for days.

before heading down the trail, take a detour to check out the bridge. Local legend holds that it's haunted, and it has become a favorite spot for thrill-seekers, especially at Halloween. Those who know the legends will sometimes refer to it as Goatman's Bridge. There are several versions of the story, but essentially they all involve a man who was killed on the bridge and comes back as a creature that is half-man and half-goat. Some accounts say he was a goatherd; others say the man lost his head and now has to wear a goat's. Most accounts say that if you honk your horn two or three times (depending on the story), you'll see the goat-man in the distance. The legends attract not only local kids but also paranormal investigators, many of whom have posted photos and reports of their investigations online.

When you're done checking out the bridge, go back to the parking lot and then left down Elm Fork Trail. The wide path travels south through an open grassy plain toward a wood on the horizon, then turns east. Butterflies, dragonflies, and crickets buzz past, hopping and flying out of your path. A few narrow trails branch off the main trail to your right, leading to fishing spots at the creek's edge. Stay on the main trail, bypassing all turnoffs. The trail eventually reaches the trees and cuts a wide path through them, keeping you clear of any shade they might cast. To your left, a wire fence partially hidden beneath vines and mesquite trees marks the outer perimeter of a ranch where cows graze lazily in their sunny pasture, watching you as you pass. You'll traverse more grassland, which is punctuated by thin groves of short trees, before reaching a creek crossing. The trail stewards have layered blocks along the creek's banks here to prevent erosion and allow hikers to step across easily without getting their feet wet.

On the other side of the creek, you'll find less grass and more trees growing closer to the trail. A lush green understory provides dense pockets of shade. Birds are much more prevalent on this side of the creek as well, and you'll hear them whistling and chirping in the background, though spotting them in the trees is fairly difficult.

The flatness of the first half of the trail is soon replaced by slight hills, and the trees give way to shrubby grassland dotted with junipers before you finally reach another creek. Continue past it and you'll soon start to hear the sounds of

Elm Fork Trail

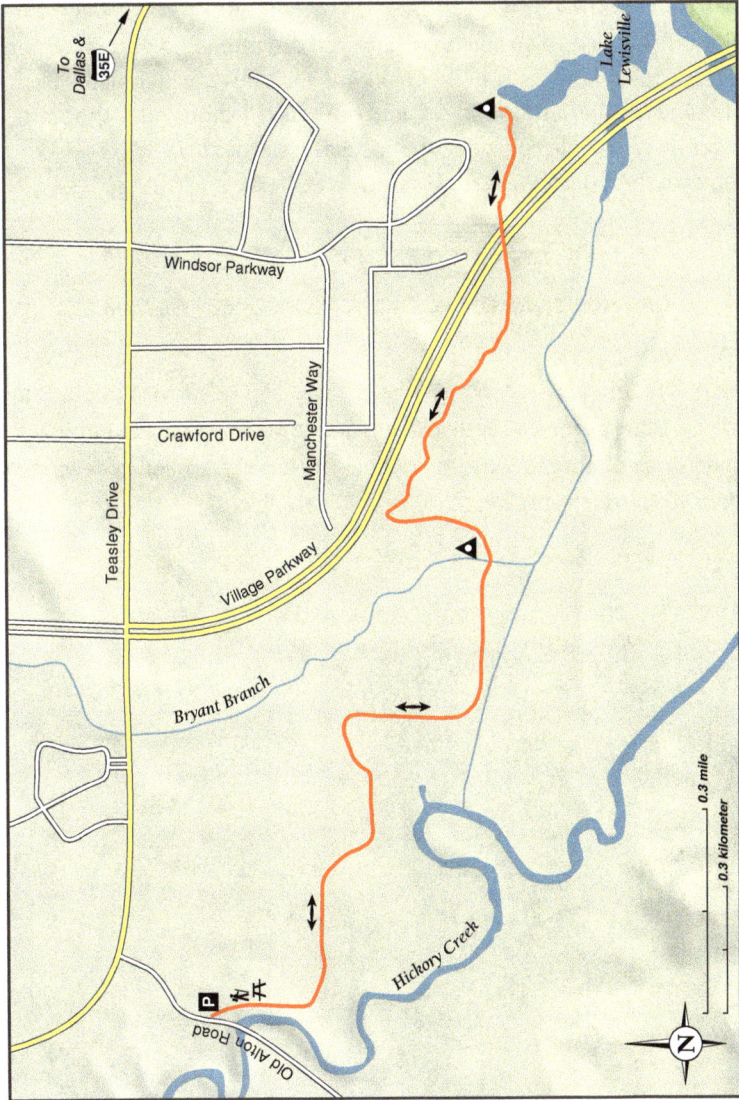

civilization; then, with some abruptness, the trail is interrupted by new road and bridge construction. At the time I hiked, the trail was still open at this point, offering access to the sandy lakeshore under the new bridge, where you can take in the views and the breezes before retracing your steps to the trailhead. Before you visit, note that access here may be limited due to the ongoing construction, but don't let that discourage you from this trail—it's a pleasant outing and hike, regardless of whether or not you can actually reach the lake.

NEARBY ACTIVITIES

Visit Denton's historic town square, where you can often find musicians performing. The square's focal point is the old County Courthouse, which dates back to 1896. Restaurants, art galleries, boutiques, and other retail shops offer shopping and dining. To get there, take I-35E south about 1.5 miles, exit at US 377/Fort Worth Drive, and then turn right onto West Hickory Street.

• •

GPS TRAILHEAD COORDINATES N33° 07.767' W97° 06.233'

DIRECTIONS From I-35E, exit onto Swisher Road and head west about 3 miles. Just after Swisher Road becomes Teasley Road/Farm to Market Road 2181, turn left onto Old Alton Road. The entrance to Old Alton Bridge Park is down a steep driveway to your left, just before you cross the bridge.

The trail is quiet and peaceful.

31 ERWIN PARK LOOP

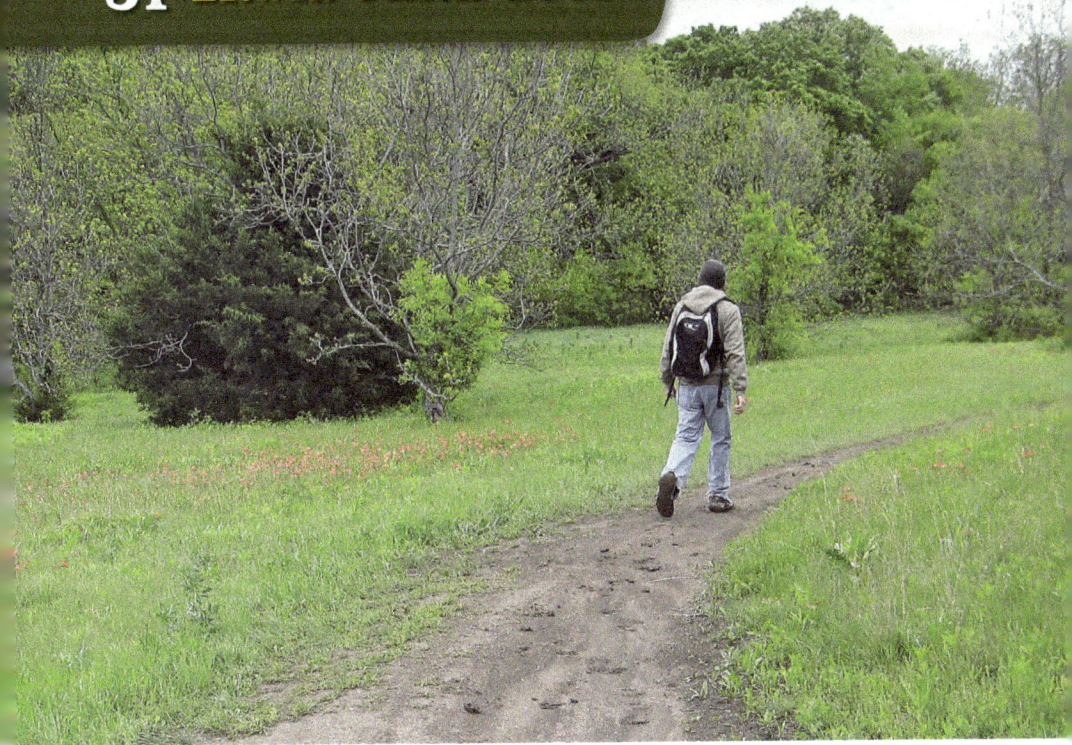

A hiker makes his way through a sunny meadow.

THIS EASY TRAIL leads you through open meadows as it loops in and out of the woods and through the preserve. Enjoy colorful wildflower displays in the spring and a variety of birdlife year-round.

DESCRIPTION

The 212-acre Erwin Park is a McKinney city park in a somewhat rural area surrounded by ranchlands, just north of Dallas–Fort Worth. Donated in 1971 to the Texas Conservation Foundation by the Erwin family, the land has belonged to the city of McKinney since 1973 and has been developed into a large park with much of its natural area preserved. It even offers overnight camping; call 972-547-2690 to make reservations.

The park's trails, maintained by the Dallas Off-Road Bicycle Association (DORBA), include about 8 miles of paths through meadows and woodlands. The trails are narrow, and you'll have to step aside to let bikers pass; however, a lot of this hike travels through open, tree-studded meadows, and you'll have no problem seeing the bikers as they approach. The trail traffic varies, and there are times when you can come here and find no one else on the trail at all. I visited on a slightly overcast

149

DISTANCE & CONFIGURATION: 2.6-mile loop

DIFFICULTY: Easy

SCENERY: Meadows, woodlands

EXPOSURE: Partially shady–sunny

TRAFFIC: Moderate

TRAIL SURFACE: Dirt

HIKING TIME: 1 hour

DRIVING DISTANCE: 6 miles from North Central Expy. and W. University Dr.

ACCESS: Daily, 8 a.m.–10 p.m.; free

MAP: dorba.org/trail.php?t=10

WHEELCHAIR TRAVERSABLE: No

FACILITIES: Toilet (closed in winter), picnic tables, water fountain

CONTACT: dorba.org

LOCATION: 4300 CR 1006, McKinney

COMMENTS: This hike can easily be extended with a second loop.

weekend morning to find the pavilion and playground full of picnickers but the trail empty except for one other hiker. Prettier days bring more bikers.

At the trailhead, you have two options: west (right) and south (left). The entire trail is actually one huge loop, and if you wanted to you could start on one side and come out 8 miles later at the other. For those wanting something a bit more manageable, there are turnaround spots that make the trail shorter, and I took advantage of that on my visit. This hike covers the southeastern corner of the park; you'll loop back to the trailhead before the turnoff into the western and northern sides of the park.

To start the hike, turn onto the trail heading left. You'll immediately find yourself hiking through an expansive meadow, which in the spring is blanketed with tiny yellow wildflowers. The terrain is not completely flat but instead dotted with gentle hills that expand to a tree line in the distance ahead of you. As you leave the vicinity of the picnic area, the sounds of folks laughing and kids playing will fade into the background and be replaced by other sounds echoing through the open clearing—woodpeckers rat-a-tatting in the woodlands up ahead and cows mooing somewhere nearby (don't worry, they're actually in an adjacent enclosed property, and you won't come face-to-face with any on the hike).

Continue toward the woods in the distance, bypassing other trails that join the one you're on. At the tree line, the path dives into the woods—a shady mixture of old and new growth, with thick vines climbing up the trees' trunks and branches. Small dips and tight twists intended to spice up bikers' rides also add interest to your trek. You'll briefly emerge into another smaller meadow before you're again enclosed by woodland.

At 0.43 mile, round a small pond hidden in the heart of the woods—one of two ponds you'll discover along the hike. If it has recently rained, the shallow dips in the path just around it can sometimes pool with water, creating mud pockets, even though the rest of the trail might be dry. They're easy to navigate unless it has rained heavily recently, in which case you might emerge a bit messier than when you entered.

A few hundred feet farther, bear left and head down a short, steep slope, where you'll find yourself walking atop a ridge beside a creek along the eastern side of the park. Stay straight at the next two four-way junctions, at 0.6 mile. The trail briefly

Erwin Park Loop

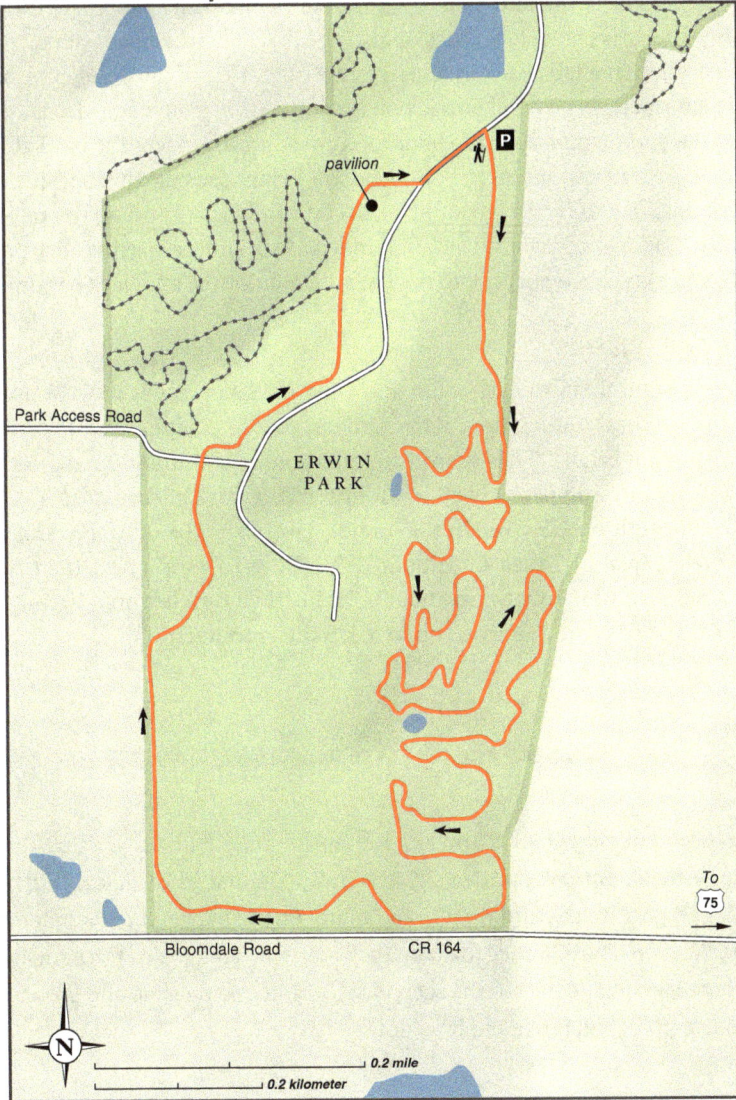

merges with the overgrown remains of an old gravel road that passes through another open, grassy clearing dotted with red, blue, yellow, and purple wildflowers. Head slightly downhill, winding through open grassland for quite a while before roots start breaking up the path and the woodlands once again enclose you. Just beyond the tree line, you'll find the second pond at 1 mile. From here, the trail heads northeast, meets back up with the creek, then heads south, following a high ridge. It then reaches a split at 1.28 miles. Bear right at the junction, bypassing a steep dip and climb intended for mountain bikers; a few of these bike dips punctuate the trail, but most have turnoffs just before them, allowing hikers to circumvent them.

The trail then winds back east, passes the other side of the pond, and curls back out into an open, grassy field as it heads south. After some sun-drenched hiking through the grass, you'll spot the park road ahead of you. Meet the road at 2.3 miles and rejoin the trail just across it. Follow the trail as it heads north alongside the road. At 2.43 miles, stay to the left to enter a final bit of woods. Through the trees to your right, you'll spot the pavilion; a few hundred feet later, a narrow dirt path bears right, leading you back out and up through the picnic area and back to your car.

NEARBY ACTIVITIES

The Heard Natural Science Museum and Wildlife Sanctuary is only 10 miles away, just to the southeast. It features plant gardens, nature exhibits, and a wildlife sanctuary with hiking trails. The Heard is open Monday–Saturday, 9 a.m.–5 p.m., and Sunday, 1–5 p.m. Admission is $8 for adults and $5 for children ages 3–12. To get there, head south on US 75. After 3.7 miles, take Exit 38A onto TX 121 S toward Fort Worth. Make a U-turn onto Spur 399 N toward McKinney, then turn right onto TX 5 S toward Fairview. Go about 0.7 mile, then turn left onto Farm to Market Road 1378 and pass the country club to reach the entrance.

• •

GPS TRAILHEAD COORDINATES N33° 15.317' W96° 39.300'

DIRECTIONS Follow US 75 N toward McKinney. Take Exit 41 (US 380/Greenville/Denton). Turn left onto West University Drive/US 380 E and go 2.5 miles. Turn right onto FM 1461 and go 2 miles. Turn right onto County Road 164, go about 1 mile, then turn left onto CR 1006. The entrance to Erwin Park is on the right. Inside the park, turn left at the end of the road and park in the second lot, next to the pavilion and picnic area. The trailhead, on the right, is marked by a kiosk.

32 LAVON LAKE: Trinity Trail

The path affords excellent views of Lavon Lake.

THIS HIKING AND EQUESTRIAN TRAIL skirts Lake Lavon, offering scenic views as it makes its way through open woodlands and prairie. The entire trail is 9 miles long and can be extended to any hiker's content.

DESCRIPTION

With an impressive 25.5 miles of trail, the Trinity Trail on Lake Lavon is long enough to challenge even the hardiest of hikers. With trailheads along the western side of the lake at Brockdale Park, East Fork, and Highland Park, plenty of options exist for adventurers who want to explore its different sections. This hike starts at the Brockdale Park trailhead and heads south, loosely following the shoreline as it traverses open woodlands and prairie. It's the perfect choice for someone interested in seeing the flora and fauna of the lake. The trail is also a good option for hikers who want a trek they can extend—the portion of trail I've mapped here is only a small segment of the 9 miles along this section of the Trinity Trail.

Once you've hiked this trail, check out other sections of the Trinity Trail. In particular, the ambitious hiker might consider visiting the Highland Park trailhead to hike the Giant Sycamore Loop Trail, a trek of about 5 miles out to a giant sycamore tree believed to be the largest tree in Texas. The tree stands 101 feet tall and

DISTANCE & CONFIGURATION: 3.2-mile out-and-back

DIFFICULTY: Moderate

SCENERY: Lake, shorebirds, grasslands, open woodlands

EXPOSURE: Partially shady–sunny

TRAFFIC: Moderate

TRAIL SURFACE: Dirt

HIKING TIME: 1.5 hours

DRIVING DISTANCE: 12 miles from TX 121 and US 75

ACCESS: Daily; free

MAP: tinyurl.com/lavonlake

WHEELCHAIR TRAVERSABLE: No

FACILITIES: Restrooms

CONTACT: trinitytrailriders.org

LOCATION: Brockdale Park, Wylie

COMMENTS: Hike this trail in spring or fall; it heats up quickly in summer. Visit www.swf-wc.usace.army.mil/lavon before you go, as flooding, construction, and maintenance can affect the operating dates and times of the lake's facilities.

measures 25.5 feet around. If you do consider this hike, leave early and bring plenty of water and snacks, as you'll be hiking about 10 miles round-trip.

Built in the early 1950s primarily for flood control, the 21,400-acre lake is on the East Fork of the Trinity River, northeast of Dallas near the town of Wylie. Some 20 parks along the lake offer myriad activities for fans of the outdoors, including bird-watching, boating, swimming, horseback riding, and camping. Lavon Lake has a reputation among anglers as an especially good spot for crappie fishing, and in the winter you'll see boats scoping the deeper waters in search of them. Hikers visiting any section of the lake would be well advised to check the U.S. Army Corps of Engineers' website (www.swf-wc.usace.army.mil/lavon) for park-closure information before visiting. Flooding, construction, and maintenance can sometimes affect operating dates and times for the lake's facilities.

Open to both equestrians and hikers, the Trinity Trail is maintained by the Trinity Trail Preservation Association, a volunteer equestrian organization that has nurtured and developed the trail into a treasure loved and frequented by not just riders but also by day hikers, photographers, walkers, and joggers. The Texas Parks and Wildlife Department has helped promote the trail as well, listing it among its Prairies and Pineywoods Wildlife Trails because of the variety of birds (herons, ducks, hawks, woodpeckers, and kingfishers), mammals (prairie dogs and bobcats), and snakes that you may spot on your visit.

The Brockdale Park trailhead is in an open section of grassland atop a small hill overlooking the lake; you'll find the trail on the eastern side of the parking lot, just beyond the white pipe gate. The area can be particularly muddy after a rainstorm, so check to see if it has rained recently; if so, give the trail plenty of time to dry out before you visit.

The trail starts out as a sunny trek through open grassland with easy lake views before curling away from the lake and into the woodlands, loosely following the shoreline as it heads southwest. The trees frame but do not envelop the trail, so

Lavon Lake: Trinity Trail

it's only partially shaded. In the patches of sun that reach through and between the trees, clumps of grass grow freely, presenting you with a primarily open woodland free of dense underbrush and thickets. Bird boxes placed along the trail attract many colorful residents. Keep an eye out for small brown creepers camouflaged among the tree trunks and for other more colorful birds, such as bluebirds and common yellowthroats.

At 0.9 mile, reach a picnic area with tables nestled in a grove of trees just off the path to your right. Continue heading straight, past the picnic area, and past a couple of little trails that branch off toward the lake.

Finally, at 1.6 miles, reach another turnoff toward the lake on the left. Turn onto the trail for a short hike to the lake's edge, where you can refresh yourself with the cool breezes sweeping off the water, enjoy full lake views, and start some impromptu beachcombing. When you've finished exploring the lake, you must decide if you'd like to continue outbound or complete the hike by retracing your steps to the trailhead. If you opt to keep going, the trail heads southeast, curving through the woodlands and teasing you with intermittent glimpses of the lake. The trail continues for miles, first passing Collin Park, with picnic tables for the weary traveler, before eventually ending at the southern trailhead in East Fork Park, 9 miles from the Brockdale trailhead.

NEARBY ACTIVITIES

Southfork Ranch (southfork.com), made famous on the TV show *Dallas,* lies just to the west of Plano. Its magnificent white mansion served as the home of the show's infamous J. R. Ewing from 1978 to 1991. The ranch was opened to the public in 1985 and continues to offer daily tours of the mansion and grounds. To get there from the trailhead, go back to the light at the Lucas Food Mart, and turn left onto Farm to Market Road 1378 (Southview Drive). After about 2.3 miles, turn right onto FM 2514 (Parker Road) and drive 2.5 miles. Turn left onto FM 2551 (Hogge Road/ Murphy Road). The entrance is about 0.5 mile down on the left.

• •

GPS TRAILHEAD COORDINATES N33° 04.383' W96° 32.950'

DIRECTIONS Take US 75 N and exit onto Bethany Drive in Allen. Turn right, heading east about 6 miles on Bethany (which becomes Lucas Road). At the stoplight next to Lucas Food Mart, turn left onto FM 3286. After 0.8 mile, turn right onto Brockdale Park Road. The gravel parking lot is about a mile down on the right, just before the boat ramp.

33 PARKHILL PRAIRIE TRAIL

A bridge connects to a section of secluded prairie.

RECONSTRUCTED AND RESTORED, this native prairie is inspiring in the spring, when the wildflowers bloom.

DESCRIPTION

If you're familiar with the opening sequence of the old TV series *Little House on the Prairie*—in which the Ingalls girls skip and frolic through a wide, open field dotted with flowers—then you have a good idea of what the Parkhill Prairie Preserve is like. The beautiful 436-acre preserve is very similar to the scenery in that unforgettable shot, offering a gently rolling, sunny grassland that is at its best in the spring, when the wildflowers bloom. The colorful display begins with prairie flowers, such as bright-red Indian paintbrush and violet-colored wine cup; late spring brings wild petunia and Mexican hat; and late summer and fall see bright-yellow goldenrod and the soft hues of the purple coneflower. The preserve has a remnant tract of blackland prairie, most of which is disappearing throughout the country as wild lands are converted to farmland.

The prairie is 60 miles northeast of Dallas in Collin County, making it one of this book's farthest hikes from the city, but it's certainly worth a visit for anyone seeking something a little different. It's fairly remote, set in the country just north

DISTANCE & CONFIGURATION: 1.88-mile loop

DIFFICULTY: Easy

SCENERY: Prairie, wildflowers

EXPOSURE: Sunny

TRAFFIC: Light

TRAIL SURFACE: Grass

HIKING TIME: 40 minutes

DRIVING DISTANCE: 32 miles from US 75 and US 380 in McKinney

ACCESS: Daily, sunrise–sunset; free

MAP: None

WHEELCHAIR TRAVERSABLE: No

FACILITIES: Toilets, picnic tables, water fountain

CONTACT: collincountytx.gov

LOCATION: CR 668, Blue Ridge

COMMENTS: Wear long pants and insect repellent if you visit in the summer—ticks love the long prairie grasses.

of Farmersville with few other houses around. From a rocky outcropping along the trail, you'll have fantastic views of the surrounding countryside, which consists primarily of gently rolling hills dotted with trees; the view is especially beautiful in the fall, when the leaves change colors.

Each season, after the spring wildflowers and grasses come in, the trail is mowed back into the prairie. You can hike here year-round, but be advised that if you come before mowing season, you're likely to see only faint hints of the trail and you'll have to navigate an overgrown path. Spikes mark the trail route at regular intervals, so even if the trail isn't mowed, you'll be able to find your way. Take care to avoid twisting your foot or stepping on snakes in the deep grass. Ideally, plan to visit after the trail has been mowed, which happens sometime after Mother's Day.

Collin County has been working with The Nature Conservancy to restore the prairie. Some of these efforts include undertaking prescribed burns—these help control intrusive nonnative plants, which can take over the prairie if left unchecked. Recent drought conditions have limited the number of burns allowed here; as conditions improve, however, more burns are planned. On your hike, you're likely to notice the charred remains of trees and shrubs.

Park in the spaces in front of the restrooms; the trailhead is opposite them and is marked by a kiosk. At the time of my visit, everything had been removed from the kiosk because the preserve was in the middle of an improvement project. Follow the mowed lane north past the kiosk, straight through the open prairie land. It's a gentle walk up and down some rolling hills, over a long wooden bridge, and through some shrubby tree growth to reach the overlook at 0.9 mile. A half-circle stone wall marks the spot atop a small rise and frames a lovely view of the rural countryside stretching out toward the horizon to the north and west.

Get back on the trail and follow it north. As you enter the northern section of the preserve, you'll notice clusters of shrubs and trees encroaching upon the prairie; you may also spot burn marks from the efforts to keep them from invading completely.

The path skirts the northern edge of the preserve. At 1.4 miles, bear left and enter a smaller section surrounded by trees. At the marker, turn right and cross the

Parkhill Prairie Trail

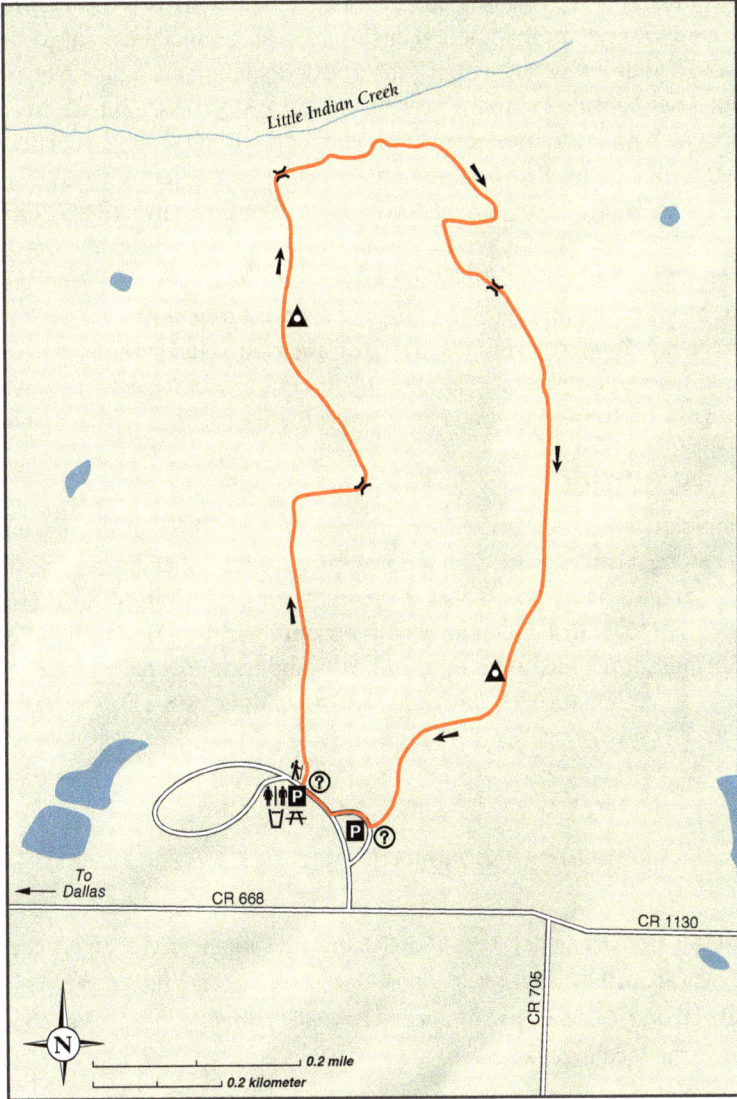

Little Indian Creek

To
Dallas

CR 668

CR 1130

CR 705

N

0.2 mile

0.2 kilometer

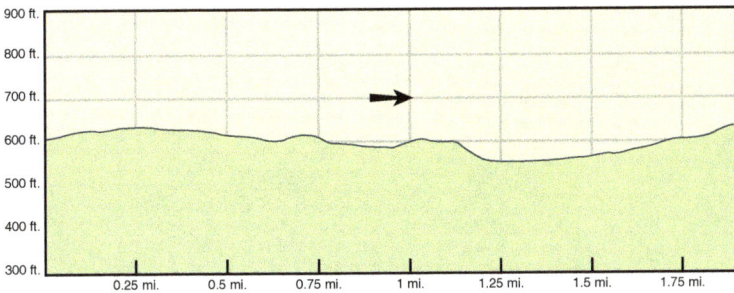

900 ft.
800 ft.
700 ft.
600 ft.
500 ft.
400 ft.
300 ft.

0.25 mi.   0.5 mi.   0.75 mi.   1 mi.   1.25 mi.   1.5 mi.   1.75 mi.

bridge to enter another small section of grassland screened by trees. Pass through a tree line and into yet another natural enclosure, which abuts the eastern edge of the preserve. To your left, a fence marks the preserve's boundaries; just beyond it, you can sometimes spot Black Angus peering curiously at you as you pass. Much to my surprise, just beside the trail here, I also encountered the skeletal remains of what appeared to be one of their herd members. How it got where I found it remains a mystery to me. Don't worry, though—you won't encounter any live steer on the trail.

You'll soon traverse the tree-lined meadow and be back on the open prairie. From here, it's a short hike uphill to the eastern rock-wall overlook, which offers picturesque views of the prairie to the north and west. From here, hike back 0.35 mile to the trailhead. You'll emerge from the prairie at a kiosk and parking area just up the road from where you parked. The parking lot and restrooms are within easy view down the road, a couple hundred feet to your right.

NEARBY ACTIVITIES

Enjoy a picnic at Caddo Park on Lavon Lake after the hike. A day-use-only park 17 miles away, it offers more than a dozen picnic sites, a handicap-accessible fishing pond, and a boat ramp. To get there, turn left onto County Road 668, which becomes CR 1130. Go 1 mile and turn right onto Farm to Market Road 36. Head south 3.8 miles, then turn right onto FM 2194 and travel 6.3 miles. Bear right onto Business TX 78, then turn left onto TX 78. Turn left onto US 380. The park is about 2 miles ahead on your right.

• •

GPS TRAILHEAD COORDINATES N33° 16.317' W96° 17.967'

DIRECTIONS From McKinney, take US 380 E toward Farmersville, then turn north onto TX 78 and go about 9.4 miles toward Blue Ridge. At CR 825, turn right and drive 4.4 miles, then turn left onto CR 668. The entrance to Parkhill Prairie is about 2 miles down on the left. Park in the second parking area.

34 PILOT KNOLL TRAIL

A red-shouldered hawk watches hikers pass by.

BIRDS DOMINATE THE WOODLANDS adjacent to this trail, which winds alongside Lake Lewisville. The trail is not the most scenic, but during hot, dry summers, the lake waters recede, leaving a marsh and exposing gnarled trees favored by vultures.

DESCRIPTION

Lake Lewisville is very popular and is often referred to as Dallas's party lake. Like many of north-central Texas's artificial lakes, Lewisville functions primarily as a flood control and water supply, but it's also well known for its recreational opportunities. In the summer, Jet Skiers, boaters, and anglers fill the waters, while the shores overflow with swimmers, picnickers, and campers. Because of its popularity, the lake is frequently in the news for its rowdiness, including boating accidents. Occasionally, alligator sightings prompt even more coverage. Game wardens advise that the gators' origins can be traced to the Trinity River. At any rate, alligators are a rarity here.

The lake dates back to the late 1920s, when the Elm Fork of the Trinity River was first dammed, creating the reservoir known as Lake Dallas. The lake was considerably smaller than today's Lake Lewisville, about a quarter of the current size. In the

DISTANCE & CONFIGURATION:
2.55-mile balloon

DIFFICULTY: Easy

SCENERY: Lake, woods, birds

EXPOSURE: Partially shady

TRAFFIC: Light

TRAIL SURFACE: Packed dirt

HIKING TIME: 45 minutes

DRIVING DISTANCE: 10 miles from
I-35W/I-35E split

ACCESS: Daily; free

MAP: tinyurl.com/elmforktrailmap

WHEELCHAIR TRAVERSABLE: No

FACILITIES: Available in Pilot Knoll Park

CONTACT: cteta.org/cteta-pilot-knoll.php

LOCATION: Pilot Knoll Park, Lake Lewisville
(South Shore)

COMMENTS: This trail can be messy after
a rainstorm. Be aware that construction of
FM 2499 may reroute portions of the trail.

late 1940s, amid concerns for flood control, a new impoundment, the Garza–Little Elm Reservoir, was created nearby by damming a number of creeks. About a decade later, Lake Dallas and the Garza–Little Elm Reservoir were combined to form the huge reservoir of today, named Lake Lewisville in the 1970s.

The trailhead for this hike is just outside Pilot Knoll Park on the east side of the parking lot, just behind the map kiosk. There is a day-use fee for the immaculately maintained park, but because the trail is not maintained by the park, you can park your car or hike the trail at no cost. A sign for Hickory Creek Trail is next to the trailhead.

The wide trail winds east through the woods, following a small access road and passing RV campsites on the right and huge private homes on the left. About 0.3 mile down the trail, reach a fork in the path and bear right, heading north down Lake Shore Trail. The trail winds through a wooded area of tangled trees before reaching another split. Head right at this second junction, passing through more woods. The trail is also open to equestrian traffic—although I didn't see any riders on my hike— so keep an eye to the ground for the occasional horse dropping.

At about 0.48 mile, a break in the trees affords an unobstructed view of the lake on the right. When water levels are low, a wide expanse of sandy beach, dotted with old, twisted tree trunks, rims the deathly-still lake. On my hike, I counted at least a dozen huge turkey vultures perched at the water's edge, surveying the watery landscape.

The trail continues, with the lake coming in and out of view on the right and a dense wood on the left. In addition to the mess of vulture feathers I found strewn across the trail, other signs of wildlife along the path are abundant, including what appeared to be deer tracks in the trail's soft dirt, and a brief glimpse of a small animal scurrying off under the trees—a raccoon, judging from the tracks. At the next junction, 1.15 miles into the hike, take the right-hand fork to head north. Go straight past another junction, and at 1.2 miles find yourself at a junction where a wide road heads toward an overlook to the right. On the left is the parking area at the end of Bishop Road, which serves as a public entrance to this overlook.

Pilot Knoll Trail

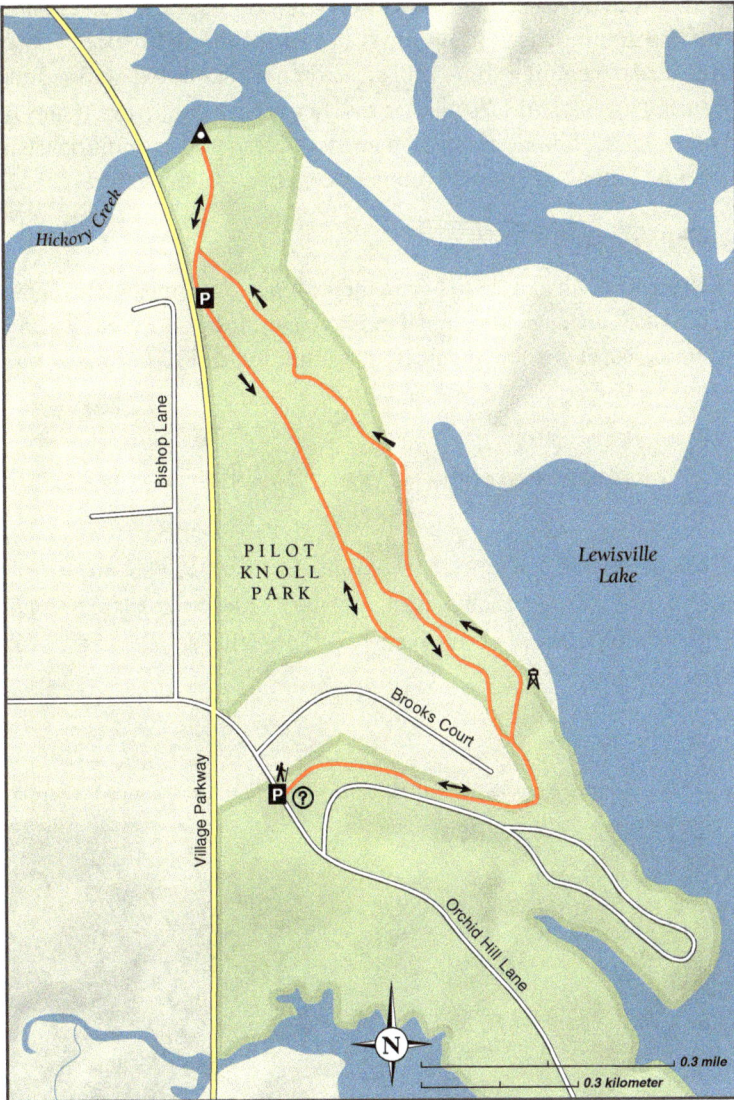

At this point, if you turn right the trail goes about 0.1 mile and then reaches the overlook—a small hill overlooking the lake (or, on a dry summer hike, the remnants of the lake). The lake's party reputation is most evident at public-access points such as these. In other words, the better the access to the lake, the more likely you are to see evidence of late-night partying.

If you've ventured to the overlook, retrace your steps (or turn left if you didn't) to the Bishop Road parking area. You'll reach a junction with signs indicating that

Hickory Trail is to the right and Lakeshore Trail is to the left. Go right onto Hickory Trail, heading south. The trail narrows and winds through woods. Look out for interesting birds, including some brilliant red ones that flitted across the trail continually during my hike. At 1.78 miles, a trail heads to the right, eventually fading out behind some private homes. Hang a left and follow the trail an additional 0.61 mile to close the loop. From here, retrace your steps 0.33 mile to the trailhead.

NEARBY ACTIVITIES

Pilot Knoll Park is a nice place to have a picnic lunch; its immaculate picnic area sits right on the lake's edge, yielding outstanding views. Just southwest, Rockledge Park at Grapevine Lake also offers picnicking, swimming, and sunning options.

GPS TRAILHEAD COORDINATES N33° 06.517' W97° 04.650'

DIRECTIONS Take I-35E and turn left (west) onto Farm to Market Road 407/Justin Road. Go about 4.5 miles to Chin Chapel Road, then turn right (north). Make a right to head east on Orchard Hill Lane, which dead-ends at Pilot Knoll Park. Parking is available just outside the park gate.

A mixture of trees and grass provides the perfect combination of sun and shade on the hard-packed trail.

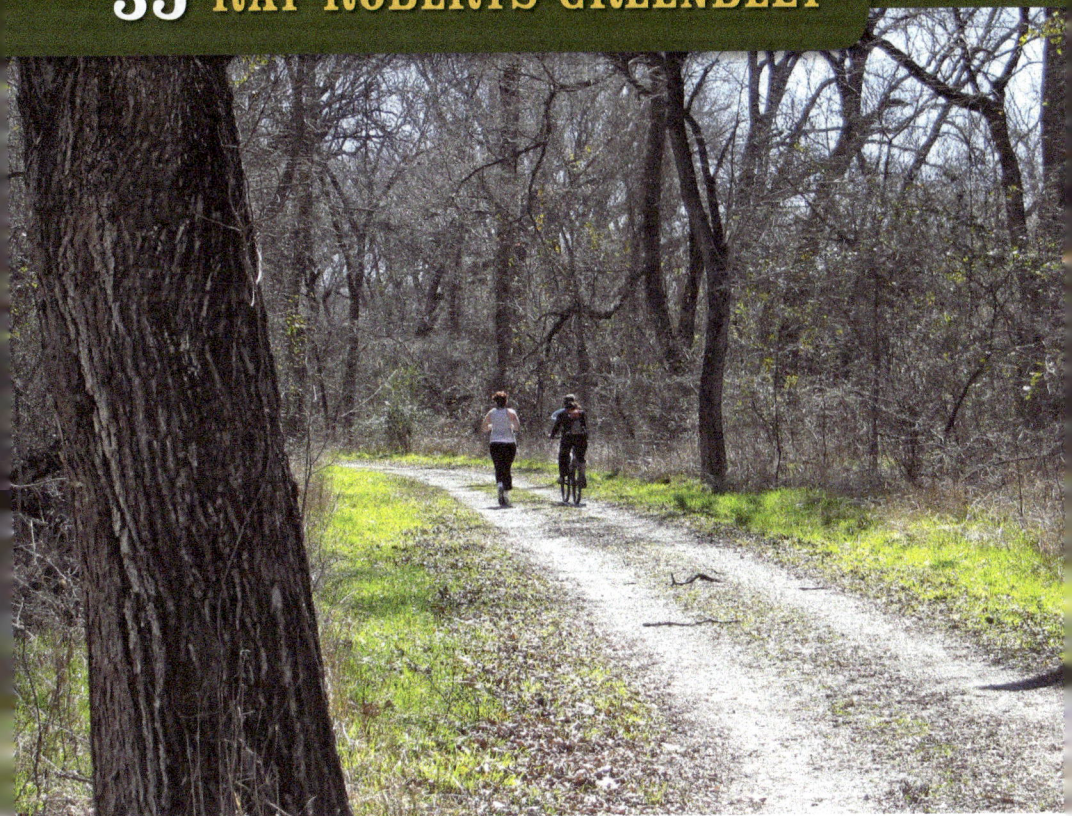

Wide, flat, and partially shaded, this trail is great for all ages.

THICK WOODS LOOM over this wide, charming trail that makes its way north from Lake Lewisville to Ray Roberts Lake. It's a great, kid-friendly hike.

DESCRIPTION

The Ray Roberts Lake–Lake Lewisville Greenbelt Corridor extends about 10 miles through a wooded section of land between the two lakes. Officially part of the state-park system, the corridor requires no entry fee from those who have a state-park pass. There are three trailheads along the greenbelt: one at the southern end, on US 380; one at the northern end, on Farm to Market Road 455; and one halfway through the corridor, on FM 428.

This trail starts at the southern end of the corridor, near the northern side of Lake Lewisville. Watch for the brown state-park sign identifying the greenbelt.

The greenbelt originally offered two parallel trails: a dirt path for equestrians and a hard-surface multiuse trail for hikers. Recently, however, the entire section of equestrian trail south of FM 455 to US 380 has been closed due to erosion. According to the Texas Parks and Wildlife Department, it will not reopen in the near future;

DISTANCE & CONFIGURATION:
5-mile out-and-back

DIFFICULTY: Easy

SCENERY: Dense woods

EXPOSURE: Partially shady

TRAFFIC: Moderate–heavy

TRAIL SURFACE: Packed gravel

HIKING TIME: 1.75 hours

DRIVING DISTANCE: 9 miles from
I-35E/I-35W split

ACCESS: Daily, 6 a.m.–10 p.m.;
$7 per person

MAP: tinyurl.com/rayrobertsgreenbelt

WHEELCHAIR TRAVERSABLE: No

FACILITIES: Recycling toilet

CONTACT: tpwd.texas.gov/state-parks
/ray-roberts-lake

LOCATION: Off E. University Dr., Denton

COMMENTS: Many miles of trail let you extend
this hike for as long as desired.

rather, proposed changes are in the works to relocate the equestrian trail to the same side of the river as the multiuse hiking trail. In the meantime, the hard-surface trail remains open and accessible to hikers.

The trailhead for this hike is in front of the gravel path next to the kiosk, on the north side of the parking lot. A self-pay booth at the trailhead allows you to deposit the small trail-use fee if you don't have a park pass. This is a great trail for youngsters because it's wide and partially shaded, has plenty of straight stretches to keep all members of the family within easy view, and is completely removed from potentially dangerous streets and highways. Encourage younger hikers to use the restrooms at the trailhead before you get under way—the other restrooms are 6.5 miles out at the FM 428 trailhead. Note also that there is no water along the trail, so make sure you've brought some, especially if it's a hot day.

I was actually much more impressed with this trail than I expected I would be. There's something special about it that's hard to put a finger on. It might be that it feels much wilder than the typical greenbelt. The land has been left in its natural state, and as you hike along, the elegance of the trees towering above and looming around you transports you into a different world. Ahead and behind you, the trail curves gently out of sight beneath the trees as it winds lazily north through the dense woods. Another part of its magic is that it's far removed from the ever-present hum of civilization. Deep within the greenbelt, you'll clearly hear the rustling of leaves and the creaking of limbs in the wind. The only sounds louder than these are the clear trills, whistles, and songs of birds watching you walk by. Surprisingly, the relaxing, peaceful atmosphere of the trail is not marred by the frequency of hikers, joggers, and dog walkers on the path. Most folks walk or jog quietly by, drinking in the calmness of the woods.

At 0.43 mile, pass an overlook to your left that offers a nice view of the Elm Fork of the Trinity River, which stays hidden from view for most of the hike. The trail follows the river as it heads north toward Ray Roberts Lake. Occasionally, signs

Ray Roberts Greenbelt

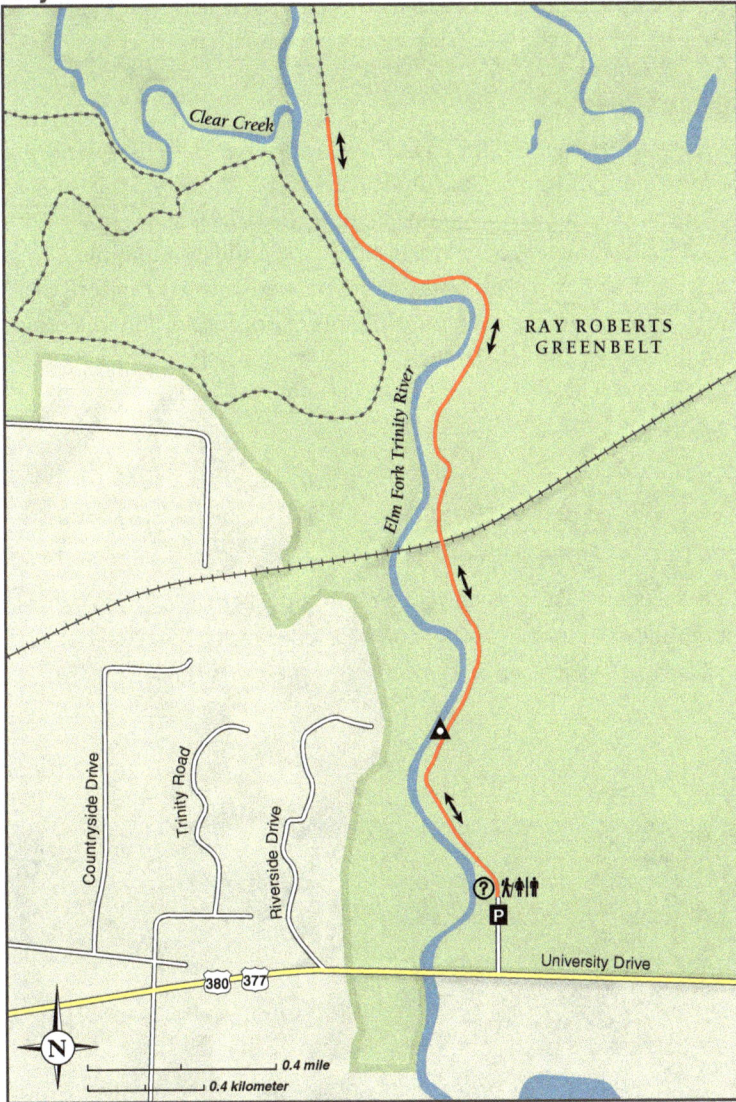

of civilization temporarily invade the beauty of the greenbelt—at 1 mile in, some power lines cross the path. Just beyond, at 1.15 miles, a railway line crosses the trail, creating another brief break in the otherwise continuous belt of woods.

The trail continues for much longer than you'll probably be willing or able to hike—10 miles in one direction. On most days, the trail is clear and quiet for as long as you're willing to walk. This trail can therefore be extended to just about any length you're comfortable with. When you're ready to head back, just retrace your steps. Reserve enough energy to make it back to the trailhead—if you're not paying attention, you could easily hike farther than you intended.

NEARBY ACTIVITIES

Stop by downtown Denton and visit the Courthouse-on-the-Square Museum, in the historic Denton County Courthouse at 110 W. Hickory St. Exhibits focus on African American families of Denton County; Hispanic families of Denton County; and special collections, such as Indian pottery, thimbles, and quilts. To get there, head back 5 miles down University Drive into downtown Denton, and turn left onto North Elm Street. Turn left onto West Hickory Street. You might also want to check out the nearby Golden Triangle Mall, with department stores, gift shops, and the Silver Cinema Theater, where you can see movies for $2.

• •

GPS TRAILHEAD COORDINATES N33° 14.433' W97° 02.500'

DIRECTIONS Follow I-35E north toward Denton and take Exit 463. Turn right onto TX 288 Loop and go about 3.5 miles. Turn right onto East University Drive. The trailhead is about 3 miles ahead on the left; keep an eye out for the brown Ray Roberts State Park sign.

Railway tracks emerge briefly from the woods.

A wide dirt path under a canopy of trees invites hikers even on the hottest day.

THIS TREK THROUGH HARDWOODS stops at interpretive signs identifying flora and leads to a pretty grove of pine trees. A spur midway through leads to a sandy lakeshore, along which you can find animal tracks and birds such as herons and egrets.

DESCRIPTION

Ray Roberts Lake, just north of Denton, is a 30,000-acre reservoir complete with boat ramps, camping, a swimming beach, trails, and a marina. The lake was originally called the Aubrey Reservoir but was renamed after a U.S. Congressman in 1980. It's a big attraction for anglers, who come to fish for crappie, white bass, catfish, and flathead, and is popular with nature lovers, who come to enjoy the various offerings of the state-park complex on its shores.

Part of the lake's state-park complex, Isle du Bois (Island of the Trees) sits on its southern shore. The park opened in 1993, making it a few years older than the neighboring Johnson Branch Unit, which opened in 1996. Within the park, you'll find miles of hiking, biking, and equestrian trails, all of which see good use. The majority of these trails run slightly inland from the shore, traveling for miles before looping back, making them ideal for long day treks. For shorter hikes, the park offers

169

DISTANCE & CONFIGURATION: 1-mile loop with spur

DIFFICULTY: Easy

SCENERY: Lake shoreline, hardwoods, pines

EXPOSURE: Shady–sunny

TRAFFIC: Light

TRAIL SURFACE: Packed dirt, sand

HIKING TIME: 30 minutes

DRIVING DISTANCE: 6 miles from FM 455 and US 377

ACCESS: Daily, 6 a.m.–10 p.m.; $7 per person for adults and children age 13 and older, free for kids age 12 and under

MAP: tinyurl.com/lostpinestrailmap

WHEELCHAIR TRAVERSABLE: No

FACILITIES: Restrooms, picnic area, playground

CONTACT: 940-686-2148, tpwd.texas.gov /state-parks/ray-roberts-lake

LOCATION: 100 PW 4137, Pilot Point

COMMENTS: This hike can be extended by walking along the lake shoreline. Bring binoculars for bird-watching.

a paved loop trail through its center and an interpretive nature trail near the park entrance, highlighted below.

The trailhead is just north of the parking area; you can see it from the lot. Pick up one of the brochures from the box at the trailhead to help you identify the flora along the trail; each plant has a numbered signpost. Heading down the trail, you'll immediately pass the first marker for Hercules' club—or toothache tree—a small tree whose bark, when chewed, can cause numbness in the mouth.

In about 400 feet, reach a small clearing and the amphitheater. Bear right, following the trail northeast through the woods. Here the trail is wide rather than singletrack, making it seem as if you've stepped into another world. At some points, I half-expected to see Little Red Riding Hood skipping through the woods on her way to a remote cottage.

Interpretive signs along the way will help you identify plants commonly found in this ecological woodland zone, known as the eastern cross timbers region. Blackjack oaks and post oaks dominate the woods; bluejack oaks and live oaks are fewer in number. Watch for colorful birds such as the eastern bluebird and American robin.

At 0.25 mile, reach a clearing amid which you'll see the remains of a chimney fenced off on the right. Elm Fork Trail, a wide path of loose dirt ideal for equestrians, intersects the nature trail here, heading west–east. Cross Elm Fork Trail and continue onto the path marked PEDESTRIAN TRAFFIC ONLY. In the shade of a dense woodland canopy, sun filters through the trees only in small patches, keeping things cool even on a hot day. Pass trees such as the Chickasaw plum, gum bumelia, and eastern red cedar as you make your way northwest. As you walk along, read the interpretive brochure, which provides interesting information regarding the historical and common uses of many of these trees.

At 0.5 mile, reach a split in the trail. Bear right onto Lake Trail and toward the water. The trail breaks from the woods and winds through tall grasses growing in the sand near the lake. When the water is low, a huge expanse of beach is exposed to stroll along. If you feel like prolonging the hike, head right or left, following the

Ray Roberts Lake State Park, Isle du Bois Unit: Lost Pines Trail

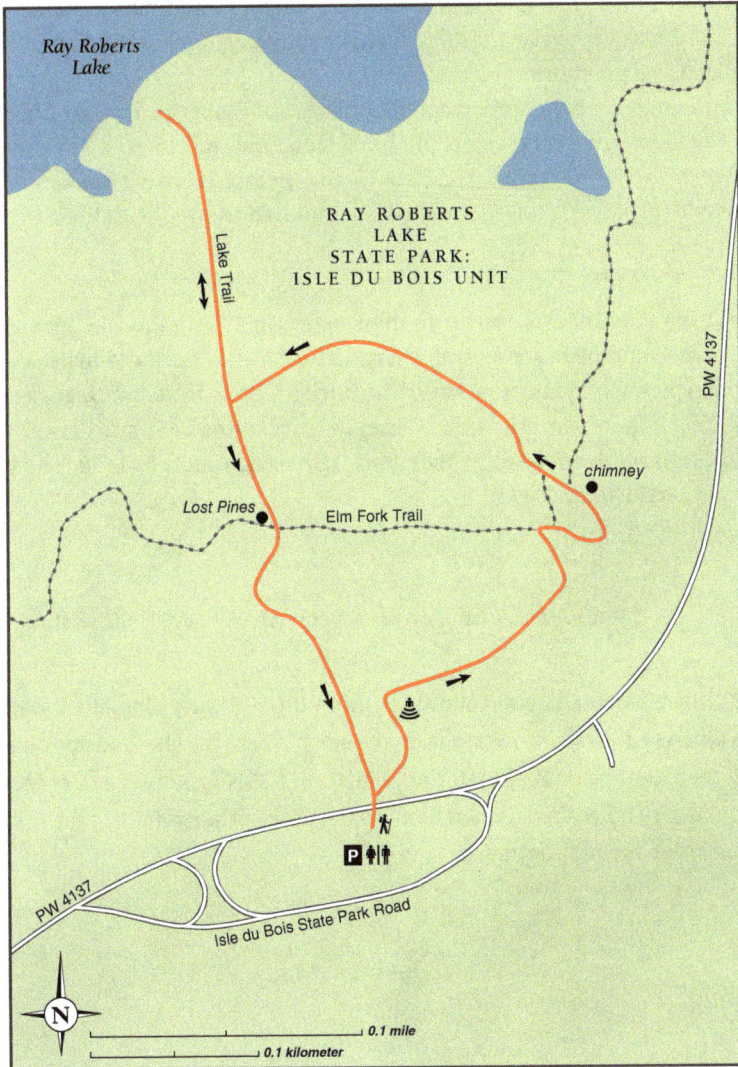

shoreline as it curves out of sight. Binoculars are helpful—this is a great spot for bird-watching. Even novices will be able to identify egrets and gulls along the water's edge. You'll see animal tracks in the soft sand at the shoreline, including the prints of white-tailed deer, which live in the area.

When you're done exploring the shore, head away from the lake, retracing your steps to the start of Lake Trail. Once you reach the trail sign, continue straight to finish the loop. Markers along the path help you identify the American elm and cedar elm. Finally, at 0.89 mile, reach the trail's namesake, a grouping of slash pines dubbed Lost Pines. The tall trees, with their needles and limbs hanging in gentle arches, present a captivating display that is completely unexpected amid the hardwood forest and greenbrier thicket.

Continuing along the trail, reach the soft dirt of Elm Fork Trail another 150 feet ahead. (Yield to horses and riders plodding along the trail.) Pass a few other native plants, such as the Texas prickly pear cactus, before reaching the amphitheater, where you'll retrace your steps the final few hundred feet to the trailhead.

NEARBY ACTIVITIES

Stop by Lake Ray Roberts Marina in the Sanger Unit along the lake for snacks or a fishing license and bait. For a small charge, you can fish from the marina's covered and lighted pier. Or try the fried catfish at Huck's Catfish Restaurant, adjacent to the marina. To get there, turn right onto Farm to Market Road 455 and drive 7 miles. At FM 2164, turn right, go 0.5 mile, then turn right again onto FM 1190. The marina is off Marina Circle, to the right.

• •

GPS TRAILHEAD COORDINATES N33° 21.967' W97° 00.683'

DIRECTIONS When reading directional signs on the highway, keep in mind that there are two different state-park units: one on the north side of the lake and one on the south side. To get to the Isle du Bois State Park Unit, take I-35 N to Sanger, exit at FM 455, and go east about 10 miles toward Pilot Point to the park entrance. Park in the first parking area, just inside the park entrance.

RAY ROBERTS LAKE STATE PARK, JOHNSON BRANCH UNIT:
Johnson Branch Trail

A picnic area with lake views offers a nice spot for lunch or a snack.

THIS FLAT, PAVED TRAIL winds through the park, passing through terrain characteristic of the eastern cross timbers region. Start with expansive views of the lake, then trek through the park toward campsites at its northern end.

DESCRIPTION

Ray Roberts Lake, just north of Denton, is a 30,000-acre reservoir with boat ramps, camping, a swimming beach, miles of trails, and a marina. The lake was originally called the Aubrey Reservoir but was renamed after a U.S. congressman in 1980. Popular with anglers, thanks to the crappie, white bass, catfish, and flathead in its waters, it also draws nature lovers who come to enjoy the various offerings of the state-park complex on its shores.

The Johnson Branch Unit is part of the state-park complex at Ray Roberts Lake and is on its northern shore in Valley View. Outdoorsy types will find both biking and hiking trails. The bike trail, which is also open to hikers, is a long trail in the western section of the park, offering loops through Dogwood Canyon and maintained by DORBA (the Dallas Off-Road Bicycle Association). For this hike, I've selected a long, paved trail that loops through the lake, woods, and camp areas on the eastern side of the park.

DISTANCE & CONFIGURATION: 3.62-mile out-and-back

DIFFICULTY: Easy

SCENERY: Elms, oaks, mesquite, lake, herons, egrets

EXPOSURE: Partially shady–sunny

TRAFFIC: Moderate

TRAIL SURFACE: Paved path

HIKING TIME: 1.25 hours

DRIVING DISTANCE: 14 miles from Chapman Rd. and I-35

ACCESS: Daily, 6 a.m.–10 p.m.; $7 per person for adults and children age 13 and up, free for kids age 12 and under

MAP: tinyurl.com/johnsonbranchtrailmap

WHEELCHAIR TRAVERSABLE: Yes

FACILITIES: Restrooms, picnic area, playground

CONTACT: 940-637-2294, tpwd.texas.gov/state-parks/ray-roberts-lake

LOCATION: 100 PW 4153, Valley View

COMMENTS: Bring your swimsuit so you can take a dip at the beach after the hike.

When you arrive, stop by the park headquarters for a map and information on free events. Although some of the events, such as campfire programs and stargazing parties (led by volunteer astronomers), occur during the evening, others, such as guided nature hikes, typically occur during the day.

Park in the large lot by the boat launch; the trailhead is just behind the fish-cleaning station, adjacent to the parking lot. Within a few steps, turn right, following the paved trail east through the trees. At 0.13 mile, reach a dirt trail turnoff on the left, with a sign identifying it as Vanishing Blackland Prairie Trail. Unfortunately, during my visit, the loop was closed. If it's open, it's worth a detour down the short trail with the interpretive guide that can be picked up at the visitor center. The small brochure describes the flora found along the trail—including trees such as honey locust, hackberry, pecan, cedar elm, and post oak, in addition to prairie grasses and wildflowers.

From the Vanishing Blackland Prairie Trail turnoff, continue straight (east) along the paved trail, which crosses the park road and passes another parking area and a picnic area before reaching a split at 0.23 mile. Head right at the split, following the trail toward the lake. The wide expanse of beach along the lakeshore is often busy with families playing ball, kids running through the sand in circles, and couples playing Frisbee. The trail makes a short loop around the peninsula, letting you take in lake views the whole way. Picnic tables along the trail tempt hikers to stay and enjoy the breeze.

At 0.28 mile, the trail splits—keep right. You'll come up behind some bathrooms, pass a playground, and then go left at 0.43 mile, looping back toward the beach. Turkey vultures can often be seen circling overhead as they search for leftover scraps of fish and other food. Also keep an eye out for water birds such as pelicans, herons, egrets, geese, and double-crested cormorants.

Turn away from the shoreline (left) at 0.55 mile, just before you reach its end. A few steps farther, bear right, then right again, following the trail north into some woods that quickly obscure the lake from view. The surrounding trees

Ray Roberts Lake State Park, Johnson Branch Unit: Johnson Branch Trail

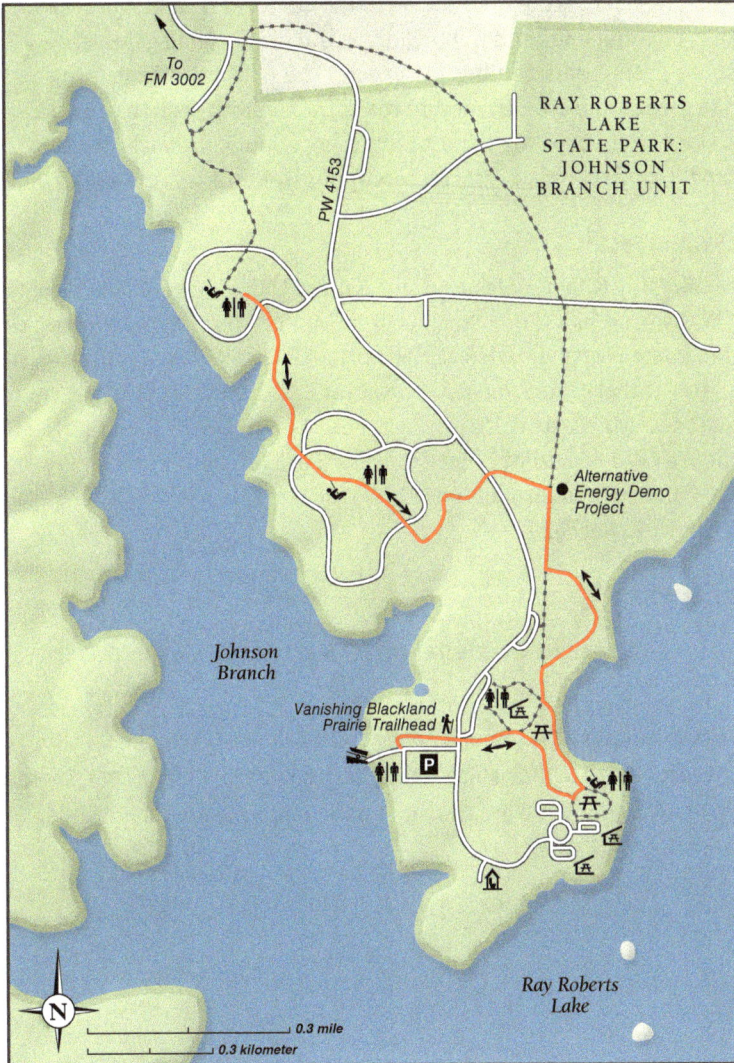

are characteristic of the eastern cross timbers region and include honey mesquite, blackjack oak, winged elm, and pecan.

At 0.65 mile, turn right at the path split. The trail winds past some camping areas tucked into the woods, then emerges again at 0.88 mile, where you'll again bear right. The trail keeps straight here for 0.33 mile, following the park road, which is hidden off to your left. Birds you may spot in the woods include the Carolina chickadee and the tufted titmouse. Also look out for flycatchers, swallows, woodpeckers, and bluebirds.

Turn left at 0.98 mile, next to a booth marked ALTERNATIVE ENERGY DEMO PROJECT. Continuing west, cross the road at 1.08 miles. Off to your right, glimpse some campsites, folks pitching tents and walking dogs, and kids playing games.

At 1.28 miles, cross another park road. The path heads northwest past a playground to the left and crosses another road. Then enter a section of dense woods and heavy shade. After you cross a short footbridge spanning a small stream, you'll reach another park road. The restrooms are just opposite. Retrace your steps to the trailhead.

NEARBY ACTIVITIES

Stop by Lake Ray Roberts Marina in the Sanger Unit along the lake for snacks and a fishing license and bait. For a small charge, you can fish from the marina's covered and lighted pier. Or try the fried catfish at Huck's Catfish Restaurant, adjacent to the marina. To get there, head 6.6 miles west on East Lone Oak Road/Farm to Market Road 3002 toward Morrow Road. Turn onto I-35 S/US 77 S and go 4 miles, then take Exit 478 (FM 455/Pilot Point/Bolivar). Turn left onto FM 455/West Chapman Drive, go 3 miles, then turn left onto FM 1190 and travel 0.9 mile. The marina is off Marina Circle, to the right.

• •

GPS TRAILHEAD COORDINATES N33° 24.567' W97° 03.000'

DIRECTIONS Follow I-35 N through Sanger, take Exit 483 onto Lone Oak Road/FM 3002, and head east 7 miles to the park, entering at the Johnson Branch Unit. There are signs, but keep in mind that there are two state-park units: one on the north side of the lake and one on the south side.

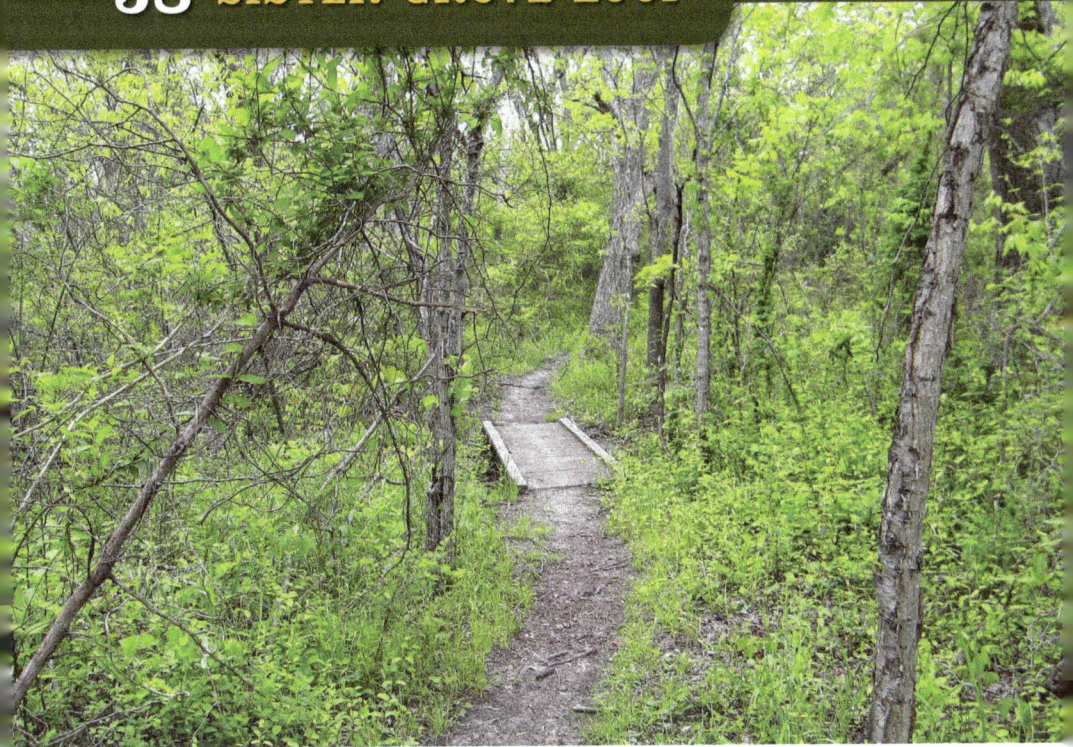

Thick vines dangle from tree limbs alongside the trail.

THIS EXCELLENT ALL-AROUND HIKE loops through a pretty, green woodland interspersed with fields and inhabited by coyotes, rabbits, and armadillos.

DESCRIPTION

This remote Collin County park, on the northeastern side of the expansive Lake Lavon, takes an unusual drive down two interconnected bridges to reach. It's a fun trail that will suit hikers whose tastes conflict—offering both open, sunny grassland and shady, lush green woodland. Expect to find some off-road bikers here—the trail is maintained by the Dallas Off-Road Bicycle Association (DORBA). It's not as popular as many of the DORBA trails closer to the city, so some days you might not find any bikers here at all. If you hike quietly, you might see some small wildlife along the trail—within a few minutes of starting the hike, I spotted a huge jackrabbit hopping alongside the path. Farther down the trail, I found what looked like coyote tracks.

The 21,400-acre Lavon Lake is operated by the U.S. Army Corps of Engineers and was impounded in 1953. More than a dozen lakeside parks dot its 83-mile shore-line. Sister Grove Park is not operated by the Corps but is part of Collin County Open Space. Its trails, started in the early to mid-1990s, have been restored and extended by DORBA volunteers continually since then. The entire trail system is

DISTANCE & CONFIGURATION: 2.96-mile loop

DIFFICULTY: Easy

SCENERY: Open fields, thick woodlands, wildflowers

EXPOSURE: Sunny–shady

TRAFFIC: Moderate

TRAIL SURFACE: Dirt

HIKING TIME: 1.25 hours

DRIVING DISTANCE: 8.3 miles from US 380 and CR 407

ACCESS: Daily, sunrise–sunset (gate is locked at sunset, and hikers can get locked in); free

MAP: None

WHEELCHAIR TRAVERSABLE: Parking area, restrooms and picnic area only

FACILITIES: Toilet, picnic tables

CONTACT: dorba.org

LOCATION: 11110 CR 562, Princeton

COMMENTS: Make sure to wear sturdy shoes.

about 6 miles long and comprises two loops—the Sister Grove Loop, which forms the northern half (and is the route for this hike), and the Lake Loop, which forms the southern half. A third trail, Hunter's Access Trail, heads south to cut directly through the two loops, directing duck hunters down to the lake. Mountain bike tires have worn a narrow groove down the middle of a couple of the softer sections of the loop trails, making it sometimes awkward to hike; wear comfortable, sturdy shoes to avoid twisting an ankle.

From the trailhead, start the loop by taking the leftmost trail, next to Hunter's Access Trail. The path heads east past a picnic area and through a sunny, open field dotted with eastern red cedar. In the spring, small clumps of purple wildflowers grow in the grass, making for a cheerful scene.

As the trail rounds a curve, you'll trade open sky for a canopy of trees as you enter a woodland full of huge, gnarled trees with vines growing up their trunks and hanging from their branches. At 0.53 mile, cross a wooden bridge, then emerge from the trees and into a small pocket of wildflower-studded grassland. The trail weaves in and out of the open and wooded areas several times; it won't be long before you find yourself heading through shrubs and back into the cool green woodlands for a more prolonged hike through the shade.

At 0.88 mile, bear right at the junction, following the Sister Grove Loop west. Stay right at the next junction. At 1.2 miles, bear right for a short detour past a small pond hidden in the woods. After checking out its still, murky, green-brown waters, which are popular with birds, loop back up and rejoin the main trail. A few hundred feet farther, pass a wide dirt path, staying on the narrow singletrack instead. Then exit yet another small pocket of grassland and find yourself entering another thick section of woodland. Tiny holes in the tree trunks provide evidence of sapsuckers and woodpeckers. Birds are plentiful: watch for the colorful plumage of the easily recognizable cardinal, and keep an ear open for the melodies of warblers and thrashers. A thick understory of saplings and small trees colors everything a vibrant green. The thick foliage engulfs the trail, making this a haven on a hot day.

Sister Grove Loop

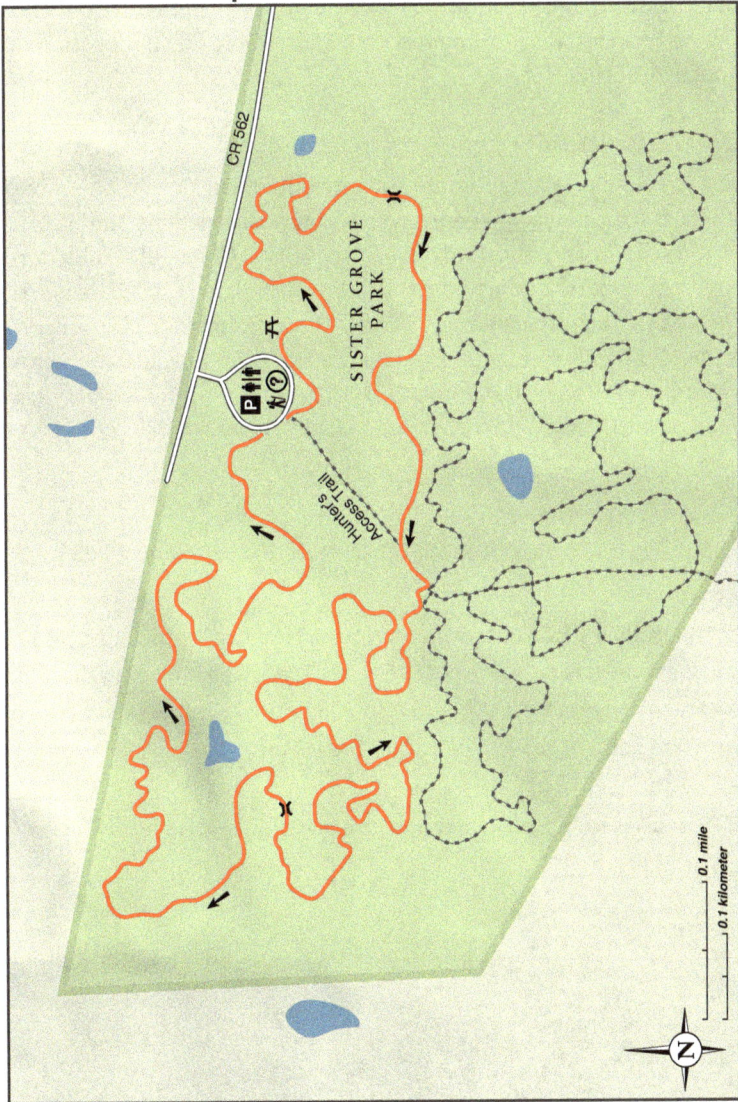

CR 562

SISTER GROVE PARK

Hunter's Access Trail

0.1 mile

0.1 kilometer

Z

Keep left at the junction at 1.65 miles and go another 0.2 mile to cross a wooden bridge and pass another small pond. Traverse a few more sections of alternating grassland and woodland pockets before you finally emerge into the main grassland near the trailhead. Look out for springtime bluebonnets in the latter couple of grassland pockets.

Although the trailhead is just to the east, there's one last woodland section to hike before you complete the trail. Heading back into the trees, you'll work your legs on a couple of small, hilly sections before climbing back uphill and out of the woods for good. At 2.9 miles, reach Hunter Access Trail, where you'll turn left to head back north to the trailhead.

NEARBY ACTIVITIES

In nearby Greenville, visit the Audie Murphy/American Cotton Museum (600 I-30, 903-450-4502, cottonmuseum.com), which comprises exhibits and displays related to the cotton industry; the Ende-Gaillard House, Greenville's oldest residence; a collection of historic military memorabilia; and various special collections. The museum is open Tuesday–Saturday, 10 a.m.–5 p.m. Admission is $6 for adults; $4 for seniors age 60 and older, military veterans, and college students; and $2 for children age 18 and under. To get there, take US 380/Audie Murphy Parkway east toward Greenville about 16 miles. Bear right onto US 69, then turn right onto I-30 E.

• •

GPS TRAILHEAD COORDINATES N33° 10.967' W96° 26.800'

DIRECTIONS Follow US 75 N toward Sherman. Take Exit 41 toward US 380 and turn right onto West University Drive/US 380 E. Travel about 12.5 miles. In the middle of the bridge over Lavon Lake, turn left onto a smaller bridge, County Road 559. After about 1 mile, turn left onto CR 561 to reach Sister Grove Park.

Be sure to wear sunscreen, as sections of exposed trail offer plenty of sunshine.

The beach at the end of the trail provides a spot for contemplation and lunch.

IF YOU'RE LOOKING for a quiet, peaceful trail where you can hike for a few miles and be rewarded for your efforts with a picnic adjacent to a small, secluded beach, then this is the hike for you. A few hours here provide an instant cure to the stresses of metropolitan life and are sure to provide you with the mental reset you've been longing for.

DESCRIPTION

Located in Denton County on the banks of Lake Lewisville, the Tribute Shoreline Trail is a fairly new trail that opened in 2013 in The Colony. Named after and part of the master-planned community of The Tribute, the trail was part of a partnership between The Colony, The Texas Parks and Wildlife Department, and the U.S. Army Corps of Engineers. The trail traverses a peninsula of Lake Lewisville, a 28,980-acre lake that is actually an impoundment of the Elm Fork of the Trinity River. The lake is a popular recreation spot on weekends and holidays, seeing frequent use from people pursuing all types of outdoor recreation activities including boating, camping, fishing, and picnicking.

The peninsula this trail traverses gives only a limited view of a small section of the lake and is fairly void of the intense recreation you might find in other sections

DISTANCE & CONFIGURATION: 4.8-mile balloon

DIFFICULTY: Easy

SCENERY: Lake

EXPOSURE: Sunny

TRAFFIC: Light

TRAIL SURFACE: Packed dirt

HIKING TIME: 2.5 hours

DRIVING DISTANCE: 9 miles from Dallas North Tollway and TX 121

ACCESS: Daily, sunrise–sunset; free

MAP: tinyurl.com/tributeshorelinetrail

WHEELCHAIR TRAVERSABLE: Yes

FACILITIES: Restrooms, water fountain, picnic tables

CONTACT: visitthecolonytx.com

LOCATION: Lebanon Rd., The Colony

COMMENTS: There are no picnic tables at the trailhead, but you will find a couple at the outermost point of the trail, so pack a lunch. Also be sure to bring sunscreen and a hat—there is little to no shade on this sun-drenched trail.

of the lake, offering a peaceful day hike. On my hike, a single fisherman was all that could be seen from the soft sandy beach at the trail's end.

The trailhead is located in a parking area near the Old American Golf Club in The Colony. Ample parking, immaculate restrooms, and benches greet you when you arrive, and interpretive signage adjacent to the parking area will help you get oriented. To start the hike, you'll head southwest down the soft dirt trail toward the distant lake. The entire trail will be as you see it here—a well-cared-for, wide, soft-packed dirt trail, great for walkers, dogs, runners, and hikers alike. It is worth noting that although The Colony cites this trail as being approximately 3 miles long, the city's mileage estimate appears to start at the entrance point to the peninsula—approximately 1 mile from the parking lot. This means that the total trail out and back consists of 4.8 miles, so plan accordingly.

As you head down the trail, you'll soon pass the Old American Golf Club—a popular spot with locals. The first mile or so of trail borders the golfing green and is shared with the golf club. It is therefore not uncommon to see golf carts passing you slowly on the wide shared path as you hike along.

At 0.15 mile, you'll reach an old storm shelter that is half buried in the ground and a sign directing you west onto the nature trail. A few steps farther and you'll reach another juncture. Don't cross the road; instead, follow the trail as it curls southward toward the lake.

At 0.45 mile you'll reach the first of many interpretive signs along the trail. Benches and trash cans at each interpretive sign provide nice rest spots regularly throughout the hike. Continuing on, the driving range fades behind you, and at 1 mile you'll reach the end of the shared trail. From here the trail becomes a hike-and-bike trail only.

At 1.15 miles, you'll reach another bench and interpretive sign. Take a moment to learn about the history of the surrounding land and peninsula.

Back on the trail, the peacefulness of your surroundings will charm you. Tall grasses surrounding the trail bend softly in the wind as you hike by. Trees dot the landscape here and there, providing spots for curious birds to rest on.

Tribute Shoreline Trail

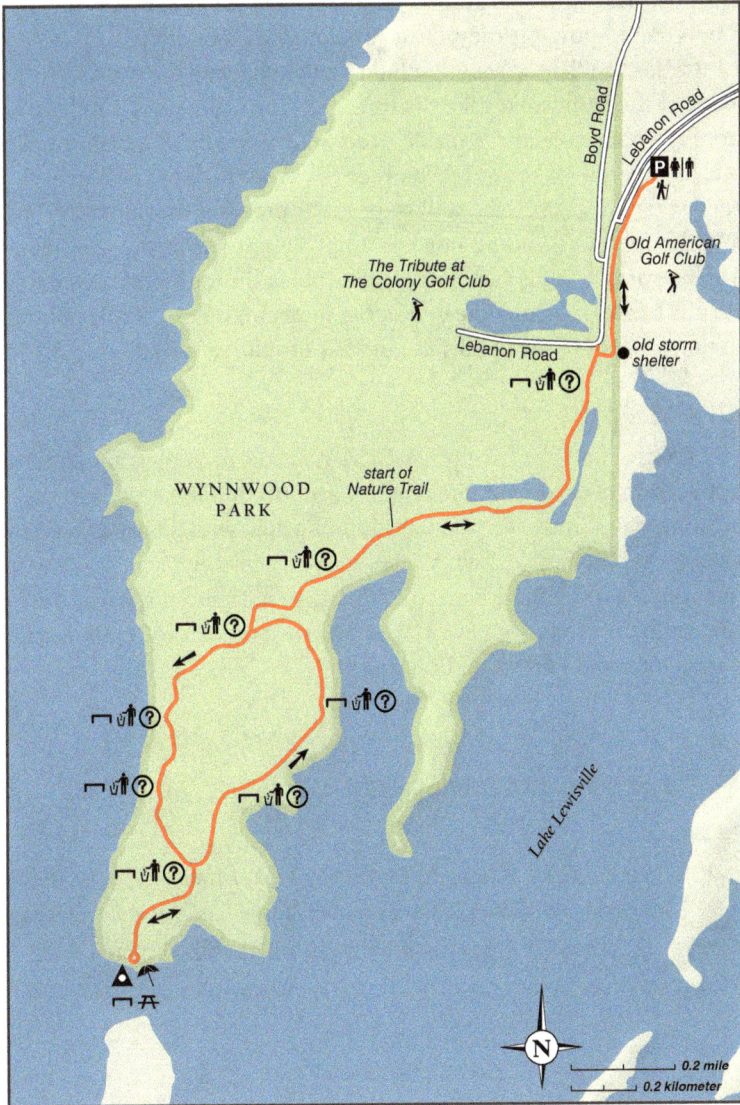

Map labels:
- Boyd Road
- Lebanon Road
- The Tribute at The Colony Golf Club
- Old American Golf Club
- Lebanon Road
- old storm shelter
- start of Nature Trail
- WYNNWOOD PARK
- Lake Lewisville
- N
- 0.2 mile
- 0.2 kilometer

Another interpretive sign at 1.3 miles describes the wildlife that inhabits the area including, raccoons, foxes, beaver, bobcats, coyotes, skunks, and white-tailed deer, to name a few. At this point, the trail splits into a loop. Head west. As you round the bend, you'll start to catch glimpses of the lake through the trees.

The trail continues heading down the peninsula. You'll pass another interpretive sign at 1.56 miles, which discusses the city of The Colony. At 1.7 miles, an interpretive sign offers an insight into the native flora of the surrounding habitat, including post oak, side oats grama, little bluestem, big bluestem, Illinois bundle-flower, bois d'arc, snow-on-the-prairie, and purple three-awn.

At 1.9 miles, you'll reach another interpretive sign and the turnoff to the lookout at the edge of the peninsula. Take the turn, heading south. At 2.1 miles you'll reach the end of the peninsula and a scenic overlook. A couple of tables, a bench, and a quiet secluded beach make an absolutely perfect spot for a picnic lunch.

When you're ready, retrace your steps to the previous trail juncture. From there, complete the loop by heading northeast up the last leg of the trail. You'll pass a couple of interpretive signs and benches describing the local birds and the surrounding wetlands before reaching the end of the loop at 3 miles. At this point, turn east back up the trail, out of the peninsula, and back to the trailhead.

NEARBY ACTIVITIES

In nearby Frisco, the Texas Sculpture Garden makes for a pleasant stroll through a unique collection of outdoor contemporary art. Just up the street from the sculpture garden, Stonebriar Centre is a popular shopping mall with plenty of places to grab a bite to eat. To get there, take Lebanon Road approximately 7 miles to Legacy Drive. Turn right on Legacy, left on Warren Parkway, then right on Gaylord Parkway. The sculpture garden is located at 6801 Gaylord Pkwy. Stonebriar Centre is a few blocks farther after you cross Parkwood Boulevard.

• •

GPS TRAILHEAD COORDINATES N33° 06.308' W96° 55.492'

DIRECTIONS Take I-35E north toward Denton to TX 121 (Sam Rayburn Tollway). Take the exit for Farm to Market Road 423/Main Street/Josey Lane, and turn left onto North Josey Lane/Main Street/FM 423. After 4 miles, turn left onto Lebanon Road. The trailhead is approximately 3 miles down on the left, just before you get to the Old American Golf Club.

40 WALNUT GROVE TRAIL

A hiker beachcombs along the lakeshore.

THIS TRAIL APPEALS to hikers looking for a quiet, peaceful walk with plenty of solitude. Although frequented by local horse owners, trail traffic is very light. Several loops to the water's edge offer opportunities to explore the wild shoreline.

DESCRIPTION

Certified as a National Recreation Trail in 1991, this pleasant trail follows the southern shoreline of Grapevine Lake, offering almost a continuous view of the water. Unlike the northern side of the lake, where waters are a little rougher and trails more crowded, this side is calm and serene, with plenty of opportunities for being alone. The gentle waters on this side of the lake do little more than lap at the shoreline, and even the view is relaxing—only the occasional fishing boat can be seen sitting out in the tranquil waters. The trail is considered a hiking and equestrian trail, and you're likely to run across a few horseback riders clopping down the path. The horses add to the bucolic mood, though you'll want to keep an eye peeled for the occasional horse dropping.

The best feature of this trail is the constant beach access. The main path traverses the shoreline slightly inland, but if you're in the mood for beachcombing, you'll find a number of paths branching off the main trail toward the lake that loop back to

DISTANCE & CONFIGURATION:
4.76-mile balloon

DIFFICULTY: Easy

SCENERY: Lake, wild beach

EXPOSURE: Sunny–shady

TRAFFIC: Light

TRAIL SURFACE: Dirt path

HIKING TIME: 2 hours

DRIVING DISTANCE: 9.3 miles from I-35W and TX 114

ACCESS: Free

MAPS: bjnc.org/wp-content/uploads/2016/09/BJNC-trail-map.pdf

WHEELCHAIR TRAVERSABLE: No

FACILITIES: None

CONTACT: www.swf-wc.usace.army.mil/grapevine

LOCATION: Bob Jones Park, Southlake

COMMENTS: The closest restrooms are at nearby Bob Jones Park.

rejoin the main trail. At 0.25 mile into the hike, reach the first of these, branching off to the left. Bear right to stay on the main trail.

The dirt trail winds past glimpses of the lake on your left and woods and shrubs on the right. At 0.3 mile, encounter the next junction, where you'll stay right as the trail winds through some dense shade then reemerges into the sun. At 0.5 mile, look for another loop heading out to the shoreline. If you decide to make a brief detour down the side trail on the left, as I did, you'll find a narrow, sandy beach with tall beach grass here and there—a completely wild and unmanicured shoreline. On my hike, I saw what is probably most typical—a couple of shorebirds standing along the water's edge and a lone woman and her dog picking their way down the shoreline. I didn't see anyone else on the shore the entire hike, until my way back, when a couple of horseback riders clopped slowly toward me then disappeared down a lake loop, presumably for a slow ride along the beach.

When you're done beachcombing, rejoin the loop, heading up and left through the tall grass back toward the main path. The next four junctions are more loops down to the water; keep on the main path, going straight to bypass them.

As you hike, keep your eyes open for wildlife, including fox, deer, coyote, opossum, armadillo, and rabbit. While I was hiking, an instructor leading a group of horseback riders passed me. She stopped to chat, commenting that on a couple of recent visits here she had spotted what she believed to be a large cougar just off the trail. She notified the U.S. Army Corps of Engineers, who told her they had already received reports of a large cat on the trail. Chances of an encounter are probably rare, but be aware of the possibility. Although I saw few animals on my hike, I found plenty of scat and tracks on the trail. If you're interested in identifying animals that have recently traipsed through, bring along an animal-scat and print-identification book. Prints are best sighted after rain (though if it's rained too hard, the trail may be too muddy to hike).

At 1.2 miles in, turn left at a fork and soon reach a clearing overlooking a sandy beach strewn with driftwood. Adjacent to the trail, about half a dozen structures

Walnut Grove Trail

resembling bat houses have been installed. At the next fork, stay to the left; at the next two forks, keep straight, following the main trail as it winds over grassy knolls with nice lake views.

At 2 miles in, reach a fork with a sign marked BOB JONES PARK/WALNUT GROVE/ CAMP BURNETT. Continue straight, following the trail as it twists uphill away from the lake. At 2.4 miles, the path forks again; a sign directs hikers to Bob Jones or White Chapel. Continue straight toward Bob Jones. A couple hundred feet farther, you'll reach the next trail sign. From here, the return loop begins, so follow the trail to the right in the direction of White Chapel. At the next fork, at 2.5 miles, bear right and follow the trail through a field spotted with prickly pear cactus. At 2.65 miles, turn right at the split and follow the fence as the trail winds back and rejoins the main trail. You'll find yourself back at the BOB JONES PARK/WALNUT GROVE/CAMP BURNETT sign, where you'll turn left to head back toward the trailhead.

NEARBY ACTIVITIES

The huge Grapevine Mills Mall—with more than 190 shops and a 30-screen AMC movie theater—is only a short drive away. You'll also find a selection of restaurants both within and around the mall. To get there, take TX 114 S 2 miles and exit at Northwest Highway/East Southlake Boulevard. Turn left onto Northwest Highway and go about 5 miles; you'll see the signs for Grapevine Mills on your left.

• •

GPS TRAILHEAD COORDINATES N33° 00.267' W97° 09.417'

DIRECTIONS Take TX 114 west into Southlake, then head right (north) onto White Chapel Boulevard. Follow the road about 3 miles past Bob Jones Park until it dead-ends in a small parking lot. The trailhead is on your right.

A hiker searches a trail for wildlife.

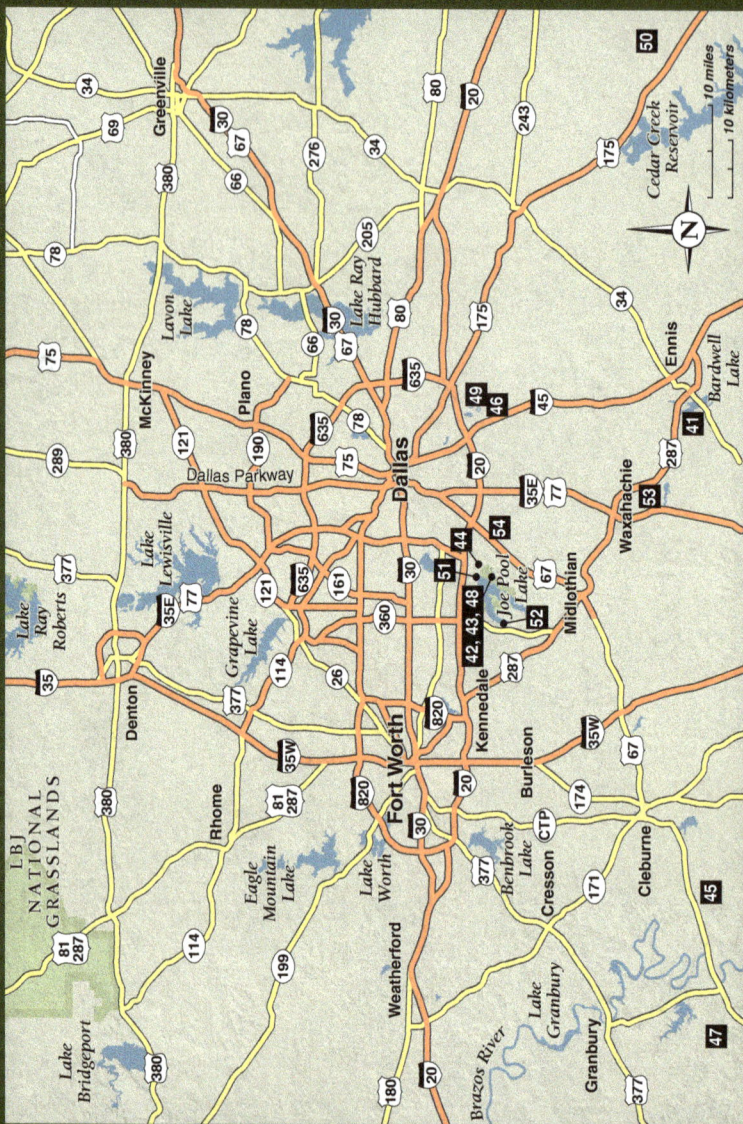

SOUTH OF DALLAS–FORT WORTH
(Including Cedar Hill, Glen Rose, and Cleburne)

Bring plenty of sunscreen, as much of the trail is exposed.

GRASSY MEADOWS AND SUNNY FIELDS take center stage on this flat hike along Bardwell Lake. The second half of the trail loops back through wooded thickets. More than 13 miles of trails offer unlimited options for those seeking a longer hike.

DESCRIPTION

On Waxahachie Creek in Ellis County, the 3,570-acre Bardwell Lake is about 40 miles south of Dallas and 60 miles southeast of Fort Worth. It was impounded in 1965 to facilitate flood control and supply water, and today it also serves as a recreational spot. A half-dozen parks lie along its perimeter, including Waxahachie Creek Park, on the southwestern shoreline—the starting point for this hike. In addition to the hiking trails, the park also offers boating, picnicking, and camping.

Many folks familiar with Bardwell Lake have heard of it while visiting nearby Ennis—the Bluebonnet City of Texas. The city's driving routes, known as the Bluebonnet Trails, lead visitors through the best of the springtime display. If you intend to tour the driving trails after you've done some hiking, you'll want to plan your visit around the end of April, when the bluebonnets should be in full bloom.

At the park entrance, pass through a gate; let the park worker there know you'll be hiking, and you should receive a general map of the trails. Admission is free for hikers,

DISTANCE & CONFIGURATION: 2.34-mile loop

DIFFICULTY: Moderate

SCENERY: Grassland, wooded thickets

EXPOSURE: Sunny

TRAFFIC: Moderate

TRAIL SURFACE: Dirt

HIKING TIME: 45 minutes

DRIVING DISTANCE: 9.6 miles from US 287 and I-45

ACCESS: Daily, 6 a.m.–10 p.m.; free

MAP: tinyurl.com/bardwelllaketrailmap

WHEELCHAIR TRAVERSABLE: No

FACILITIES: Toilets, picnic tables

CONTACT: www.swf-wc.usace.army.mil/bardwell

LOCATION: Waxahachie Creek Park, Bozek Rd., Ennis

COMMENTS: Trail etiquette gives equestrians the right-of-way.

but if you plan to camp, you'll need to pay. Once you pass through the gate, turn left and park in the lot on the westernmost side of the park, near the boat launch. Although the huge parking lot can easily accommodate a large number of cars, on my visit it was completely empty because most hikers were primarily campers who just walked over.

The Army Corps of Engineers website advises that this trail is within a hunting area, and hikers should be wary during hunting season. I did speak with a park ranger regarding safety issues, and he advised me that the trail receives a fair amount of traffic from campers, hikers, equestrians, and bikers year-round and that they have never encountered any type of a problem, even during hunting season. I felt very safe and would readily visit again at any time of year. Those still concerned, however, can check the dates of hunting season for Ellis County available in the Texas Parks and Wildlife *Outdoor Annual.* A couple of general tips for hiking close to or within a hunting area: wear brightly colored clothing in shades not found in nature, and stay on designated trails.

At the trailhead, take the path that heads straight out from the gate toward the west. A couple hundred feet down, bear right at the junction and hike through a grassland clearing dotted with cactus and eastern red cedar. The path winds up and down a couple of low, grassy hills where butterflies and dragonflies come to greet you as you pass. Off to your right, thick woodlands surround the lake to the north, forming a shield that prevents any glimpse of the water.

At 0.48 mile, reach a wide, grassy lane running through the center of a long stretch of grassland meadow. Bear right onto the flat, sunny route, heading west. This is an excellent trail to hike with the family, because the comfortable width of the trail allows you to walk three or four abreast. With the woodlands still to the far right, tree-dotted hillsides to the far left, and nothing but a grassy corridor before you, you'll be able to take in the peaceful scenery while still maintaining a conversation. Equestrian riders love the trail for just this reason, and you're likely to pass a few along this portion of the hike.

Bear left at 1.1 miles, leaving the grassland and heading south onto the narrow path through the short trees and berry-laden shrubs. The path winds slightly uphill

Bardwell Lake Multiuse Trail

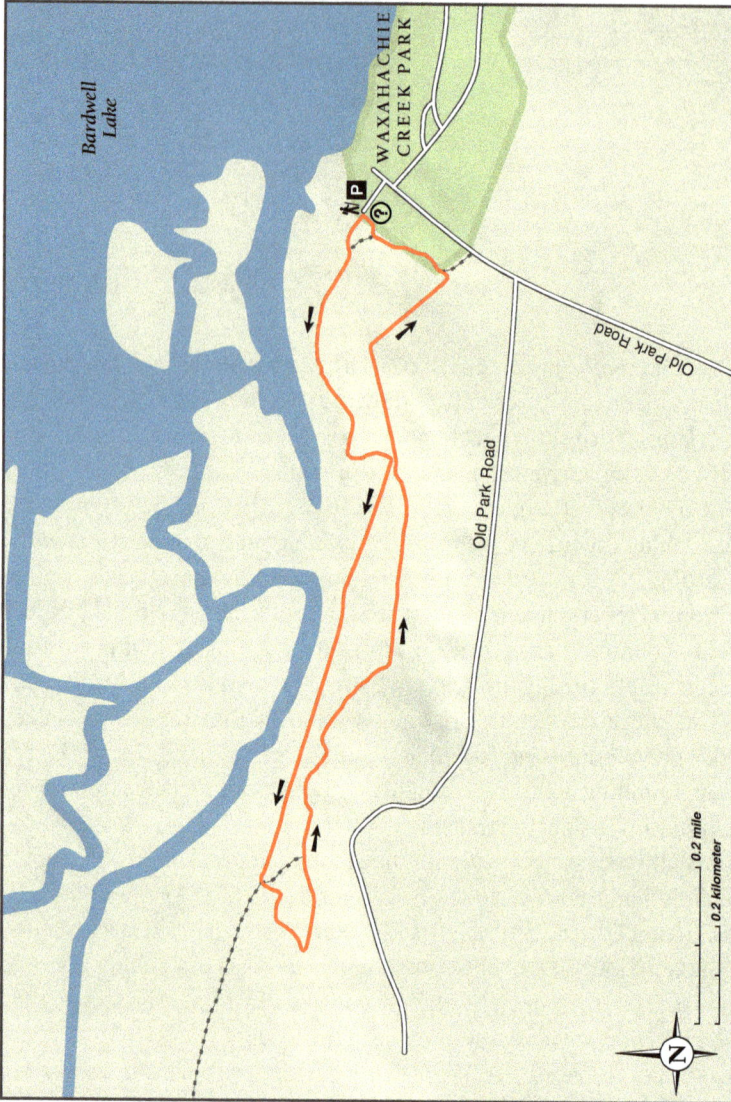

and curves back east through the gently rolling, shrubby woodlands. You'll eventually emerge from the woods and back into the grassland, hiking parallel to the trail you came in on, which is hidden by the tall, dry grasses on your left.

Merge back onto the wide path at 1.9 miles, where you'll turn right, following the trail uphill. It's a pleasant walk through more open grassland until you reach 2.2 miles, where an alternate trailhead intended for equestrians appears. Bear left at the junction and follow the trail back to the final right turn at 2.3 miles, where you'll find the trailhead.

Tree-dotted grasslands line the path.

For hikers wanting a longer trail, instead of turning off the wide, grassy path at 1.1 miles, continue straight. The trail heads northwest past the Ennis Rotary Club, then turns east, leading all the way out to Mustang Point on the edge of the lake; in total there are more than 13 miles of trail.

NEARBY ACTIVITIES

For lunch, don't miss Bubba's Bar-B-Q & Steakhouse (972-875-0036) in Ennis, spotlighted in *USA Today* as an excellent roadside eatery. It's right off I-45 at Exit 251.

If you're here in spring, don't miss Ennis's Bluebonnet Trails driving routes, which take you past fields of wildflowers. Springtime also brings the Bluebonnet Trails Festival, where you'll find arts, crafts, food, and music. Visit the city's convention and visitor bureau for the exact dates, or check online at visitennis.org.

• •

GPS TRAILHEAD COORDINATES N32° 17.767' W96° 41.817'

DIRECTIONS Take I-45 S toward Corsicana. In Ennis, take Exit 251A and turn left onto Creechville Road/Farm to Market Road 1181. Creechville Road becomes TX 34. Continue about 4.5 miles and turn right onto Bozek Road to reach Waxahachie Creek Park. The entrance to the park is about 1.5 miles down Bozek. Park in the westernmost parking lot, adjacent to the boat launch.

Interpretive signs along the trail identify points of interest.

THIS PLEASANT HIKE winds along an interpretive trail where markers help you identify native plants and grasses, then loops around a small pond. A couple of overlooks along the trail provide peaceful spots to enjoy the scenery.

DESCRIPTION

Since Cedar Hill State Park's opening in 1991, it has become one of the most visited state parks in the state of Texas, in large part because it's so close to both Dallas and Fort Worth (about 20 miles from the former, and about 25 miles from the latter). Adjacent to Joe Pool Lake, the park's expansive 1,826 acres attract millions of outdoor enthusiasts each year. Although Joe Pool is not the most scenic of lakes, it's justifiably popular as a catalyst for getting outside and enjoying the park's array of activities, which include hiking, camping, biking, fishing, picnicking, and boating.

The park's several miles of trails include some open to both mountain bikers and hikers, and a couple open only to hikers. Before the hike, stop by the visitor center at the park's entrance and ask for the interpretive brochure for the Talala Trail. The small booklet is not usually out with the other park maps and information, but the park rangers do have brochures if you ask. The pamphlet, which describes native wildlife and plants at numbered posts along the trail, is useful at the beginning of this hike.

DISTANCE & CONFIGURATION: 3.7-mile figure eight with spurs

DIFFICULTY: Easy

SCENERY: Native plants, wildflowers, pond

EXPOSURE: Partially shady

TRAFFIC: Light

TRAIL SURFACE: Packed dirt

HIKING TIME: 2 hours

DRIVING DISTANCE: 9 miles from I-20 and US 67

ACCESS: Daily, 6 a.m.–10 p.m.; $7 per person

MAP: tinyurl.com/talaladuckpond

WHEELCHAIR TRAVERSABLE: No

FACILITIES: Restrooms, water fountain, picnic area

CONTACT: 972-291-3900, tpwd.texas.gov /state-parks/cedar-hill

LOCATION: 1570 FM 1382, Cedar Hill

COMMENTS: Bring insect repellent in spring and summer. Pack a picnic to enjoy at a lakeside table.

You'll find the trailhead adjacent to the parking lot. The first part of the hike is along the Talala Trail, which loops through a hilly terrain where you can use the interpretive brochure to identify points of interests. This trail is best hiked on a cooler day because much of the trail is exposed; small trees and brush cast partial shade on only some portions. I strongly suggest bringing a GPS or compass along, as it can be easy to get disoriented at the many junctions and secondary paths along the trail.

Starting down the trail, reach a split in the path at 0.13 mile and turn left, following the trail as it curves south through a grassy meadow with a few trees. At 0.18 mile, come to a wooden bridge (which, on my hike, spanned a dried-up creek), across which you'll find another trail junction, where you'll bear right. The next junction is at 0.21 mile and has the first marker, identifying the clasping coneflower, a yellow annual with a long, cone-shaped head.

The trail slopes slightly downhill, crosses another small, wooden bridge, and passes through some hackberries. A few steps farther on is the marker for giant ragweed, which flowers in late summer. For the next mile, the trail winds slightly uphill past trees such as the honey locust and grasses such as Texas wintergrass. In the spring, markers indicate that you can see wildflowers, including Indian paintbrush. You'll also see posts identifying the wildlife that lives in the area, including the painted bunting, red-tailed hawk, and cattle egret, along with larger animals such as the bobcat.

At about 1.1 miles, reach a clearing and see a small red outhouse intended for primitive campers, as well as a trail split, where you'll bear right. Watch for a marker identifying the mesquite tree, recognizable by its spiny branches. About 150 feet farther is the next junction, where you'll go right. Continue straight until you reach 1.18 miles, where the path splits. Head right to reach Lake Overlook, which offers a view of the glistening waters of Joe Pool Lake in the distance. This is a nice place to rest for a minute on the bench and take in the scenery. Retrace your steps to the overlook turnoff, taking a right (southwest) to resume the trail. The path widens, still winding through the trees. You'll see a campground over to the left, and then

Cedar Hill State Park: Talala–Duck Pond Loop

Joe Pool Lake

South Spine Road

Coyote Crossing Camping Area

CEDAR HILL STATE PARK

South Spine Road

Plum Valley Overlook

Belt Line Road

Duck Pond

DP Duck Pond Trail
PV Plum Valley Trail
TT Talala Trail

N

0.2 mile
0.2 kilometer

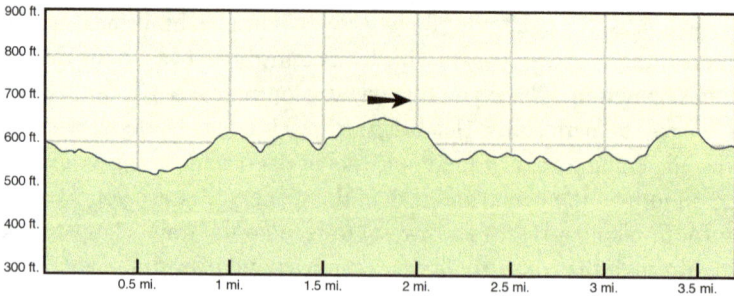

you'll cross over a small road that heads past the campsites. Cross the street and pick up Duck Pond Trail at the yellow gate just to the left of some restrooms. The path winds downhill through the trees, crosses a bridge, and then starts to wind back uphill through grassy terrain.

At 1.88 miles, cross South Spine Road and resume the trail on the other side. A couple hundred feet farther, reach the next junction. To the left, the trail dead-ends at Plum Valley Overlook, where a bench is tucked away beneath some vine-covered trees and you can relax and enjoy the views of the surrounding hillsides.

When you're ready, head back to the overlook turnoff, then follow the trail southwest as it curls downhill through trees and native grasses and over a couple of long, wooden bridges spanning ravines. The path slowly winds uphill and then, at 2.63 miles, reaches a junction marked by another red outhouse, indicating another area for primitive camping. When I was here, however, I saw no evidence of any such adventurers.

Turn right onto a wide gravel trail peppered with cacti. At 2.7 miles, reach the loop junction. Turn left onto the loop. The trail crosses a wooden bridge and then heads through some tall trees before passing two more bridges and finally reaching Duck Pond. The small pond is like an oasis amid the woods. There's only one small vantage point between the trees, however, discouraging anything more than a short rest.

Continuing past the pond, cross a bridge and turn right at the split at 3.18 miles. At 3.25 miles, you'll have completed the pond loop. From here, retrace your steps to South Spine Road. Turn right onto the road and walk along the grassy shoulder. The trailhead and parking lot are about 0.29 mile ahead on the left.

NEARBY ACTIVITIES

Within the park, you can explore Penn Farm Agricultural History Center, a restored farm exhibit. Ask at the visitor center for a self-guided interpretive booklet.

About 8.5 miles northwest of the park, you can visit Trader's Village—the largest weekend flea market in the state—open weekends from 8 a.m. to sundown. Thousands of booths sell all manner of products. To get there, take I-20 W to Exit 454, and turn right onto South Great Southwest Parkway. After 1 mile, turn left onto Mayfield Road. Trader's Village is about 0.3 mile down on the right.

• •

GPS TRAILHEAD COORDINATES N32° 36.983' W96° 58.883'

DIRECTIONS Take I-20 to exit Farm to Market Road 1382 toward Cedar Hill. Cedar Hill State Park is about 4 miles south on the right. The trailhead is on the south side of the park. From the park entrance, turn left at the first intersection, onto South Spine Road. Continue straight, past some campsite turnoffs on the right, before you reach the trailhead parking lot, also on the right.

A welcome sign greets hikers on this scenic woodland trail.

THIS PLEASANT TRAIL winds slowly uphill through a dense woodland. It's a nice hike for kids just getting interested in hiking because the size and terrain are easy to manage, but it's still wild and secluded enough to feel like an accomplishment.

DESCRIPTION

The Cedar Mountain Nature Preserve, a 110-acre section of hilly woodland next to Joe Pool Lake, draws a fair number of visitors, despite its proximity to larger trail systems, such as the Cedar Ridge Preserve (aka the Dallas Nature Center) and Cedar Hill State Park. This is in part due to Cedar Mountain's convenient, appealing location. Parking for the preserve is located in the same parking lot as for the Dogwood Canyon Audubon Center. A kiosk adjacent to the parking area signals the entrance to the preserve's trails. Many of the hikers lured into the preserve are on their way to or from the lake, a reservoir named after a 1960s congressman instrumental in its establishment. The lake lies just to the west of the preserve. Organized events are always happening somewhere along the lake and include bike rallies, fishing tournaments, outdoor-club meet-ups, and activities such as camping, picnicking, and bird-watching.

DISTANCE & CONFIGURATION: 1.2-mile balloon

DIFFICULTY: Easy

SCENERY: Woodlands, cedar trees

EXPOSURE: Mostly shady

TRAFFIC: Light

TRAIL SURFACE: Packed dirt

HIKING TIME: 45 minutes

DRIVING DISTANCE: 8.4 miles from I-20 and US 67

ACCESS: Daily, 6 a.m.–sunset; free

MAP: None

WHEELCHAIR TRAVERSABLE: No

FACILITIES: None

CONTACT: cedarhilltx.com/1716 /cedar-mountain-nature-preserve

LOCATION: 1300 FM 1382, Cedar Hill

COMMENTS: Make sure younger hikers know what to do if they see a snake. Bring insect repellent. Bikes are prohibited on this trail.

Because the trails in the preserve are not incredibly lengthy, visitors don't stay long. It's popular with folks walking their dogs and families with children, who appreciate its manageable size.

In front of the parking lot, a kiosk displaying a map of the preserve gives you a chance to get oriented before the hike. To get to the trailhead from here, go past the kiosk, following the sidewalk north. The trail curves away from the parking lot and, at about 0.1 mile, reaches the trailhead—a dirt path branching north off the paved trail. A sign here advises that bicyclists are prohibited and cautions hikers of the presence of venomous snakes. The dirt trail heads northwest onto the wide, grassy strip alongside Farm to Market Road 1382. Although the sounds of cars whizzing past drown out the sounds of crickets, the trail is well off the roadway and feels safe. Just as you start to wonder where you're going and become concerned that you may have missed some vital turn, the trail veers west, away from the road and toward an opening in the woods, at about 0.27 mile. A rustic sign mounted between two tree trunks marks the entrance where the trail disappears into the trees.

The trail climbs slightly and then descends, twisting and turning as it makes its way through the woods. The closely packed trees do an excellent job of shrouding the trail in shade. Although we did pass a couple of folks on the trail—one group with children and one couple—the trail still had a feeling of solitude and remoteness to it.

You'll soon reach a grove of trees where an intoxicating scent hangs thick in the air. A few deep breaths will help you identify it as the rich smell of cedar. In the summer, flying insects buzz regularly around the path. Apply plenty of insect repellent for your walk through this wooded hillside. I also found it impossible to ignore the thick spiderwebs that stretched across the ground and between trees, bridging gaps between logs, across branches, amid leaves, and in every trunk's knothole. Fortunately, most of the spiders stay in the woods, and unless you're one of the first hikers on the trail, their webs don't obstruct the path. The woodlands are also home to raccoons, coyotes, and armadillos.

At about 0.55 mile, head right onto the beginning of the trail loop, which makes a slow, mild uphill climb. The path passes an interesting section where a number of

Cedar Mountain Preserve Trail

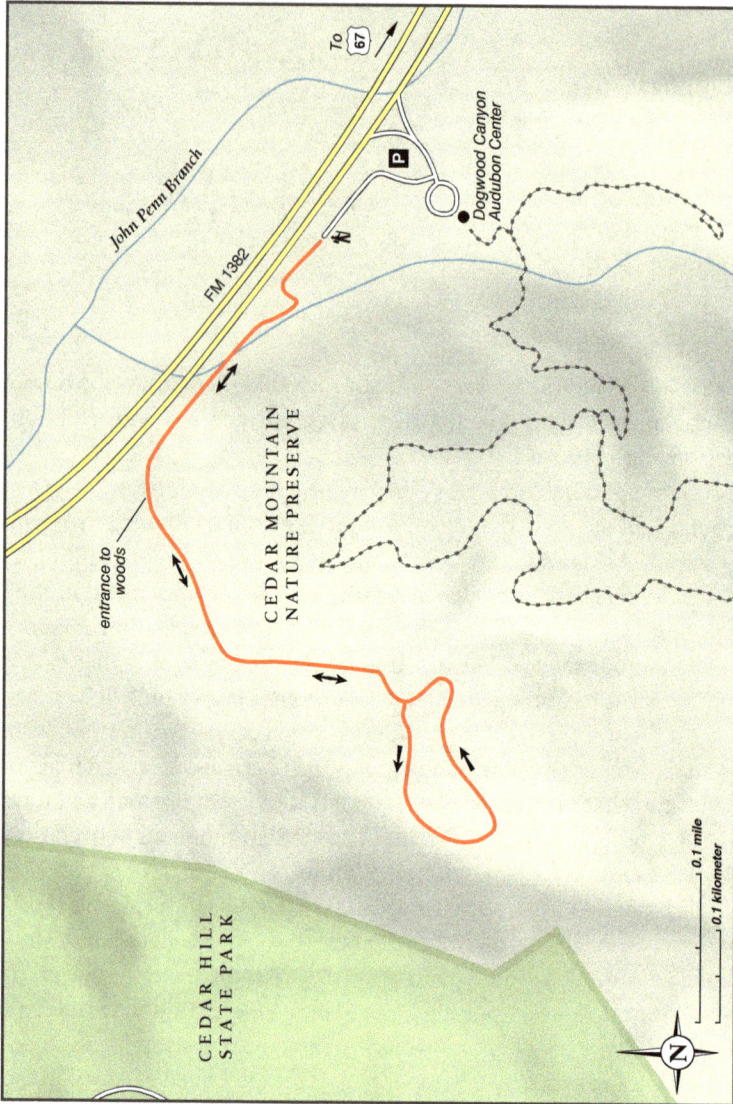

To 67

P.

Dogwood Canyon
Audubon Center

John Penn Branch

FM 1382

entrance to
woods

CEDAR MOUNTAIN
NATURE PRESERVE

CEDAR HILL
STATE PARK

0.1 mile

0.1 kilometer

N

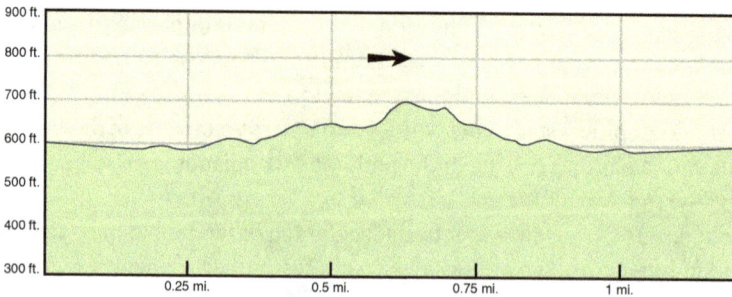

900 ft.				
800 ft.				
700 ft.				
600 ft.				
500 ft.				
400 ft.				
300 ft.				

0.25 mi.   0.5 mi.   0.75 mi.   1 mi.

old, dead trees litter the ground, then bypasses a dried-out ravine. After you duck under a low-hanging branch that spans the trail, reach the top of a hill. Although you haven't climbed high enough to get above the trees for any kind of a view, the surrounding wilderness rewards you with a sense of being deep in the woods.

The trail then loops east, heading back downhill before rejoining the trail. At about 0.88 mile, you'll be back at the loop junction. From here, retrace your steps to the trailhead. To extend the hike, detour onto the paved pathway loop through the woods and back to the parking lot.

NEARBY ACTIVITIES

Just up FM 1382, Cedar Hill State Park (see Hike 42, page 196), which lies along Joe Pool Lake, is popular with anglers, boaters, picnickers, campers, and birders. Inside the state park you'll also find the Penn Farm Agricultural History Center, a restored farm exhibit.

· ·

GPS TRAILHEAD COORDINATES N32° 36.917' W96° 58.317'

DIRECTIONS Located at 1300 FM 1382 in Cedar Hill, take I-20 and exit onto FM 1382 toward Cedar Hill. The trail is in Cedar Mountain Preserve, about 5 miles south on the right, just past Cedar Hill State Park.

A view of Cattail Pond

THIS RIGOROUS HIKE takes you through varied terrain on some of the most enjoyable trails in the area. Hike up a modest hill, trek down a fossil trail, traverse a pond enclosed by hundreds of cattails, and meander down excellent bird-watching footpaths.

DESCRIPTION

A 10-mile network of paths of varying difficulty keeps the Cedar Ridge Preserve—a park that can be fairly busy on weekends—uncrowded and even desolate in parts. In spring the preserve is a great place to see butterflies, migrating and breeding birds, and beds of bluebonnets. In addition to hawks circling overhead, you may see a snake or two, as I did on a recent hike here. Signs clearly posted at several points along the trail warn of copperheads, rattlesnakes, water moccasins, and coral snakes; obviously, sticking to designated trails is a must.

Formerly known as the Dallas Nature Center, Cedar Ridge Preserve is managed by the Dallas Audubon Society, which has done an excellent job of maintaining the park. The amenities in particular are excellent and include picnic tables, restrooms, well-marked trails, and water fountains . . . even one at ground level for hikers of the four-legged kind!

DISTANCE & CONFIGURATION: 3.25-mile loop

DIFFICULTY: Moderate

SCENERY: Pond, creek, abundant birdlife

EXPOSURE: Open–shady

TRAFFIC: Light

TRAIL SURFACE: Dirt, rock

HIKING TIME: 2 hours

DRIVING DISTANCE: 5.3 miles from I-20 and US 67

ACCESS: Tuesday–Sunday, 6:30 a.m.–dark

(approx. 30 minutes after sunset); donations accepted

MAP: tinyurl.com/cedarridgepreserve

WHEELCHAIR TRAVERSABLE: Yes

FACILITIES: Restrooms, benches, water fountains

CONTACT: 972-709-7784, audubondallas.org /cedar-ridge-preserve

LOCATION: 7171 Mountain Creek Pkwy., Dallas

COMMENTS: Bring sunscreen.

From the parking area, enter the preserve and stop to orient yourself at the visitor kiosk. The trailhead starts just behind the kiosk, so once you're ready to go, follow the main trail a few steps until you see a sign for Cattail Pond Trail. The trail is well kept, and you'll note that much of the first 0.5 mile is strewn with mulch, which makes walking fairly easy. You will, however, want to watch for low branches and exposed roots, especially as you venture farther down the trail and deeper into the preserve. Most of this section is enclosed by trees and shrubbery, keeping hot sun to a minimum. But you should expect it to be warm, even on an otherwise cool day, because trees tend to block the wind.

Follow the trail past prickly pear cacti and signs warning of poison ivy, until you reach a trail split at about 300 feet into the hike, where Possumhaw Trail branches off to the left. Continuing straight on Cattail Pond Trail, a short hike quickly leads you to another junction, where you can access Cedar Brake Trail (a 1.7-mile loop). For this hike, stay right on Cattail Pond Trail, which briefly descends a rocky path then climbs gently. The path meanders through low trees and brush, past the spot where Cedar Brake Trail rejoins Cattail Pond Trail, and then over a small wooden bridge that spans a dry ravine. The preserve is particularly well known among birders; many birds visit and live here, particularly in the spring, including warblers, flycatchers, buntings, vireos, bluebirds, and hawks. The bridge is a good vantage point to catch sight of one of these residents, the Carolina wren—a small, rust-colored bird distinguished by a thin white stripe over its eye, further described on a plaque adjacent to the bridge.

A little more than 0.5 mile into the hike, turn left onto the path marked FOSSIL VALLEY TRAIL. The trail curls downhill before starting a steep ascent. As you begin the uphill trek, scan the ground for fossils, which you may find embedded in rocks along the trail if you have a keen eye. The next 0.25 mile is the most challenging part of the hike—the trail climbs steeply to the summit of a small hill, passing a couple of benches, some grassy patches with dragonflies buzzing past and butterflies darting about, a wide shallow creek, and another wooden bridge. When you reach

205

Cedar Ridge Preserve Trail

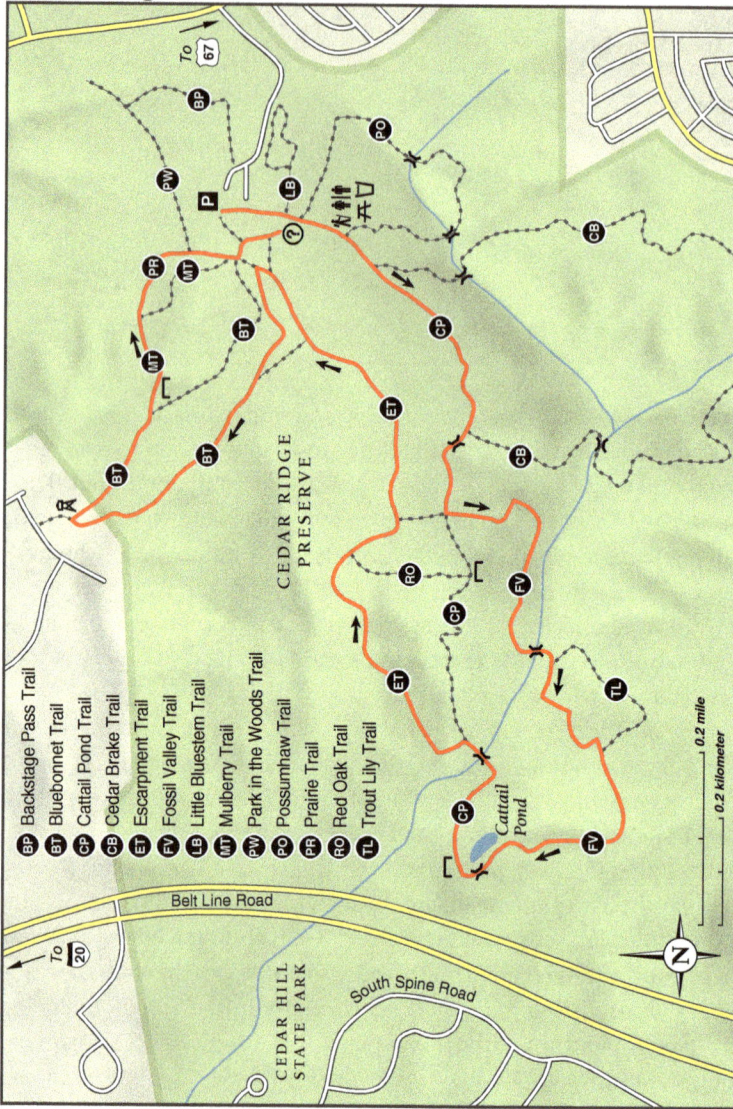

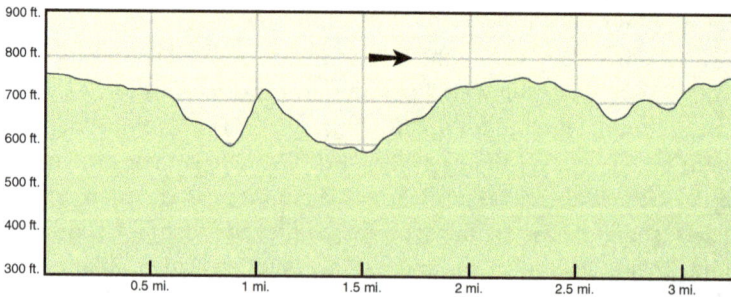

To 67

BP

PO

PW

P

LB

CB

PR MT

?

CP

BT

ET

MT

CB

BT

BT

RO

FV

CP

ET

TL

CEDAR RIDGE PRESERVE

CP

Cattail Pond

FV

BP Backstage Pass Trail
BT Bluebonnet Trail
CP Cattail Pond Trail
CB Cedar Brake Trail
ET Escarpment Trail
FV Fossil Valley Trail
LB Little Bluestem Trail
MT Mulberry Trail
PW Park in the Woods Trail
PO Possumhaw Trail
PR Prairie Trail
RO Red Oak Trail
TL Trout Lily Trail

0.2 mile

0.2 kilometer

Belt Line Road

To 20

Z

CEDAR HILL STATE PARK

South Spine Road

900 ft.
800 ft.
700 ft.
600 ft.
500 ft.
400 ft.
300 ft.

0.5 mi.   1 mi.   1.5 mi.   2 mi.   2.5 mi.   3 mi.

Trails are well maintained and easy to follow.

an unmarked trail split, with both paths continuing steeply uphill, take the path to the right for a more moderate climb. A short climb later, reach a small clearing that marks the hill's summit. Although trees obstruct the view of the surrounding terrain, there are several viewpoints on the descent that make the climb worthwhile. This is an excellent spot (with a conveniently placed bench) for taking a breather before you begin the downhill trek.

Your route downhill winds past a couple more benches before emerging into a small meadow teeming with purple wildflowers and offering excellent views of the surrounding hills and the surprisingly close highway. When you reach the bottom of the hill, you'll find yourself on the other side of Cattail Pond, which is hidden by hundreds of 6-foot-tall cattails. As you wind your way around the pond, take time to enjoy the scenery. You may discover animal tracks or spy the elegant great blue heron. This portion of the trail is much more exposed to the sun, so be prepared.

At the next trail split, look for signs for Escarpment Trail to the left and Cattail Pond Trail to the right. Head left down Escarpment Trail, which quickly widens and follows the remnants of an old wagon trail. This portion of the trail has a few scenic overlooks on its way slowly up another hill.

At about 1.85 miles into the hike, you'll reach the intersection of Red Oak Trail and Escarpment Trail. Continue right, up Escarpment Road Trail, then bear left onto Bluebonnet Trail. The past couple of summers have seen few bluebonnets, but if you're hiking in spring, you should see at least some bordering the trail. At the next trail split, take a hard left, continuing along Bluebonnet Trail. At the next unsigned junction, bear right. A few steps up this trail, at 2.75 miles into the hike, you'll find an observation tower that affords excellent views of the surrounding hills and woodlands. A few steps up the trail from the tower, turn left onto Mulberry Trail, where you'll find yourself at the top of a set of steep stairs built into the trail, overlooking what is one of the most striking parts of the hike. Tall trees threaded with vines rise out of a small valley and tower overhead, casting deep shadows on the trail and the surrounding dense, green vegetation. This little section of trail makes you feel as if you're deep inside a forest. The most curious feature—an old tree that has somehow curled in upon itself to form a C before reaching for the sun—is definitely worth a closer look. A few benches tucked next to the trail offer a spot from which to enjoy the special beauty of this portion of trail. At this point, you're close to 3 miles into the hike.

The final portion of the hike follows the trail until it reaches an unmarked split, where you turn left. The trail then emerges into an open meadow, where the trail splits, strategically circling the meadow—ideal for bird-watching. Turn left at the split to reach the trail's end, behind the restrooms; head toward and around them, and you're back at the trailhead.

NEARBY ACTIVITIES

Just 3 miles away, Cedar Hill State Park, which lies along Joe Pool Lake, is popular with anglers, boaters, picnickers, campers, and birders (see Hike 42, page 196). Inside the state park you'll also find the Penn Farm Agricultural History Center, a restored farm exhibit. To get there, head north on Mountain Creek Parkway for 1 mile, then turn left onto Eagle Ford Drive. About 0.8 mile ahead, turn left onto South Belt Line Road; the park entrance is about 1.7 miles ahead on the right.

• •

GPS TRAILHEAD COORDINATES N32° 38.200' W96° 57.533'

DIRECTIONS From I-20 W, take Exit 458, then turn left onto Mountain Creek Parkway and follow it 2.8 miles to the Cedar Ridge Preserve. Access the preserve via a turnoff on the right where there is a small sign—keep an eye out for it. Follow the road into the preserve and turn right at the fork to enter the main parking lot; the left fork terminates at a smaller lot reserved for persons with disabilities.

45 CLEBURNE STATE PARK LOOP TRAIL

A short climb offers outstanding views of the spillway below.

THIS ROCKY TRAIL loops through the woods of the park's outer perimeter, offering a few steep sections that will raise your heart rate. Its highlight is an overlook with a view of an elaborate masonry spillway adjacent to the park's small Cedar Lake.

DESCRIPTION

The 528-acre Cleburne State Park opened in 1938, thanks in part to the work of the Civilian Conservation Corps, who constructed the elaborate masonry spillway adjacent to spring-fed Cedar Lake. The park's amenities include camping and fishing (though at only 116 acres, the lake is quite small) and more than 5 miles of hiking trails. These trails, with names such as Whispering Meadow, Fossil Ridge, and Spillway, can be combined to form a loop circumnavigating the park.

To get to the trailhead for the loop, enter the park, pass the bathrooms on the left, and pull off into the first small parking area on the right, just off the park road. The trail curls downhill through trees and brush and crosses a creek. Across the creekbed, continue straight (east). The trail starts to ascend a rough, rutted path strewn with small rocks.

At about 0.1 mile, bear left at the trail split. The path proceeds parallel to the creek you crossed and climbs toward an overlook. Be prepared for uneven footing;

DISTANCE & CONFIGURATION: 5.86-mile loop

DIFFICULTY: Strenuous

SCENERY: Spillway, lake, woods, meadow, fossils

EXPOSURE: Partially shady

TRAFFIC: Light

TRAIL SURFACE: Packed dirt

HIKING TIME: 2.75 hours

DRIVING DISTANCE: 25 miles from I-35W and US 67

ACCESS: Daily, 7 a.m.–10 p.m.; $5 per person

MAP: tinyurl.com/cleburnesptrailmap

WHEELCHAIR TRAVERSABLE: No

FACILITIES: Restrooms, benches, and picnic tables in nearby day-use area

CONTACT: 817-645-4215, tpwd.texas.gov /state-parks/cleburne

LOCATION: 5800 Park Road 21, Cleburne

COMMENTS: Bring a walking stick, and wear good hiking shoes.

this ragged section of trail resembles a gully more than a path. Small bushes adjacent to the path cling to the hillside, offering little by way of scenery.

After a short climb, at 0.3 mile you'll come to the overlook, from which you'll have an exceptional view of the ravine and spillway. When I first reached this spot, I was unprepared for the spillway's size and beauty. Masonry built onto the sides of the bluff on the far side of the ravine accentuates a matching spillway that rises gradually in three massive tiers, looking more like an ancient pyramid than a common spillway. Pick your way along the bluffs for a couple of great lookout spots.

Continue down the trail, following the sign reading TO OVERLOOK AND LAKE LOOP, and bear right at the 0.35-mile junction. The path makes another short, strenuous climb up a rock-strewn stretch before reaching an old, gnarled tree clinging to the edge of the bluff, beyond which is another fantastic view of the lake and spillway.

The trail continues through elm, mesquite, oak, and juniper; keep an eye out for exposed tree roots. Bear right at the next couple of trail splits. You'll then begin a downhill trek through woods of mesquite, ash, oak, and elm. From here, the trail traces the state park's perimeter, marked by a barbed-wire fence. Note that, when in doubt at a trail split, keeping the fence to your right will keep you on the correct trail. The fence is almost invisible at most points, thanks to an overgrowth of vines and trees, and does not detract from the scenery.

Keep right at the next two junctions, continuing through terrain characterized by short, steep, rocky hills. The trail eventually flattens somewhat; however, it remains rocky and uneven for almost the entire hike. The path winds through the shade of the woods, keeping the sun from overheating you.

Pass a sign marking a huge, beautiful old live oak tree before reaching a junction at 1.25 miles; bear right. Continue across a babbling brook, then turn right at the next junction, where you'll trek through a small, cheery meadow. Briefly glimpse some private houses to the right before the next split at 2 miles, where you continue straight. In 0.35 mile, reach a paved road in Shady Spring's camping area; if you've brought your lunch, you might stop at one of the shaded picnic tables for a rest.

Cleburne State Park Loop Trail

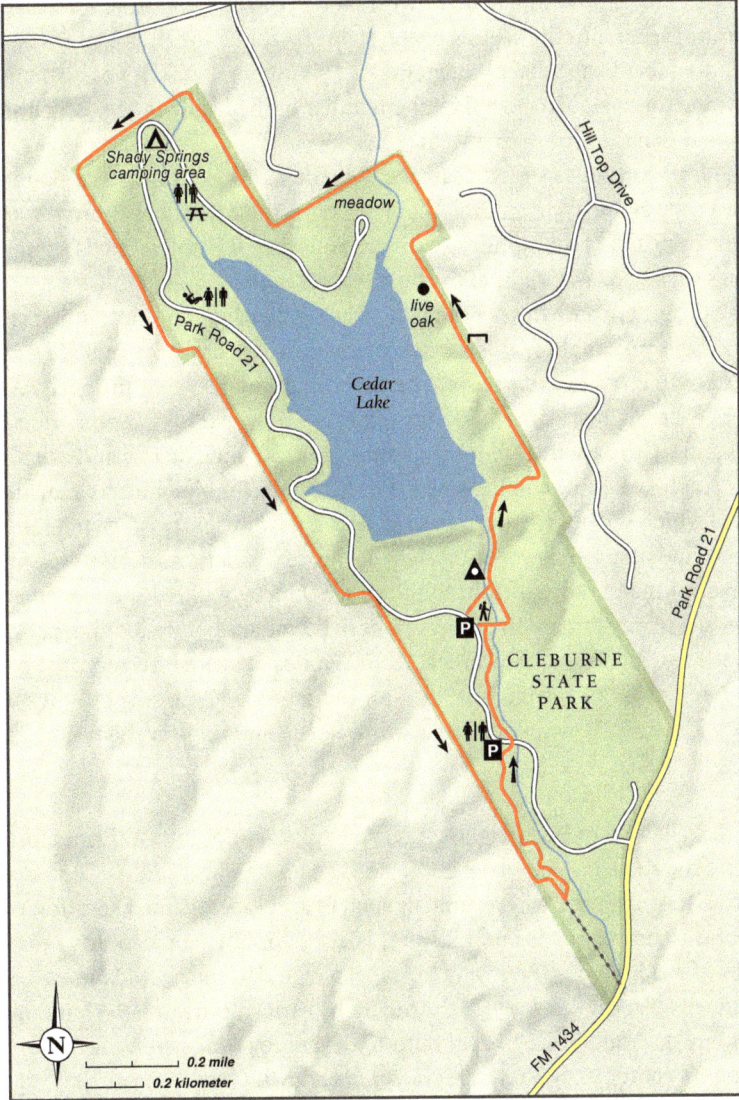

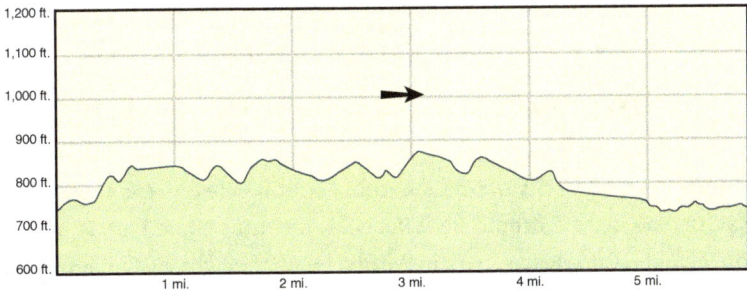

Shady Springs
camping area

meadow

live
oak

Park Road 21

Cedar
Lake

CLEBURNE
STATE
PARK

Park Road 21

FM 1434

N

0.2 mile
0.2 kilometer

1,200 ft.
1,100 ft.
1,000 ft.
900 ft.
800 ft.
700 ft.
600 ft.

1 mi.   2 mi.   3 mi.   4 mi.   5 mi.

Hill Top Drive

To resume the trail, head southwest along the road and look for a narrow dirt trail disappearing into the woods to the right. It will be the first trail you see, only a few hundred feet from where you emerged. It is unmarked, so it's easy to miss. You'll know you're on the correct trail by the familiar barbed-wire fence, which reappears a few feet down the trail on the right.

The trail continues straight, adjacent to the park's southwestern boundary and along a rocky slope appropriately named Fossil Ridge Trail. I spotted a couple of excellent imprints of ammonites (extinct mollusks with spiral shells) embedded in the trail's rock bed. Stay right at the next few junctions.

The property southwest of the park is being developed for its natural resources, and at various points along this section of the park's boundary you'll see signs advising you not to cross out of the state park and into the adjacent property. A barbed-wire fence clearly marks the boundary; be sure, however, youngsters don't get too curious and try to explore—the adjacent property is a lime quarry and can be dangerous. As you hike south, you'll also start to hear the rumble of heavy machinery, the source of which is a huge natural-gas rig on the next property off to the right.

Continue past the rig, bearing right at the next junction, at 4.3 miles, where the path reaches the park road. The sound of machinery will fade. The trail continues straight, stretching toward the southern park boundary before looping back through the woods and along a narrow creek. At 5.53 miles, it again intersects the park road, which you'll cross to resume the trail on the far side. Continue another 0.33 mile alongside the densely wooded creek before finally emerging at the trailhead.

NEARBY ACTIVITIES

Dinosaur Valley State Park, where you can explore dinosaur footprints fossilized in the park's riverbed, is in nearby Glen Rose. The Fossil Rim Wildlife Center, an 1,800-acre drive-through park where animals such as antelopes, rhinos, giraffes, ostriches, and zebras roam the fields and hillsides, is also close by. You can drive through the 10 miles of road in your own vehicle, or take a guided tour, which must be booked in advance. To get there from Cleburne State Park, return to US 67 and head west about 15 miles. You'll see a brown state-park sign for Dinosaur Valley on your right. The wildlife center is about 3 miles beyond it, down County Road 2008, on the left. Hours vary by season. For more information, call 254-897-2960.

• •

GPS TRAILHEAD COORDINATES N32° 15.550' W97° 33.183'

DIRECTIONS Take US 67 S toward Cleburne. About 6 miles past Cleburne, follow the brown state-park signs left onto Park Road 21. Cleburne State Park is about 6 miles down on the right. Once inside, park in the first lot on the right, just after the restrooms.

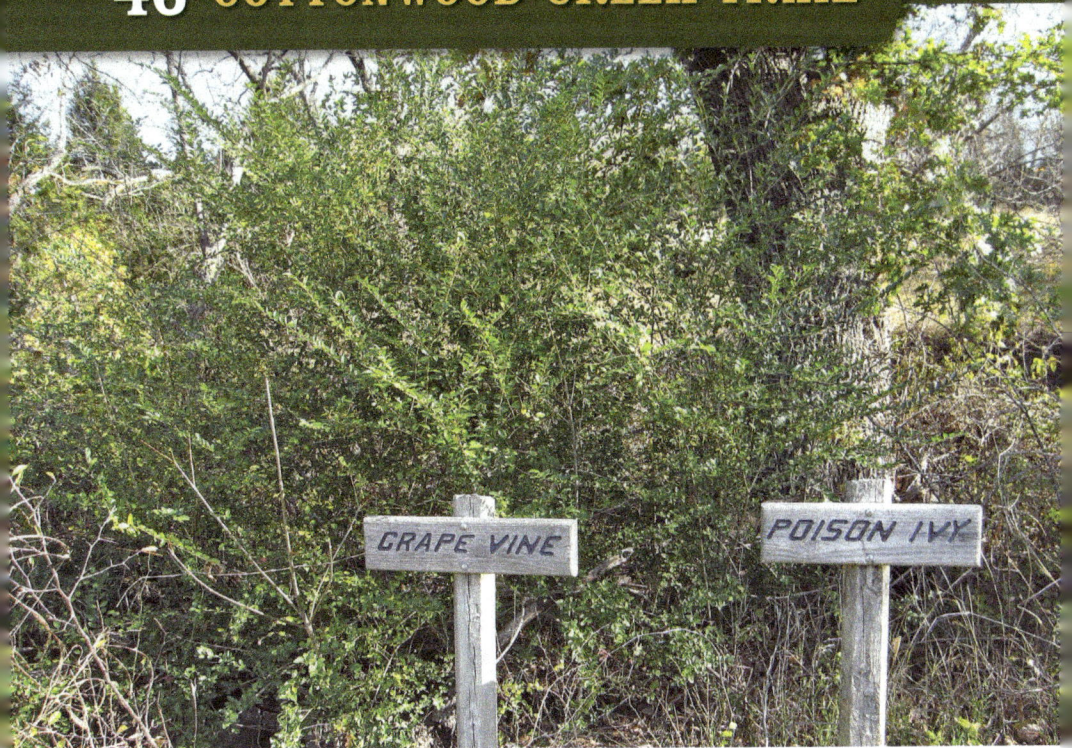

Interpretive signs along the trail identify native flora.

THIS PEACEFUL TRAIL winds alongside a creek toward a tall pecan grove. Interpretive signs along the way identify the flora, and a bridge at the far end crosses the creek to take you back to the beginning.

DESCRIPTION

Hidden down a small, bumpy road behind an old neighborhood in Wilmer, the 220-acre Cottonwood Creek Preserve was private land before it was given to the city. Its original owner planted the land with pecan trees. The pecan grove, which remains, comes as a pleasant surprise halfway through the hike.

During your visit, you'll probably see only one or two other hikers, more because of the hidden location than anything else. We came to an empty parking lot and empty trails and took our time enjoying the scenery before having a leisurely lunch at the picnic table. It wasn't until we were about to leave that others arrived—one local who quietly let his dog out for some romping, then left shortly thereafter, and another local couple who arrived with pecan pie in mind; they headed down the trail to quietly collect a few nuts from the thousands strewn through the grove.

From the parking lot, take the road past the entrance gate toward the creek. Initially it can be difficult to determine where the trail is: on your right, a low cable

DISTANCE & CONFIGURATION: 2.17-mile loop

DIFFICULTY: Easy

SCENERY: Pecan grove, creek

EXPOSURE: Shady–sunny

TRAFFIC: Light

TRAIL SURFACE: Grass

HIKING TIME: 40 minutes

DRIVING DISTANCE: 7 miles from I-20 and I-45

ACCESS: Daily; free

MAP: None

WHEELCHAIR TRAVERSABLE: No

FACILITIES: Picnic tables

CONTACT: 972-441-6373

LOCATION: Cottonwood Creek Preserve, Wilmer

COMMENTS: Watch your step if you leave the trail; there are patches of poison ivy along the creek.

strung between some posts cordons off the road from the rest of the landscape. A small wooden sign reading CREEK TRAIL sits in the grass against the creek, with seemingly no trail in sight. This is in fact the end of the trail loop. In many places along the hike, the trail—though marked with regular wooden signs pointing the way—is poorly defined, being nothing more than a mowed strip in the tall grass. You need not worry about getting lost, though, because the trail simply follows the creek out, crosses a bridge, then comes back along the other side. Helpful signs along the way identify trees and point to the trail.

The trailhead is down the road and over the creek a few hundred feet past the CREEK TRAIL sign. Turn right onto the mowed, grassy strip, and you'll see a sign identifying the path as the Green Trail, which is where the hike starts. A sign next to it advises that archaeological remains, which you may see in the preserve, are not to be disturbed.

The trail heads northeast. To your right, between the trees, catch sight of the wide creek running along the bottom of a deep gully. Trees loom on either side, forming a shady canopy over the water. To your left, a small treeless meadow soaks in the sun, stretching alongside the path. Lime-green, softball-sized fruits known as horse apples (sometimes referred to as green brains because of their mottled appearance) litter the trail. An old farm road, now mostly grass, runs a couple dozen feet off to the left along the length of the trail. It stays mostly hidden from view, except at 0.2 mile, where the trail curves to join the road temporarily before veering east back toward the creek.

Along the trail, you'll spot a number of wooden signs in front of various plants and trees. The signs identify the honey locust, a thorny tree identifiable by its long brown seedpods; the grapevine, a climbing vine; the saw greenbrier, a vine that can form thick thickets; and poison ivy. Other signs along the trail advise that the area is a venomous-snake habitat.

The trail continues along the creek, offering a couple of nice overlooks with views of the water on the right. Pass more signs identifying native plants, including coralberry, chittamwood, and privet. The meadow ends as you enter a large grove of pecan trees where the creek curves. In the fall, leaves litter the ground, hiding the trail.

Cottonwood Creek Trail

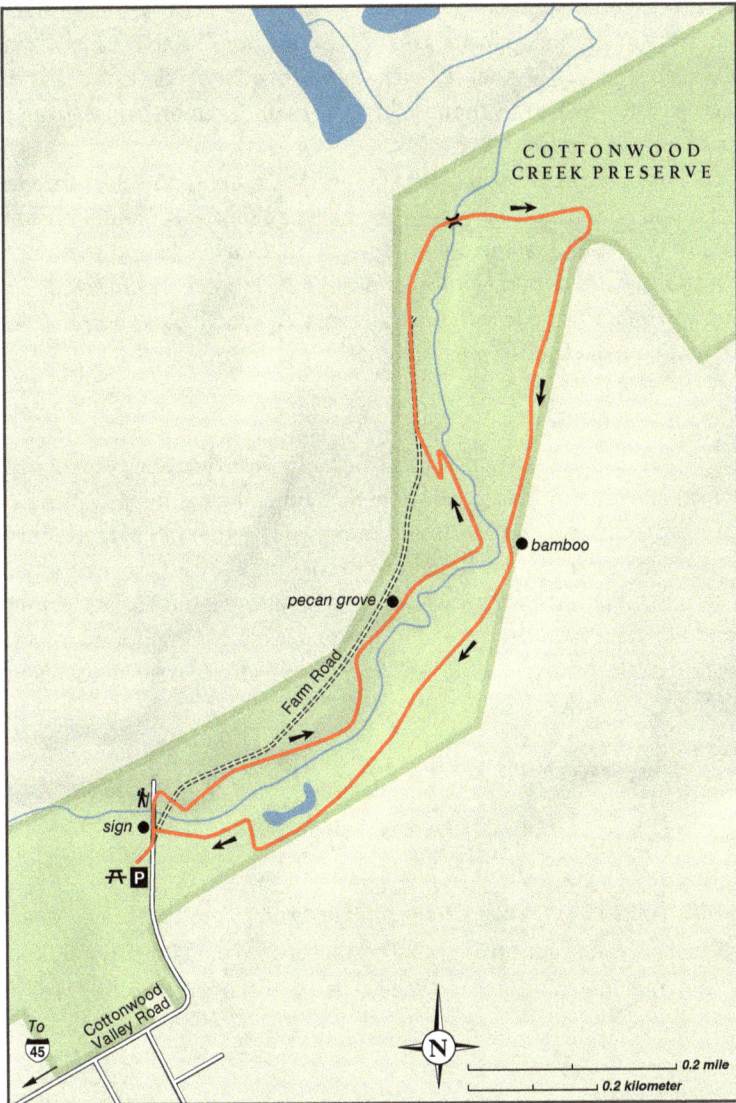

COTTONWOOD
CREEK PRESERVE

bamboo

pecan grove

Farm Road

sign

To
45

Cottonwood
Valley Road

N

0.2 mile
0.2 kilometer

Continue alongside the creek, traversing the outskirts of the grove. On the banks you'll spot trees such as chinaberry, dogwood, cedar elm, and hackberry. At various points, the trees open a little, and you can peer into the creek and see the intricate patterns of exposed tree roots clinging to the sides of the steep bank.

The preserve narrows into a lane with the creek on the left and a fence on the right. The trail then merges onto the park road, overgrown and barely discernible, before it curves toward a wooden bridge. The bridge, built atop two huge logs that bounce with each step, marks the hike's halfway point. Cross the bridge and follow the trail signs on the opposite side of the creek for Creek Trail. The path winds through another grove, then curves back south along the creek. In the fall, the grove's small leaves turn a brilliant yellow. When they fall in the breeze, the sun glints off them, in an entrancing, snowlike effect.

At 1.5 miles, traverse a patch of bamboo. At 1.6 miles, the trees recede and the trail is exposed to sun as it passes through a small meadow of tall grass. Droves of crickets and grasshoppers, including some up to 2 inches long, live along this section. With your every step, they spring up and fly out of the way in a wide spray. Stay in the mowed area alongside the creek. Before long, you'll pass another CREEK TRAIL sign and find yourself back at the trailhead.

NEARBY ACTIVITIES

The Rogers Wildlife Rehab and Farm Sanctuary is in Hutchins, only 6 miles away. The facility is a nonprofit organization that rehabilitates injured birds and farm animals. Visitors are welcome to roam the property free of charge; donations are accepted. On the grounds, you'll find dozens of outdoor cages serving as temporary homes for rehabilitating hawks, owls, blue jays, vultures, and herons, among others. Geese and pheasants wander around unfettered. To get there, follow I-45 N 2 miles and take Exit 274 (Dowdy Ferry Road). Stay on the service road about 0.5 mile, then turn right onto East Cleveland Street.

• •

GPS TRAILHEAD COORDINATES N32° 36.167' W96° 40.383'

DIRECTIONS Follow I-45 S toward I-30 and take Exit 270 onto Belt Line Road. Turn left onto East Belt Line Road and go 0.4 mile. Then make a left onto North Goode Road and go 0.3 mile. Turn right onto Cottonwood Valley Road to reach Cottonwood Creek Preserve.

A 45-foot-tall T. rex and a 70-foot-tall apatosaurus guard the entrance to the park.

THIS HIKE GAINS a little altitude to offer excellent overlooks of the park then winds down to the riverbed, where you trek along million-year-old fossilized dinosaur tracks.

DESCRIPTION

Dinosaur Valley State Park is known internationally for the well-preserved dinosaur tracks in the riverbed that runs through the park. The tracks date back about 110 million years to the Cretaceous period. It is believed that at that time this area was a shoreline along which the dinosaurs may have been migrating or feeding. The mud tracks of these huge creatures eventually fossilized and were buried by limestone and sandstone in what is now the Paluxy riverbed. Today, the river cuts through these sheets of rock, exposing the tracks buried within. In summer, the river dries out and many of the tracks are exposed on the dry, stony riverbed. The park allows you to roam freely among these sites, and in summer you'll find hordes of visitors closely examining the imprints left by these prehistoric reptiles.

Although the park is heavily visited, you'll find that the hiking trails are fairly empty, because most folks head straight for the main track sites or for a dip in the nearby swimming hole. In fact, the day we set out on this hike, we passed no other

DISTANCE & CONFIGURATION: 4.31-mile loop

DIFFICULTY: Moderate–strenuous

SCENERY: Hills, valley, river, dinosaur tracks

EXPOSURE: Partially sunny

TRAFFIC: Light

TRAIL SURFACE: Packed dirt

HIKING TIME: 2 hours

DRIVING DISTANCE: 7 miles from TX 144 and US 67

ACCESS: Daily, 7 a.m.–10 p.m.; $7 per person

MAP: tinyurl.com/dinosaurvalleytrailmap

WHEELCHAIR TRAVERSABLE: No

FACILITIES: Restrooms, picnic area, store

CONTACT: 254-897-4588, tpwd.texas.gov /state-parks/dinosaur-valley

LOCATION: 1629 Park Road 59, Glen Rose

COMMENTS: If the water level is high, be prepared to ford a couple of shallow rivers. Bring your suit for a dip in the swimming hole after the hike.

hikers on the trail, although footprints and bike marks in the dirt indicate that the trails do see some use. Those who don't venture onto the hillside trails are missing out on one of the more fun hikes in the area.

The route I've selected starts with a decent workout as it climbs into the hills alongside the river, offers inspiring views of the surrounding hillsides midway through, and finally rewards you with the excitement of discovery as you reach the ancient dinosaur tracks at its end. When you arrive, stop by the park's headquarters at the main entrance to pick up a trail map, check out the interpretive display, and find information on any ranger-led talks or events happening during your visit.

The hike will start by following the Cedar Brake Outer Loop. Parking is a short drive from the main entrance; find the trailhead on the east side of the parking lot, adjacent to a kiosk with a map displaying the various trails. Take a moment to examine the map; you'll see the trails are referenced by color. On the hike, the trail's corresponding color appears every few hundred feet on a tree. Watch for these markings to ensure you're on the correct route—it's easy to get lost. The park's trail maps are a good reference, though they are slightly outdated and can be confusing. For reference, this hike will start on the Cedar Brake Outer Loop, connect briefly to the Denio Creek Trail before joining the Black-capped Vireo Trail, wind over to the Overlook Trail, head down the Limestone Ledge Trail, then finish back on the Cedar Brake Outer Loop by the Main Track Site.

To start the hike, follow the trail past the kiosk through a grassy field dotted with trees. When the path splits at 0.18 mile, keep left to follow the main trail. Descend a brief switchback and a few steep stairs before reaching the riverbed. Hop across the rocks or wade through the shallow river to resume the trail on the opposite bank. If you've come late in summer, as I did, chances are the river will be dry, allowing you to stop and investigate Track Site 4, which is in the riverbed about 500 feet to the left. Look for the three-toed tracks, which are about a foot long, on the left bank of the river. Many of them are so well defined that it's hard to believe they're not fresh and that one of the huge beasts isn't waiting around the bend for you.

Dinosaur Valley Trail

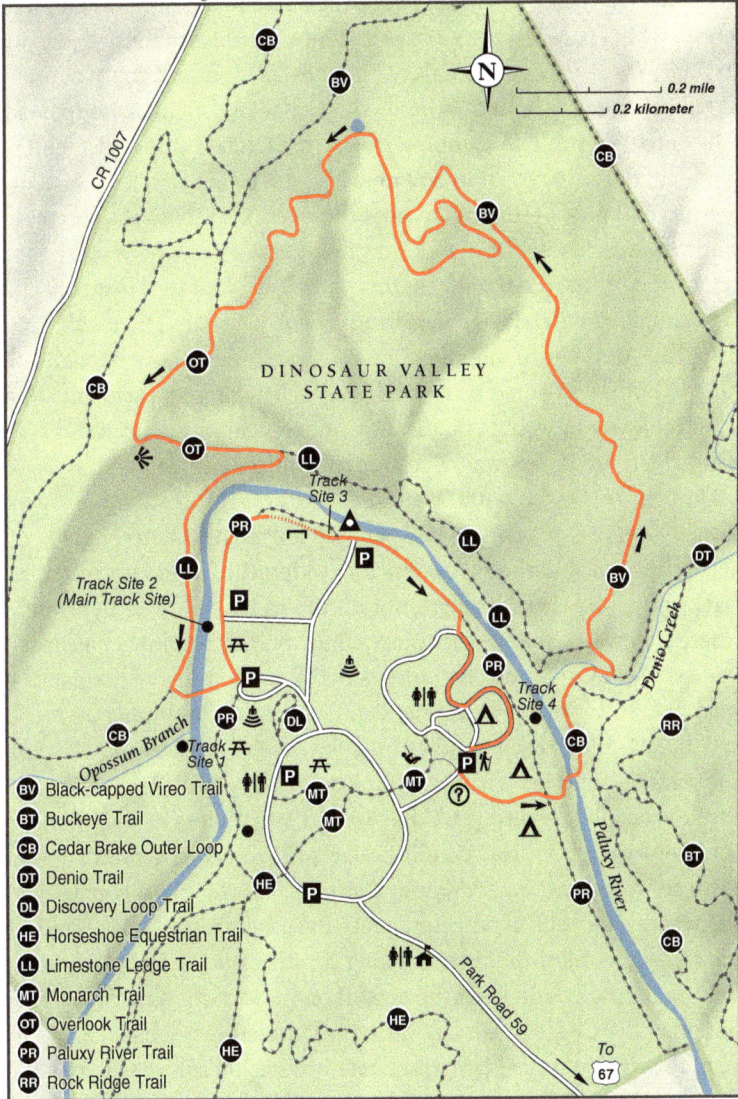

Map legend:
- 0.2 mile
- 0.2 kilometer

CR 1007

DINOSAUR VALLEY
STATE PARK

Track Site 3

Track Site 2
(Main Track Site)

Opossum Branch

Track Site 1

Track Site 4

Denio Creek

Paluxy River

Park Road 59

To 67

BV Black-capped Vireo Trail
BT Buckeye Trail
CB Cedar Brake Outer Loop
DT Denio Trail
DL Discovery Loop Trail
HE Horseshoe Equestrian Trail
LL Limestone Ledge Trail
MT Monarch Trail
OT Overlook Trail
PR Paluxy River Trail
RR Rock Ridge Trail

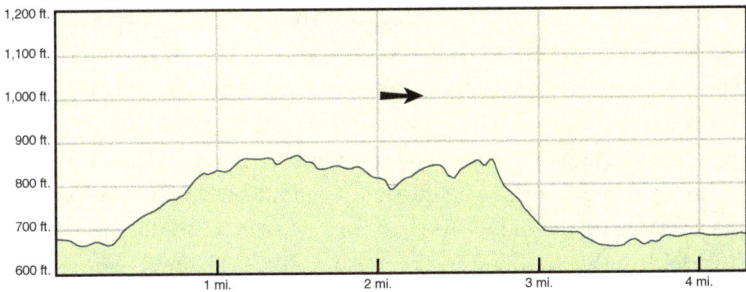

Elevation profile: 1,200 ft. to 600 ft.; distances 1 mi., 2 mi., 3 mi., 4 mi.

After you cross the river, you'll pick up the trail and continue on the Cedar Brake Outer Loop, which parallels the river as it climbs steadily up through a wooded hill. Keep straight, ignoring any secondary paths branching into the woods, until you reach a trail juncture at about 0.36 mile. The Cedar Brake Outer Loop heads southeast (right) into the primitive-camping area; to the left is the Denio Creek Trail. Take the left branch, following the trail downhill into the Denio Creek riverbed. Cross the shallow river, and pick up the trail across the river, slightly to the right. Head back uphill until you reach another junction at about 0.43 mile, where you bear left onto the Black-capped Vireo Trail. Stay on this path, following it as it slowly climbs into the hills, through woodlands peppered with grassy clearings and cacti.

During the summer, dragonflies, crickets, and—curiously enough—flies buzz across the trail often, so you'd be well advised to bring insect repellent along. As for animals, in the early morning you can hear movement in the brush adjacent to the trail as they clear out of your way. The area is home to deer, armadillos, coyotes, and skunks. Though we spotted nothing more than lizards (of which there are many), we came close to seeing a raccoon, as indicated by the fresh scat on the trail.

The trail passes a barbed-wire fence marking the boundary of the park then switchbacks downhill. Pass a small pool on the right, followed by some excellent unobstructed views of the surrounding valley, before reaching the next junction at 2.41 miles. To the right, catch glimpses between the trees of the park's entrance down below. A better overlook is not far off; stay left, continuing on the Overlook Trail, and at 2.61 miles reach another junction, with a path heading steeply downhill to the right. Again, stay left, continuing on the Overlook Trail, and at 2.81 miles come to the overlook, where you'll have a bird's-eye view of the Main Track Site below and the scores of visitors bending over to examine the ground.

As you continue, the trail descends and then, at 2.96 miles, reaches yet another junction, where you will head right, onto the Limestone Ledge Trail. The trail descends steadily toward the river peeking through on the left. At 3.29 miles, just past a field on the right, you'll see the turnoff on the left to get to the river; this is the continuation of the Cedar Brake Outer Loop. Turn left here, and at 3.36 miles reach the edge of the river and the Main Track Site, where you can see the tracks of theropods (three-toed prints from large carnivorous dinosaurs) and sauropods (elephant-like prints from gigantic herbivorous dinosaurs resembling brontosaurs).

The trail resumes on the left, adjacent to the entrance steps, on the other side of the river. In summer you probably won't have to ford the river to get there but can simply walk across the dried-out riverbed, examining the tracks as you go. You might even catch one of the park rangers giving an impromptu presentation there. When you're done exploring, continue on the trail. At about 3.69 miles, reach some benches and stairs climbing up out of the riverbed, and at about 3.71 miles, pass a parking lot and an overlook to the theropod tracks at Track Site 3. The trail continues along the

The sculptures offer visitors a sense of the size of the area's previous inhabitants.

sidewalk through the woods and to the camping area. At about 3.96 miles, arrive at the camping area, where you'll turn left onto the road, following it 0.35 mile past the restrooms and back to the trailhead.

NEARBY ACTIVITIES

The nearby Fossil Rim Wildlife Center is an 1,800-acre drive through a park where animals such as antelopes, rhinos, giraffes, ostriches, and zebras roam the fields and hillsides. You can drive the 10 miles of road in your own vehicle. Guided tours are also available with advance booking. To get there from Dinosaur Valley, take US 67 southwest 3 miles and turn left onto County Road 2008; it's about 1 more mile to the park. Hours vary by season. For more information, call 254-897-2960.

• •

GPS TRAILHEAD COORDINATES N32° 14.983' W97° 48.750'

DIRECTIONS Take US 67 south to Glen Rose and Dinosaur Valley State Park. Just before you leave Glen Rose, turn right onto Farm to Market Road 205 (Barnard Street); the Dinosaur Valley sign is small, so watch for it. At about 3 miles, bear right at the fork onto Park Road 59. The park entrance is about 1 mile farther. When inside the park, take the first two right turns, following the signs toward the camping area. The parking lot is on the right, just before the campsites.

A perfectly placed bench alongside a scenic overlook provides a great spot to stop and enjoy the view.

BE PREPARED FOR a vigorous hike on this trail that switchbacks from the canyon floor to the canyon rim, offering outstanding views of Joe Pool Lake and the surrounding countryside. A 0.5-mile stroller- and wheelchair-friendly trail on the Canyon Floor offers a pleasant cooldown and completes the hike.

DESCRIPTION

It's hard to say what to like most about the Dogwood Canyon Audubon Center. Could it be the 200-plus acres of protected wildlife and habitat that call the area home? Or is it the scenic trail that meanders to more than 150 feet above the canyon floor, rewarding hikers with magnificent views of the surrounding countryside? Or perhaps it is the fact that this pocket of wilderness and adventure is conveniently accessible—only a short 20-minute drive from downtown Dallas. Whichever turns out to be your reason for visiting, there is no doubt that Dogwood Canyon will quickly become one of your favorite hiking spots in the metroplex.

The newer of the two Audubon Centers in Dallas County, the Dogwood Canyon Audubon Center opened in 2011. Although dogwood trees are not commonly found in the area, the canyon does indeed have a grove of its namesake tree deep within the preserve. The grove can only be viewed by joining an organized annual hike coordinated by the Audubon Center. Hikes are usually scheduled annually in spring when the dogwoods are in bloom.

DISTANCE & CONFIGURATION:
2.2-mile balloon

DIFFICULTY: Moderate

SCENERY: Panoramic views

EXPOSURE: Partially shady

TRAFFIC: Moderate

TRAIL SURFACE: Packed dirt

HIKING TIME: 1.5 hours

DRIVING DISTANCE: 7.6 miles from US 67
and I-20

ACCESS: Tuesday–Sunday, 9 a.m.–5 p.m.; free

MAP: tinyurl.com/dogwoodcanyonaudubon

WHEELCHAIR TRAVERSABLE: Yes
(0.5 mile of trail)

FACILITIES: Restrooms, picnic tables, visitor
center, children's play area

CONTACT: 469-526-1980,
dogwoodcanyon.audubon.org

LOCATION: 1206 W. FM 1382, Cedar Hill

COMMENTS: Leashed dogs are permitted on the
trails on Sundays.

A 6,000-square-foot visitor center anchors the Audubon Center and serves as the entrance and starting point to the scenic canyon trails. The small entrance fee that was originally charged when the center first opened has been eliminated, and visitors are welcome to visit and explore the grounds admission-free. Programs and events such as academic field trips, Girl Scout outings, and yoga workshops are regularly hosted there. In addition, guided day and night hikes are also occasionally sponsored by the center. The website has a calendar of events that is regularly updated for those interested in finding out what activities are available.

Inside the visitor center, you'll find a small gift shop, maps of the preserve's trails, and for the birders, a beautifully designed enclosed balcony surrounded by windows and bird feeders—the perfect retreat before or after your hike.

The trails start behind the visitor center next to a couple of bird enclosures that house the center's resident raptors—an American kestrel and a barred owl. Both were rescued and rehabilitated but failed reentry into the wild. They now offer visitors a chance to appreciate and learn about the region's native birds of prey.

Adjacent to the bird enclosures, you'll find the trailhead, where you can start either of the center's two main trails. To the southeast is the Canyon Floor Trail, a relatively flat 0.5-mile ADA-accessible trail, and to the west is the West Loop Trail, a 1.65-mile hike that winds up to the canyon rim. The hike I've selected will start with the more vigorous West Loop Trail, then return to this juncture and cool down by following the Canyon Floor Trail. If you've visited this trail specifically for the ADA-accessible portion, you'll want to forgo the West Loop Trail and head southeast down the Canyon Floor Trail.

Start the hike by heading west down the West Loop Trail. Wooden posts along the trail's edge mark your progress in 0.1-mile increments, helping you track your progress. A couple hundred feet into the trail, you'll cross a bridge and follow the path as it switchbacks up the canyon in a moderately strenuous 150-foot climb to the top of the canyon ridge. On your climb, keep an eye on the trail to avoid loose rocks and dirt as well as native wildlife; on my hike, a large rattlesnake curled on the side of the trail was easily bypassed but might have been an unwelcome surprise for the less observant hiker.

Dogwood Canyon Audubon Trail

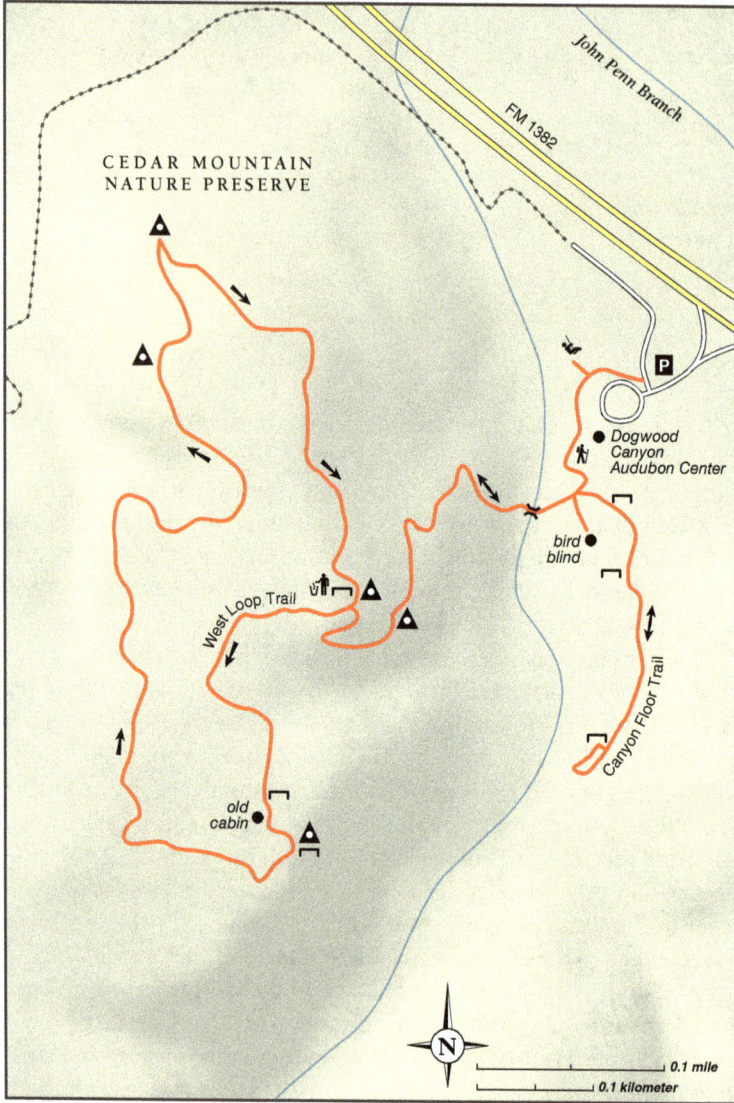

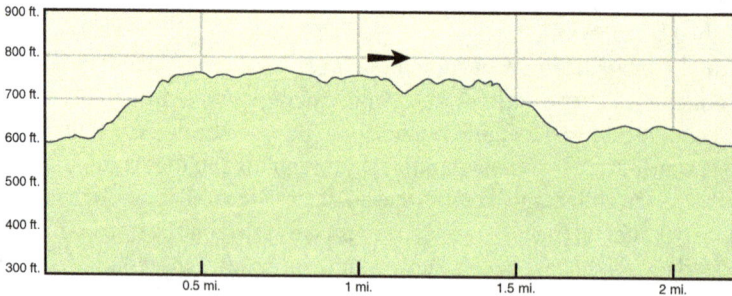

CEDAR MOUNTAIN NATURE PRESERVE

John Penn Branch

FM 1382

Dogwood Canyon Audubon Center

bird blind

West Loop Trail

Canyon Floor Trail

old cabin

N

0.1 mile

0.1 kilometer

At approximately 0.25 mile, you'll reach the canyon rim, where conveniently placed trash cans serve as a reminder to leave no trace behind. From here, the trail splits into a loop, allowing you to go west or north—either direction you choose, you'll return to this spot on your descent. On the hike I've outlined here, turn west. The trail is relatively flat and easy, winding through the trees before coming upon a bench and an old metal cabin. Long since abandoned, the cabin is closed; however, you can peer into the windows as you hike by and see the remnants of a former life, allowing your imagination to wander and wonder what life might have been like in such a remote region.

As you continue your hike, you'll pass another bench that faces an overlook toward Farm to Market Road 1382. After a brief break to admire the view, continue on the trail as it loops toward the edge of the canyon rim. You'll soon reach a scenic overlook with fantastic views of Joe Pool Lake, Cedar Hill State Park, and even the Cowboys Stadium. A conveniently placed bench makes this an ideal spot to take a break and have a snack or lunch. As you take in the views and relax, keep your eyes to the sky for glimpses of oft-sighted birds such as red-tailed hawks and turkey vultures.

When you're rested, continue back on the trail as it follows the canyon rim back to the start of the loop. At the trail juncture, head east back down the switchback toward the canyon floor, where you'll retrace your steps back to the trailhead.

By the time you reach the trailhead, you should be ready for a cooldown. Head southeast down the Canyon Floor Trail for an easy hike to wind down your muscles. The geography on this section of trail is markedly different from the rim—vines hang loosely from trees and brush, forming a lush canopy. A couple of conveniently placed benches along the trail offer spots to sit and observe birds and enjoy the peace and tranquility of the forest. The trail ends at 0.25 mile, marked by a bench and a small loop. From here, retrace your steps to the trailhead.

NEARBY ACTIVITIES

Just 0.5 mile up the road, Cedar Hill State Park is popular with anglers, boaters, picnickers, campers, and birders. Inside, you'll also find Penn Farm Agricultural History Center, a restored farm exhibit. To get there, turn left (west) onto FM 1382 (Belt Line Road). The park is about 0.5 mile down on the left.

• •

GPS TRAILHEAD COORDINATES N32° 36.787' W96° 58.263'

DIRECTIONS From Dallas, take I-35E south to US 67 S. Exit onto FM 1382, and turn right, heading west 2.2 miles. The Audubon Center is just past Northwood University.

From Fort Worth, take US 287 south to I-20 E. Take Exit 457 for FM 1382/Belt Line Road. Turn right (south) onto FM 1382. The center is 4.4 miles down.

Although there are no goats here, plenty of wildlife and outstanding views of the Trinity River are highlights of this trail.

THIS TRAIL RUNS along an old road in one of the largest preserves in Dallas County. The flat, straight path is ideal for walkers and joggers, and it offers a scenic overlook onto the Trinity River.

DESCRIPTION

There is perhaps no easier way to motivate someone to join you on a hike than by telling them you are going to Goat Island Preserve. The name itself is exotic and intriguing, arousing an immediate desire to explore and prompting a string of thought-provoking questions: *Are there goats? Are there islands? Why would there be goats on an island? And how far is it from Dallas–Fort Worth?*

Remarkably, although Goat Island Preserve is the second largest preserve in Dallas County, very few people are even aware of its existence. It has been part of the county's open space program since 1993; however, for most of its existence it has gone largely unnoticed. Only in the past few years has it been revitalized with a network of trails for hikers and bikers.

The 348-acre preserve is located on the Trinity River in Southeastern Dallas County, and is maintained by Dallas County, who has partnered with The Dallas Off-Road Bicycle Association (DORBA) to develop and maintain more than 9 miles of natural-surface trails open to hiking and biking.

DISTANCE & CONFIGURATION: 2.54-mile out-and-back

DIFFICULTY: Easy

SCENERY: Trinity River

EXPOSURE: Sunny

TRAFFIC: Light

TRAIL SURFACE: Old dirt/gravel road

HIKING TIME: 1.25 hours

DRIVING DISTANCE: 6 miles from the intersection of I-20 and I-45

ACCESS: Daily, 6 a.m.–sunset

MAP: dorba.org/trail.php?t=41

WHEELCHAIR TRAVERSABLE: No

FACILITIES: None

CONTACT: dorba.org

LOCATION: 2800 Post Oak Rd., Hutchins

COMMENTS: Feral hogs, raccoons, and even the occasional alligator have been spotted down on the banks of the river; practice good trail etiquette, and give wildlife plenty of space. Be sure to check the DORBA website (dorba.org) after a rain for trail closures.

Although the preserve itself is not an island, it is named after one of two islands on the river. Though it may disappoint some, I'm sorry to say that you won't find any goats on the island or anywhere else in the preserve. So why the name? Unfortunately, the actual history of why the island was named Goat Island is not well documented.

Though it is fairly close to Dallas, you'll find that this is one of the less visited corners of the county, and ideal for those looking for something off the beaten track. The main trail is an old soft-surface farm road that roughly follows the Trinity River, running from the trailhead on Post Oak Road northeast to the dams near South Belt Line Road. From this "main" trail, smaller singletrack trails branch off and rejoin, offering bikers and hikers the choice of staying on the wider farm road or branching off onto the smaller side shoots to get deeper into the preserve. Because of this choice, your outing can be a relaxing stroll or a more adventurous hike through the Trinity River forest, depending on your mood.

The trail has outstanding views of the Trinity River and a surprising amount of wildlife. Occasional evidence and sightings of a variety of animals, including armadillo, deer, bobcat, snakes, feral hogs, raccoons, and even alligators, are not uncommon. Practice good trail etiquette by giving any animals that may cross your path—especially feral hogs—plenty of space.

Because the preserve is in a floodplain, be sure to check for trail closures if there have been rains in the days prior to your visit. DORBA monitors trail conditions closely and will post closures on the trail's website.

The trailhead is adjacent to the parking lot and has signage reminding you that you are entering "one of the very few wilderness areas left in Dallas County." Disappearing north into the preserve behind the signage, an old farm road marks the main trail for this hike. Follow the path, and after a few hundred feet, you'll find a trail marker with an arrow directing you off the main path and onto a side trail. There are many side spur trails such as this along the main farm road, providing you with opportunities to delve deeper into the preserve. After a period, these trails redirect themselves and merge back onto the road.

Goat Island Preserve Trail

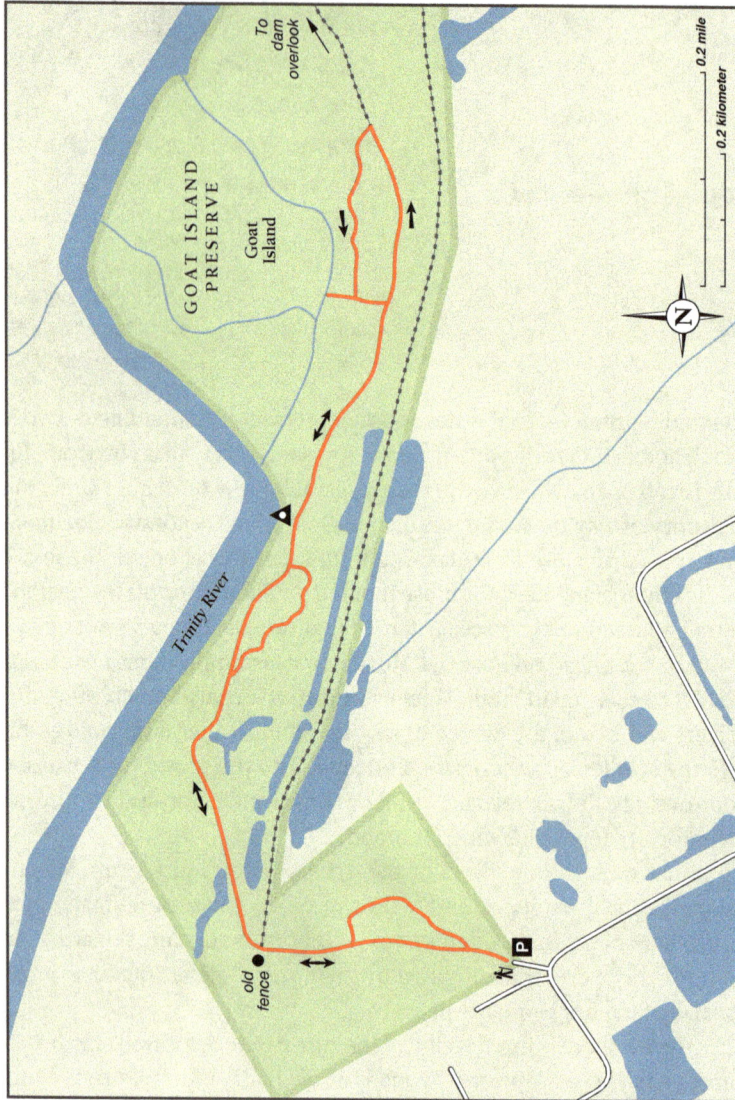

For this hike, head down the Bevo trail to get an idea of what the preserve is like. The trail heads through some grass and into a forested canopy, where the chirping of birds and rustle of leaves will charm and lull you into forgetting the stresses of city life. Before long, and after a few twists and turns, the trail will emerge back onto the main farm road.

Continue down the farm road and you'll reach an old piece of fence. Turning east will take you along the top of an old levee. Bypass the detour, and continue your hike down the farm road. You'll eventually reach the Owls Trail, heading south off the main farm road. By now you're likely ready for a little more adventure, so head off into the trees onto the Owls Trail. The sights and sounds of the forest will again surround you before you eventually emerge back onto the main path. At 0.8 mile, you'll reach an overlook with fantastic views of the Trinity River. When you're finished admiring the view, continue back on the trail, following the road another 0.2 mile until you reach a trail marker marking a wide, grassy path heading north. Follow the side trail a few hundred feet, bypassing the Eagles Trail, and you'll reach a river channel with a concrete crossing. This is the crossing to Goat Island. When you're done exploring the island, retrace your steps back to the Eagles Trail marker and continue through the forest heading east. Just when you've convinced yourself you're lost in the middle of the preserve, the Eagles Trail emerges from the forest back onto the main path.

At this point I chose to return to the trailhead by heading west back down the farm road in the direction from which I originally came, but this hike can be extended by several miles by continuing to follow the trail southeast. At the preserve's south end, you'll find an overlook onto an old lock and dam in the Trinity River.

NEARBY ACTIVITIES

Just 25 miles south down I-45 is Ennis, the Official Bluebonnet City of Texas. Ennis is famously known for its Bluebonnet Trail—a 40-mile drive through some of the prettiest wildflower blooms the state has to offer. In April, when the bluebonnets are in bloom, tens of thousands of visitors drive the route. Visit the city's convention and visitors bureau for the dates, or check visitennis.org. If you're visiting at a different time of year, the city also has a drive-in theater; the Ennis Railroad and Cultural Heritage Museum; and Bubba's Bar-B-Q & Steakhouse, one of the state's best road-side eateries (972-875-0036). Bubba's is right off I-45 at Exit 251.

• •

GPS TRAILHEAD COORDINATES N32° 37.988' W96° 39.734'

DIRECTIONS Take I-45 south toward Hutchins, and take Exit 273. Turn right onto Fulghum Road, and follow it back left under the highway. Continue 1.8 miles. Fulghum Road will then become Post Oak Road. The trailhead will be on your left at a bend in the road.

A small boat explores the lake's shoreline.

THIS SHADY TRAIL loops through the woods in an area used for primitive camping. Several access points to the water and a photo blind make it a good morning hike for bird-watchers.

DESCRIPTION

Almost exactly 60 miles from Dallas, Purtis Creek State Park is known specifically for its excellent fishing. The waters, stocked with largemouth bass (catch-and-release), catfish, and crappie, attract anglers from throughout the metroplex. The lake has speed limits and permits only 50 boats on the water at a time, resulting in a quiet, mellow atmosphere. The park was acquired in 1977 and opened to the public in 1988. It includes a 355-acre lake with a swimming area, fishing pier, boat ramp, and bait shop. If you're interested in getting out on the water after the hike, you can rent a canoe or a kayak.

According to the Texas Parks and Wildlife Department, the Caddo and Wichita tribes originally inhabited the area, and some petroglyphs have been found nearby. The petroglyphs cannot be viewed from the park, however, because they are on private land. Pick up a map, an interpretive brochure, and a pamphlet on the park's history from the rangers in the park headquarters. The brochure, in conjunction with numbered signposts along the trail, will help you identify the local flora.

DISTANCE & CONFIGURATION:
1.73-mile balloon

DIFFICULTY: Easy

SCENERY: Woods, lake

EXPOSURE: Shady

TRAFFIC: Light

TRAIL SURFACE: Packed dirt

HIKING TIME: 40 minutes

DRIVING DISTANCE: 20 miles from I-20 and FM 47

ACCESS: Daily, 7 a.m.–10 p.m.; $5 per day for adults and children age 13 and older

MAP: tinyurl.com/purtiscreektrailmap

WHEELCHAIR TRAVERSABLE: No

FACILITIES: Restrooms, playground, water fountain

CONTACT: 903-425-2332, tpwd.texas.gov /state-parks/purtis-creek

LOCATION: Intersection of FM 316 and CR 2938, Eustace

COMMENTS: Pets are allowed but must be leashed. A couple of days a year (in winter) are for hunting only. Before your visit, check tpwd.texas .gov/state-parks/purtis-creek for trail closures. Canoes and kayaks are available for rent.

The trailhead is adjacent to the parking area. Head southeast down a narrow dirt path bordered by dense thickets. Plants you'll spot along the trail include the American beautyberry, which bursts with purple berries in the fall. Also look for the flowering dogwood. In the fall, this short tree produces small, red fruits that look like berries; in the spring, they sport hundreds of small, white flowers.

The trail continues, winding its way through the woods before reaching a lookout over a swampy inlet of the lake. Across the water, you can sometimes spot hikers peering out of the narrow slats of a wooden photo blind on the opposite bank.

Back on the trail, cross a couple of bridges spanning small streams before reaching the first trail junction. Bear right at the path split, then right again at the next split. This portion of the trail loops through the woods and around a primitive-camping area. As you venture onto the loop trail, you'll first reach the photo blind you glimpsed earlier on the hike. When waters are low, the narrow inlet in front of the blind is very shallow, exposing numerous tree stumps. The main portion of the lake is farther left. This is a nice spot for spying some of the park's birds. More than 200 species inhabit the area, including the downy and hairy woodpeckers, the warbling and red-eyed vireos, belted kingfisher, and yellow-billed cuckoo. I lingered in the photo blind a while and spotted a turkey vulture, an egret, and some mallards. Farther down the trail, a fellow hiker spied what he believed to be a red-tailed hawk before it disappeared behind the trees. Birders can pick up a complete list of all bird species found in the area at park headquarters.

Continue along the loop, which follows the shoreline. The trail stays inland, offering only brief glimpses of the water through the trees. Pass a number of shorter side trails shooting off to the right from the main trail. These trails lead to primitive-camping spots at the water's edge and provide nice overlooks and access to the water. Investigate as many of these trails as you'd like; each gives a different view of the lake. Just be sure no campers are settled into the sites you explore. Each of

Purtis Creek Trail

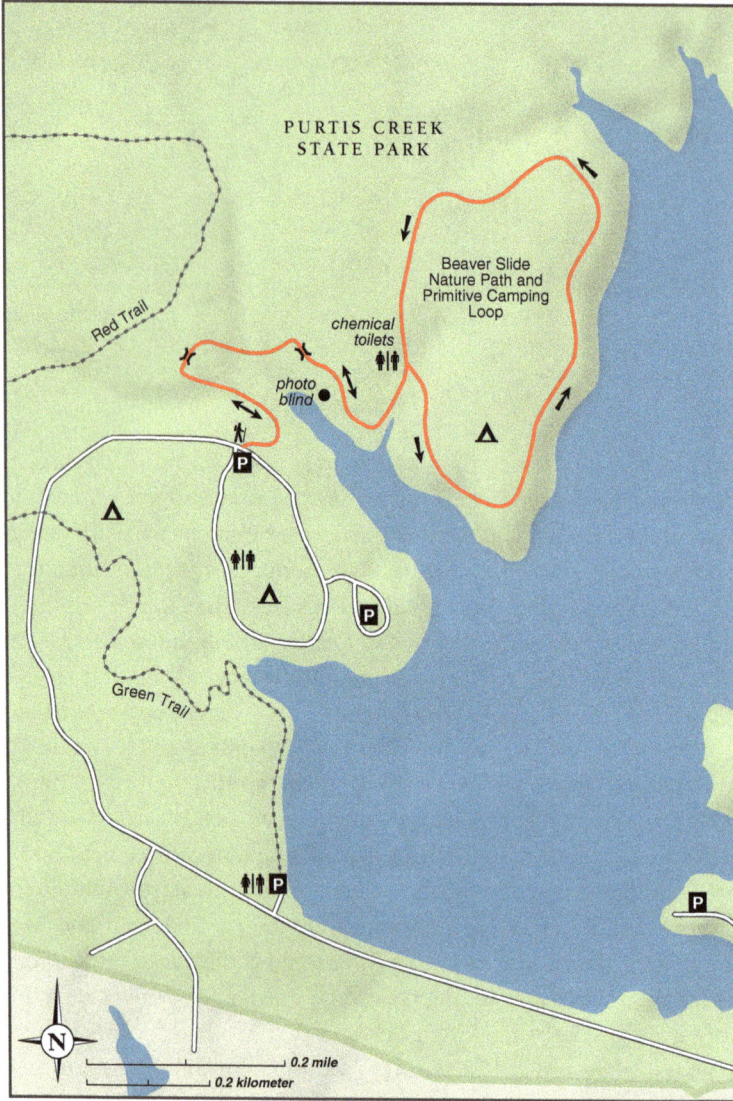

PURTIS CREEK
STATE PARK

Beaver Slide
Nature Path and
Primitive Camping
Loop

Red Trail

chemical
toilets

photo
blind

Green Trail

N

0.2 mile
0.2 kilometer

these sites is designed for boat (and pedestrian) access. Trails lead from the campsite itself to small beaches along the adjacent shoreline. Small numbered signposts on the water's edge allow boaters to float up to their site from the lake.

The trail continues through dense woods that close in on both sides. If you've failed to spot any birds, you won't fail to hear the cawing of crows as you walk along. Old, gnarled trees in a couple of spots along the trail add interest to the mass of woodlands.

If you enjoy geocaching—using a GPS unit to locate items hidden in various public places—pick up a handout from the park headquarters that describes a few caches hidden here.

Pass some chemical toilets, then find yourself back at the beginning of the loop. From here, retrace your steps to the trailhead.

NEARBY ACTIVITIES

If you're interested in getting on the lake after the hike, rent a canoe, kayak, or paddleboat. Outside the park, stop by the Texas Freshwater Fisheries Center, which has a hatchery, an aquarium, a wetlands trail, and a 1.2-acre lake, where rods and bait are provided (closed Mondays; 800-792-1112; tpwd.state.tx.us/spdest/visitor centers/tffc). To get there, turn left (south) onto US 175, then take Loop 7 E to Farm to Market Road 2495, where you'll turn left and go about 3 miles.

• •

GPS TRAILHEAD COORDINATES N32° 21.833' W96° 00.167'

DIRECTIONS From Dallas, take US 175 to Eustace. Follow the signs to Purtis Creek State Park, exiting left (north) onto FM 316 to travel 3.5 miles. From the park entrance, take the first left, pass the fish ponds, and head into the camping area. Take the left fork and park in the small parking lot on the left.

Looking through the photo blinds for birds

Cool breezes and unobstructed lake views are hallmarks of this trail.

THIS FLAT TRAIL runs across the top of Joe Pool Dam, rewarding you with unobstructed views of the lake. The trail is kid-friendly, dog-friendly, and bike-friendly.

DESCRIPTION

Though not the prettiest lake in the metroplex, Joe Pool Lake has, since its recent completion in 1989, been surprisingly popular—and for good reason. The lake is ideally located, about 20 miles southwest of Dallas and about 25 miles southeast of Fort Worth. A state park and several city parks border the lake, making it a natural choice for summer outings. Large and sprawling amid nondescript tree-filled terrain, the lake is unlikely to inspire awe. But what it lacks in beauty, it makes up for in activities: the parks offer everything from camping and hiking to boating, fishing, and swimming. Organized events are always happening somewhere along the lake and include bike rallies, fishing tournaments, and outdoor-club activities.

Named after a 1960s congressman instrumental in its establishment, the lake is a huge reservoir created by impounding creek waters with a long embankment dam. The dam is made of earth fill, composed of compacted soils that form a raised wall on the northern side of the lake. An old road that runs along the top of the dam and over the lake is popular with cyclists and joggers—this is the route for the following hike.

DISTANCE & CONFIGURATION: 3-mile out-and-back

DIFFICULTY: Easy

SCENERY: Lake, spillway

EXPOSURE: Sunny

TRAFFIC: Moderate

TRAIL SURFACE: Paved

HIKING TIME: 1.5 hours

DRIVING DISTANCE: 9 miles from I-20 and US 67

ACCESS: Daily, sunrise–sunset; free

MAP: None

WHEELCHAIR TRAVERSABLE: No

FACILITIES: Restrooms at trailhead

CONTACT: 972-291-3900, tpwd.texas.gov /state-parks/cedar-hill

LOCATION: FM 1382, Cedar Hill

COMMENTS: Bring plenty of water, a hat, and sunscreen—there's no shade on this trail.

The trail is flat and there is little nature along the route, but that's why it's an excellent spot for those who want to hike with their dogs and those looking for an easy walk. From any point along the trail, you have unparalleled views of all lake activity, and thanks to nearby Cedar Hill State Park, which is just 1 mile south on Farm to Market Road 1382, there's always something to see on the waters, be it kayakers, sailors, anglers, or seabirds. Wear plenty of sunscreen—the trail is completely sun-drenched, though a strong breeze helps keep the trail cool on even the hottest days.

Adjacent to the parking area, a long walkway twists back and forth, leading to the restrooms and ending at an overlook, which curiously enough looks out onto nothing but grass and shrubs. Several trails disappear into the brush from this area, heading toward the lake. This hike starts at the trailhead just to the right of the restrooms and is marked by a sign advising that all pets must be leashed. The trail heads into the trees and within 100 feet ends at a service road, where you'll turn left toward the lake. This road serves as the trail for the duration of the hike and is open only to pedestrian and bicycle traffic. At 0.25 mile, the trail meets the lake's edge and continues straight along the top of the dam toward the far side of the lake.

On a clear, sunny day the opposite bank looks close, making you think you can reach the other side of the lake fairly quickly. The distance, however, is greater than it appears, and as much as you walk, the far side of the lake is likely to stay just out of reach. In fact, the trail continues along the dam for 1.5 miles before reaching the far side of the lake, where it continues another couple miles inland.

As you hike along the dam, enjoy unobstructed views of the lake on the left and a vacant, low-lying floodplain on the right. A pair of binoculars comes in handy— the vastness of the lake makes it hard to see much detail along the shoreline. Without binoculars you'll be able to make out little more than some of the closer tents pitched by state-park visitors.

Wildlife along the route consists of only a few butterflies and birds, although nearby Cedar Hill State Park's website (tpwd.texas.gov/state-parks/cedar-hill) identifies more than 200 types of birds that have been found here, including several

235

Visitor's Overlook: Joe Pool Lake Dam Trail

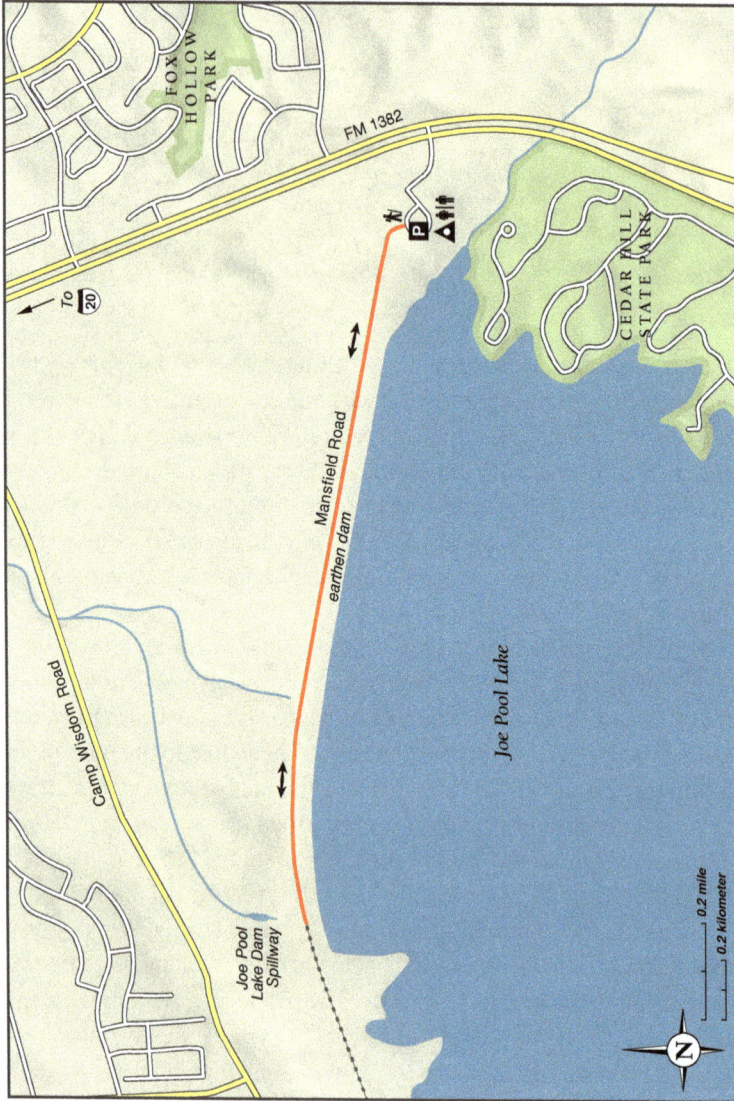

varieties of hawks, herons, and pelicans, and more than a dozen types of sparrows. The bald eagle even makes the list, although on my hike I saw only a few gulls swooping over the water.

At 1.5 miles, reach the far side of the lake and the end of the dam, marked by a tower and a concrete spillway. This is a good place to turn around—from here the trail quickly heats up as you leave the water and lose the breeze coming off it.

A view of the spillway from the trail

NEARBY ACTIVITIES

Visitor's Overlook is adjacent to Cedar Hill State Park, which is only 1 mile south down FM 1382. The state-park visitor center is a good place to get maps and brochures. Check with the staff for event information; the park also regularly schedules nature walks and talks.

• •

GPS TRAILHEAD COORDINATES N32° 38.467' W96° 58.567'

DIRECTIONS From I-20, head west toward Fort Worth. Exit onto FM 1382 and turn left (south). The entrance is 3 miles down on the right and has a small sign identifying it as Visitor's Overlook.

237

The wide, packed-dirt trail winds through woods.

A SHADY TRAIL with multiple overlooks for bank fishing follows the creek through the woods. After the hike, enjoy a picnic overlooking Joe Pool Lake; the picnic area is just down the road in the northern section of the park.

DESCRIPTION

Loyd Park, on the northwest banks of Joe Pool Lake in Grand Prairie, is operated by the city's parks and recreation department. The lake is a reservoir named after a 1960s congressman instrumental in its establishment. Cedar Hill State Park sits on the shores on the opposite side of the lake.

At this scenic park, aside from hiking and equestrian trails, you'll find more than 200 campsites, eight cabins, a beach, a designated swimming area, a boat ramp, fishing piers, and an assortment of picnic areas along the lakeshore. The park sometimes appears empty, but a quick drive from end to end reveals considerable activity; the amenities are fairly spread out, and so too are the visitors. From the hiking trailhead on the west side of the park, you'd never know how many boaters are coming and going at the easternmost side or how many kids are romping on the beach just to the west. Leashed pets are allowed in the park, except at the swimming beach and playgrounds.

There is an admission fee, which may seem a bit high for just a day hike, considering the other options. However, you'll find this park spotlessly clean and the trail

DISTANCE & CONFIGURATION: 2.16-mile out-and-back

DIFFICULTY: Easy

SCENERY: Woods, lake

EXPOSURE: Shady–sunny

TRAFFIC: Light

TRAIL SURFACE: Sections of loose- and packed-dirt trail

HIKING TIME: 45 minutes

DRIVING DISTANCE: 6.4 miles from I-20 and TX 360

ACCESS: Daily; open 24 hours (quiet time after 10 p.m.); $10 per vehicle per day, $15 per vehicle on holidays and holiday weekends

MAP: None

WHEELCHAIR TRAVERSABLE: No

FACILITIES: Restrooms, picnic area, fishing pier, swimming beach

CONTACT: 972-237-4120

LOCATION: 901 N. Day Miar Rd., Grand Prairie

COMMENTS: Up to 6 people per car for the 1 entrance rate. There is a special senior citizens rate of only $2 per person.

well maintained. And after the hike you can enjoy the roped-off swimming beach and other amenities. Another tip: come with a couple of friends—the charge per car is the same whether you have two people in the car or six.

The trail starts on the park's west side. A small wooden WALNUT CREEK TRAIL sign welcomes you onto a wide path that disappears into the trees. Tall grasses beneath the towering trees provide good cover for snakes. I didn't spot any, and you're unlikely to have a problem, but it's always a good idea to watch where you step. The trail is easily wide enough to walk two abreast and allow you to step around anything you might see. Because the trail also welcomes equestrians, you'll want to keep an eye out for horse manure, although I found little evidence of horses. At the first trail junction, bear right.

The trail winds through the woods; bear left at the next junction to follow it alongside a creek connected to the lake. There are a couple of water overlooks at the beginning of the hike; after that, the water is hidden from view behind the trees to your left. Plenty of paths lead over to the water, though, and you'll pass a number of spurs from the main trail heading left toward the bank. The spurs, which are marked with BANK FISHING signs, attest to the trail's popularity with anglers. I ventured down some of these trails and found a father fishing with his son at one, a young teen fishing alone at another, and only the soft rustling of leaves at the third. It comes as no surprise that anglers like the area—most of the trail has a quiet, mellow feel, the only sounds being the wind rustling in the leaves and the occasional bird chirp.

Because most of the trail winds through the woods, the fall is an excellent time to hike here. The reds, yellows, and greens of the changing leaves add to the trail's beauty. This is also a good hike for a bright, sunny day, because the trees cast most of the trail in deep shade. Pick a different trail if it rained the day before your hike; some sections of the trail are loosely packed soil, making for a muddy walk if the trail gets even slightly wet.

Walnut Creek Trail

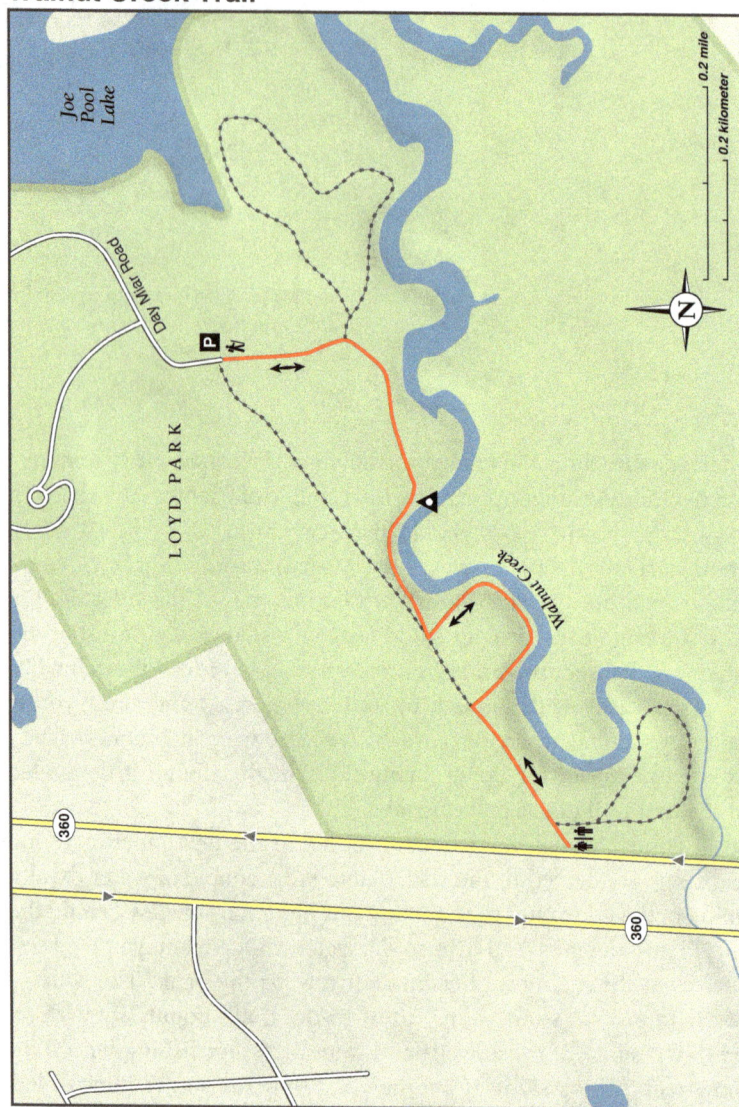

At 0.63 mile, the trail emerges from the woods onto a grassy maintenance road. Head left and pick up the trail that disappears back into the woods on the left. Wind through more woods before you finally reemerge onto the maintenance road at 0.9 mile. Go left down the service road. You'll hear the sounds of cars coming from US 360, which you'll see ahead, beyond the park's boundary.

At 1.08 miles, within view of the highway, reach a small building—the Walnut Creek Restroom. This is a good turnaround spot; just retrace your steps to the trailhead. If you'd like to extend the hike, you can pick up the trail just beyond the restroom, where it continues its peaceful meander through the woods.

Note: Crossing the bridge at the last intersection will take you to the Blackland Federation Trail. This section is very confusing, with many junctions that can easily get you lost. I highly suggest bringing a compass or GPS if you choose to explore the section across the bridge.

NEARBY ACTIVITIES

Lone Star Park, site of the 2004 Breeders' Cup, is a huge racetrack that offers horse racing in the spring, early summer, and fall (800-795-7223, lonestarpark.com). The park also hosts special events such as live music throughout the spring and fall. To get there, follow TX 360 N 6 miles and exit at I-30/Six Flags Drive toward Dallas. Go 3 miles and take Exit 34. Turn left onto Belt Line Road. Lone Star Park will be on your right.

• •

GPS TRAILHEAD COORDINATES N32° 35.867' W97° 04.100'

DIRECTIONS Follow I-20 W toward Fort Worth and take Exit 453B onto TX 360 S toward Frontage Road/Watson Road. Go about 3 miles and turn left onto Arlington Webb Road/County Road 2017, which becomes Ragland Road. The entrance to Loyd Park is on your right. The trailhead is on the western side of the park; to reach it, turn right after you enter the park.

A hiker enjoys the sunny trail.

THIS SURPRISINGLY CHARMING HIKE starts down a rural path alongside Waxahachie Creek and ends at the remnants of the historic Interurban Railway. The lush, green setting and abundance of bird boxes make this trail a must-visit for birders.

DESCRIPTION

Dubbed Gingerbread City, thanks to the ornate carpentry on some of its Victorian-style homes, Waxahachie is the seat of Ellis County. It also has the distinct honor of being associated with the Texas state shrub, having been designated the Crape Myrtle Capital of Texas. A third nickname refers to the city as the Movie Capital of Texas, thanks to a number of feature films having done location shooting here. About 30 miles south of Dallas and 40 miles southeast of Fort Worth, the city is easy to reach from anywhere in the metroplex.

The Texas Parks and Wildlife Department helped fund the trail, which currently offers about 6 miles of paved path. The trailhead is hidden just outside downtown Waxahachie in Lion's Park, a small city park that's dominated by soccer and softball fields. As you enter the park, you'll see a huge field with a pavilion at the northeast end. Park in the small lot adjacent to the pavilion, where you'll find the trailhead.

DISTANCE & CONFIGURATION: 5.54-mile out-and-back

DIFFICULTY: Easy

SCENERY: Historic bridges, rail tracks, creek, birds

EXPOSURE: Partially sunny

TRAFFIC: Moderate

TRAIL SURFACE: Paved

HIKING TIME: 1.75 hours

DRIVING DISTANCE: 3 miles from I-35E and US 77

ACCESS: Daily, sunrise–10 p.m.; free

MAP: None

WHEELCHAIR TRAVERSABLE: Yes

FACILITIES: Restrooms, picnic tables, benches

CONTACT: waxahachie.com/departments /parks_and_recreation

LOCATION: Lion's Park, 2303 Howard Rd., Waxahachie

COMMENTS: A good option if it has recently rained.

The trail heads a few hundred feet northeast until it meets Waxahachie Creek, then turns left, following the curves and bends of the creek as it heads northwest. For the duration of the hike, the creek gurgles and babbles just beyond the hardwoods to your right. Lions Park soon disappears from view and is replaced by fenced pastures where horses graze and trot lazily through sunny fields. The trail is very well maintained, and in addition to trash bins placed discreetly at various points along the trail, you'll find large, handsome stone mile markers at quarter-mile intervals, helping you keep track of where you are on the trail.

As you hike, you'll hear the near-constant chirping and whistling of birds, many attracted by the wooden bird boxes that have been set up at various points along the trail. Benches at key spots overlooking the creek offer opportunities for you to rest and pull out your binoculars. Especially in spring, this trail is so full of life that even if you don't have any binoculars, you won't leave disappointed—the birds swoop and flit across the trail, disregarding hikers. Watch for colorful cardinals, bluebirds, robins, and warblers. If you're lucky, you'll even spot a few hummingbirds—as I stood taking a swig from my water bottle, a couple of them buzzed boldly past me, seeming to ignore my very existence.

At 0.38 mile, a small clearing offers a scenic overlook where you can view the creek. Trees loom on either side, partially shading its clear waters. If you look carefully, you're likely to spot turtles warming themselves in the small patches of sun that filter through the tree branches. Just ahead, environmentalists have built a bat house. Just beyond it and behind the trees across the river, glimpse some railroad tracks paralleling the creek.

At 1.53 miles, reach the short, wooden Continental Bridge. Beyond it, the trail continues to curl lazily through the lovely rural setting, framed by pastures on the left and a dense clustering of hardwood trees growing up against the creek on your right—a combination that is utterly peaceful and entirely relaxing without being boring.

The trail crosses Matthews Street at 2.15 miles; if you glance to the right as you cross the street, you'll see the top of the Ellis County Courthouse towering in the

Waxahachie Creek Hike and Bike Trail

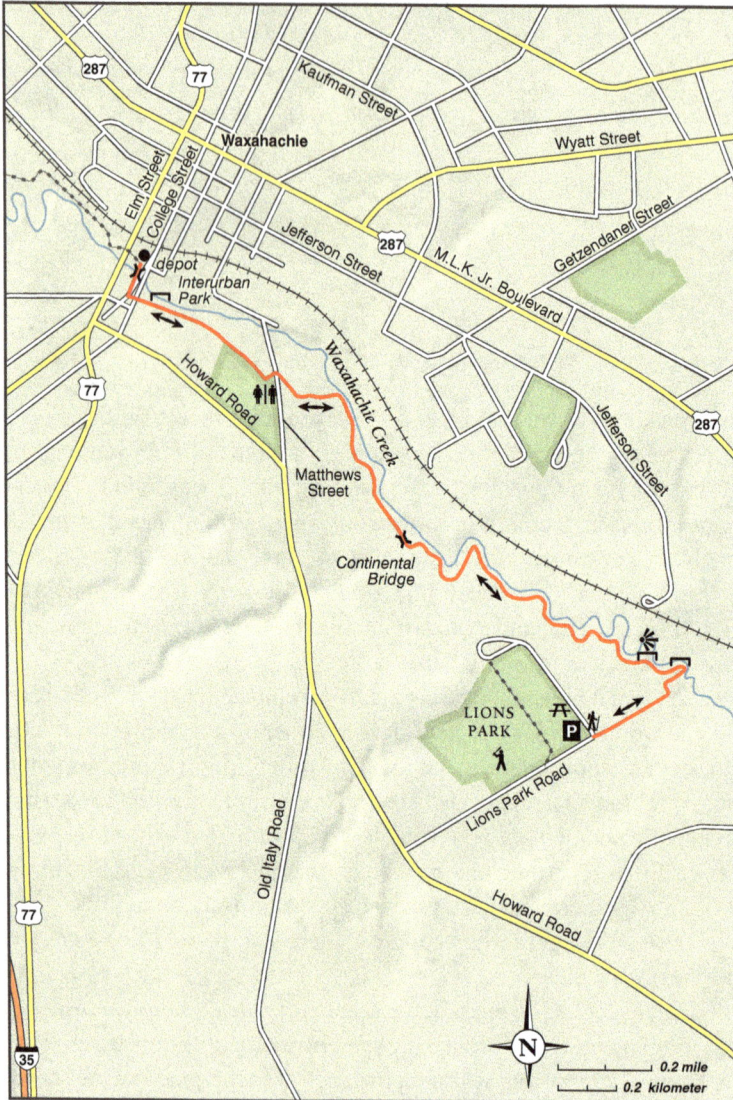

distance. Continuing along the trail, hike another 0.3 mile to Interurban Park, named for the Interurban Railway (aka the Texas Electric Railway), which ran from Dallas through Waxahachie to Waco until December 31, 1948. Signposts show old photographs of the 1,442-foot trestle bridge that spanned Waxahachie Creek here. Though the bridge is long gone, the supports are still intact. The scenery hasn't changed much since the photographs were taken, and with a little imagination you can almost see the bridge disappearing north toward downtown.

Continue northwest down the trail until you reach College Street, at 2.58 miles. Cross the street and turn right toward the old red metal truss bridge, known as the Rogers Street Bridge. This Texas Historic Bridge, now open only to pedestrians, was built in 1889 when the area was first settled; vehicles used it until 1990, when a newer bridge replaced it. Cross back over Rogers Street and explore the old depot. Adjacent to the depot, an old feed store reminds you of the city's agricultural roots. This is an ideal spot to turn and retrace your steps to the trailhead. If you want to extend the hike, the trail continues northwest to Getzendaner Park.

NEARBY ACTIVITIES

Stop by Waxahachie's Downtown Historic District, where you can shop, visit the Ellis County Museum, and admire the courthouse, which dates to 1895. To get downtown, turn right onto Howard Street, then right onto South Elm Street.

• •

GPS TRAILHEAD COORDINATES N32° 22.083' W96° 50.017'

DIRECTIONS Follow I-35E south toward Waxahachie and take Exit 408 onto US 77 S. Go about 9 miles, then turn left onto Howard Road. Lions Park is about 1.3 miles ahead on the left. Park in the lot next to the pavilion, at the northeast end of the road.

Horse-filled pastures line this pretty trail.

A bridge connects two sections of trail.

THIS SHADY TRAIL loops through a small, heavily wooded preserve, making it an excellent spot for hiking on a hot, sunny day. Though not especially scenic, the trail appeals to those who enjoy exploring because the myriad junctions allow you to digress with little risk of becoming too lost.

DESCRIPTION

The local community lobbied to get this plot of land set aside, and now, thanks to their efforts, it is part of the Dallas County Trail and Preserve Program. The 72-acre nature preserve has a large network of trails crisscrossing the woods and is well used by those in the area.

Be prepared for a network of paths branching left and right as you hike along the trail. Though these unmarked trails split off in different directions every few hundred feet, it's almost impossible to get lost for long because almost all trails eventually lead back to the center of the preserve, where a trail runs west–east through its center. All trails funnel into this central trail and go across the Stevie Ray Vaughan Memorial Bridge, which divides the western side of the preserve from the eastern side. The bridge honors the famous 1980s blues-rock guitarist Stevie Ray Vaughan. Vaughan played lead guitar on David Bowie's *Let's Dance* album and became very popular with his own band, Double Trouble. The guitarist died in a

DISTANCE & CONFIGURATION: 1.6-mile figure eight

DIFFICULTY: Moderate

SCENERY: Woodlands, bridge

EXPOSURE: Mostly shady

TRAFFIC: Light

TRAIL SURFACE: Packed dirt

HIKING TIME: 50 minutes

DRIVING DISTANCE: 3 miles from US 67 and I-20

ACCESS: Daily, 6 a.m.–10 p.m.; free

MAP: None

WHEELCHAIR TRAVERSABLE: No

FACILITIES: None

CONTACT: 972-230-9653

LOCATION: 1410 N. Duncanville Rd., Cedar Hill

COMMENTS: Leashed dogs and mountain bikers are welcome on this trail.

helicopter crash following a concert on August 26, 1990. Vaughan is memorialized here because he was born and raised in Dallas.

The trail I've mapped out is a rough loop around the preserve and has lots of small ups and downs through hilly terrain, providing a nice workout. If you miss a turn—highly possible with so many trails branching out—don't become overly concerned. Explore as you wish, and you'll eventually find yourself back at the bridge, which is a good reference point.

There are two main entrances from the parking lot. Take the trailhead on the right (the one on the left is where you'll come out at the trail's end). Immediately, you'll be on a somewhat rocky trail. The scenery for most of this hike is what you see here: dense woods that shade much of the trail. About 250 feet into your trek, the trail splits; bear right. At the next trail split, at 0.13 mile, bear left. At this point, the trail has some small steep uphill and downhill climbs. The ruggedness here appeals to mountain bikers, who maintain the trail. On my hike, however, I didn't see a single biker, just a couple of hikers whose dogs were thoroughly enjoying their workout.

At the next junction, 0.28 mile into the hike, continue straight and downhill. The preserve abuts some backyards, and through the trees you'll catch sight of houses before the trail returns to the woods. Finally, 0.55 mile into the hike, come to the Stevie Ray Vaughan Memorial Bridge, a brick-red truss bridge spanning a dry creekbed.

Cross the bridge and a small gully, then turn right at the next split, at about 0.65 mile. This will take you on a 0.5-mile loop through the eastern half of the preserve. Hang a right at the junction at 0.8 mile, and the trail will loop through a piney grove and emerge into a small field with a few pine trees.

At the next juncture, continue straight before reaching another trail split. If you were to turn right, the trail heads up a short, steep, rocky hill and exits the preserve. You should turn left, bypassing this back entrance.

The trail continues north through underbrush, trees, and the occasional dog walker before reaching another juncture, where you'll turn left. Cross a wooden

Windmill Hill Preserve Trail

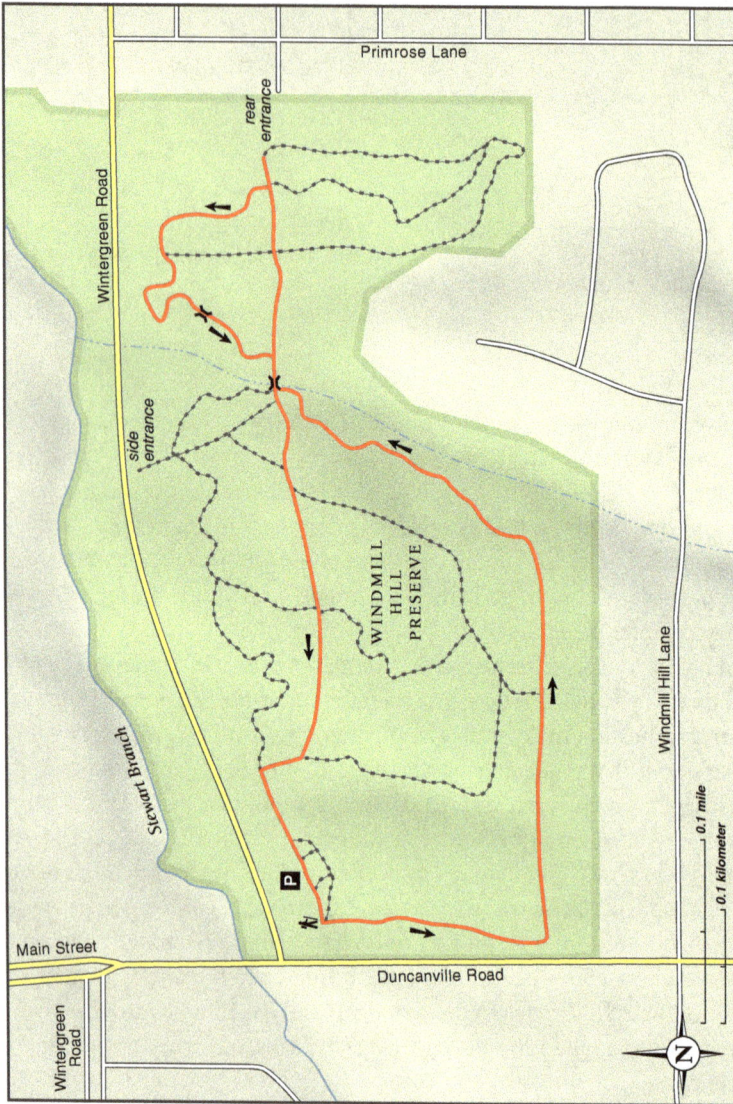

bridge, then hang another right and you're back at the Stevie Ray Vaughn Bridge. Cross back over the bridge and take a moment to orient yourself. To your left is the trail you initially came in on. To your immediate right (heading north) is a short trail that leads to a back entrance to the preserve. Directly in front of you is a third option, which heads west. Proceed down the trail heading west.

Turn right at the next juncture, traversing rough, rocky terrain. A couple hundred feet farther and you'll find yourself back at the trailhead.

NEARBY ACTIVITIES

Joe Pool Lake, along which lies Cedar Hill State Park, is nearby and is popular with anglers, boaters, picnickers, campers, and birders. Inside the state park, you'll also find Penn Farm Agricultural History Center, a restored farm exhibit. To get there, take US 67 South. After about 1.5 miles, exit to the right, onto Pleasant Run Road. Turn right onto South Belt Line Road (FM 1382). The park is about 2 miles down on the left.

• •

GPS TRAILHEAD COORDINATES N32° 37.017' W96° 54.483'

DIRECTIONS Take US 67 south toward Cleburne, and exit at Duncanville Road/Main Street, turning left. Head south on Main about 0.75 mile; the parking lot is at Windmill Hill Preserve on the left, at the corner of Wintergreen Road.

The Stevie Ray Vaughan Memorial Bridge was erected in honor of the famous Dallasite.

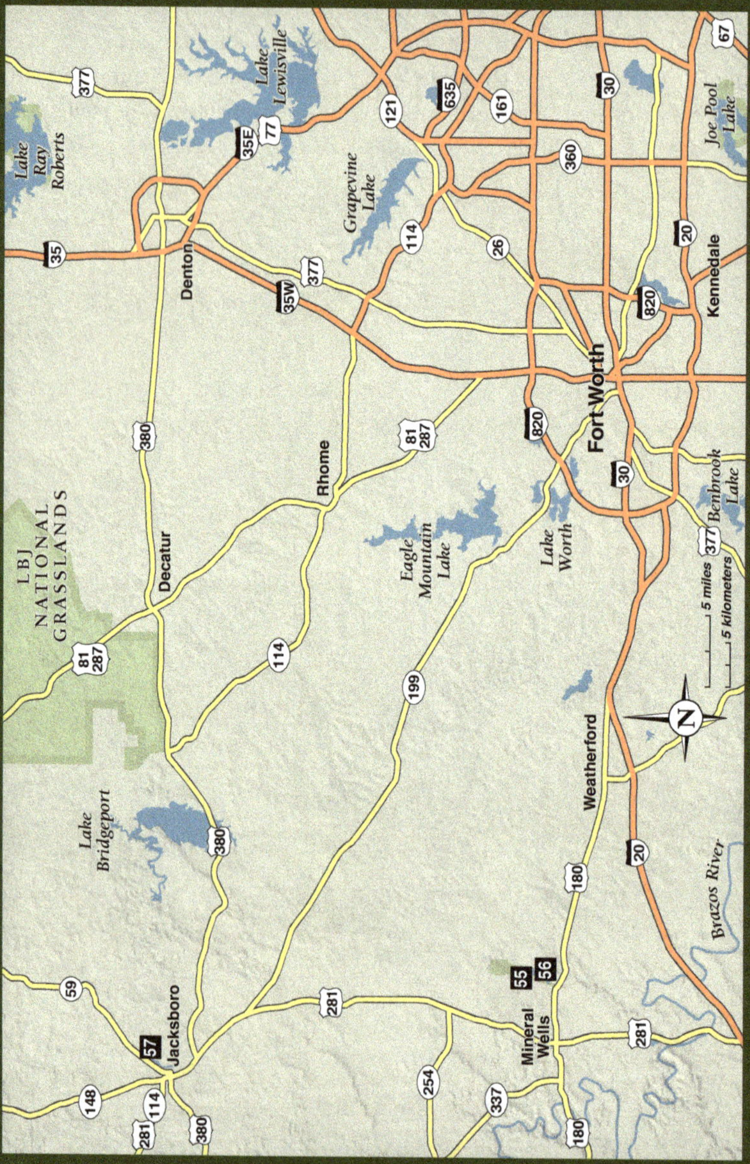

Lake Ray Roberts

377

35

Denton

35E
77

Lake Lewisville

Grapevine Lake

121

635

161

30

67

Joe Pool Lake

360

35W   377

114

26

820

20

Kennedale

380

Rhome

81
287

Fort Worth

820

30

Bennbrook Lake

377

Decatur

114

Eagle Mountain Lake

Lake Worth

5 miles
5 kilometers

LBJ NATIONAL GRASSLANDS

81
287

199

N

Weatherford

Lake Bridgeport

380

180

20

Brazos River

59

Jacksboro

281

55   56

254

57

148

114

380

281

Mineral Wells

337

281

180

WEST OF FORT WORTH

55 LAKE MINERAL WELLS STATE PARK:
Cross Timbers Trail

Animal tracks crisscross the path the day after a rainstorm.

THIS WIDE TRAIL is great for spotting animal tracks after a rainstorm—check with the park, though, to ensure the path has dried out enough to hike. The route starts in a wooded area, then loops through some sunny cactus-dotted grasslands.

DESCRIPTION

About 46 miles west of Fort Worth, Lake Mineral Wells State Park is popular among outdoor enthusiasts for good reason—not only does it have a generous trail system that welcomes bikers, hikers, and equestrians, but it also has a fishing pier, which attracts anglers; beach access for lake swimming; and, most uniquely, a section of canyons and boulders open to rock climbers. The park, which opened in 1981, covers more than 3,200 acres, including the 646-acre Lake Mineral Wells. The lake was originally designed to supply water to the expanding city of Mineral Wells. It served its purpose for 40 years before an alternate water supply was found in 1963.

On the northwest side of the lake, find the park's camping areas and the backcountry trail this hike traverses. On the southeast side of the lake, locate the trailhead for the Lake Mineral Wells State Trailway and the rock-climbing area, known as "Penitentiary Hollow." Its narrow, rocky canyons are in stark contrast to the wide, open grasslands of the trail; before or after the hike, be sure to stop by for a look.

DISTANCE & CONFIGURATION: 4-mile balloon

DIFFICULTY: Easy

SCENERY: Rocks, cactus, grasslands

EXPOSURE: Sunny

TRAFFIC: Light

TRAIL SURFACE: Packed dirt, rock

HIKING TIME: 1.5 hours

DRIVING DISTANCE: 5.5 miles from US 180 and US 281

ACCESS: Daily, 6 a.m.–10 p.m.; $7 per person

MAP: tinyurl.com/crosstimberstrailmap

WHEELCHAIR TRAVERSABLE: No

FACILITIES: Restrooms, picnic tables

CONTACT: 940-328-1171, tpwd.texas.gov /state-parks/lake-mineral-wells

LOCATION: Park Road 71, Mineral Wells

COMMENTS: Bring along an animal-tracking and scat-identification book. The trail is closed when wet, so call ahead to check trail conditions.

Running down a stone stairway to the canyon floor is a trail that rock climbers and rappellers use to access climbing spots with names such as Scrambled Egg Boulder, The Cave, and Pee Wee's Playhouse. If you're interested in exploring (or rock climbing), pick up a map at the entrance to Penitentiary Hollow. Rock climbers bring their own equipment, are required to sign a liability release, and must pay a $3 climbing fee. If you're not up for another hike and just interested in taking a look, a scenic overlook only a couple dozen feet down the rock-climbing trail offers fantastic views of the canyon and lake. You're likely to see a rock climber or two scaling the far walls.

To get to the trailhead from the park entrance, take a sharp left at the first road juncture, then follow the road across the spillway. At the next intersection, stay left. The road dead-ends at the parking area, and you'll find the trailhead on the northeast side of the lot.

The path is very wide and stays this way for most of the hike, easily accommodating both hikers and equestrians. You'll also find that the combination of partially rocky surface and sunny exposure allows the trail to dry quickly after rain. I encountered few problems with mud or puddles, even though I visited at the end of a rainy week. And because I hiked it just after it had rained, I was rewarded with some of the best animal tracks I've ever encountered on a trail—clear prints from raccoons, opossums, white-tailed deer, coyotes, and birds zigzagged all across the path throughout the entire length of the hike. Though I did not spot any of the animals themselves, I had a lot of fun reconstructing the scenes of skirmishes, crossings, and encounters that I imagined had occurred the night before my visit.

The trail is bordered by cacti to your right, beyond which the woods shroud all but brief glimpses of Lake Mineral Wells in the distance. To your left, a chain-link fence marks the boundary of the state park.

The trail soon curls away past the fence, and at 0.5 mile, you'll find yourself at a split, where you should veer right. You'll soon pass the junction to a small singletrack hiking trail that heads off to the primitive camping area. Bypass this, staying on the wide trail as it heads slightly uphill through rocky terrain. Close examination of the

Lake Mineral Wells State Park: Cross Timbers Trail

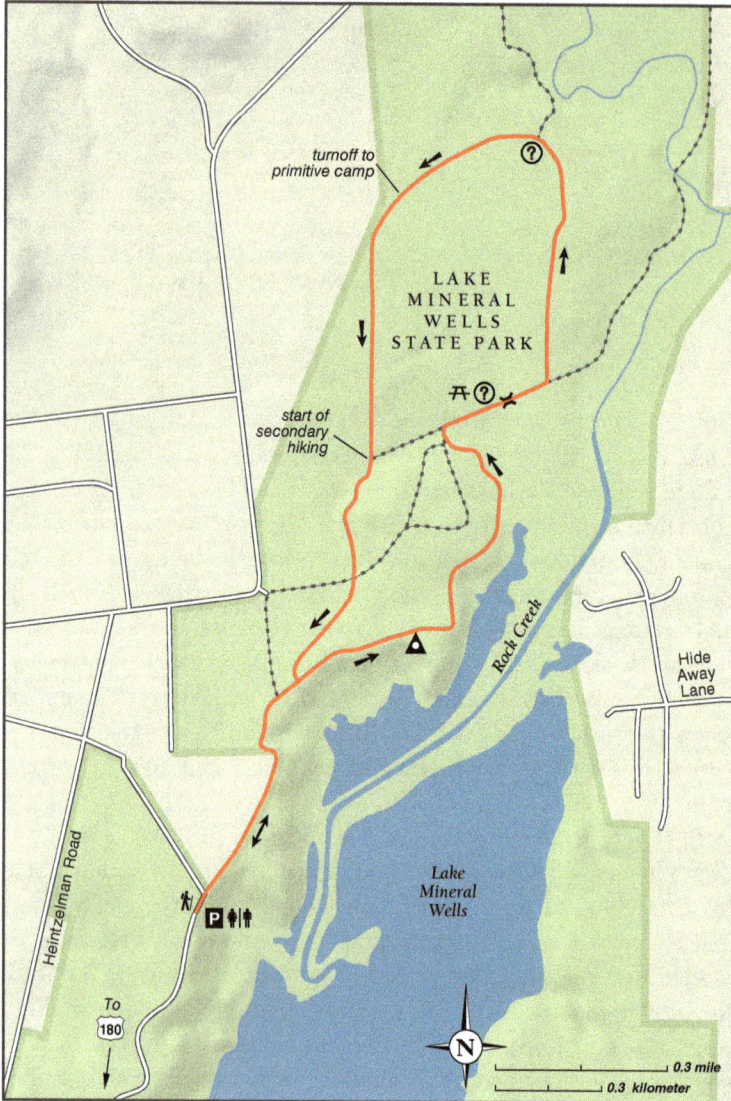

ground reveals the rocks to be varying shades of pink, glittering with flecks of mica or some other mineral.

To the right you'll catch glimpses of the surrounding hillsides through breaks in the trees. You'll find a better vantage point at 0.8 mile, where a small path to the right leads to an overlook.

Continuing, you'll bypass a turnoff heading back the way you came. A few dozen feet beyond, a trail forks; veer right. Rest areas have been placed at each of the major trail junctures, and at 1.68 miles you'll reach the first one, which has both a kiosk with a map of the entire backcountry trail and a shady picnic table just off the trail.

At 1.85 miles, veer left at the next trail fork. The trail passes through a sun-baked grassland dotted with the occasional tree. In the winter, the flatlands can be uninspiring, but in the spring, wildflowers peek from tall grasses, adding interest and beauty to the setting. At 2.28 miles, reach another junction and rest area with a kiosk. Turn left (south) to begin the trek back toward the trailhead. If you wanted to extend the hike another few miles, you could instead turn right (north) to follow the trail onto another loop.

The trail back continues through grassland another 0.8 mile, passing the turn-off to the primitive camping area and another split, where you'll continue straight. Finally, at 3 miles, reach a junction with a smaller singletrack hiking trail. For a change of scenery, veer right into the trees and onto the narrow trail; it winds slightly uphill through dense woods. The path crosses the wide trail once, disappearing into the woods on the far side. At 3.5 miles, it crosses back onto another section of the main trail you just left. This time you should veer right, back onto the main trail, to retrace your steps to the trailhead. Alternatively, if you're enjoying the woods, you can cross the wide trail and pick the singletrack path where it runs through the woods back toward the trailhead parallel to the main trail.

NEARBY ACTIVITIES

You can buy bottled mineral water and souvenirs at Mineral Wells' Famous Mineral Water Company. The company was founded in 1904 by the pharmacist Edward Dismuke, who believed the town's mineral waters could cure ailments—including his own. At the age of 40, he was told he had only a short time left to live; he ended up dying at the age of 97, attributing his longevity to the mineral waters. The Texas Historical Commission has honored the building with a historical marker.

To get there, take US 180 W 4 miles. Turn right onto Northwest Sixth Street; the building is number 209. The hours are Monday, 10 a.m.–3 p.m.; Tuesday–Friday, 8 a.m.–5:30 p.m.; and Saturday, 9 a.m.–5 p.m.

• •

GPS TRAILHEAD COORDINATES N32° 50.067' W98° 02.167'

DIRECTIONS Follow I-20 W toward Abilene. Take Exit 414 onto Fort Worth Highway/US 180 W toward Mineral Wells. Continue about 21 miles (about 14 miles past Weatherford), then turn right onto Park Road 71, following the brown state-park signs. To get to the trailhead, enter Lake Mineral Wells State Park and make a sharp left, crossing over the spillway. Bear left at the next juncture. The parking lot is at the end of the road.

An interpretive sign identifies native wildflowers.

THIS PACKED-GRAVEL TRAIL runs atop an old railway bed and connects the cities of Mineral Wells and Weatherford. It will appeal most to folks looking more for exercise than for scenery.

DESCRIPTION

With four access points along its 20-mile route, Lake Mineral Wells State Trailway stretches between Mineral Wells and Weatherford along a converted railway line. The multiuse trail, which opened in 1998, runs through countryside peppered with ranches. Because of its length, it is well suited to joggers and to walkers looking for a good section of uninterrupted trail upon which to stretch the legs. Access points for bicyclists, hikers, and equestrians are, from east to west, just outside Weatherford, in Garner, and at Lake Mineral Wells State Park. The fourth access point at the far western end of the trail is in the Mineral Wells; access here is restricted to hikers and bicyclists.

Besides the trailway, you'll find an excellent backcountry trail within the park, which I've also highlighted. The park's more unusual attraction, however, is a rock-climbing area known as Penitentiary Hollow—a section of narrow canyons on the eastern side of the lake near the trailhead for this hike. See Hike 55, Cross Timbers Trail (page 252), for more details about the area.

DISTANCE & CONFIGURATION: 3.16-mile out-and-back

DIFFICULTY: Easy–moderate

SCENERY: Hills, grass, chaparral, old railway bed

EXPOSURE: Sunny

TRAFFIC: Light–moderate

TRAIL SURFACE: Packed gravel

HIKING TIME: 1 hour

DRIVING DISTANCE: 5.5 miles from US 180 and US 281

ACCESS: State park open 6 a.m.–10 p.m.; trail open sunrise–sunset; $2 adults, $1 senior citizens over age 65 and children under age 12; $7 state-park admittance fee

MAP: tinyurl.com/lakemineralwellstrailway

WHEELCHAIR TRAVERSABLE: Yes

FACILITIES: Restrooms, benches

CONTACT: 940-328-1171, tpwd.texas.gov /state-parks/lake-mineral-wells

LOCATION: Park Road 71, Mineral Wells

COMMENTS: You can extend this hike for just about as long as you like—there are about 20 miles of trail.

To get to the trailhead, stay to the right at the first fork after you enter the park. A short drive down on the right, you'll find the huge parking lot. There is a small trail fee, and a self-pay box has been set up adjacent to the trailhead for hikers' convenience.

As you head down the paved trail, the path immediately starts to switchback down a steep hill. After you pass an amphitheater off to the right, the trail turns into packed gravel. This section of trail is actually a small spur that connects the state park with the trailway itself, which is 0.6 mile southeast. The spur curls toward the main trail, cutting through grassy fields peppered with cacti and the occasional isolated tree.

At 0.38 mile, pass a bench alongside an interpretive sign identifying native wild-flowers of the area. The sign advises you to keep an eye out for the vivid hues of more than a dozen wildflowers, including the Texas bluebonnet, the standing cypress, and the Texas yellow star. Unfortunately, when I visited (in the middle of winter), the dry grasses were devoid of all color but brown. Although in winter it's not at its most picturesque, it is at its most pleasant, temperature-wise. Sections of this little-shaded trail—which would normally be baking midday in summer—are mild and gentle, even on a late-winter afternoon.

Continuing, the trail switchbacks down another hill. As you descend, you'll have a charming view of the trail snaking away into the distance against a backdrop of small wooded hills. The path cuts through grasslands and passes another interpretive sign identifying the red-tailed hawk, a common resident. Finally, at 0.63 mile, reach the main juncture with the trailway. The trail splits here, extending 14 miles to the left (east) to Weatherford, and 6 miles to the right (west) into Mineral Wells.

I opted for a shorter hike, heading right toward Mineral Wells. Both directions are equally pleasant, offering wide, paved trails atop an old railway bed, suitable for comfortable walking shoes, strollers, or bikes. The trail runs parallel to a road, so expect the sound of cars occasionally passing as folks head to and from their ranches.

Lake Mineral Wells State Trailway

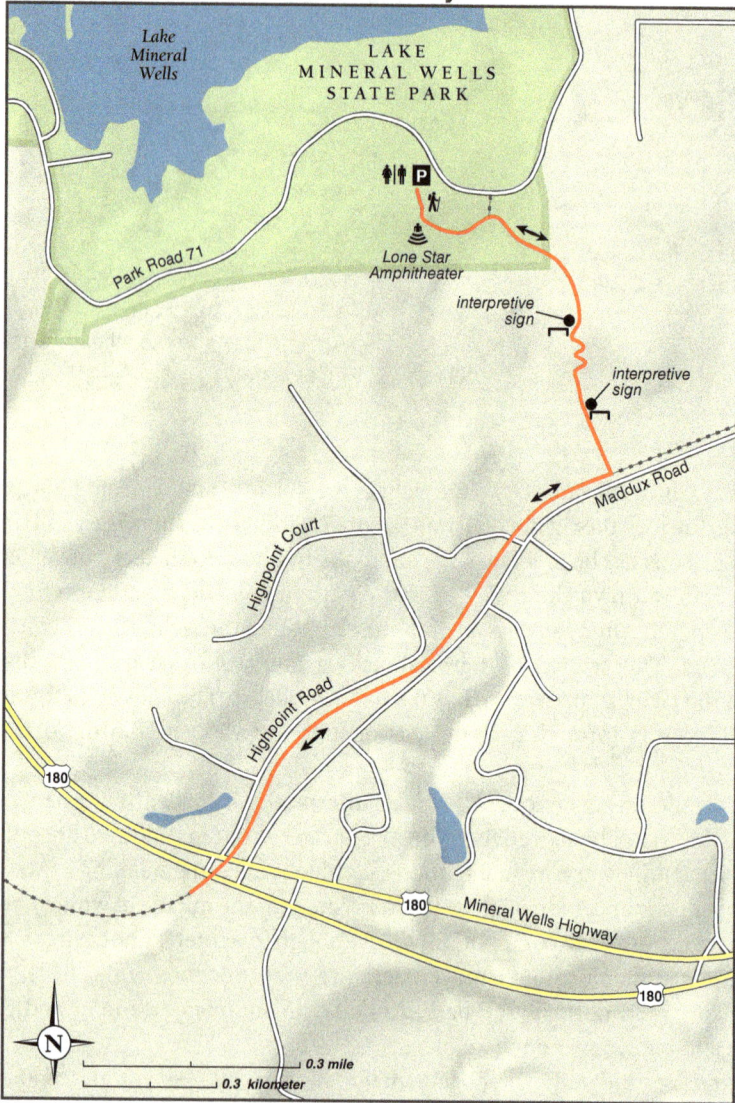

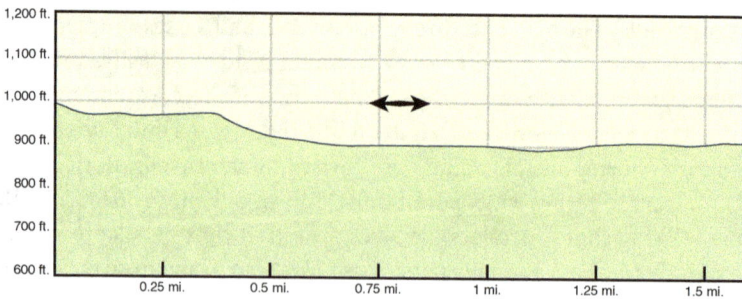

A local resident surveys his domain.

Traffic is light, however, and not distracting. The section of trail between Garner and Weatherford on the far eastern portion of the trailway does not run near any roads, something to consider if you're looking for a more remote feel.

Turn right (west) onto the trailway. The scenery along the trail is mostly trees and shrubs, and, unlike the hilly spur from the state park, this section is fairly level. As you near US 180, the trail starts to climb gradually to cross the highway via an overpass. The other side of the bridge marks exactly 1.5 miles into the hike and is the point where I turned around. If you're interested in continuing, the trail stretches another 4.5 miles west into downtown Mineral Wells.

NEARBY ACTIVITIES

You can buy bottled mineral water and souvenirs at Mineral Wells' Famous Mineral Water Company. See page 255 for details.

· ·

GPS TRAILHEAD COORDINATES N32° 48.800' W98° 01.900'

DIRECTIONS Follow I-20 W toward Abilene, then take Exit 414 onto Fort Worth Highway/US 180 W toward Mineral Wells. Follow the highway about 21 miles (about 14 miles past Weatherford), then turn right onto Park Road 71, following the brown state-park signs. To get to the trailhead parking, enter Lake Mineral Wells State Park and stay right at the junction. The parking lot is on the right.

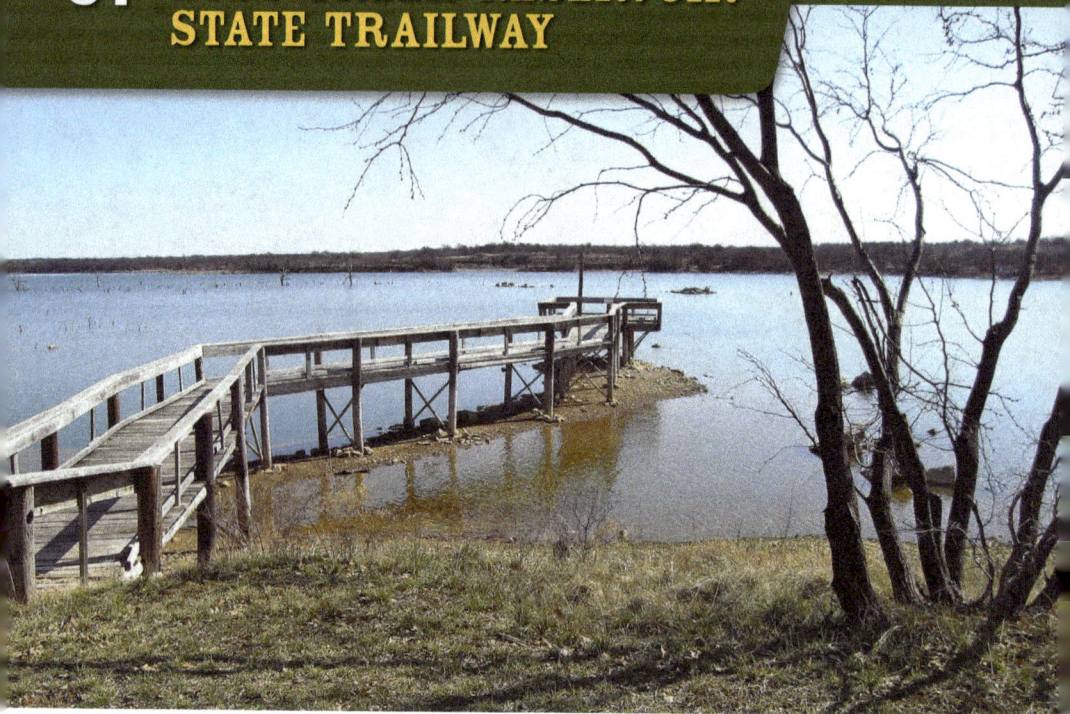

A wooden fishing pier attracts anglers.

IN AN AREA rich with the history of the North Texas frontier settlement, this sunny, peaceful hike winds through grasslands and over the dam of the Lost Creek Reservoir toward Fort Richardson State Park. Ranchlands abut the trailway, and you'll sometimes be greeted by the curious stares of bulls or livestock as you hike along.

DESCRIPTION

In Jacksboro, along the banks of Lost Creek, the Fort Richardson State Park, Historic Site, and Lost Creek Trailway's amenities include fishing, hiking, and camping. The trailway portion opened in 1998 and is about 10 miles long (one way), connecting the state park with the Lost Creek Reservoir. Trailheads are at both the park and the reservoir. The reservoir trailhead is a few miles away from the state park and historic site, a short drive northeast.

If you want to explore Fort Richardson itself, it will require a separate stop before or after the hike but is well worth it. Consider making a weekend of this trip—not only is there a lot to explore, but the state park has been named one of the top 100 family campgrounds among U.S. federal and state parks.

The fort was established to protect frontier settlements against raids from Southern Plains Indian tribes after the Civil War. Named after Civil War general Israel Bush

DISTANCE & CONFIGURATION: 5.35-mile balloon

DIFFICULTY: Easy

SCENERY: Grassland, ranches, reservoir, dam

EXPOSURE: Sunny

TRAFFIC: Light

TRAIL SURFACE: Pavement and crushed rock

HIKING TIME: 2 hours

DRIVING DISTANCE: 2.5 miles from TX 59 and S. Main St. in Jacksboro

ACCESS: Daily; $3 per person

MAP: tinyurl.com/lostcreekreservoir

WHEELCHAIR TRAVERSABLE: No

FACILITIES: Composting toilet and picnic tables near the swimming beach

CONTACT: 940-567-3506, tpwd.texas.gov /state-parks/fort-richardson

LOCATION: TX 59 near Lake Jacksboro, Jacksboro

COMMENTS: This trail can be very hot in summer; bring a hat, sunscreen, and plenty of water—there are no drinking fountains .

Richardson, it is associated with many battles, including the Salt Creek Massacre (aka the Warren Wagon Train Massacre). The massacre involved a bloody raid against a wagon train by a group of Kiowa and Comanche. The chiefs were eventually arrested and tried for murder—the first trial of its kind. In 1878, 11 years after its establishment, the unsettled frontier plains were secured and the fort was finally abandoned.

In 1963 the fort was named a National Historic Landmark. In 1968 the Texas Parks and Wildlife Department claimed it, opening it to the public as a state park and historic site a few years later. A few of the buildings from the fort's original complex have been restored or preserved, including the commanding officer's quarters, the post hospital, and the magazine. Pick up a walking-tour pamphlet at the visitor center to guide you around the site. The tour starts at the Interpretive Center, where you'll find displays and information about the fort's history.

This hike starts at the trailhead at the reservoir. If you want to pick up a map or other park information, be sure to stop by the state-park visitor center before heading to the trailhead; the trailway is unmanned. A self-pay booth allows you to pay the marginal trail fee; state-park pass holders should just hang their pass inside their car. Park rangers do patrol the area, so be sure you've paid your dues. The trail is open to hikers, bikers, and equestrians, though on the gorgeous weekend day I visited, I encountered no one.

When you arrive, you'll find a huge parking area with trailheads on both the east and west sides of the lot. Head down the trail on the west side; facing the back of the lot, it'll be the trail at the back on the right. The path is actually a paved one-way park road bordered by woods and shrubs, which loops downhill toward the reservoir. Within a few hundred feet of starting down the path, you'll see the waters come into view and will pass a charming wooden fishing pier stretching into the still blue-green waters; anglers come here to fish for channel and blue catfish. Looking across the reservoir, the opposite shoreline is dotted with trees and shrubs and is pleasantly devoid of development or construction.

Lost Creek Reservoir State Trailway

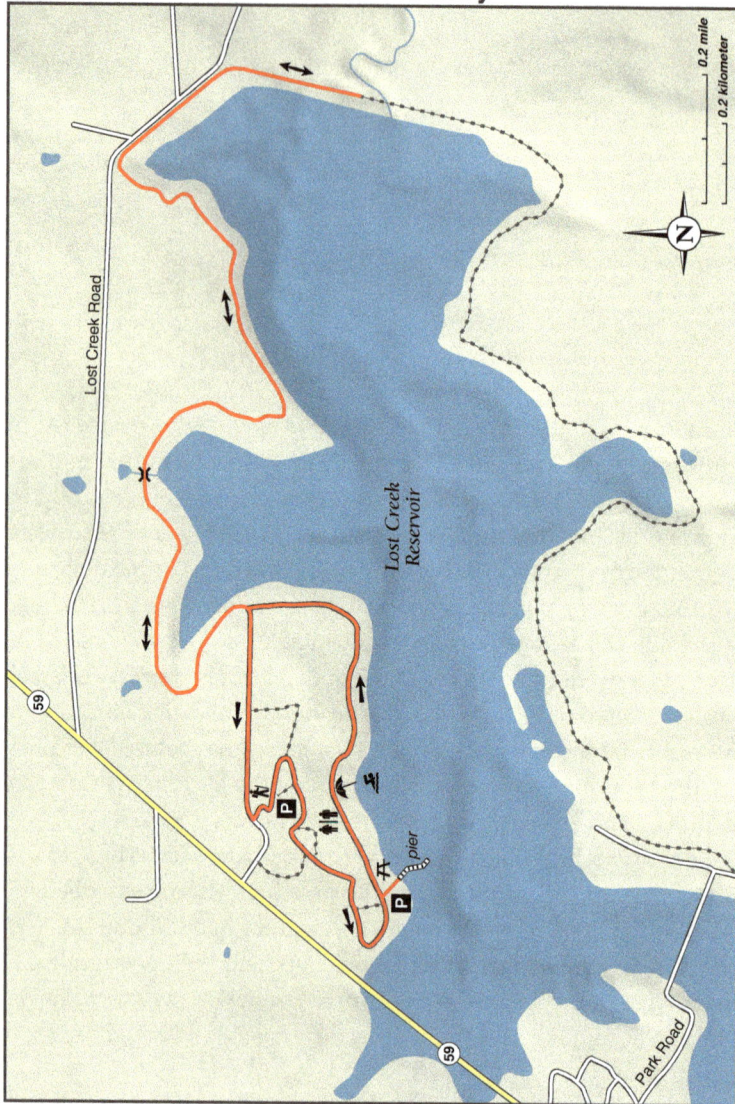

Just past the pier, you'll pass a huge day-use area replete with a long pavilion and picnic tables overlooking the water. Just before and below it, a swimming beach with a wide stretch of sand beckons visitors on hot days. The park road continues its loop then splits at 1.45 miles; follow the crushed-limestone multiuse trail. (Continuing to the left—on the road—would take you back to the parking lot and the opposite trailhead.) To the right, the reservoir's water is still visible, glinting in the sunlight just beyond the tall prairie grasses.

The trail winds around a small inlet of the reservoir and heads east through flat prairie lands dotted with the occasional tree. To the left, a fence marks the boundary of a local ranch. On the sunny day of my visit, I was greeted here by the steady gaze of a couple of huge bulls eyeing me through the fence.

At 2.1 miles, reach a large old metal bridge nestled among the prairie grasses, mysteriously spanning nothing more than flat grassland. Cross the bridge and continue following the trail east. The scenery is mostly trees and rocks to the right, blocking the nearby reservoir from view, and ranchland to the left. Eventually, the eastern edge of the reservoir comes into view between the trees to the right, and you have a glimpse of the dam. The trail winds toward them atop the dam. From the middle of the dam, you'll have a fabulous view of a lush green valley to the left. I spotted some type of livestock grazing there (though from the height of the dam, they looked like nothing more than white dots). To the right, the reservoir spreads out before you, shimmering in the sunlight. This is a great spot for taking a break and enjoying lunch before retracing your steps to the trailhead. If you want to extend the hike, you can follow the trail about 6 more miles across the dam, around the southern side of the reservoir, past the local airport, and to the state park.

NEARBY ACTIVITIES

If you're hiking the trailway, be sure to stop by Fort Richardson itself before or after the hike to explore the old buildings on the fort grounds. Within Jacksboro, you can visit the Jack County Museum, a historical house with period furnishings. It's near the town square, at 237 W. Belknap Street.

• •

GPS TRAILHEAD COORDINATES N33° 14.700' W98° 08.300'

DIRECTIONS Take Jacksboro Highway/TX 199 west toward Jacksboro. Fort Richardson State Park is on the left, just off the highway, about 1 mile outside Jacksboro. To get to the trailhead itself, bypass the state park and continue straight into downtown Jacksboro. Turn right onto East Belknap Street; the road curves left and becomes Bowie Street/TX 59. The parking lot is about 2 miles ahead on the right.

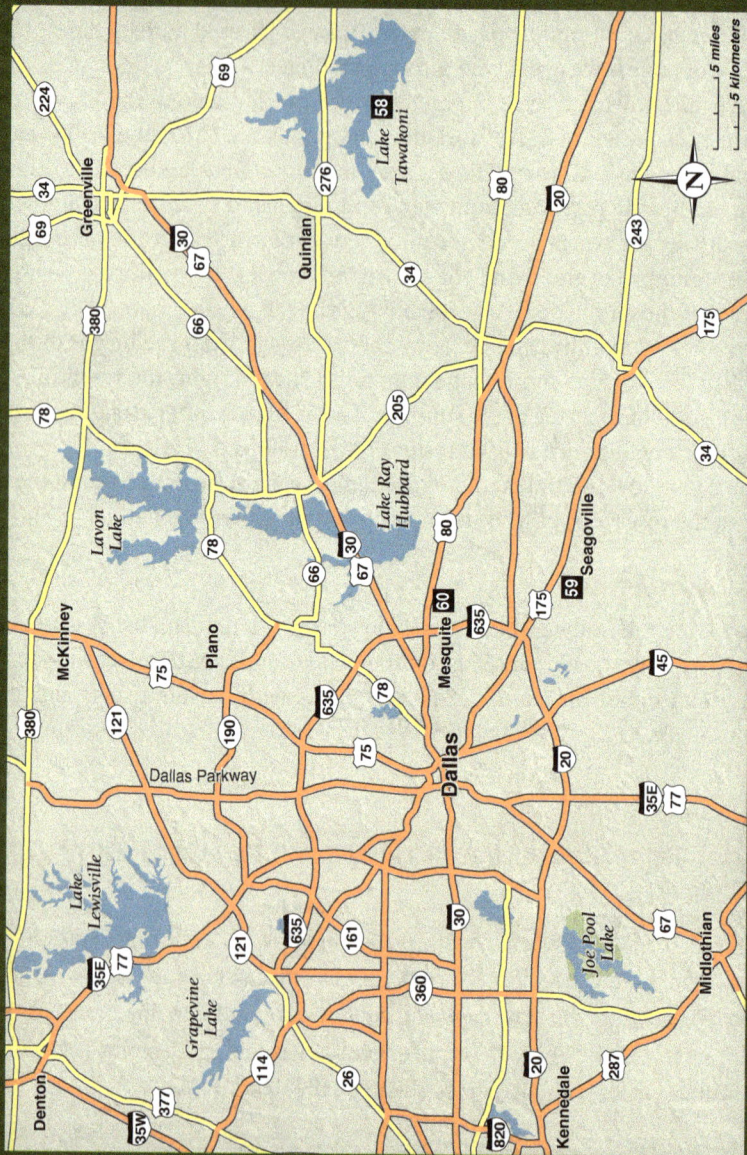

EAST OF DALLAS

On a sunny day, the towering trees provide pleasant shade.

NEAR THE BLUEBIRD CAPITAL OF TEXAS, this trail winds through the woods near Lake Tawakoni and is great for bird-watching.

DESCRIPTION

The 36,700-acre Lake Tawakoni (tuh-WOCK-o-nee) is a huge reservoir on the Sabine River occupying the corners of three counties—Hunt, Van Zandt, and Rains. Its dam (the Iron Bridge Dam) and spillway are 5.5 miles long. The reservoir serves as a municipal and industrial water supply and a recreational spot. Along its 200-plus-mile shoreline, boaters will find half a dozen boat ramps, hunters will find three units of the Tawakoni Wildlife Management Area, and hikers and campers will find a state park. The lake is also known as an excellent spot for catfishing in particular; striped, largemouth, and white bass can also be found in good numbers.

At only 376 acres, Lake Tawakoni State Park sits like a tiny speck on the reservoir's southern shoreline. Opened in 2002, the state park is refreshingly remote, being just a 20-minute drive down a secondary road. Even the closest town—Wills Point—has fewer than 5,000 people. Although it's a drive to get there, the effort will reward you with a couple of charming trails, including a short loop along the lake's shoreline and a longer trail through woodland adjacent to the lake. The park's atmosphere is laid-back and will appeal most those looking for a mellow, quiet hike. In

DISTANCE & CONFIGURATION:
1.72-mile balloon

DIFFICULTY: Easy

SCENERY: Hardwood forest, birds

EXPOSURE: Partial shade

TRAFFIC: Light

TRAIL SURFACE: Packed dirt

HIKING TIME: 45 minutes

DRIVING DISTANCE: 56 miles from downtown Dallas

ACCESS: Daily, 7 a.m.–10 p.m.; $5 per person age 13 and older, free for children age 12 and under

MAP: tinyurl.com/laketawakonisp

WHEELCHAIR TRAVERSABLE: No

FACILITIES: Restrooms, picnic area, benches

CONTACT: 512-389-8900, tpwd.texas.gov /state-parks/lake-tawakoni

LOCATION: 10822 FM 2475, Wills Point

COMMENTS: Look for the unusually knobby bark of a couple of trees along the first half of the trail.

winter, it's not unusual to find yourself one of only a handful of visitors in the park, and certainly the only one on the trails. The unusual name of the lake and park are a reference to the Tawakoni Indians who originally inhabited the area.

The trailhead is in the far left corner of the parking lot, marked with a NATURE TRAIL sign and a notice that it is only open for use when dry. The singletrack path winds southwest through the woods. A thick mixture of American elms and post oaks provides a pleasant canopy of shade as you hike.

At 0.3 mile, come to a split in the trail, and turn right, heading west through more hardwood forest. Vines hang thick from the surrounding tree limbs, shrouding any wildlife in the vicinity from view. Occasionally, however, a rustling in the leaves indicates something is nearby—typically birds hopping through the underbrush. As you continue, keep an eye out for poison ivy.

The trail continues west, crosses a bridge spanning a small creek, heads slightly uphill, then reaches a juncture at 0.57 mile. The entire trail is open to both bike and foot traffic, with one section exclusively for bikes. If you were to head left at this juncture, you'd reach the loop reserved for mountain bikes. You should therefore veer right, following the path 1 mile farther, where you will reach a three-way juncture. The first trail, to the right, loops to the south, from whence you just came. The second trail, straight ahead, loops north toward the lake, curls around, and comes back out onto the third trail to your right. Continue straight, following the second (middle) trail north, where you'll find the hardwood trees starting to mix with junipers such as eastern red cedar. The elevation is slightly higher than that of the lake, and as you reach the farthest point of the loop, you'll catch glimpses of the water to the left through the trees. Before you loop back, you'll find a couple of benches at 0.83 mile and 0.93 mile just off the trail, beneath the trees. These provide ideal shade-covered spots for bird-watching, so you may want to bring your binoculars. Keep an eye out for the eastern bluebird, which is commonly found in the park; the nearest town of Wills Point is called the Bluebird Capital of Texas. State park materials indicate more than 200 species of birds have been identified here.

Lake Tawakoni Nature Trail

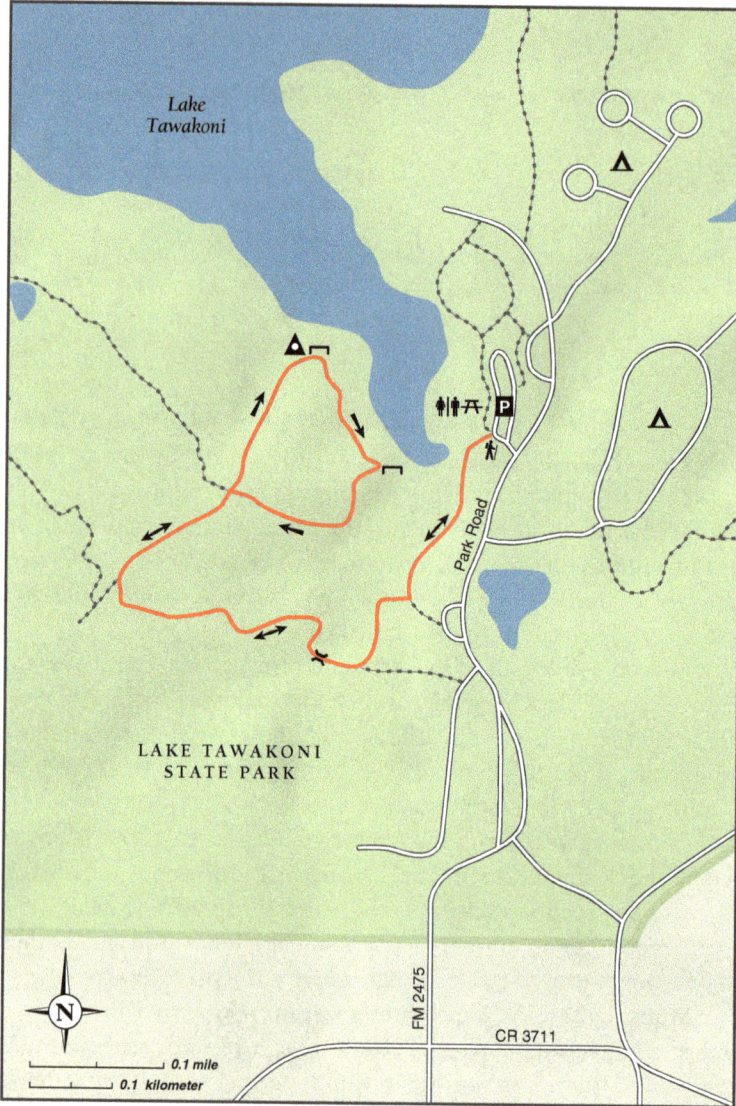

At 0.93 mile, veer right, following the red arrow, and after about 500 feet, you'll be back at the start of the loop. From here, retrace your steps to the trailhead. If you're interested in extending the hike, drive to the northern end of the park and pick up the trailhead just to the right of the swimming beach to hike along the lake. The first half of the trail hugs the shoreline, providing inspiring views of the lake before looping back through the woods, making it a little more than 1 mile round-trip. Keep an eye out for bird-attracting plants such as the American beautyberry,

a shrub that produces clusters of berries in the autumn, and yaupon holly, a berry-pro ducing evergreen shrub.

NEARBY ACTIVITIES

In 1995 Wills Point was officially proclaimed the Bluebird Capital of Texas. The town hosts an bluebird festival, with food, exhibits, and entertainment. Visit wpbluebird festival.org to see if your visit will coincide with the April event. Year-round, you can explore the town's historic buildings, Depot Museum, and pioneer cabin.

• •

GPS TRAILHEAD COORDINATES N32° 50.733' W95° 59.650'

DIRECTIONS Take US 80 east toward Terrell. When you reach Wills Point, turn left onto Farm to Market Road 47/North Fourth Street, bear right, and go approximately 5 miles. Turn left onto FM 2475, then travel about 4 miles, following the brown state-park sign to enter Lake Tawakoni State Park. You can pick up a map of the park at the headquarters as you drive in. As you head into the park, stay to the left at the first junction, and you'll reach the day-use area on your left, where you should park in the first parking lot.

The curious bark of a prickly ash tree encourages closer study.

Take a brief rest and watch for birds on the shores of a small pond midway through the trail.

ON THIS SHADY HIKE looping through a pretty preserve, the first half traverses a predominately thickly wooded area, whereas the second half winds among smaller clearings of native grasses.

DESCRIPTION

As part of an effort to provide students with environmental learning programs, the Dallas Independent School District established the Environmental Education Center. In southeast Dallas County, in the small town of Seagoville (named for its founder, T. K. Seago), the center was established in the 1970s and offers students an outdoor education experience; in addition, there is a museum complete with ecosystem exhibits, learning labs, and interactive video stations. Although the center is mainly intended for students, it also manages the Post Oak Preserve, which is just across the street, where this hike begins. The preserve's namesake, the post oak, is a small, acorn-producing, drought-resistant tree, commonly used to make fence posts.

Open to the public, the preserve offers nature trails winding through a small remnant of post oak savanna. The 334-acre preserve is also regularly used by the center as an extension of its outdoor classroom, and if you visit on a weekday, you may encounter students or teachers along the trail. This is an excellent trail for younger hikers because wooden signs at various points along the trail instruct less

DISTANCE & CONFIGURATION: 1.69-mile loop

DIFFICULTY: Easy

SCENERY: Pond, thickets, woods, meadows

EXPOSURE: Partly sunny

TRAFFIC: Light

TRAIL SURFACE: Dirt

HIKING TIME: 45 minutes

DRIVING DISTANCE: 19 miles from downtown Dallas

ACCESS: Daily; free

MAP: None

WHEELCHAIR TRAVERSABLE: No

FACILITIES: Picnic tables

CONTACT: 972-749-6900

LOCATION: 1501 Bowers Rd., Seagoville

COMMENTS: Birding is excellent around the small lake.

experienced hikers, providing general reminders and tips, such as keeping an eye out for snakes, being cautious of poisonous plants such as poison ivy, and keeping wildlife wild by not feeding the animals. In addition, the trail is wide and flat—easy for small, curious feet to maneuver.

Start the hike by heading past the picnic area and bearing left onto the trail heading east (the path on the left is where you'll exit at the end of the hike). The trail winds through a thick woodland dotted with cedars and sporadic clumps of prairie grasses. Faced with all these trees, many of you may wonder, as I did, where the savanna is. Interestingly, natural fires and grazing bison are the two key forces in maintaining a savanna. The former keeps the woodlands at bay, allowing the prairie grasses to thrive, while the latter spreads the seed. Without these forces, the woodlands start to take over. As you hike along, you'll pass some educational signposts that indicate that a woodland takeover is what you're seeing here.

As you continue, the trail becomes more densely wooded. Thick vines tangle themselves in the branches of the surrounding trees, hiding all signs of wildlife from view, though occasional rustling in the leaves and branches hints at their presence. At 0.3 mile, a small sign with bright-green lettering marks the split for the easy Wee Folks Trail. Stay to the left, bypassing the turnoff. As you continue along, the trees will start to thin, and you'll catch a few brief glimpses of water sparkling in the distance before you reach a signpost marking the "moderately easy" Lake Shore Trail. Another 0.27 mile down the trail, reach a quiet overlook of the preserve's 12-acre lake. A large old tree offers a shady spot for you to sit and observe the birds that frequent the small oasis. Most commonly, you'll spot teams of ducks paddling through the marshy waters or herons wading along the shoreline. If you glance up, you're likely to spot at least one slow-circling bird peering down at you—most likely a resident turkey vulture monitoring the ground for any food it can scavenge.

Back on the trail, you'll notice the scenery start to change as the woodlands thin dramatically and mix with patches of cactus and clumps of prairie grasses. At 0.92 mile, turn left onto a wide, paved road framed by short trees and shrubs. The road heads west and passes a picnic area before reaching another juncture a few

Post Oak Trail

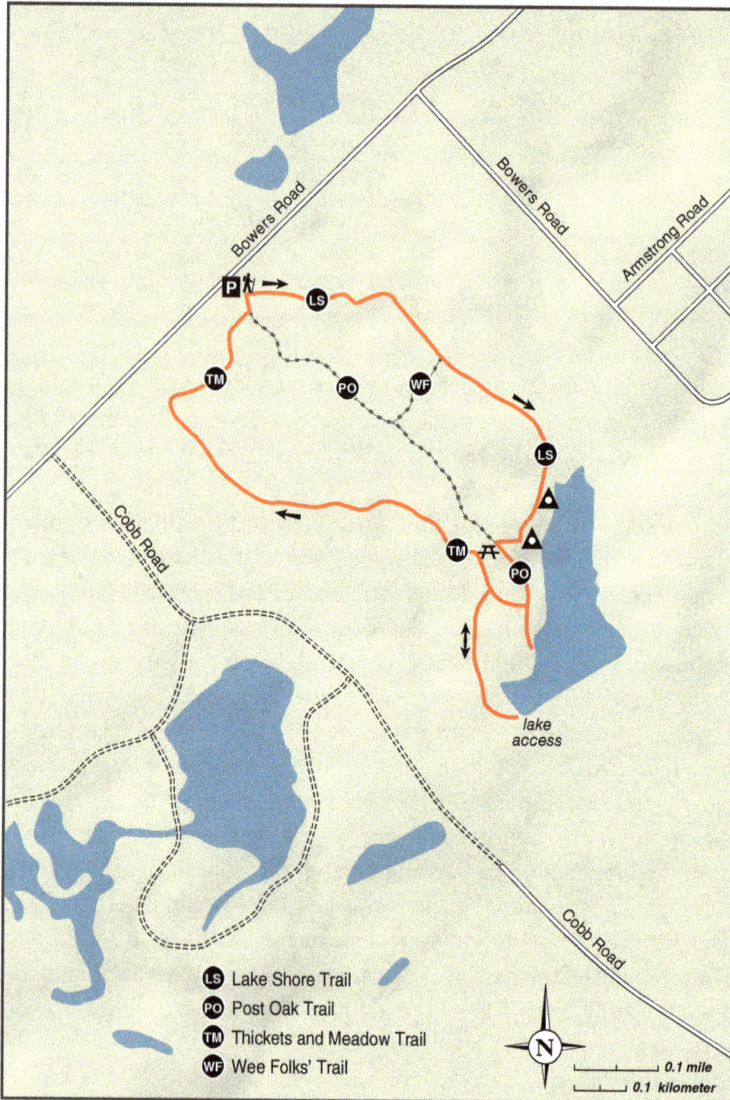

LS Lake Shore Trail
PO Post Oak Trail
TM Thickets and Meadow Trail
WF Wee Folks' Trail

0.1 mile
0.1 kilometer

hundred feet down. Bear left, following the paved path to its end, where it fades to join the soft, sandy banks of the lake. The gentle, sandy slopes offer you another chance to take a brief break and scope the pond-sized lake for waterfowl.

After exploring the short shoreline, head back up the trail and bear right at the next juncture to head northwest. The trail winds through patches of grassland dotted with small shrubs and cedar trees, markedly different from the dense woodlands character-izing the first half of the trail. You'll start to notice the shrubs and trees thin out, and then a sign advises that you've entered the Thickets and Meadow Trail. Throughout this section of trail, you'll find a couple of small, sunny meadows, framed by bright blue skies. Dragonflies and butterflies buzz and flutter around you as you round the final bend and turn back northeast toward the trailhead. From the final turn, it's a mere 0.2 mile before you emerge back at the trailhead, completing the loop.

NEARBY ACTIVITIES

The Rogers Wildlife Rehab and Farm Sanctuary is located in nearby Hutchins, about 14 miles away. The facility is a nonprofit organization that rehabilitates injured birds and farm animals. Visitors are welcome to roam the property free of charge; donations are accepted. On the grounds, you'll find dozens of outdoor cages serving as temporary homes for rehabilitating hawks, owls, blue jays, vultures, and herons, among others. Geese and pheasants wander around unfettered. To get there, turn left, heading west on Simonds Road approximately 1.6 miles, then bear left onto Belt Line Road and drive 4.6 miles. Turn right onto I-45 N, and go 3.6 miles to Exit 274, Dowdy Ferry Road/Palestine Street. Stay on the service road for about 0.5 mile, then turn right onto East Cleveland Street. The sanctuary is about 1 mile down on the left.

• •

GPS TRAILHEAD COORDINATES N32° 38.467' W96° 34.133'

DIRECTIONS Take US 175 east toward Kaufman. In Seagoville, take the exit for Simonds Road/Kimberly Drive. Turn right onto Simonds Road and travel 2 miles to Bowers Road, then turn left. The Post Oak Preserve is about 1.5 miles down on the right, across from the Environmental Education Center.

Vintage tractors provide a fun diversion at the farm's entrance.

THIS CHEERY HIKE through an old farm traverses a couple of meadows and offers plenty to see, including a windmill, log cabins, and vintage tractors.

DESCRIPTION

Located just off the service road of busy US 80 in Mesquite, Samuell Farm may seem like an unlikely spot for an enjoyable hiking experience, but don't let its location mislead you. The 340-acre farm is surprisingly beautiful, with miles of hiking trails and scores of birds. The farm is often used as an educational resource for school field trips and is also a regular monthly walk on the Dallas Trekkers Walking Club agenda. The atmosphere on the farm switches easily from festive and active to quiet and peaceful, so be prepared for either. I arrived one afternoon to find the huge gravel parking lot teeming with schoolkids and families. I set off expecting a lively hike; however, within 30 minutes of my arrival, the school buses had packed up and driven off, leaving me almost the only visitor on the entire farm. I enjoyed a couple hours of quiet hiking and exploring and encountered only one other family, just as I was leaving.

The City of Dallas inherited the land in 1937 from the late Dr. W. W. Samuell. In 2001, budget constraints forced its closure, and it has reopened in the past couple of years only with help from the nonprofit Friends of the Farm.

DISTANCE & CONFIGURATION: 2.93-mile triple loop

DIFFICULTY: Easy–moderate

SCENERY: Ponds, meadows, woods, birds, antique tractors

EXPOSURE: Sunny

TRAFFIC: Light on weekdays, heavy on weekends

TRAIL SURFACE: Packed dirt

HIKING TIME: 1.5 hours

DRIVING DISTANCE: 13 miles from downtown Dallas

ACCESS: Tuesday–Sunday, 9 a.m.–5 p.m.; free

MAP: None

WHEELCHAIR TRAVERSABLE: No

FACILITIES: Restrooms, picnic area

CONTACT: dallasparks.org

LOCATION: 100 US 80 E, Mesquite

COMMENTS: Hike in the morning to avoid the heat of the day on this sunny trail.

Enter the farm through the gate just to the left (east) of the main building. To your left, you'll see a small wooden building housing the restrooms. Begin the hike by turning right to take the dirt path passing in front of the main building. A picnic area dotted with colorful vintage tractors and a few tables fills a large expanse of grass off to your left. On your right, you'll pass a small working garden, then the trail splits in several directions.

Follow the wide, dirt path to the right as it curves back toward the highway between a small pond and the parking lot. The trail heads toward the highway and at 0.57 miles reaches a windmill, where you'll turn left. The trail then narrows, following a faint grassy trail between the highway on the right and a meadow on the left. (Although the cars are distracting, the trail is safe for all ages—there is a wide grassy expanse in addition to a fence between hikers and the roadway.)

When you reach the trees that border the meadow on the west, turn left, away from the highway, following the treeline. Hike along until the treeline ends, then turn right, away from the meadow. Pass through a gate and continue 0.1 mile until the next split, where you'll turn left. The trail then loops back southeast alongside a wide meadow dotted with trees. Insects are abundant, so be sure you've applied repellent. On a sunny day, you may see small yellow butterflies flitting across the trail. Crickets and grasshoppers are also abundant and are likely to smack you in the chest as they hop out of your way and back into the tall meadow grasses. The meadow also attracts birds and is a good spot to see the scissor-tailed flycatcher, easily identified by its forked tail.

Straight ahead, you'll see the Texas Pioneer Homestead, a picturesque old log cabin, whose cramped quarters and tiny rooms are open to exploration. Continue along the path past a small pond, to the next split at 1.5 miles, where you'll turn right, following the gravel trail south. The trail heads slightly downhill into a dip where a shallow creek cuts the trail and prevents further progress. Instead of wading through the water, cross the grass to your right, following the creek a few dozen feet to a small red footbridge hidden behind the trees. Rejoin the trail, keeping the gazebo to your left. Another pond off to the right sets the bucolic mood as you pass

Samuell Farm Trail

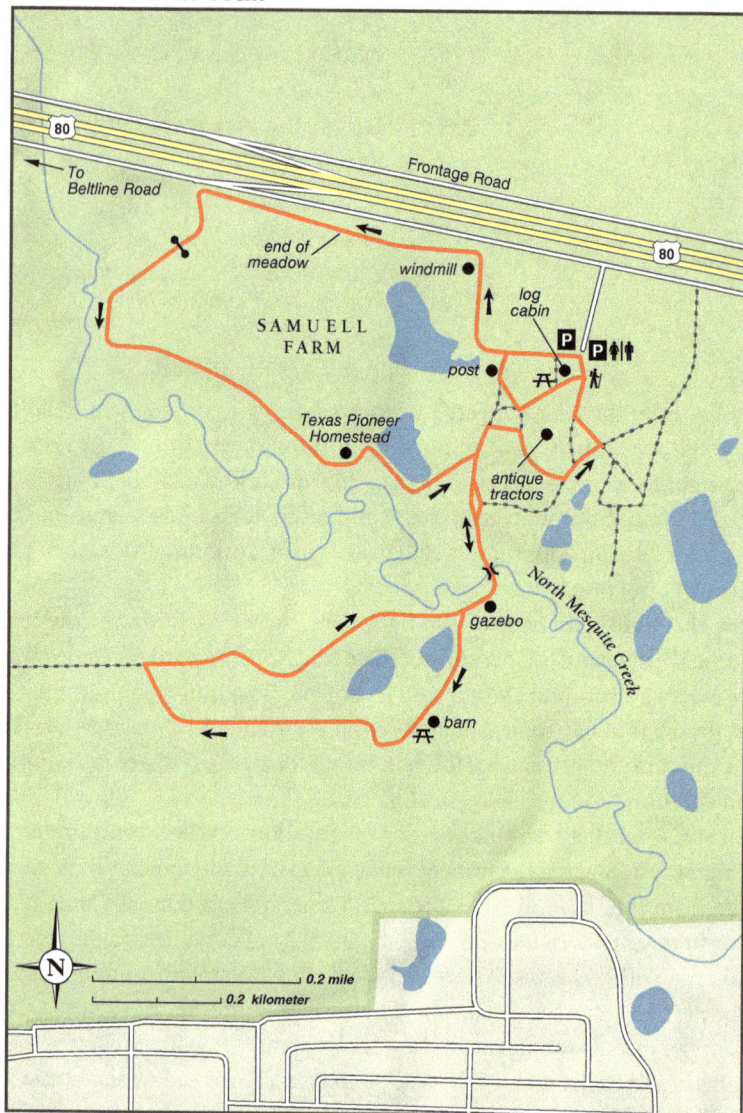

rolls of hay and approach a large barn. At 2.15 miles, follow the trail to the right, passing the barn and a picnic area. The trail continues past a huge sunny meadow with tall grasses and brilliant yellow sunflowers.

You'll soon reach the next trail split, where you'll hang a right, following the shady remnants of a wide dirt road. Stay to the right at the next path split at 2.33 miles. After about another 0.2 mile, the gazebo will pop back into view. Before you reach it, bear left back onto the footbridge and cross the creek heading back toward the entrance.

You can explore the rooms of the Texas Pioneer Homestead, an old log cabin.

At 2.7 miles, turn right on the path just before the picnic area. If you've brought lunch, grab a table and a bite; otherwise, continue along the trail, which passes between dozens of antique tractors. Take the next two lefts to do a small loop. Another picnic area and a small log cabin to the right invite closer inspection. From here, it's just a few hundred feet back to the trailhead.

NEARBY ACTIVITIES

From spring through early fall, you can catch the Mesquite Championship Rodeo, which features bull riding, chuckwagon races, clowns, cowboys, and cowgirls. Shows typically start in the early evenings. Be sure to check the website (mesquite rodeo.com) for the current season's hours and rates. The rodeo is 8 miles away. To get there, take US 80 E west 3 miles. Merge onto I-635 S and travel 2 miles, then exit at Scyene Road/TX 352. Stay on the service road about 0.5 mile, then turn right onto Rodeo Drive.

• •

GPS TRAILHEAD COORDINATES N32° 47.200' W96° 35.033'

DIRECTIONS Take I-30 east to US 80 E toward Terrell. Exit at Belt Line Road. Cross Belt Line Road and continue 0.3 mile on the service road. The entrance to Samuell Farm is just off the service road on the right and is marked by a huge tractor.

APPENDIX A: Outdoor Shops

ACADEMY SPORTS + OUTDOORS
academy.com

6101 I-20 (at Bryant Irvin Road)
Fort Worth, TX 76132
817-361-1240

8050 Forest Lane
Dallas, TX 75243
214-355-3200
(See website for more locations throughout the metroplex.)

BASS PRO SHOPS
basspro.com

2501 Bass Pro Drive
Grapevine, TX 76051
972-724-2018

5001 Bass Pro Drive
Garland, TX 75043
469-221-2600

CABELA'S
cabelas.com

12901 Cabela Drive
Fort Worth, TX 76177
817-337-2400

1 Cabela Drive
Allen, TX 75002
214-383-0502

CAMPING WORLD
campingworld.com

10100 South Fwy.
Fort Worth, TX 76140
866-393-6441 or 817-568-1991

5209 I-35 N
Denton, TX 76207
800-527-4812 or 940-898-8906

2764 I-30
Mesquite, TX 75150
888-271-5205 or 972-279-8110

3825 N. Main St.
Cleburne, TX 76033
888-310-2373 or 817-500-0050

DICK'S SPORTING GOODS
dickssportinggoods.com

Parks at Arlington
3891 S. Cooper St.
Arlington, TX 76015
817-987-4800

13838 Dallas Pkwy.
Dallas, TX 75240
972-239-5455

8030 Park Lane
Dallas, TX 75231
214-696-5800
(See website for more locations throughout the metroplex.)

MOUNTAIN SPORTS
mountainsports.com

2025 W. Pioneer Pkwy.
Arlington, TX 76013
800-805-9139 or 817-461-4503

The North Face
8687 North Central Expy.
Dallas, TX 75225
214-987-1436

REI
rei.com

5929 E. Northwest Hwy.
Dallas, TX 75231
214-368-1938

2424 Preston Road
Plano, TX 75093
972-985-2241

5924 Convair Drive
Fort Worth, TX 76109
817-732-9539

1011 E. Southlake Blvd.
Southlake, TX 76092
817-416-0948

SUN & SKI SPORTS

sunandski.com

1100 W. Arbrook Blvd.
Arlington, TX 76015
682-433-0027

11170 N. Central Expy.
Dallas, TX 75243
214-442-7007

2943 Preston Road, #1400
Frisco, TX 75034
214-494-4288

3000 Grapevine Mills Pkwy.
Grapevine, TX 76051
972-355-9424

4941 Overton Ridge Blvd.
Fort Worth, TX 76132
682-747-0418

WHOLE EARTH PROVISION CO.

wholeearthprovision.com

5400 E. Mockingbird Lane
Dallas, TX 75206
214-824-7444

Grab a pair of hiking boots and pick your favorite trail—it's time for a hike!

APPENDIX B: Places to Buy Maps

GARMIN
garmin.com

KAPPA MAP GROUP
universalmap.com

NATIONAL GEOGRAPHIC
natgeomaps.com

ONE MAP PLACE INC.
onemapplace.com
1620 Surveyor Blvd.
Carrollton, TX 75006
972-416-5071

REI
rei.com

TRAILS.COM
trails.com

USGS MAP STORE
store.usgs.gov

TEXAS PARKS & WILDLIFE
tpwd.state.tx.us
*(Free downloads of many
Texas state park maps)*

USDA FOREST SERVICE
fs.fed.us/r8/texas

APPENDIX C: Hiking Clubs

AMERICAN HIKING SOCIETY
americanhiking.org

DALLAS SIERRA CLUB
dallassierraclub.org

FORT WORTH SIERRA CLUB
sierraclub.org/texas/greater-fort-worth

TEXINS OUTDOOR CLUB
meetup.com/texins-outdoor-club

TEXAS OUTDOORS-WOMAN NETWORK
towndallas.org

Wildflowers bloom alongside a trail in spring.

INDEX

ABOUT THE AUTHOR

Photo: Andrew Sánchez

Avid hiker, camper, and traveler **Joanie Sánchez** first fell in love with the outdoors when she had the opportunity to work one summer with the Youth Conservation Corps in Yosemite National Park. The following year, she served as a leader of the group, teaching and mentoring as she shared her passion for nature. Since then, her adventures have taken her backpacking across Europe, on a state-to-state biking tour across New England, and hiking in the Caribbean islands. She has traveled extensively throughout Mexico and has written an adventure guidebook to its Gulf Coast. A graduate of Yale University, Sánchez grew up and lives in the Dallas area. She spends her free time showing fellow hikers the beauty that Texas trails have to offer.

DEAR CUSTOMERS AND FRIENDS,

SUPPORTING YOUR INTEREST IN OUTDOOR ADVENTURE, travel, and an active lifestyle is central to our operations, from the authors we choose to the locations we detail to the way we design our books. Menasha Ridge Press was incorporated in 1982 by a group of veteran outdoorsmen and professional outfitters. For many years now, we've specialized in creating books that benefit the outdoors enthusiast.

Almost immediately, Menasha Ridge Press earned a reputation for revolutionizing outdoors- and travel-guidebook publishing. For such activities as canoeing, kayaking, hiking, backpacking, and mountain biking, we established new standards of quality that transformed the whole genre, resulting in outdoor-recreation guides of great sophistication and solid content. Menasha Ridge Press continues to be outdoor publishing's greatest innovator.

The folks at Menasha Ridge Press are as at home on a whitewater river or mountain trail as they are editing a manuscript. The books we build for you are the best they can be, because we're responding to your needs. Plus, we use and depend on them ourselves.

We look forward to seeing you on the river or the trail. If you'd like to contact us directly, visit us at menasharidge.com. We thank you for your interest in our books and the natural world around us all.

SAFE TRAVELS,

Bob Sehlinger

BOB SEHLINGER
PUBLISHER

CPSIA information can be obtained
at www.ICGtesting.com
Printed in the USA
LVHW05*1050241018
594634LV00001B/1/P